Edited by **David J. Rachman**

Associate Professor of Marketing
Bernard M. Baruch College,
City University of New York

RETAIL MANAGEMENT STRATEGY

Selected Readings

Prentice-Hall, Inc., Englewood Cliffs, New Jersey

13-778787-1

Library of Congress Catalog Number: 79-107600

Current Printing (last number)
10 9 8 7 6 5 4 3 2 1

PRENTICE-HALL INTERNATIONAL, INC., *London*
PRENTICE-HALL OF AUSTRALIA, PTY., LTD., *Sydney*
PRENTICE-HALL OF CANADA, LTD., *Toronto*
PRENTICE-HALL OF INDIA PRIVATE LIMITED, *New Delhi*
PRENTICE-HALL OF JAPAN, INC., *Tokyo*

Printed in the United States of America

TO MARLI AND NANCY

PREFACE

My first problem in attempting to collect readings for a retailing book was to develop a philosophy. As I note below, I decided to limit my readings to those that will contribute to a reader's understanding of the difficult decisions faced by retail management. However, for the reader who hasn't faced the task of compiling a readings volume, let me describe both the psychological and practical problems involved in this undertaking.

The first practical problem is how far back into the literature shall one collect readings. Although I have dubbed this a practical problem, one soon learns that he must delve into the psyche of the reader. Thus, if the editor goes back, let us say, to 1938 and rescues an article from sure oblivion, he must judge the reaction of the reader who, in the middle of the article, is told that the Gross National Product of the United States was $85.2 billion during that year. In order to save the reader from traumas, the decision was made to limit the readings to years following 1950, with preference given to those of a more recent vintage.

My second practical problem, which was easily solved, was shall I include the so-called classical articles—that is, those that any self-respecting pedant would be almost forced to include in his readings assortment simply because they are universally recognized as milestones in retailing. Although one may recognize a slip or two, on the whole, *conventional wisdom* was by-passed—and the articles that coincided with the thesis of being of interest to retail management prevailed.

The next problems concern the judgments as to the actual choice of articles. The first situation one is faced with here is what to do with articles on the subject of retail management written by friends? Following the theory that "everyman thinketh his own fleas gazelles," one is well aware of the reactions of his closest friends when he chooses to ignore their contributions to the retailing dogma.

Another sticky problem one has, is what to do with articles written by authors he admires. One should admit that there are certain authors who can do no wrong. Thus, everything they write seems adequately suited to a readings book. If one follows this path, he is faced with a moral obligation to appoint those he admires as co-authors.

I would like to thank my colleague and friend, Houston "Tex" Elam, who helped me solve some of these problems. I would also like to thank Professor Richard Embertson, Western Michigan University, and Professor Bernard J. LaLonde, Ohio State University, for their useful comments and detailed criticism of the manuscript. Many of their suggestions were incorporated. Helen Schriefer typed the manuscript and, demonstrating her versatility, helped in the preparation of some of the instructional materials. For her four years of assistance, patience, and good judgment, she deserves endless accolades.

DAVID RACHMAN

CONTENTS

INTRODUCTION

It is somewhat arbitrary to divide any management job into different parts. While recognizing, however, that management does not operate in a vacuum and that all decisions are the result of the weights and interrelationships of many factors and values, it is still important to realize that (1) all of these elements exist and (2) some are within the power of management to control or manipulate, while others are uncontrollable.[1] For this purpose the book has been divided into two main parts: the *Retailer's Environment* (Part II) and the *Internal Organizational Mix* (Part III).

The *Environmental* readings embrace those areas that the retailer must contend with but that are beyond his ability to control. In this grouping are competition, social pressures, the law, and, of course, the major area of concern, the whimsical consumer.

The internal organization of the firm is the only aspect of the retailer's business that he can control. It includes the goods and services offered to the consumer, the size of inventories and the location of stores, and the selection of means of communication with the consumer—newspaper advertising, television, direct mail, personal selling, or self-service. In the operation of these functions the retailer exercises his decision-making abilities by choosing among his many alternatives. Planning and developing a proper strategy constitutes the day-in, day-out task of retail management. Management's choice of alternatives is, of course, guided substantially by the environmental factors described in Part II. Thus, the internal organizational readings include several selections on retail research, the feedback mechanism through which management gains information concerning the most uncontrollable aspect of the firm's environment, the consumer.

The other two parts of the book are intended to supplement the reader's understanding of retailing philosophy and of some of the special problems in the constantly changing retail environment. Part I contains readings that demonstrate both the differences in outlook of the retailer and the manufacturer and the many similarities. Part IV, the last section, includes se-

[1] For a more detailed discussion, see David J. Rachman, *Retail Strategy and Structure* (Englewood Cliffs, N.J.: Prentice-Hall, Inc., 1969), Chap. 1.

lections about one of the most important problems of the sixties: retailing in the ghetto areas of our cities. There are also articles about the one problem faced by all businessmen, namely, change. This is discussed in terms of automatic vending, franchising, and other problems that make any businessman's life an uneasy one.

PART I

RETAILING PHILOSOPHY

RETAILING PHILOSOPHY

Retailers represent the most numerous institutions in the distribution field. It is also important to remember that retailers usually look at consumers, merchandise, and their organization in a different manner than do manufacturers. Some of the flavor of this philosophy is captured in the article "Misunderstanding the Retailer" by Warren J. Wittreich. On the other hand, the retailer sometimes approaches his problems in the same way as the manufacturer. William Lazer and Eugene Kelley, in their article "The Retailing Mix: Planning and Management," indicate that the marketing concept, which manufacturers have found useful as a system of business action, can also be applied to retailing. Eugene Fram makes the same point by reviewing the possible implications of the marketing concept in "Application of the Marketing Concept to Retailing."

1

Misunderstanding the Retailer

Warren J. Wittreich

There is no question that manufacturers generally acknowledge the *necessity* for communicating with the retail dealer. This is clearly evidenced by the dollars spent for advertising and promotion aimed directly at retail dealers (over and above dollars expended in personal selling effort) as well as the generally high number of articles

Reprinted from *Harvard Business Review*, Vol. 40, No. 3, May-June 1962, pp. 147–59.

and speeches which reaffirm management's recognition and interest in the problem.[1]

Yet, despite the large amount of such communicating and the importance attributed to it by management, within the complex distribution system of *all* owner-operated retailing outlets we generally find the same phenomenon: *the people who manufacture the goods and the people who move the goods into the hands of the ultimate consumer do not share the same business philosophy and do not talk essentially the same language.* Nevertheless, corporate management in the manufacturing organization (which obviously depends on the retailer for ultimate sales) continues to operate on the assumption that *there is no problem*—that it and the retailer have the same goals and use and understand the same words.

In this article, I shall explore these twin dimensions of the serious breakdown in the communications system between manufacturer and retailer. These dimensions I have identified as (1) the problem of *crossed purposes,* and (2) the problem of *confused languages.* Then, I shall offer several specific examples to illustrate how this communications failure adversely affects the achievements of manufacturers' distribution goals at the retail level.

Crossed Purposes

To understand the problem of crossed purposes, it is necessary to analyze and understand the differing points of view held by most members of corporate management, on the one hand, and by most retail owner-operators, on the other.

By and large, corporate management's point of view is characterized by a *growth psychology.* A key to understanding why this is so can be found in thinking about *who* gets to be top management.

Reams have been written about the characteristics of successful managers. For our purposes here, however, the most important finding about top managers is that generally they are people who identify their own personal goals with the goals of the corporation. While this fusion of personal and corporate goals can manifest itself in a number of ways, the essential fact remains that the people guiding our major corporations today are those individuals whose personal objectives in life are intellectually and emotionally intertwined with the goals of the organizations they command.

The significance of this rather obvious fact can best be understood against the broad background of our country's past history, present position, and

[1] For example, see the editorial in *Sales Management,* October 20, 1961, p. 7; E. B. Weiss, "Outdated Ad Presentations to the Trade," *Advertising Age,* September 11, 1961, p. 122; W. J. Regan, "Full Cycle for Self-Service?" *Journal of Marketing,* April 1961, p. 15; W. Lazar and E. J. Kelley, "The Retailing Mix: Planning and Management," *Journal of Retailing,* Spring 1961, p. 34; "Ads Not Enough; Retailer Must Be Sold," speech by G. E. Mosley before the Boston Advertising Club and the Point of Purchase Advertising Institute, April 1959.

RETAIL DEALERS

The "retail dealer" referred to here is a very specific kind of businessman. He is found in the small to medium-size retailing operation which is both owned and operated by a single independent businessman. Such retail outlets are numbered in the hundreds of thousands and constitute a significant portion of the total consumer retailing efforts in this country. For many large manufacturers of consumer goods or services this type of retail store constitutes their *only* outlet.

Examples of this kind of retail operation would be the automobile dealer, the hardware store, the drugstore, the small grocery store, the specialty food shop, the package store, the tavern, the "specialty shop" in both men's and women's clothing, the small appliance dealer, the specialist flooring outlet, the retail outlet, the gift shop, the retail lumber dealer, and so on.

We are *not* concerned with the kind of outlet whose manager is a captive employee, as is the case in a massive retailing organization (supermarket, department store, or discount chain) or with the company-owned retail outlet. Actually the development of these two types of outlets over the past ten or fifteen years reflects to some degree a solution to the problems with which this article is concerned.

---

expected evolution over the years ahead. The growth which is the keynote of modern management's thinking is in reality a part of the over-all growth which has characterized our country's history from the outset. Our society is riding the crest of a wave which began to gather strength hundreds of years ago and shows no signs of abatement—neither now nor in the foreseeable future. Our population, our government, and our corporate economy have grown, are growing, and will undoubtedly continue to grow in the future. In short, all of the basic elements of our over-all social structure are at this moment reflecting a basic, pervading, continuous thrust of expansion.

The consequence of this inexorable growth process for the individual corporation is the fact that the principle of growth is basic to the fused goals of top management and corporate organization. The age-old question of cause and effect—whether the leader produces, or merely manifests, the basic characteristic of the society—is unimportant. What *is* of importance is that our business leaders, as individuals, are characterized by an assortment of personal goals, all of which are focused on, contingent on, and superseded by the basic objective of achieving more tomorrow than was achieved today.

It really does not matter whether the individual's objectives in life are income, status, power, security, fame, self-satisfaction, or any other conceivable, understandable, and worthwhile human goal. What does matter is the fact that these goals are never finite—there is no satisfactory end point. Today's accomplishments quickly become history—rapidly become the plateau from which tomorrow's gains will be reached. *The psychology of our business leaders is a growth psychology;* the men who succeed to the positions of top management are men who are constantly striving for something more—for themselves and for the organization for which they are responsible.

Such is not the psychology of the typical retail dealer. Unlike corporate management, the individual retail dealer is characterized by a psychology essentially *static* in nature. Again, to understand the kind of thinking and philosophy which characterizes the dealer, we must understand the kind of individual who becomes an independent "owner-operator" retail dealer.

He is *not* the same kind of person that succeeds to the top management of a major corporation. He is a very different kind of person. Within the framework of this difference lies a large part of the fundamental problem.

While the various goals of the top corporate executive can be characterized as constantly evolving and never reaching a satisfactory terminal point, the goals of the typical retail dealer are far more circumscribed. Like the executive, the dealer's goals may also be income, status, power, security, fame, self-satisfaction, or other aims similar in kind to those of his corporate counterpart. However, regardless of the similarity of goals, the critical difference is that in the large majority of instances *there is a relatively easily defined end point to the objectives.* If money is a goal, at some not-too-difficult-to-define level of income this goal becomes satisfactorily achieved. If status is important, owning one's own business, becoming president of the local chamber of commerce, and other similar kinds of accomplishments provide the required satisfactions. If power is a drive of significance, the manipulation of a very few employees can usually satisfy the need. The same is true with other goals I could list here. The dealer's achievements can almost invariably be pegged at a clear and easily defined level of accomplishment. Once that level is reached, the fact that it has been reached provides the necessary degree of satisfaction as years go on.

In essence, then, the key to understanding management's problem of crossed purposes is the recognition that the fundamental goals in life of the high-level corporate manager and the typical retail dealer in the distribution system are quite different. The former's goals can be characterized as being essentially dynamic in nature—continuously evolving and emerging; the latter, which are in sharp contrast, can be characterized as being essentially static in nature—reaching a point and leveling off into a continuously satisfying plateau.

Confused Languages

The differences between the fundamental goals in life of most corporate managers and most retail dealers are only part of the over-all problem. The other part can best be summarized in a rather simple, but disturbing, sentence: *Corporate management tends to talk in a language comprehensible only to itself!*

Actually, this fact reflects a phenomenon which tends to characterize *all* new scientific disciplines and professions. The field of management has been and is still undergoing the "pangs of professionalization," a process invariably accompanied by the development of a body of terms with meaning primarily (all too often, exclusively) for members of the professional "in-group."

As a professional psychologist, I can point to no better (or poorer) example of this phenomenon than that evidenced by psychology itself. Such terms as "ego," "id," "cathexis," "goal gradient behavior," "oral regression," "tension reduction" (regrettably the list is interminable) are meaningful and understandable to psychologists. To others they are relatively incomprehensible and all too often appear to be unnecessary gobbledygook.

While psychologists may be particularly prone to accusations of talking clearly and lucidly to no one but themselves, the same faults can be found in other scientific disciplines. Physicians, mathematicians, chemists, physicists, data-processing experts, and all other professional groups cannot escape the charge of professional lingo. Regardless of what the causes may be for this phenomenon, the simple fact remains that it exists. *Management is no exception.*

The language of modern industry revolves around words like *profit*, *profit margin*, *profit-ability*, *merchandising*, *marketing*, *promoting*, *quality control*, *delegation*, *line-and-staff functions*, and all the other "modern" terms of the new science of management. Are these terms clear and meaningful? The answer is very definitely "yes" if we mean: Are they clear and meaningful to members of the management fraternity? However, if we raise the question as to their clarity and meaning for a very large proportion of individual owners of retail businesses, the answer is by no means "yes."

Manufacturers make the assumption that because "owner-operator" retailers are also "businessmen," the latter very quickly understand the words that corporate management uses with regularity. This assumption is no more valid than the assumption that such retailers share the same personal and business goals as does corporate management.

At times the differences in the meanings ascribed to words, or the kinds of words which are used most comfortably, may appear to be trite. In theory they may indeed be trite, but as the specific illustrative examples outlined below will indicate, in actual practice these differences can be critically important.

THREE EXAMPLES

Any business or industry which operates a distribution system of retail outlets which is made up entirely, or in part, of individual "owner-operated" establishments presents essentially the same phenomenon.

Three examples are offered here, representing very different kinds of products, maketing approaches, and broad business problems. Specifically, they are:

- The brewing industry and the retail tavern owner.
- The appliance industry and the retail dealer.
- The building products industry and the retail lumber dealer.

Each industry yields essentially the same evidence: a failure of corporate management to recognize the dissimilarity of its own goals and the goals of the retail dealer, a failure of corporate management to talk to the retail dealer in a language that the dealer understands.

Tavern Owners

I have deliberately chosen the brewing industry as my first example because it illustrates the fundamental problem in boldest relief.

The brewing industry is undeniably a major American industry. It manufactures and markets a specific product. While its marketing procedures vary according to the laws of different states, one of its major retail outlets is the "tavern." The tavern owner is then a "retail dealer"—an end point of the distribution system which places the product in the hands of the ultimate consumer. What kind of a person is the typical tavern owner? What are his goals? What language does he speak?

The typical tavern owner is essentially *not* a businessman. He is *not* used to thinking in terms that are familiar to the businessman. To him "profit" is a highfalutin' esoteric word used by wise guys who think they are better than he is. Being in business to "make money," he is more likely to respond to arguments or appeals which will help him do that than to arguments or appeals which are supposed to lead to "better profits." By the same token, talk about "merchandising" or "promotion" is likely to sail over his head. In order to get him to act, you have to speak to him in terms which are familiar and meaningful to him and which promise concrete rewards that he can grasp and understand.

The brewing industry is interested in growing. Individual brewers in the industry are interested in expanding their businesses. One of they ways that the brewing industry as a whole can grow is through successful promotion of the use of beer in the home. Consequently "takeout" business in taverns is promoted by all brewers. The obvious avenue of growth for the individual brewery is for more people to drink its particular brand of beer.

However, the tavern owner, as the "retail dealer" of beer, does not necessarily see the above objectives as consistent with his own. He sees the promotion of the use of beer in the home as hurting his own business. He is not interested in having people drink beer at home; he is interested in having them drink beer in his establishment. Regardless of all the "rational" arguments to the contrary, as far as he is concerned, encouraging beer drinking at home means less business for him. Similarly he has little interest in the promotion of any particular brand of beer. He is simply interested in giving his customers what they ask for.

In short, a situation of conflicting interests and misunderstanding exists between the brewer and the tavern owner. The latter generally does not feel that brewers are genuinely interested in his problems. He sees industry "take-home" advertising as undermining his business. He sees the individual brewer as primarily interested in pushing his own brand—something in which the tavern operator is not interested because pushing one brand over another does not really add to *his* over-all business.

At the same time that an analysis of the situation within the brewing industry indicates the existence of rather serious problems of both crossed purposes and confused languages, these problems can be, and often are, satisfactorily resolved on a very practical level. One such resolution is illustrated from the following excerpt, describing a highly successful beer salesman, from a report I made on a survey of various practices pursued by the brewing industry in selling its products through taverns:

It quickly became apparent that Lou personified the most essential characteristic of success as a beer salesman—namely, the ability to operate comfortably on the same level as the tavern owner. The latter is often a rough, uncouth, uneducated man who is in business "to make a buck," and whose attitude is essentially "what's in it for me?"

Without any question Lou talked a language that the tavern owner understood. He never mentioned profit; he always talked about "making money." He never mentioned merchandising or display; he simply talked about getting the product out where the customer could see it. If the tavern owner shouted at him, he shouted back. If the tavern owner called him a "no-good s.o.b.," he called the tavern owner a "no-good cheap b . . . ."

His basic approach to the tavern owner in trying to sell him on the idea of take-out beer was: "Look, you gotta stand behind this bar all day long. You can't go anyplace so you might as well make some money when you're here. If a guy comes into your place for a shot and a beer and he's got an extra buck and a quarter in his pocket, he's going to spend that buck and a quarter someplace else if he doesn't spend it here. So you gotta figure out a way to get him to spend that money here. Remember, if you don't get that money, somebody else will.

"Maybe he figures he might like to take home some beer in case he has company drop in that evening. If you don't have the beer out where he can see it, he's not going to ask you if you have it. Don't give me that junk about him knowing you've got it; you gotta have it where he can see it in order to get him to buy. Did you ever try to smoke a cigarette with your eyes closed? Try it. You know you're smoking; but if you can't see the cigarette and the smoke, you don't get any enjoyment out of it. It's the same thing with the beer. Just knowing you got it isn't enough; you gotta be able to see it.

"You also gotta have a price on it. Supposing he's only got a dollar ten in his pocket and he doesn't know what you charge for a six-pack. He isn't going to ask you because he knows he's going to be embarrassed if your price is more than what he's got. But if he's got the money and you don't have the price where he can see it, then he won't ask and he won't spend the money in your place, either. Remember, if he doesn't spend it in your place, he's gonna spend it somewhere else. You gotta get his money while he's there.

"Put up a display. Put all your beers up there. Put my competitor's beer up right beside my company's beer. I don't care. All I care about is that you put up the display so you'll make some money for yourself. If you do that, then I know I'm gonna get my percentage of your business. As long as I get my percentage, I'm happy. I can't make money if you don't make money."

This account describes someone who is obviously an unusual and exceptionally capable salesman. It is doubtful whether many other beer salesmen operate in similar fashion. Lou was essentially expressing his own personality in his sales approach. While others naturally would have to base their approaches on what was comfortable and natural within the framework of their own personalities, nonetheless the essential principles that make Lou successful *are* transmittable to others. His success as a beer salesman was based on two factors, both integral to solving the problem of communications breakdowns:

1. The willingness to deal with the tavern owner on the latter's own level and within the framework of the latter's value system.
2. The willingness to talk to the tavern owner in a concrete down-to-earth language which the latter understood.

In short, Lou understood the goals and values of the individual tavern owner. His approach to the latter was within his—the tavern owner's—framework. He did not try to push management's philosophy or marketing strategy down the tavern owner's throat, but instead *translated* his firm's philosophy and strategy into an approach which make the tavern owner feel that Lou was on his side and understood the problems he had in running his tavern. And while Lou talked in terms which were perhaps somewhat "rough" and not befitting someone on the "management team," those terms got the point across to the tavern owner in a clear and unmistakable fashion.

Appliance Retailers

I have chosen my second example to contrast with the first. It is easy to say that the first study only illustrates a problem unique to the brewing industry: the fact that the so-called "retail dealer-tavern owner" is often an ex-bartender without a great deal of education or sophistication, and hence in a category unto himself. As our second example will indicate, the problem is *not* unique to the brewing industry. The underlying problem and its ramifications can be found in *any* major industry's distribution system.

The retail appliance dealer is far more a respected member of the "business community" than is the tavern owner. The products he sells—radios, television sets, phonographs, refrigerators, freezers, washing machines, ranges, and so on—are all highly "respectable" items. Consumer ownership of one or more of these items often conveys a degree of status—certainly far more status than does drinking beer in a tavern.

Similarly, the retailer who sells these items is generally a man of greater stature in his community than the local tavern owner. He is more likely to have a better education and a higher level of intelligence, to live in a better section of the community, to have a position of importance on the local chamber of commerce, and all of the additional accouterments of status and class. While it was easy to write off the tavern owner as not really being a businessman in the true sense of the word, it is not so easy to dismiss the retail appliance dealer from the business fraternity.

Nevertheless, the same kinds of differences in understanding, or lack of understanding, between the manufacturer and the retail dealer as were found in the brewing industry can also be found in the appliance industry. Compare the following brief analysis of the nature of the retail appliance dealer's business with the basic dimensions of the tavern owner's business:

- The typical appliance dealer handles a number of different products from a number of different manufacturers. Seldom do we find a dealer who handles exclusively the products of one manufacturer only. Hence, one of the appliance industry's basic elements is the constant competition among manufacturers for the favor of the retail dealer (just as different breweries are constantly competing for the favor of the tavern owner).
- Further, the retail appliance dealer's primary focus is on satisfying his (the dealer's) customers (just as the tavern owner is interested primarily in giving his customers what they want).
- Finally (and this is perhaps the most critical point) the retail appliance dealer evaluates whatever the manufacturer does from his (the dealer's) point of view. The latter point of view is *not* the same as the manufacturer's.

Product Quality. To illustrate this important difference in viewpoints let us take a specific example. Product quality is a concept which we can rightly assume to be of importance to both the manufacturer and the retail dealer. The former is interested, of course, in having a high-quality product. In the great majority of instances, individual manufacturers sincerely believe that their product—dollar for dollar—is superior in quality to competitive products. In those aspects of product quality where they can be convinced that their particular product falls short of competitive products, they strive to raise the quality level up to, or hopefully above, the level of competition. And in advertising, selling, and promoting their products they constantly hammer home their conviction that their offering is the "best" on the market.

Similarly it is self-evident that product quality is of critical importance for the retailer. The dealer's interest in selling quality products (at a competitive yet profitable price) is of course simply a reflection of self-interest. Therefore, the obvious question arises: If both the manufacturer and the retail dealer have a strong interest in product quality, wherein lies the difference between the two as far as product quality is concerned?

The crucial difference lies in the differing meanings that this term has for the two:

To the manufacturer, quality is something that is measured in terms of the performing characteristics of the appliance. If the product is a refrigerator, quality is reflected in such things as maintenance of constant temperature, avoidance of excessive "frosting," and other such refinements of today's modern systems of home refrigeration. If the product is television sets, their quality is measured in terms of picture clarity, pulling power, tonal effect, and similar kinds of yardsticks. The principle is essentially the same for all other kinds of appliances: quality is measured in terms of the various aspects of the performance objectives of the particular product.

To the retail appliance dealer, there is no question as to the importance of quality in the products that he sells; numerous studies of dealer attitudes have consistently underscored this fact. However, these same studies have also shown that product quality has a special meaning for the dealer.

The dealer has very little genuine interest in and concern with the quality "refinements" claimed by the different manufacturers. While the retailer may espouse these very same claims when a prospect is being sold a particular appliance, these product "merits" are not what he views as product quality. It is the *consequences* of product quality that are important to him—the fact that the construction of a good appliance *results* in a high level of consumer satisfaction and a minimizing of customer complaints and servicing problems.

As far as the dealer is concerned, he is relatively unimpressed by the claims of competitive manufacturers. What *does* impress him is a product which gives him little in the way of headaches through recurrent servicing calls and complaints, a product which brings a satisfied and pleased customer back into his store to provide him with a steady flow of sales dollars.

Differences between the manufacturer and the retailer in the appliance industry are by no means restricted to differing meanings ascribed to product quality. The evidence accumulated so far indicates that the whole range of policies and decisions made by manufacturers in regard to the dealers are often viewed by the latter in terms far different from those the manufacturer ever intended. This is not to say that policies or decisions are made without regard to how they will affect the dealer, but that all too frequently they are made without any real understanding of how they will be looked upon by the dealer as an individual. In most instances management decisions which affect the entire distribution system are made with some consideration for all of the various links which go to make up that system (producer, distributor, dealer, and ultimate consumer). At the same time the assumption is all too often made that what is good for the system as a whole will be just as good for each link in the system. This assumption is by no means true—at least not from the point of view of that link which is represented by the dealer.

Dealer Incentives. To illustrate this point, let us look at another specific example. Dealer "incentives" find widespread favor among managements of appliance manufacturers. These generally take the form of financial stimuli to the dealer to increase his dollar volume of sales. An example of such an incentive would be the "volume discount," whereby an increasingly larger percentage discount on purchases is given to the dealer as his volume of sales increases.

If management is sometimes puzzled as to why such discounts fail to produce the anticipated and desired results, the answer lies in the simple fact that in a large percentage of cases these discounts are not seen as any sort of an incentive on the part of the dealer, but rather are viewed as an "irritant."

To understand such a puzzling point of view, we should recall one of the two basic points stated at the outset of this article—that while management is characterized by the unrelenting surge of expansion, the dealer is often not the least bit interested in growing beyond the level of business he has achieved. The latter, enjoying a good living as far as he is concerned, is not only satisfied to stay at his present level, but is annoyed at what he considers a supplier's "prodding" him into moving beyond that level. Furthermore, he not only resents such prodding, but considers it to be "unfair discrimination" in favor of dealers who are bigger than he is. Often, to the owner-dealer the need to maintain some degree of cost equivalence with larger appliance outlets *does* prod him into purchase, but with frequent consequent discontent over increased inventories and slow-moving items.

To place this point in proper perspective, we stress that we are by no means implying that management should determine policy on the basis of always pleasing the dealer. In a system where the retail dealer is but one of a number of units, this would be quite unrealistic. However, management should (but seldom does) set policy within the framework of a serious and realistic consideration of how any given policy will be looked upon by the retailer—from the latter's point of view. Not only should management know and consider what this point of view is; management should also take into consideration *how* such policies are communicated to the dealer. What is called for is an explanation which provides the retailer with the feeling that his point of view *has* been considered, and he is *not* being treated in an unfair or discriminating manner. Furthermore, what is communicated to the dealer should be stated in the *dealer's* terms.

Retail Lumber Dealers

Our third example again demonstrates that investigation of any major American industry which distributes through owner-operated retail establishments will reveal evidences of the overriding problem with which this article is concerned.

With the postwar building boom, the building materials industry has reaped the benefits of a particularly vigorous period of expansion. Of paramount importance to our analysis is the degree to which the "do-it-yourself" movement has boomed in the past fifteen years. The butterfingered breadwinner of prewar years has transformed himself into a professionally "amateur" carpenter, reconstructer, and restorer; even the "better half" has become a builder of improvements and additions to the family home. In short, where formerly local carpenters and contractors provided the retail lumber dealer with the bulk of his business, today it is *the consumer* who makes up a large part of the dollar volume of the lumberyard.

Manufacturers of building materials have, of course, had a high degree of interest in this "do-it-yourself" boom. The phenomenon is related to the goals of the managements of these firms, since the trend to amateur activity involving usage of their products has had a great deal to do with the growth of their business. As a consequence, these managements have undertaken various programs designed to expand this portion of their dollar sales. One of these programs has involved an attempt to "upgrade" the retail lumber dealer—to get the latter to recognize the same tremendous growth potential in consumer business as does corporate management.

The results of this program of upgrading have been widely varied. Examples can be cited where "forward-looking" lumber dealers have capitalized on the do-it-yourself trend. However, such examples are notable in their lack of frequency. It does not require many visits to very many lumberyards to verify this observation. The typical retail lumber dealer presents a showroom which at times is an almost unbelievable mishmash of assorted products in assorted displays. The attempts of far too many retail lumberyards to merchandise their products to the consumer provide a textbook example of how *not* to market to the consumer.

Typical of the retail lumber dealers' confusion engendered by manufacturers' aggressive marketing efforts is the following case history, drawn from my study of a problem-laden retail lumber dealer. At the time of the study, the dealer was doing a total annual business of over $2 million but was earning a return of less than 2% on his invested capital. The lumber dealer, a postwar graduate of an Ivy League college, had recently taken over the business from his father. His objective was obvious: to make substantial improvements in the company's earnings position.

A study quickly revealed that the dealership was really not certain as to "who" it was supposed to be. It had been originally developed through sales to building contractors and carpenters. Since the war, recognition that consumers also represented a worthwhile market had gradually crept into the dealer's way of doing business. Three branch outlets had been opened up. Two of these outlets sold primarily to the consumer; the third did the large majority of its business with the aforementioned contractors and carpenters.

All three branches had done quite well—far better than the main lumberyard and retail showroom. However, it was the showroom's business which still made up the bulk of the sales volume and which was yielding the poorest earnings. Thus, attention was focused on the latter outlet as the key to the problem.

The main showroom, in attempting to adapt to the opportunities inherent in consumer business, had ended up by being *neither a satisfactory source of supply for contractors and carpenters, nor a soundly conceived store for the consumer*. The elder dealer had never really accepted or grasped the growth objectives of the suppliers who were providing him with an ever-increasing flow of products suited to the consumer. His marketing efforts were in essence attempts merely to accommodate or adjust his business to an emerging consumer market, without any real plan. The showroom's over-all volume had remained relatively constant for a ten-year period. By becoming involved in a growth market when he himself had no real desires to participate in this growth, the dealer had succeeded only in diluting his formerly profitable business.

His suppliers had been communicating to him for some time the marketing opportunities in "do-it-yourself." Never having shared their basic objectives of expansion, and never really understanding their modern marketing concepts and the terminology associated with them, he had half-willingly followed what he felt was a reasonable course of action. The result of his efforts to follow the marketing guidelines suggested to him was the slow erosion of what had once been a solid and profitable business.

If we focus on one product line that this dealer was carrying, we can achieve an even sharper insight into his dilemma:

> Acoustical ceiling materials were being sold in the dealer's main showroom for direct consumer purchase. These materials were relatively poorly displayed, and his sales personnel evidenced both lack of understanding and lack of enthusiasm in selling them.
>
> Five years ago no such materials would have been found on the dealer's showroom floor. Acoustical ceilings were installed almost exclusively by contractors and carpenters primarily in commercial establishments. At about that time, the management of one of the larger corporations manufacturing building supplies recognized the marketing opportunity in promoting acoustical ceilings for use in the home. Their leadership in entering and developing this new market was quickly followed by other acoustical ceiling manufacturers, to the extent that today such ceilings are rapidly becoming accepted as attractive and useful additions to the home.

The link in the distribution system which must ultimately place products such as acoustical ceilings in the hands of the consumer—as amply illustrated by this particular retail lumber dealer—has only reluctantly and lethargically capitalized on this marketing opportunity. The reason again is obvious:

primarily because the "opportunity" is to the manufacturer another significant opportunity to achieve his growth objectives, but the "opportunity" for the typical dealer is all too often just one more confusing element in what used to be a stable, satisfying, and easily understood business.

CONCLUSION

These three examples were deliberately chosen as illustrative of differences in products, markets, and the nature of the retail outlet itself. The tavern owner, the retail appliance dealer, and the lumber dealer are all, on the surface, quite different kinds of people in very different kinds of businesses. Yet in spite of these differences, the same problems emerge: the goals of these people and the language they speak are quite different from the objectives and terms of their corporate suppliers. Selection of any other business or industry distributing through individually owned and operated retail outlets would produce the same findings; the essential point is that the problem exists, it is a critically important one, and corporate management ought to be aware of it and be undertaking constructive steps to deal with it.

To some degree it is appalling that top-level management is so far out of contact with certain realities of the distribution system. In far too many cases, the retailer is nothing more than a statistic or some sort of depersonalized component of the "channels of distribution." There is no disputing the fact that large numbers of retailers constitute an impressive and essential set of statistics with which management *must* deal. There is no denying that management must *also* operate the total distribution system as effectively as possible. But it is equally true and important for management to recognize that these statistics—this "component of the system"—are made up of individual human beings!

Accomplishment of management's goals depends to a large degree on proper understanding of these human beings. To continue to operate on the implicit assumption that these people share the goals of management and understand the language with which management talks to them is simply wrong. Every bit of evidence with which I have had contact clearly indicates it to be wrong.

At the same time, no suggestion is being made that management should formulate policy solely in terms of what is good for, or meaningful to, the individual dealer. Setting policy for the distribution and marketing of products—like the setting of any other kind of basic corporate policy—requires an intelligent reconciliation of frequently conflicting or competing points of view. However, intelligent policies cannot be set if points of view are unknown or assumed to be something that they are not. If what is clear, worthwhile, and meaningful to corporate management is *not* viewed or understood in similar light by others on whom management depends for the accomplishment of its goals, then these goals cannot and will not be achieved in the most effective manner possible. In short, corporate management has a clear-cut responsibility *to itself* to achieve considerably better understanding of the retailer than exists at the moment.

QUESTIONS

1. In what ways does the psychology of the retailer differ from that of the manufacturer?
2. How can this difference affect the distribution problems of the manufacturer?
3. Why do these differences exist?

2

The Retailing Mix: Planning and Management

William Lazer and Eugene J. Kelley

Some retail managers have been observing the rapid growth of the marketing management concept in manufacturing firms with considerable interest. This concept of marketing is resulting in the acceptance of a new perspective for business activities in which marketing is viewed as the basis of an integrated system of business action. Adaptation of the marketing management approach has significance for retail managers concerned with designing a total retail capability to achieve realistic and attainable objectives.

The marketing management concept in retailing is characterized by:

1. *Planning.* An emphasis on planning to achieve clearly defined retailing targets, this is the key concept. It stresses that retailing objectives can be identified and that an integrated program of action be designed to achieve these objectives through orderly retail planning.
2. *Customer Orientation.* The customer orientation is adopted as the focus for retail decision making. A philosophy of customer orientation is more important than any body of retailing techniques, personnel policies, or organizational arrangements. It ensures that retail decisions are viewed through the consumer's eyes.

Journal of Retailing, Vol. 37, No. 1, Spring, 1961, pp. 34–41.

3. *Systems Approach.* The systems perspective of retailing action is used. In this approach, a retail organization is viewed as a total system of retail action. The interaction between the components of the retailing system is stressed as is the functioning and structure of the whole organization. This approach focuses on the integrated use of all retail resources to satisfy current market needs and future opportunities.
4. *Change.* Change is recognized as the "constant" in planning, organizing, and controlling retailing activity. The prime managerial responsibility is seen as that of adapting retailing organizations creatively to conditions of accelerating change. Retailing leadership's charge becomes that of planning for and managing change.
5. *Innovation.* There is a new emphasis on research and innovation. Innovation is seen as the basis for retailing action. The important fact is that innovation is becoming programmed and a basic part of the retail management process. In short, research, a system of commercial intelligence, and innovation are becoming standard factors in modern retail action. This is resulting in the application of findings from the behavioral and quantitative sciences to retailing. The effect is new techniques of retail control, better management of inventories, improved communications, and a greater awareness of the usefulness of theory in understanding and solving retailing problems.

The crucial factor for retail management to recognize is that socioeconomic developments are operating so as to stimulate the emergence of more accurate and intellignent planning on the part of retail executives. Retailing executives are operating in an economy which is characterized by rapid change and explosive cultural and economic developments. The increasing degree of competition from both downtown and suburban areas, the impact of population shifts, trends in income and expenditures, the degree of innovation in both areas of products and services, the availability and utilization of more information about customers and markets, are examples of forces which require retail management to accept change as a normal way of life and to assign high priorities to developing creative adaptations to change. It is in such a climate that the marketing management movement, with prime emphasis on planning, has made its greatest headway.

To manage retailing effort effectively in such an environment requires planning. Yet retail planning is more than just a tool of growth. It is a rational means of achieving continuing profitable adjustment of the retail system to current and future marketing conditions.

Retailing planning, in its broadest terms, may be thought of as the utilization of analysis and foresight to increase the effectiveness of retail action. Planning retailing effort, therefore, is necessarily concerned with the objectives and goals that the retailing organization seeks to attain, the development of retailing systems, the operating system, through which retail management is attempting to achieve these goals, the availability of capacity and resources within the firm and existing facilitating agencies to exert the quantity and quality of effort necessary for their achievement. The planning proccess in retail management is portrayed in Chart I. Although this chart is necessarily a simplification, it does indicate the requisite arrangements of various factors in retail planning.

Retail plans must be conceived as functioning within an external framework determined by various forces beyond the control of the management of a given retail enterprise. This is one reason why it is becoming increasingly important in retail planning to consider environmental business factors as well as to identify the many retailing inputs, their interactions, and expected outputs.

THE PLANNING PROCESS IN RETAIL MANAGEMENT

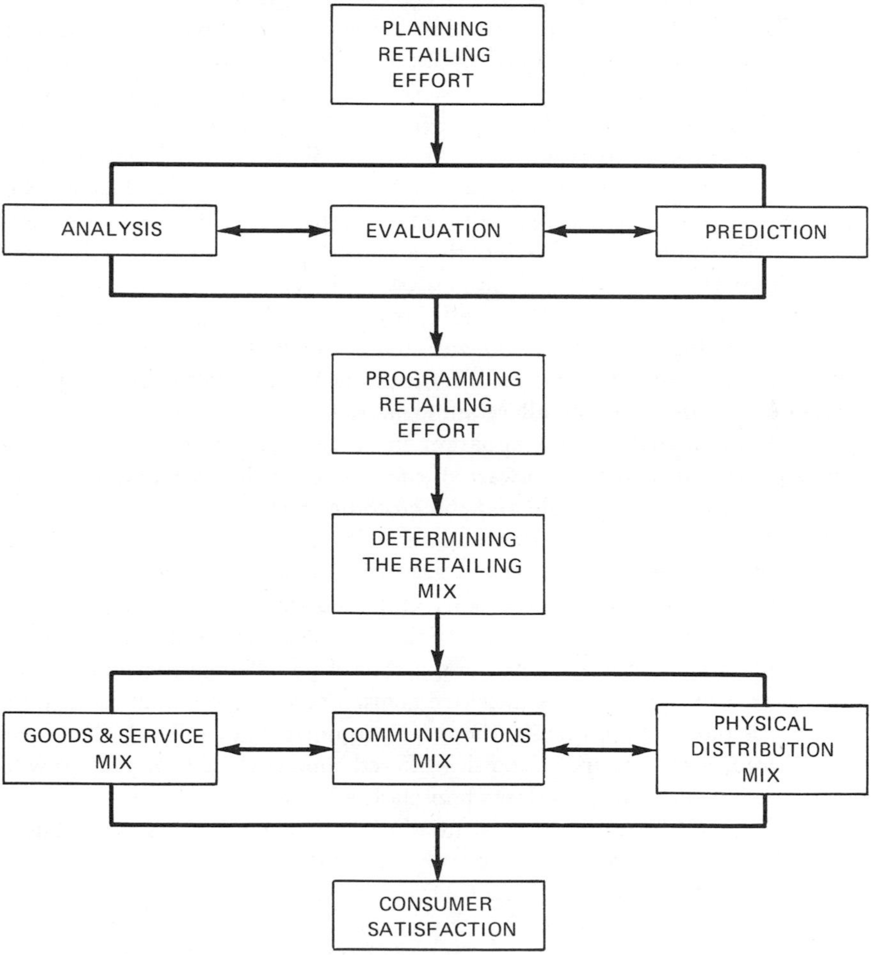

CHART I

The retail planning process involves at the first level three actions on the part of executives: analysis, evaluation, and prediction. The analysis of available information, and an evaluation of trends and relationships will give retail management the frame of reference from which to perceive current and future problems. It will afford executives a perspective of the future. Past data is useful to management mainly as it helps predict the future.

RETAILING MIX

The analysis and evaluation of data and the predictions made place executives in a position of being able to program total retailing effort. Retail programming is achieved through the determination of a retail store's retailing mix. Such a mix becomes the total package of goods and services that a store offers for sale to the public. The retailing mix, then, is the composite of all effort which was programmed by management and which embodies the adjustment of the retail store to its market environment.

The retailing mix, as such, is comprised of three sub-mixes: a goods and service mix, a communications mix, and a distribution mix. Consumer satisfaction is achieved through optimal sub-mix blending. It is through the achievement of a high customer satisfaction that a store prospers and grows. Some of the components of each of these sub-mixes are depicted in Chart II.

In Chart II the consumer is presented as the focus for all market planning and programming. The retail program is designed specifically to bring the offerings of a retail organization into line with the wants and needs of its customers and the natural market areas. The established program, therefore, sets the tone for all retailing activity.

The sub-mix that is most apparent in retailing is the *Goods and Service Mix*. Retailers are often well aware of the impact of the variety and assortment of goods offered for sale and the customer services that are extended. Other components of the goods and service mix are various credit plans that are offered, the price lines that a store will adhere to, the guarantees that are made and exchanges, alterations and adjustments, the image of the store and the goods it offers for sale, delivery, sales service, and parking facilities. The total goods and service mix should be so integrated that it will tie in with the store's own marketing goals. For example, if the image of the store is one of high quality then the customer lines offered, the price lines offered, and the types of service offered should be such that they will blend in with this concept, rather than clash with it.

The *Physical Distribution Mix* essentially has two components: a channels of distribution component and a physical distribution component. The channels of distribution component is concerned with the number and type of retail outlets that comprise the total retailing complex. For example, the number and type of branch stores that are part of the retail enterprise, and the types of suburban stores that are members of the organization, are part

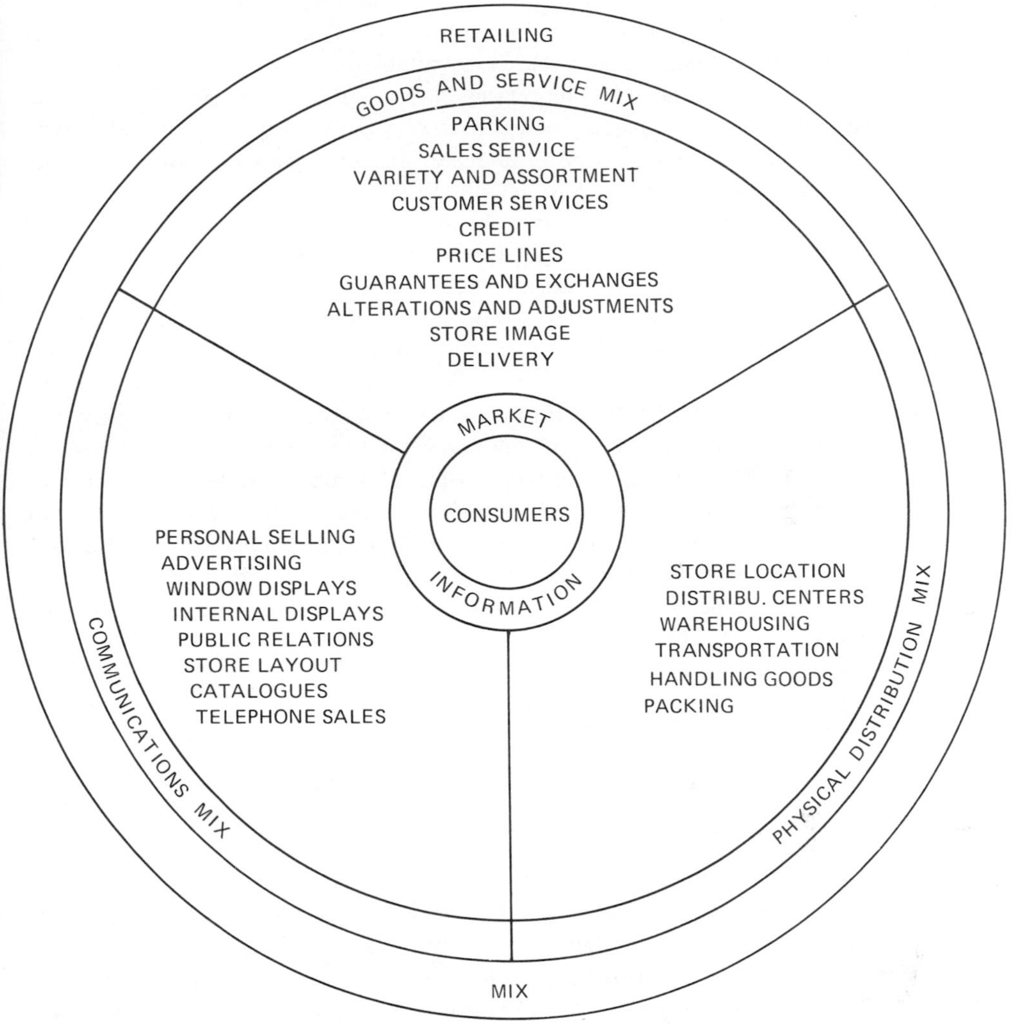

CHART II

of the mix. The physical distribution part of the distribution mix is concerned with integrating the warehousing, handling, and transporting of goods. It is evident, therefore, that the distribution mix is concerned with such factors as store location, the establishment of distribution centers, breaking bulk, warehousing, transporting, physically handling the goods, and packing them. This group of activities has been traditionally grouped under the authority of an operations manager or a store operations manager.

The *Communications Mix* is the third sub-mix. The retailer is separated in time and space from the ultimate consumer. He attempts to overcome these barriers by obtaining information about the market and by communicating information to it. The provision of information about the retail store and the goods and services available for sale constitute the crux of the communications mix. The retailer has a variety of tools for communicating with the market place. Included among these tools are personal selling, advertising, window displays, internal displays, public relations efforts, store layouts, catalogues, and telephone sales.

The communications mix is extremely important in adjusting the goods and services that are offered for sale to consumer demand. It can convince consumers that the retail store's program is primarily satisfactory to the consumer. The communications mix should be such that it ties in with the image and reputation of the store and the goods that are offered for sale.

It should be noted that the consumer is separated in Chart II from the retail program. A gap exists that must be bridged by the total retailing mix. Here marketing research helps management to adjust the mix and become aware of future trends in order to plan and make rational decisions. As retail organizations grow larger, develop more branches, and become more decentralized, the existing gap between top retail management and consumers becomes wider. Therefore, more pertinent and readily available marketing information becomes a requisite for proper programming and control of retailing effort.

THE RETAIL MANAGEMENT SYSTEM

Planning an optimal retailing mix involves viewing a retailing operation as an integrated action system affected by both internal and external forces. The success of a retail system depends not only on proper selection of each element and sub-mix but on the interaction between them.

The retail management system can be perceived as an input-output system. All of the ingredients of the retailing mix may be viewed as the inputs which flow through the retail organization and attain the outputs realized by the retailing organization. Hopefully, the outputs achieved match the accepted objectives of the organization. The response of consumers in the market place ultimately determines whether or not the store actually achieves its objectives, or the outputs planned by the programmer. In this sense, consumers hold the veto power over the entire retail system.

The retail management system, as an organization, has been studied in various books and research studies. It is composed of various levels of "departmental" managers. In Chart III, five levels are depicted from the actual selling department to top management. The department manager is concerned with management and cultivation of a particular market area. He is immediately concerned with selling and sales tactics. The group manager co-ordinates the departmental marketing effort of several departments. Therefore, his is an integrative function to alleviate dysfunctioning

THE RETAIL MANAGEMENT SYSTEM

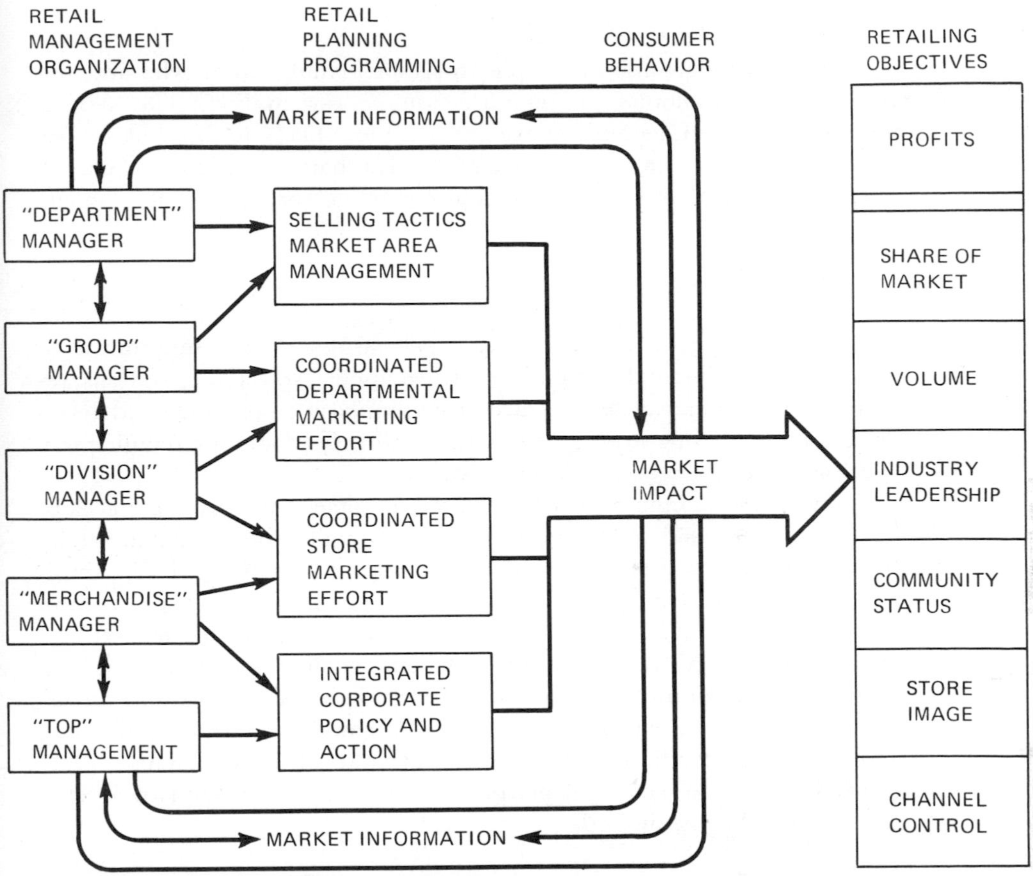

CHART III

between the departments. The division manager has a higher-level integrative point of view and is concerned with co-ordinating the store marketing effort with the marketing effort of a number of departments. The merchandise manager is more concerned with integrated corporate policy and action as it relates to the total marketing effort within the store. Top management, of course, is concerned with the broader corporate issues including store adjustment to non-controllable environmental forces.

The consumer reactions to the retailing mix determine the profits that are achieved by the organization, its volume, its share of market, its image as an industry leader, its status in the community, and the degree of channel control that retail management earns. If the proper planning has taken place, the outputs that are achieved through consumer behavior will be in line with the retailing objectives originally planned by management. If this alignment does not occur, then retail management has three alternatives:

1. Alter the objectives of the retail organization
2. Adjust the retailing mix
3. Combine the two

The systems view also has implications for manufacturers who are concerned with developing a retailing-customer orientation. The systems view of retail planning and management is more likely to foster a genuine customer-retailer orientation by manufacturers than the product or process orientation typical of many manufacturers selling through retailers today.

CONCLUSION

The marketing management approach assigns high importance to planning. This philosophy of business, when applied to retail operations, requires that retail managements place heavy emphasis on planning and developing a total retailing strategy: Only then will they program a retailing mix which achieves predetermined objectives.

Sound retail planning, in other words, becomes the basis for developing co-ordinated and goal-directed systems of retail action. Fundamentally the main functions of retailing leadership are similar to those of other business areas. Retail management must plan, organize, actuate, and control market and customer-related factors to achieve clearly defined market and organization objectives. They must view their retailing operations as a total system of action comprised of the goods and services, communication and distribution mixes, geared to the satisfaction of consumers' wants and needs, and be willing to adjust quickly to the demands of market change. Only through such enlargement of perspective can the profit thrust of a retail organization be maximized.

QUESTIONS

1. The authors point out that retail plans function "within an external framework determined by various forces beyond the control of the management of a given retail enterprise." What are some of these external factors?
2. Does the concept of a retailing mix apply to a corner grocery store?
3. What is the role of research in the retailing firm? Give an example of its use. Should it differ fundamentally from the research role in a manufacturing firm?

3

Application of the Marketing Concept to Retailing

Eugene H. Fram

Much has been written in business journals about the benefits that can be derived by organizations which use the marketing concept as a base for planning and operating. Current textbooks devote space to the subject, and numerous top executives have urged all to further its use.[1] However, in all of this activity little has been said about the marketing concept itself and its potential benefits for larger retailers.[2] The purposes of this article are to indicate that many large retailers focus their operations on products, not customers, and to present some suggestions to remedy the situation through retailer adoption of the marketing concept.

WHAT IS THE MARKETING CONCEPT?

The marketing concept has been described as a "corporate state of mind" under which management requires that all marketing functions be integrated.[3] It demands that company policies be built on the base that customer needs and wants are the starting points for all efforts. These points are different from those derived from an operating philosophy based on the company's product. Under the latter situation, the organization begins with a product which it *thinks* has a good chance of selling, and the sales division is given the responsibility of determining and effecting the promotional efforts necessary to do the job.

The integration taking place under the marketing concept is best explain-

Reprinted from *Journal of Retailing*, Vol. 41, No. 2, Summer 1965, pp. 19–26.

[1] For examples see Peter F. Drucker, "The Economy's Dark Continent," *Fortune*, 65 (April 1962), p. 103, pp. 265–70; Hector Lazo and Arnold Corbin, *Management in Marketing* (New York, McGraw-Hill Book Company, Inc., 1961), pp. 3–32; Robert Lear, "No Easy Road to Market Orientation," *Harvard Business Review*, 41 (September-October 1963), pp. 53–60; Richard Christman, "Standards of Measurement for the Marketing Concept," *Journal of Marketing*, 26 (April 1962), pp. 80–81; J. B. McKitterick, "Focus on Profit Opportunities, Not Efficiency," in *Long-Range Planning For Management*, ed. David W. Ewing (New York: Harper and Row, 1964), pp. 74–78.

[2] One exception to the last statement is the article by William Lazer and Eugene Kelley, "The Retailing Mix: Planning and Management," JOURNAL OF RETAILING, 37, No. 1 (Spring 1961), pp. 34–42.

[3] Arthur Felton, "The Marketing Concept in Action," *Business Horizons*, 4 (February 1961), pp. 14–21.

ed in the following quotation from the 1952 General Electric Annual Report.

> . . . the marketing man (enters) at the beginning rather than at the end of the productive cycle and (therefore the integration of) . . . marketing into each phase of business (is possible). Thus marketing, through studies and research, will establish for the engineer, the designer, and the manufacturer what the customer wants in a given product, what price he is willing to pay, and where it will be wanted. Marketing would have authority in product planning, production scheduling, and inventory control as well as in the sales distribution and servicing of the product.[4]

Here marketing exists not in parts but as an umbrella to coordinate all skills in the organization to maximize profits over the long-range period. In terms of this article, ". . . the principal task of the marketing function . . . is not so much to be skillful in making the customer do what suits the interests of the business, as to be skillful in conceiving and then making the business do what suits the interests of the customer."[5]

Although results from use of the marketing concept are difficult to evaluate precisely, nearly all those speaking and writing about it seem to be favorably impressed. For example, a Dun and Bradstreet survey has indicated that executives of 170 large successful corporations believe that a marketing orientation has been basic to their favorable records.[6] However, one detractor, Pierre Martineau of the *Chicago Tribune*, termed it a "hoax" because he felt it can lead to too much control being centered in too few people in the home office.

THE MARKETING CONCEPT—SUMMARY

An articulate spokesman for the concept has been Theodore Levitt at the Harvard Business School.[7] He has stated the thesis that too many businesses have been *product oriented* rather than *marketing oriented.* This has resulted in most having placed the emphasis on selling products (product orientation) instead of marketing goods and services to consumers (marketing orientation).

In total, the marketing concept operates on the well-known assumption that "the consumer is king." Although many will quickly acknowledge the importance of placing the consumer at the beginning of company planning, analysis of practice has indicated that, in fact, the product is placed first.

[4] Cited in Peter F. Drucker, *The Practice of Management* (New York: Harper and Row, 1954), p. 39.

[5] J. B. McKitterick, "What is the Marketing Management Concept?" *The Frontiers of Marketing Thought and Science* (Chicago, Ill.: The American Marketing Association, 1957), p. 77.

[6] Cited in "Crying Need for New Ways to Sell," *Sales Management*, 78 (June 1, 1962), 35–38.

[7] Levitt's major work is *Innovation in Marketing* (New York: McGraw-Hill Book Company, Inc., 1962).

Peter Drucker has summarized the situation well with the following statement:

> Despite its obvious importance, few businesses today, I am afraid, are really geared to effective marketing. The major reason is perhaps that so few top managements have as yet acquired a marketing view, let alone turned it on their own business. Despite all the speeches made about "marketing orientation" or "customer orientation," most businesses are still primarily product- or process-oriented rather than market-oriented.[8]

DOES THE MARKETING CONCEPT APPLY TO RETAILING?

It can be conceded that retailing organizations are different from those already mentioned in that they generally are not involved with manufacturing products. Consequently, this raises the question as to whether or not retailers could be product-oriented, since they are totally within the marketing process. However, retail businesses have much in common with others in that they are all organs of society and, as such, their basic reason for existence lies outside their own organization, *i.e.*, they exist to serve consumers and therefore *must fully understand movements in consumer wants.*

Since there is this common element between retailing and manufacturing organizations, it can be concluded that retailers can focus on operating problems instead of on customer needs. The thesis being presented here is that the former situation is the prevailing practice for the majority of retail organizations. In other words, retailers are defining their businesses too narrowly by stating that they are in the "retail business" when they should consider themselves to be in the business of "marketing goods and services to consumers."

To illustrate the difference in definition, all one has to do is to look to the reactions of the traditional department and chain stores to the innovations which have taken place in the last fifteen years. In the department store field, the writer knows that many executives were not concerned with the growth of the discount house until an article appeared in *Life* magazine in August 1954. This article quoted a representative of a drug trade association as saying that the discount house would be gone within a year![9] E. B. Weiss reports that during the same period chain stores had to be forced into major changes wanted by customers—more night hours, credit operations, catalog selling, telephone selling, and in-home selling. Weiss concluded that the only change they made with a high degree of energy was to imitate one another.[10]

Had these organizations been aware of the movements that were taking place in consumer demand (been "marketing goods and services to cus-

[8] Lazo and Corbin, *op. cit.*, pp. vi-vii.

[9] Herbert Brean, "Discount Houses Stir Up a $5 Billion Fuss," *Life*, 37 (August 9, 1954), 55–61, at p. 61.

[10] E. B. Weiss, *A Reappraisal of New Retail Trends* (New York: Doyle, Dane, Bernbach, Inc., 1964), pp. 9–10.

tomers" instead of being in the "retail business"), they would not have moved so slowly as to reap the following results:

1. Traditional department stores—*on balance*—have been totally unable to reverse their ten-year downtrend in capital return percentage and net profit percentage.
2. The food chains—*on balance*—have shown a declining trend in these two crtitical yardsticks for the better part of ten years.
3. The drug chains—*on balance*—have fared even worse by these two basic measurements of business performance than the food chains.
4. As for the variety chains—their ten-year record by these two measurements, is *even more dismal* than that of either the food chains or the drug chains. Among the major variety chains, there is no exception to this consistent downtrend in net profit and capital return ratio.[11]

In summary, an organization in the "retail business" attempts to sell products to customers while one which is "marketing goods and services to consumers" begins with the determination of consumer needs.

Of course, as with any group of businesses, one can find exceptions, and in the industry as a whole, they appear to be in some of the giant organizations. Sears is one good example. This firm has indicated the broad view it takes of its customers by diversification into insurance, service stations, personal loans, and mutual funds—all of which are not normally thought to be chain store "retail" functions.

Evidence to support the points being made can be located in many places. A quick look at the manner in which many buyers work provides an illustrative set of supporting facts.

1. *The Buyer Seeks Products.* One of the major activities of a variety chain and department store buyer is to "check the market." In this process he decides which items to buy out of the many offerings. These decisions are often made with a limited knowledge of what the customer might want and with heavy reliance on the proposition that his best "resources" will know customer demands. In supermarket chains, some buyers may not leave the central office, but wait for salesmen to call—the market comes to them! A recent study of the fashion buyer reveals the fact that this group is very prone to take the word of the vendor's salesmen in making buying decisions.[12] Through this method of operation, the buyer assumes only the responsibility for selling products, one part of the marketing process. In turn, this contributes to the product orientation of his organization. Of course, there is some prior consumer probing by the manufacturer, but is this sufficient, considering the reliance placed on it by the buyer?
2. *The Buyer Relies on His Records.* Most persons familiar with department stores will readily acknowledge the importance placed on "black books"—

[11] *Ibid.*, p. 6.
[12] Beatric Judelle, "The Fashion Buyer," *Stores*, 46 (September 1964), 21–36, at p. 33.

inventory records of what has and has not been sold. Soft goods buyers take them along on market trips. In central operations, chain personnel place even heavier emphasis on records because of their distance from stores. Although limitations to this situation are rather clear, heavy reliance on records continues. Use of these tools is important in all marketing areas (especially with the staple items), but very heavy use of historical data leaves little room for open marketing vision.

3. *The Buyer Watches His Customers.* In discussing customers, most buyers will state that they have a fairly good idea of what their customers want. But if one probes further he will find the department store buyer is talking about customers observed on the selling floor, the chain store man is talking about purchasers observed in the headquarter's city and many store managers and resident personnel refer to consumers in New York City. Certainly, these are good sources of data on consumer needs, but unfortunately, the bases for observation are not broad enough, meaning that *potential* customers may be elsewhere or *regular* customers not purchasing sufficient amounts because buyers are not aware of the changes that are taking place in their needs.
4. *The Buyer Uses Buying Office Reports and Talks with Other Buyers.* Like the other items, these are also valuable sources of data to aid in decision-making. But they are "in store" rather than "by consumer" in viewpoint.

Credit operations in department and chain stores provide an additional example indicating the lack of knowledge of customer needs and desires in sales supporting areas. The following questions can be raised to illustrate the point. Why is the credit office very often poorly located in terms of customer access? Why can't a system be devised so that minor problems can be settled on the main floor or at another more convenient location? How many credit personnel are really prone to help the customer make the best use of credit? If seriously investigated, changes could probably be made in line with these points without any appreciable increase in cost. A good marketing view of credit has been given by one writer with the following statement:

> In selling on credit, sellers provide a service which must be regarded like any other service they perform. It is offered for the satisfaction of the market; for the differentiation of their market offering; and for additional income, either indirectly through increased sale of products or directly through a charge made for the credit service.
>
> Credit service must be marketed like any other service or product. The character of market demand for it must be ascertained. Operating costs are incurred in the performance, and these must be taken into consideration in setting price or in estimating profit.[13]

[13] Robert Bartels, "Credit Management as a Marketing Function." *Journal of Marketing*, 28 (July 1964), 59–61, at p. 59.

The above examples support the idea that many retailers operate with too little information about consumers and their changing needs. What can be done to make retailers more marketing oriented will be presented later, but first the following question must be explored:

SHOULD RETAILERS HOLD A MARKETING VIEW?

Some retailers may agree with the analysis given and conclude that these methods of operating are sufficiently good. They also may state that the manufacturer should continue to do a basic job of consumer probing in order to determine the customer's needs, and add that if a vendor does the marketing job well, benefits will accrue to the retailer. In the sales supporting area, they may feel credit (as used in the example) could be improved, but it has been doing reasonably well to date.

There are several reasons why these arguments have little validity. First, since there are regional differences that are very important to retailers, they must seek to understand more fully their own customer groups. Second, no amount of reliance on vendors' market knowledge, records, and *some* customers will shed light on the major question of what are the new markets for goods and services. If Sears had relied on resources for market data, none of the diversified areas cited before (insurance, service stations, mutual funds, personal loans) would have been discovered.

The need for the marketing concept in retailing was dramatically shown through recent research studies. Major findings indicated that half of those who enter stores with buying intentions never make a purchase and that walkouts occur because of a number of biological, sociological, economic, and psychological factors.[14] What greater proof is needed to indicate the loose manner in which retailers view customer needs?

WHAT CAN THE RETAILER DO TO BECOME MARKETING ORIENTED?

As with most things, doing is harder than talking. However, difficulty in the retail situation is somewhat lessened because marketing of some merchandise is more related to product category than to the consumer. For example, in merchandising of many ready-to-wear items, fashion dictates of the designers are so strong as to shape feminine desires.[15] What woman will lower her skirts when Dior and others order a hemline rise? On the other side, even in this area, needs of women in terms of size, fit, and laundering are best approached by beginning with the customer.

[14] "Retail Research Institute," *Stores*, 46 (February 1964), 15–18, at p. 15.

[15] For an opposite point of view on this statement, see Louis Cheskin, *Business Without Gambling—How Successful Marketeers Use Scientific Methods* (Chicago, Ill.: Quadrangle Books, 1963).

For specific recommendations, there are five major steps most retailers can take to build a marketing concept within their organizations.

1. *More Research.* Persons in and out of retailing become uneasy when the word "research" is used. This brings visions of chart-carrying statisticians speaking in incomprehensible mathematical terms. Research as it is used here adds up to FACTS. It is the customer investigative tool needed to make decisions which place the consumer in the proper focus. The executive using the marketing concept at all times researches the customer first. His objective is to obtain a wide range of *usable* facts on how customers are living, where they spend their leisure, family situations, and many other items that set "life style" patterns, and which, in turn, determine needs and desires for goods and services. At present this kind of activity is limited to some giant organizations when in the process of investigating new locations. The type of information that can be gleaned was recently reported in a *Harvard Business Review* article on market segmentation.[16] The author concluded that women can view value in four different ways—when they pay more money for better quality, pay a sale price, pay the lowest possible price, and buy seconds or discounted merchandise. Learning where one's own and potential customers fit into these groups can be of invaluable help if the store uses the findings as guides for critical examinations of current sales promotion and buying policies and then experiments with new approaches derived.
2. *Be More Alert to Changes in Customer Wants.* For years, retailers have thought themselves purveyors of specific types of goods and services to customers. However, the potentials in quickly meeting the changes in consumer wants should be always uppermost in the minds of management. Management people should be innovators who are attuned to developing shopping habits. For example, there are the current infant trends of leasing and banking services which are open for consideration. One analyst points to the potentials for leasing as growing out of a desire for service rather than ownership based on a consumer shift in thinking from a desire for owning products to a desire to buy time.[17] E. B. Weiss thinks that retailers have a tremendous potential in the area of banking services because customers will find it convenient to "buy" these services in retail outlets.[18] The Christmas Club Plan initiated two years ago by Hess Brothers is a good example of the application of this thinking. Under the operations of the plan, customers deposit money weekly at the Hess store and at Christmas time are able to withdraw it to buy merchandise at a discount. Broad

[16] Daniel Yankelovich, "New Criteria for Market Segmentation," *Harvard Business Review*, 42 (March-April 1964), 83–90, at p. 88.

[17] Ferdinand F. Mauser, "The Future Challenges Marketing," *Harvard Business Review*, 41 (November-December 1963), 169–88.

[18] E. B. Weiss, *Twenty-Five Challenges to Accepted Marketing Traditions* (New York: Doyle, Dane and Bernbach, Inc., 1964), pp. 6–8.

and perceptive consideration of new areas is a must for retail application of the marketing concept.

3. *Consider Market Integration.* Retailing is only one step in the marketing process, but many organizations have hesitated to assume functions performed at other levels in the field. However, some retailers have found that they can profitably integrate other functions. For example, one chain has discovered that it is desirable to enter the transportation business by renting a fleet of trucks to carry its merchandise throughout the country from its central distribution center. The trucks attempt to pick up incoming loads from resources for the return trip—a nice cost saving for the chain. It is not easy for the retailer to take on other marketing activities, but if done well, it can be profitable.

4. *Orientation of Sales-Supporting Personnel.* How customer conscious are copywriters, alteration, credit, and other personnel? Even though they may not necessarily come in daily contact with them, their attitudes toward consumer needs and desires are important. A perfect alteration job may satisfy the tailor in terms of his own skill satisfactions but may not satisfy the customer in terms of delivery timing. Ask sales-supporting people to concentrate on the things about which the customer does not complain or with which he is only mildly satisfied.

   Try to build in all sales-supporting personnel the attitudes that they are not in the credit, alterations, delivery, etc., businesses but are there to help customers buy more through the work they do. There is quite a difference in the two viewpoints, although it may sound like a semantic difference on the surface.

5. *Organizational Changes.* To effect the marketing concept in retailing, responsibility for its growth must rest with someone at top level. Staff Office for Market Planning might be a good title for the function. It would have as its duties the development of proposals for broadened marketing activities and for better marketing coordination between the organization's various divisions. General Electric began its marketing emphasis in 1946 with this kind of innovation.

In this section five major areas have been presented to indicate what retailers can do to become better oriented toward placing the consumer first in their operations. This list is only a beginning. Individual companies can add to it in order to meet their own special needs.

THE PLACE OF TOP MANAGEMENT

Retailers who want to look to manufacturing firms for ideas on how to initiate the marketing concept as an operating philosophy will find that it will grow only if top management desires to move from a "common sense" approach to a "formal concept" approach. In making the move, top management must assume certain responsibilities.

1. *Create the Atmosphere or State of Mind.* Management must set the "style" in the organization by making sure that all concerned with solving problems have sufficient data, based on reasonably good investigation, on which to make decisions. Top executives also should set an example by working on some formal investigations of their own.
2. *Think in Terms of Long-Range Plans.* Urge management to consider the potentials of where the company could be five or ten years from now by using the broader marketing philosophy recommended. Although there will be some resistance to this type of activity because of daily pressures, the long haul benefits are rather evident.
3. *Establish and Support a Marketing Planning Office.* Have the Office for Market Planning regularly analyze market opportunities, develop consumer objectives (*i.e.*, how can your store mean more to your community?), develop marketing programs for sales-supporting divisions, etc. Place at the head of the office a person with diversified experience and have him use his time for the future planning and control of the marketing effort and for the development of subordinates.

SUMMARY

The marketing concept has become increasingly important in industry since 1946. The consensus seems to be that it has been instrumental in yielding greater profits for the pioneering firms which have used it—General Electric being the outstanding example. Most larger retailers should reorient their thinking from the "in-store" product view that has been utilized for many years and should adopt the marketing concept to realize greater benefits for themselves and their consumers.

QUESTIONS

1. Since a retailer does not actually produce a product, how is it still possible for him to apply the marketing concept to his business?
2. What are some indications that the retailer is in need of this approach?
3. What are some of the actual changes that would occur in a department store were the firm to apply the marketing concept? Be specific.

PART II

THE RETAILER'S ENVIRONMENT

A. COMPETITION AND SOCIAL PRESSURES

B. THE LAW

C. THE CONSUMER

A. COMPETITION AND SOCIAL PRESSURES

One of the characteristics of retailing is the ease with which competitors can enter the field. This is due to the relatively small capital requirements in retailing. Furthermore, many types of retail organizations establish a cash business, which minimizes still further their capital requirements.

Since entry into retailing is rather easy, retailers who engage in price competition soon find that because of the number of rival firms it becomes self-defeating to continue competing on a price basis over a long period of time. Lawrence Lockley, in his article on "Avoidance of Direct Competition at the Retail Level," addresses himself to this problem; Louis Wagner disputes some of his conclusions.

The article extracted from the report of the National Commission on Food Marketing gives an indication of the diverse institutions that compete in the food retailing field and of the organizational growth of cooperatives, chains, and the independent retailer.

In the last two articles, William Kelley and Stanley Hollander address themselves to a more subtle, but nevertheless important, consideration in competition among retailers—namely, social pressures. Kelley discusses the competitive pressures to maintain similar prices and ways of doing business in a small town. Hollander examines the many customs and social pressures that any retail or service organization must consider, not only in setting prices but in the manner in which business is conducted.

4

Avoidance of Direct Competition at the Retail Level

Lawrence C. Lockley

OPPORTUNITIES FOR RETAIL COMPETITION

. . . There are few areas of commerce where the opportunities for competition are better than in the field of retailing. Retailing is a field in which entrance and exit have been, for the most part, uninhibited. Only a few occasions have seen a limitation on the establishment of retail stores, and such occasions have been temporary. Small stores have been opened frequently, even though they have opened with very poor prospects for survival.

Because retailing is the final step of the marketing process, it must be performed in places convenient to the ultimate consumer. Retailing, then, has been ubiquitous enough to give a large proportion of stores access to customers; and it may be supposed that those stores which are poorly enough located as to deny their proprietors adequate access to customers are so because of the lack of wisdom or resources of the proprietor. In the same fashion, most retailers are able to buy a full range of the merchandise they wish to deal in, without worrying about restrictive agreements between sources of supply and other retailers.[1]

Moreover, the nature of retailing business is such that the operator of a store has a wide variety of options in the combinations of service and price which he can use to attract trade and maximize his profit opportunities. The fact that stores vary in location and in size does not limit the possibility of competition, though these factors may focus competition into a stratified pattern.

TENDENCIES TO AVOID DIRECT COMPETITION

In spite of what appears to be an ideal basis for competition, we find a considerable amount of agreement between various classes of stores as to

Reprinted from *Marketing: A Maturing Discipline*, Proceedings of the Winter Conference of the American Marketing Association, December 28, 29, 30, 1960, edited by Martin L. Bell, pp. 143–48.

[1] Some cognizance must be taken of restricted or exclusive distribution policies of some manufacturers, but even in such cases, it is a particular brand rather than a classification of merchandise that is unavailable to a given retailer.

uniformity of action in policies which might be the basis of competition and as to steps to prevent direct price competition.

Private Branding

In the first place, retailers have long sought an umbrella to protect themselves against price competition. The tradition goes back to the days of the craft guilds, when price, specifications, materials, and all possible variables were not only controlled by guild regulation but were held uniform for all craftsmen, so that intentional competition was virtually impossible. In our own day, one of the first efforts to avoid direct price competition was the development of private (or more properly, distributors') brands. It was not until our manufacturing techniques had made possible the processing of large quantities of consumers' goods, and until advertising was well enough advanced to help popularize particular brands that price competition on equivalent merchandise became more or less inevitable. Since that time, the rise of private brands has been rapid. These brands offer equivalent or approximately equally acceptable merchandise under the brand-sponsorship of a retailer or a wholesaler. Mail order firms, department stores, large chain grocery firms, supermarkets, soft-goods chains, and drug retailing organizations have adopted private or distributors' brands widely.

Particularly during the nineteen-thirties, strenuous efforts were made to promote the use of government grade labelling as an alternative to manufacturers' brands. One association of some eighty smaller food packers maintained an office in New York City for a number of years to spearhead a national campaign to "educate" food buyers on the preferability of grade labelling to manufacturers' brands. In an interview with the headquarters staff of this organization, the author learned that the purpose of the organization was to destroy any price premium enjoyed by established brands so that price competition could be avoided or minimized.

So many private brands have been offered by so many large retailers and chain store companies that it is difficult to make price comparisons in large sectors of the range of consumers' goods.

Fair Trade

Another main attack on the possibility of price competition came with the *fair trade laws*. These laws, concerning as they do the price behavior of local retail establishments, had to be state laws. The first is said to be the California Act of 1931.[2] However, the pressure behind the idea of fair trade laws was so great that ultimately we had such acts in forty-five states. The acts in the various states differed only slightly from the original California statute. Palamountain's comment makes the point excellently:

[2] Vaile, Grether, and Cox, *Marketing in the American Economy* (New York: The Ronald Press, 1952), p. 426.

> Within an eight-year period, 1933–1940, the National Association of Retail Druggists secured the passage of resale price maintenance acts in forty-four states—half again as many as passed chain taxes. In one year alone, 1937, twenty-eight states passed such laws. That this was a centrally directed and carefully organized campaign is indicated by the fact that the acts of sixteen states are closely modeled on the California statute, which had been passed at the insistence of the organized retail druggists of that state, and those of twenty states are direct or close copies of the NARD's "Model Act." These acts were such close copies and were pushed through so hastily that sixteen states repeated California's wrongful use of the word "content" where "container" was intended, and eleven states actually copied a stenographic error in the California act which made an important section of the law unintelligible, substituting "in delivery" for "any dealer."[3]

Typically the fair trade acts allowed a manufacturer or a wholesaler to establish minimum resale prices for the vendor's merchandise. When minimum resale price agreements have been signed by a small number of retailers, the number varying among the states, but usually being fewer than ten retailers, and often five or seven, these minimum resale prices have the force of law.

Because some of the merchandise which was "fair traded" moved across state lines, federal enabling legislation was necessary. Sufficiently strong pressure was available to get such legislation passed. As various of the state courts have upset the laws in these states, a new enabling act was needed from Congress; it was forthcoming in the McGuire Act of 1952.

We have, in the history of fair trade legislation, a clear case of avoidance of price competition on the part of a number of groups of retailers. Of course, the application of minimum pricing is limited to branded merchandise which can be specifically identified. From this point of view, it fits in very well with the increased reliance on private or distributors' brands. The retailer relying on the established manufacturers' brands finds himself, when the merchandise is fair traded, unable to cut price; and the retailer relying on private brands finds himself not forced to!

The drug trade was the most active group to push for fair trade legislation. One of the most frequent arguments for the support of the campaign for fair trade legislation was that retailers would price-war themselves into insolvency, thus injuring the economy and depriving consumers of a necessary service. Comparisons made by the present writer with census figures on the drug trade in Missouri and Texas, where fair trade legislation was not legal, with figures for the drug trade in various other areas which appeared to be reasonably comparable suggested that the trade was more profitable without the protection of fair trade legislation though it may be it required more managerial ability and industry.

[3] J. C. Palamountain, Jr., *The Politics of Distribution* (Boston: Harvard University Press, 1955). pp. 235–36.

Robinson-Patman Act

It is probably important to mention the Robinson-Patman Act which prohibits price discrimination on the part of vendors who sell to retailers. Although the subject of price control is so complex a one that no law can cope with it adequately or control price discrimination or price cutting completely, the interest of retailers in getting the act passed emphasizes their efforts to prevent the opportunity for price competition at the retail level, or at the least, between retailers in the same trade classification.

UNIFORM STORE PROCEDURES

Even in areas of store operation it is not uncommon to have competitive retailers, or retailers who should be competitive, acting by agreement. In some cities, possibly in a great many, hours of doing business, Sunday openings, check cashing, and other customer services are offered only after an agreement among retailers, and no retailer offers customer services that his "colleague" retailers do not offer.

Established merchants make every effort, apparently, to avoid direct price competition. Even now, local and regional associations of pharmacists in Northern California have apparently agreed on pricing schedules for prescriptions which not only assure an adequate gross margin, but also avoid the possibility of any direct price comparison or competition.[4] Currently, the Federal Bureau of Investigation and a Federal Grand Jury are investigating the possibility of collusive practices.

By choice of merchandise, by brand policies, by trade association activity, and by legislation when possible, retailers aspire to the same freedom from competition among themselves as was enjoyed by the members of the craft guilds. We can look for competition only between merchants of different trade classifications.

IS NONPRICE COMPETITION SUBSTITUTED FOR PRICE COMPETITION?

In the absence of price competition, is there any major reliance on nonprice competition? That is, do merchants of the same trade classifications use elaborateness of store building or selling space, advertising, display, and personal selling as a means of competing with each other? As Professor Perry Bliss indicates,[5] it is difficult to separate price and nonprice competi-

[4] *San Francisco Chronicle,* November 23 and November 24, 1960.

[5] Perry Bliss, *Non-Price Competition at the Department Store Level,* Journal of Marketing, April 1953, pp. 357–65.

tion; but the total effect of the "mix" of competitive actions is primarily to shift the demand curve to the right, so that the result of the "mix" will be the sale of a greater number of units at about the same prices.

It can be said that the larger retailing units probably watch the comparison of their current operating and profit figures with those of the previous years more carefully than they watch their competitors. It is also probably true that, if a retail establishment fails to do well, the cause for its failure is more likely to be found in its own operations, in its failure to adapt its methods to the chaniging needs of its customers, or to the development of alternative types of satisfaction for retailing needs, than to the competitive actions of its colleague stores. . . .

5

Discussion

Louis C. Wagner

Professor Lockley's paper emphasizes that the field of retailing presents opportunities for competition superior to that provided in most other fields of commerce, but as he points out, "in spite of what appears to be an ideal basis for competition, we find a considerable amount of agreement between various classes of stores as to uniformity of action in policies which might be the basis of competition, and as to steps to prevent direct price competition."

One of the most important areas of infringement is in the field of marketing legislation restricting pricing freedom. It is interesting to note that while much early federal and state legislation regulating competition attempted to protect competition and pricing freedom, the most recent laws covering this area have been aimed at protecting retailers from certain types of price competition. Much of the legislation enacted in the past thirty years has been supported by retailing groups who fear aggressive price competition. "Fair trade laws," "unfair trade practices acts," directly, and the Robinson-Patman Act, indirectly, tend to restrict the pricing activities of those retailers who wish to use low prices as a primary method of appealing to the customer.

While many marketing experts may consider the pricing restrictions made

Marketing: A Maturing Discipline, Published by American Marketing Association. Proceedings of the Winter Conference of the American Marketing Association, Dec. 28, 29, 30, 1960, edited by Martin L. Bell, pp. 161–65.

possible by fair trade laws more stringent than those imposed by the Robinson-Patman Act or unfair trade practices acts, recent developments have tended to widen the scope of these laws over price competition. While one of the purposes of the Robinson-Patman Act was to prevent unfair or discriminatory price discounts which could not be justified on a cost basis, some court rulings have tended to limit the size of discounts to large buyers even though these discounts can be justified from a cost standpoint by the seller.

While unfair trade practice acts were passed to attempt to eliminate sales below cost or the use of predatory price cutting, particularly in areas in which fair trade laws were ineffective, unfair trade practice acts have been difficult to enforce. As a result, many states have yielded to pressures exerted by retailing groups to fix prices or minimum markups in fields in which price cutting has been prevalent. The state of Washington, as a result of active retailer support, passed an Unfair Cigarette Sales Act setting the minimum wholesale margin on cigarettes at 4½ percent and the minimum retail margin at 10 percent.[1] The act provides a system of licenses which may be revoked by the Tax Commission for failure to comply with the minimum specified markups.

In the case of fluid milk pricing, freedom has completely disappeared in many areas where prices are fixed by governmental agencies operating under milk-marketing orders.[2] In some states, legislation has been passed eliminating price competition in the retailing of gasoline. Rather than permitting retailers to provide consumers with products at the lowest prices, such legislation forces retailers to emphasize forms of nonprice competition and often encourages excessive duplication of outlets.

Lockley makes the point that the opportunity for price competition in retailing is aided by the relatively greater freedom of entry than in other fields. However, it should be pointed out that in some areas this freedom is being curtailed by legislation or limited by the necessity for a much larger investment.

While ability to enter retailing in the United States is not restricted to the extent that is true in many European nations, there are some areas in which entry by individuals is restricted or forbidden. Many states restrict the sale of packaged liquor, exclusive of beer or wine, to government controlled liquor stores. While these operations usually make a substantial contribution to state revenue, they do so at the sacrifice of customer convenience as far as hours, location, and product choice are concerned. It is also doubtful whether these monopoly stores are as efficiently operated as they might be if they had to face active competition. In addition, state liquor stores tend

[1] Guy G. Gordon, "The Impact of Washington State Legislation on Effective Retail Competition," unpublished paper.

[2] S. C. Hollander, "Retail Price Policies," in *The Relationship of Prices to Economic Stability and Growth*, Joint Economic Committee, 85th Congress, 2nd Session (Washington, D. C.: U.S. Government Printing Office, 1958), p. 422.

to price their products higher than private stores in nonmonopoly states.

In the interest of controlling the sale of liquor by the drink, many jurisdictions also restrict the issuance of licenses to sell beer or other liquor by the drink. As a result, price competition is reduced and licenses to retail these products sell for large sums of money.

While the public needs protection from unscrupulous or unqualified operators in fields associated with health, licensing of entry into these fields tends to reduce the number of outlets and to restrict the opportunity for price competition.

Even in types of stores in which freedom of entry is not influenced by local or state legislation, it is difficult for an operator to launch a new store today. In spite of a rapid expansion in total retail sales during the past twenty years, the number of stores has not increased. For example, since 1939 dollar retail sales have increased fivefold, while the total number of stores has shown no increase. In many lines, in spite of a rapid increase in dollar sales, the number of retailers has actually declined.

In the retailing of foods, for example, the number of stores has decreased substantially, while the typical store has expanded its floor space. The number of food stores declined from 600,000 in 1939 to 400,000 in 1958. However, these 400,000 stores do a volume of over $47 billion compared with $10 billion in 1939. During the past 20 years the size of the average supermarket increased from an average of 1,200 square feet to an average of 15,000.[3] As a result, a much more substantial investment in capital is needed to open a grocery store which has a reasonable chance of being successful.

There is also evidence to support the position that in many areas of retailing, a larger share of the business is controlled by fewer firms. Professor Entenberg makes the point that multi-unit firms increased their market share only slightly from 1951 to 1959: from 18.0 percent to 21.7 percent. However, the domination of chains in some fields is substantial. In 1954, the Census shows that multi-units accounted for nearly 80 percent of the variety volume and 66 percent of all department store business.[4] While it is true that the nation's largest retailer, the Atlantic & Pacific Tea Company, absorbs less than 9.0 percent of the grocery market, this firm and other chains may exert a local degree of penetration far in excess of this national percentage. In the city of Seattle, for example, the leading chain, Safeway, enjoys the favored patronage of nearly 26 percent of the market.[5]

If we take into consideration both formal and informal groupings of retail stores—chains, voluntary chains, department store buying groups, and leased

[3] N. R. Collins and J. A. Jamison, "Mass Merchandising and the Agricultural Producer," *Journal of Marketing*, 22, No. 4 (April, 1958), p. 358.

[4] U. S. Census of Business, 1954, Retail Trade, Bulletin R–2–4, Single Units and Multiunits, 1957.

[5] *The Seattle Times 1960 Consumer Analysis.*

departments—it is estimated that 50 percent of our retailing volume is controlled by about 400 organizations. Dominance of such a large share of the nation's retailing by these firms influences the choice of merchandise available as well as the degree of price competition possible.

It also appears that retailers have exerted collective efforts to avoid certain types of nonprice competitive devices which may have a set and measurable cost and which cannot be dropped easily once they have been used. In many areas retailers, by agreements or through the assistance of local regulations which they actively support, have been instrumental in limiting store hours and Sunday openings. In addition, they have supported making uniform charges for or eliminating various customer services, such as check cashing, making alterations to garments, and provision of gift boxes and gift wrapping.

As an additional example, in Washington state, retailers have actively supported legislation which makes the use of trading stamps ineffective. A state law requires that each retail unit must pay a $6,000 license fee to redeem stamps with merchandise. Since cash redemption is relatively unattractive to consumers as compared with the usual merchandise redemption provided in most areas, this legislation practically discourages retailers from using trading stamps as a competitive device. This fall the Wyoming State Supreme Court upheld a law outlawing the use of trading stamps in that state.

The adoption of private brands by retailers may be looked upon as a device sometimes aiding and sometimes hindering price competition. While private brands may be employed by retailers in order to make price comparisons difficult or to avoid active price competition, often merchants have used private brands as a competitive tool. Retailers have adopted private brands to enjoy greater pricing freedom than they enjoy on manufacturers' brands subject to price restrictions. There is evidence to support the position that the existence of private brands in some areas has forced more reliance on price competition by those selling manufacturers' brands. . . .

In conclusion, I wish to take a position . . . that the field of retailing is more competitive than many other segments of our economy. However, too many retailers are concerned with preventing their competitors from engaging in active price competition or even in certain forms of nonprice competition which they consider too risky. As a result, they support legislation or agreements which deny their competitors pricing freedom or freedom to elect some types of nonprice competition. Fortunately, as long as new types of retailers have an opportunity to enter and actively to compete with older higher-cost retailers, the consumer's interest is reasonably well protected from excessive prices. As students of marketing, however, we should view with alarm any increased pressure by established retailers or other groups to restrict freedom of entry or to fix retail margins. . . .

QUESTIONS

1. Is it true that retailers avoid price competition? Why?
2. It has been stated that retailers prefer nonprice over price competition. Assuming this is true, why would they take this position?
3. Do you agree or disagree with Professor Wagner's statement that ". . . the field of retailing is more competitive than many other segments of our economy"? Discuss.

6

Small-Town Monopoly - A Case Study

William T. Kelley

Industrial monopoly and imperfect competition have been subjects of continual discussion and interest. Observations on the decline of competition purportedly occurring in this country are usually linked to such aspects as the increased aggregation of financial power and ownership. Advertising is pointed to as a powerful factor making possible brand control, which results in further imperfections on the market. Pricing systems of various kinds (such as basing-point pricing) are also mentioned as contributors to the situation.

RURAL MONOPOLY

There is one kind of imperfection, however, about which little has been written: the kind of quasimonopoly that arises from circumstances of geographical isolation and socioeconomic control often found in the small-sized rural community.

It is interesting to note that this kind of monopoly has probably been declining in modern times. It must have been much stronger in America prior to the twentieth century, when most of the population was rural or semirural; when the small market centers serving such areas were much more remote and isolated due to poor transportation; and when retailing was almost exclusively in the hands of the small, independent merchants, rather than shared with chain stores, mail-order houses, and other large-scale

Journal of Retailing, Vol. 31, No. 2, Summer 1965, pp. 63–66, 101–2.

retailers. Accordingly, the monopolistic elements present in such communities are well worth analyzing and studying as still another example of the decline of competition in America.

Perhaps because the field of social science is so ubiquitous, trained people in the profession have failed to bring this question of small-town monopoly under analysis. By employing the observational techniques common to the sociological field, the author was able to study such a situation at firsthand during one summer spent as visiting professor at a small liberal arts college. For obvious reasons, the town in question will be given the pseudonym "Collegeville." The reader is assured that such a town actually exists, as do thousands of similar small market centers throughout the country. The observations made, of course, are subject to the usual limitations found in any case study: human error in observation and author bias. An attempt has been made to keep both down to reasonable proportions.

LIFE IN COLLEGEVILLE

Collegeville is a pleasant community of approximately 2,000 people, situated in gently mountainous country. It is the seat of a small liberal arts college and is an agricultural collecting center for a number of prosperous general farms within a radius of several miles from the town. There are a few small factories on the outskirts of the town, but the factory workers constitute a small minority. The rest of the population consists chiefly of teachers and personnel of the college, retired farmers, merchants, and the families of these groups. A great number of the farmers in its trading area consider Collegeville to be the traditional shopping center for their needs, and a good business volume accrues to the local retail merchants from this source. In addition, the college brings a great deal of money into the area. Finally, much business is intracommunity, generated by the mutual purchases of the families of the local merchants and business men.

Collegeville's main competition for the retail dollar is Citytown, a manufacturing community of about 50,000, located twenty miles away. Citytown has a large shopping center and offers a number of competitive retail stores in each merchandise line, including a small department store. Other cities are too remote to compete with Collegeville stores in most merchandise lines. There are a number of other towns about the same size as Collegeville, to which Collegeville inhabitants could travel by automobile. However, the quality and price of offerings in such towns are seldom sufficiently advantageous to be competitive with the local stores.

The store population of Collegeville is carefully adjusted to what the local merchants consider the most profitable potential of retail business. There is a well-defined main street, along which is located one each of the following types of retail establishments: variety (nonchain), general merchandise (mainly soft line), drug, hardware and appliance, motion picture house, dairy (with ice cream parlor), garage (with gasoline pumps and farm appliance agency), restaurant, dry cleaning, feed and farm supply, and coal-lumber-millwork-ice. Only in the grocery line was this one-of-a-kind pattern broken. There were five grocery stores—four independent, and one small chain outlet of an obsolete service type.

MEANS OF CONTROL

This pattern is not the result of fortuitous circumstances as might seem to be the case at first glance. Investigation into existing institutional arrangements revealed a very interesting form of trade control. All business properties on the main commercial thoroughfare were owned or controlled by the local businessmen of Collegeville. The merchant group within Collegeville was closely integrated socially by feelings of responsibility and often by family connections. Local inhabitants, not members of the business in-group, told of instances in which outsiders had attempted to secure ownership or control by lease of business locations on Collegeville's main street, with the purpose of opening a competing type of store. In each case, the property owners had steadfastly refused to sell or rent their properties, even though the offers in some cases had been very attractive. The same sources reported that very strong social pressure in each case had been brought to bear on the property owner by his merchant colleagues. The opinion was expressed that a kind of social ostracism would have followed any yielding to temptation on this score.

Outsiders had been known to acquire property on side streets intersecting with the commercial section and to open retail establishments in competition with those of the in-group. Without exception, such stores had failed, usually within a relatively short period of time. Reasons given for this high mortality rate were: (1) unfavorable location—people "just don't shop off the main street"; (2) social solidarity—the merchant group's influence in the town's social structure was so great that townspeople, at least, tended to remain loyal to "old Joe, the druggist," or "Pete, the dry cleaner"; (3) innate conservatism—the farmer shoppers, especially, were reluctant to switch from dealers whom they knew, and, presumably, trusted; (4) cooperation from the wholesale stage in the channel.[1]

[1] The author observed a case of this. A college student with a wife and baby to support had developed a profitable little business delivering ice and bottled soft drinks to Collegeville householders. He secured both items from the sole wholesaler of these articles in Citytown. When he drove up one day to the wholesaler's warehouse in his Army surplus jeep, this young retailer was informed by the wholesaler that he could no longer supply him with merchandise. The wholesaler candidly admitted it was because of pressure brought to bear on him by the sole Collegeville retailer of these items. Thus was the neophyte retailer driven from business.

PRICES IN CITYTOWN

An informal investigation of prices charged by Collegeville retailers as compared with Citytown prices indicated that they were appreciably higher for most items. Surprisingly enough, in the one area in which one might except some price competition—groceries—prices were quite similar among the five Collegeville grocery stores. Generally, they were a few cents higher on low unit-cost convenience items than they were in the Citytown supermarkets. For instance, the price on a popular brand of canned tomato soup was fifteen or sixteen cents a can in the Collegeville groceries (including the chain). Simultaneously, the same item was being sold in Citytown supermarkets at two cans for twenty-five cents. The local cleaner charged $1.25 for cleaning and pressing a man's suit, while cleaners in Citytown were offering the service at prices ranging from eighty-nine cents to $1.00. The druggist carried only a few national brands of aspirin, for which he charged the full manufacturer's suggested price. Chain drug stores were offering a wider choice in brands, including little known ones at very substantial reductions in price.

These instances demonstrate the general price pattern. The tendency was not to charge outrageous prices, but rather "manufacturers' suggested" or fair-trade prices for all nationally branded articles which would afford "fair" or traditional margins. Few private brands were to be had on the Collegeville market.

No merchant wanted to obtain the reputation of being a "price gouger" among his fellow villagers. Moreover, he was constantly aware that most of his customers were automobile owners who could travel to Citytown if the difference in prices made a rather long automobile ride worth the time and trouble. Indeed, the few dealers in big ticket items—the farm implement and appliance dealers—charged little or no premium over their independently owned city competitors, since such a difference would be an obvious one to the purchaser.

CUSTOMER BUYING HABITS

There are a great many cases in this country in which price competition tends to be reduced due to the influence of geographical location and isolation. Imperfect competition is heightened because of the remoteness of the trading area from competing trading areas. This may be termed lack of intertrading area competition.

Patterns of behavior probably contribute to some extent to this lack of interarea competition. The farm families around Collegeville, for generations, had been accustomed to travel to that market center for their supplies.

Occasionally, they went to Citytown for items not obtainable in Collegeville, particularly for shopping goods. However, such trips, while exciting, involved a great deal of travel time over roads partly congested by heavy traffic. They clearly preferred the shorter trip to Collegeville, where they often formed friendships of long standing with the merchants. They knew what to expect from a Collegeville shopping excursion, while one to Citytown always had that strong element of uncertainty tied up with less familiar patterns of behavior.

OTHER FACTORS LIMITING COMPETITION

There are also cases, probably more numerous than generally supposed, in which price competition is limited by the absence of intratrading area competition. The one-of-a-kind retail pattern which was found in Collegeville is perpetuated by such factors as:

1. Group solidarity. There may not be overt collusion among the local merchants, but each is on friendly terms with his colleagues, and channels of communication are very free. Moreover, the best commercial properties, as in the Collegeville example, may be owned or controlled by the local business interests. Accordingly, when competition from outside threatens, the group exerts strong pressure to keep out the intruder. When these factors are present to any large degree, one strong element of monopoly control is implemented; *i.e.*, denial of entrance into the field.
2. Adjustment of the retail population to the market. Although the author doubts that Collegeville retailers ever heard of marketing research, they seemed to have an innate grasp of the principle of adjusting the store population to the potential business in the trading area. Such expressions as "There's not room for two drug stores" and "More than one hardware dealer would starve here" were heard whenever the merchants were questioned on the subject. To the extent that lack of intra-area competition is attributable to intelligent adjustment of store population to volume potential, charges of monopoly lose much of their force. The question always arises, however, as to whether such adjustment is merely a by-product, incidental to a motivation noncompetitive in nature.
3. General sentiment against price cutting. Merchants and even many townspeople expressed opinions that "a man has a right to a fair profit" and seemed to reflect a sentiment against price cutting much stronger than that usually held by city dwellers. This live-and-let-live attitude probably explains in part the lack of price competition in those retail lines carried by two or more Collegeville stores, e.g., groceries. If the trading area of the town had been sufficiently great to attract a chain supermarket to Collegeville, this behavior on the part of grocery retailers might have changed a good deal. The sentiment may also explain the

willingness of the customers to accept prices based on a full, traditional markup.

4. Lack of legal sanctions. Federal and state antitrust laws have not been enforced generally against cases of local restraints of trade. Although restraint is prevalent there is a great variation in degree. It often seems inconsequential since prices are not visibly too far out of line to the casual observer. If the situation is hard to detect, it would be even more difficult to prove; overt collusion and control are seldom practiced.

There are strong limiting factors which set a ceiling beyond which prices charged by local merchants will not rise. These limiting factors are:

1. Competition from distant trading areas. There are probably few small trading areas in the United States so isolated that the competition of larger, distant trading areas is not felt in this day of widespread automobile ownership and good highways. The price differences between convenience goods in Collegeville and Citytown were proportionately greater than they were for larger unit-cost shopping or specialty items. The local merchants know well that their customers will weigh the price economy of going to Citytown for an item or bill of items against the effort and expense of making the trip. Accordingly, their ability to price above the city market must be nicely calculated against these imputed and actual costs. People will discount the convenience and social approbation of dealing with the local merchants if it becomes financially unrewarding. This is the strongest limiting factor.
2. Increased value of commercial properties. If the prices charged by the local retailers get too high and their profits too great, outside enterprisers will be attracted to the area. Based on expected earnings, it will be worth while for the outsiders to offer high rentals for existing properties. Someone in the business group will give way since social solidarity can stand only a limited amount of financial temptation. Then the outsiders will offer sufficient competition to drive down the prices. (Prices were never sufficiently high in Collegeville, nor profits so great, as to cause this rise in the value of commercial property.)
3. Growth of the trading area. If the population and income of the area grow sufficiently the potential volume of business will then attract large-scale retailers such as supermarkets and chain drug and variety stores. If acceptable commercial properties are not available, such institutions can afford to locate in newer areas, perhaps on the outskirts of the town. Through advertising, low price offers, and parking facilities, these retail organizations can change shopping patterns and break the little monopoly rather easily. It would all depend on the critical size and volume potential of the area. (Collegeville had a relatively stable population and income, never growing beyond the point where it would attract such institutions.)
4. Ethical forces. The prevailing ethical sentiment against price cutting

may also work against price gouging. No merchant in Collegeville wanted his fellows to consider him a profiteer. He wanted only to make a "fair profit." As the last war indicated, public opinion can be a strong force to keep the monopolist from charging as high a price as he might. This factor may exert some force in the case of the local monopoly.

QUESTIONS

1. In what ways do small-town retailers control competition?
2. It has been stated that it is not possible for small towns to control competition as they did twenty years ago. Support this statement.

7

Social Pressures and Retail Competition

Stanley C. Hollander

The most ambiguous, the most accommodating and changeable, and yet the most pervasive and potent forces that control retail competition are custom, consumer expectations, and social pressure. Suppliers frequently try to direct their dealers' behavior. Retail unions and other worker groups have sought, sometimes successfully, to influence store hours, services, and operating methods. The market in many ways limits what retailers can do. The wares that merchants offer must be adjusted to customer needs and tastes: the sale of antifreeze at the equator and of bathing suits at the Arctic Circle usually are not viable merchandising alternatives. Similarly, price policies must be adapted to the incomes and spending habits of the market. But in some sense even more fundamental than the market is the set of ideas that both merchants and the public share as to what is the proper way for a retail business to be conducted.

In some cases the public's concept of what is appropriate retail action becomes crystallized in legislation. Legislative action may result when the behavior of some retailers differs substantially from what an influential segment of the public believes to be fitting and proper conduct. Aside and apart from formal legislative codes, however, custom and expectations

Reprinted from *MSU Business Topics*, Winter 1965, pp. 7–14, by permission of the publisher, the Bureau of Business and Economic Research, Division of Research, Graduate School of Business Administration, Michigan State University.

create very real, even if somewhat vague, limits on the competitive alternatives that the retailers can successfully adopt.

The relationship between retailing and its environment is complex. It is difficult for us to perceive that relationship as it operates within our own culture, since our questions and expectations of retailing are very largely determined by that same culture. A sort of cross-cultural anthropological economic analysis is needed to discover the social determinants of retailing. In the past few years marketing specialists and anthropologists alike have become increasingly interested in that sort of analysis; and so we have recently had, for example, some fascinating studies of the social forces that determine trading relationships, the use of credit, and merchandising practices in Indonesian villages. British economists have tried to establish statistical relationships between socioeconomic variables, on one hand, and, on the other, the number and kind of stores that will operate within a given community. Many other interesting studies are becoming available,[1] and while they still are exploratory rather than definitive, they do much to suggest society's role in shaping the limits of competition.

SOCIETAL CONTROLS

Most merchants are even unlikely to conceive or consider alternatives outside those limits, a fact that in turn reinforces the original impact of the social controls. Few merchants in America today, for example, would consider as a competitive tool the use of a "puller-in," that is, a man stationed at the doorway to coax window shoppers into the store. The use of these men was once a common competitive tactic, yet today it is simply outside the average merchant's frame of reference.

The August fur sale illustrates the self-reinforcing nature of many retail customs. At one time very few furs were sold in August, which is what one would expect to have been the case in the days before air-conditioning. Apparently some furriers tried offering drastic price inducements to offset this normal seasonal slump in business. Their competitors followed suit, and eventually a large, price-conscious segment of the market began to do its fur shopping in August. Consequently, the merchants who wanted to attract this segment had to offer their more attractive specials that month, before the customers purchased elsewhere. The concentration of specials, in turn, tended to strengthen the consumers' belief that August was the time to buy, and so on in circular fashion.

A similar illustration of self-reinforcement appears in the recommenda-

[1] See the sources cited in Stanley C. Hollander, "Retailing: Cause or Effect," in William S. Decker (ed.), *Emerging Concepts in Marketing* (Chicago: American Marketing Association, 1962), pp. 220–32. Also see Robert Bartels, *Comparative Marketing* (Homewood, Illinois: Richard D. Irwin, Inc., for the American Marketing Association, 1963), pp. 1–6, 283–308, for a discussion of comparative analysis in wholesaling.

tions that the American Newspaper Publishers' Association offered to the retail trade for many years. Although the Association's Bureau of Advertising has recently modified its position somewhat, it used to suggest that retailers concentrate their advertising of each type of merchandise in those months when the consumer purchases of that merchandise were greatest.

Of course, societal forces shape all businesses, not merely retailing alone. As one economist has put it:

> No less important is the unconscious influence provided by the mores, folklore, customs, institutions, social ideals, and myths of a society which lay the foundation for formal organization. More immediately relevant to any one firm's behavior are the standards and values of the groups with which it comes into contact as an organization, as well as the groups, communities and organizations to which its members belong. It should be clear that the preference system of the firm, as well as the attitudes of the participants in the firm's organization toward such things as cooperation, efficiency, innovation, etc. must be profoundly affected by the broader community within which the firm operates.[2]

The totally public nature of retailing and of some of the service trades does nevertheless create some special problems for businessmen in those fields. Often a factory or a wholesale establishment in an isolated or unfrequented location, for example, may operate at full force on Sunday subject to possible resentment only among its own employees and their families. The storekeeper who opens on Sunday, however, is more likely to come to the attention of, and to irritate, segments of the general public that may include both voters and potential customers. Local sentiments, which vary from place to place, determine whether clothing merchants must cover their windows when changing the garments on the display dummies.

In an entirely different sense as well, dealing with the ultimate consumer probably leaves the retailer more susceptible to the influence of custom and tradition than most other businessmen. For over two hundred years economists, marketing specialists, and psychologists have debated whether habit and past practice are more important in guiding the purchases of consumer buyers than those of the supposedly more rational industrial and commercial buyers. This debate has often centered around the supposedly more crucial role of customary prices in consumer markets than in commercial ones. The argument is by no means settled, but the only question in all the debate has been whether consumer dependence on tradition is greater than or only equal to that of business buyers. No one has ever seriously urged that it is less. The retailer's problem is that his public is indeed *the* public.

Caplow has argued that the prevailing customs and expectations influence the retailer's entire relationship to his customers and, to a considerable ex-

[2] Andreas G. Papandreou, "Some Basic Problems in the Theory of the Firm," in Bernard F. Haley (ed.) *A Survey of Contemporary Economics* (Homewood, Illinois: Richard D. Irwin, Inc., 1952), II, 192.

tent, even his behavior outside the store. In contrasting the occupation of shopkeeper with that of factory worker, he says:

> the control of occupational behavior is entirely different, being at once much wider and much more diffuse. Indeed, it is the popular belief that self employment in a small business carries with it freedom from personal coercion which constitutes the principal appeal of retail trade, just as it is often the impact of impersonal coercion which subsequently disillusions the neophyte proprietor.

He describes the coercion as originating with suppliers, creditors, and customers. Then he goes on to say:

> [Compared to the rigid system of control exercised by suppliers and other creditors], the control which the customer exerts upon the occupational comportment of the merchants is very informal. It is none the less important. Particularly since the restrictions of price and quality competition, personal relations with customers are often the decisive factor in the history of a retail business.
>
> The "rules" are essentially these:
>
> 1. The merchant is expected to minimize his status and exaggerate that of the customer by exaggerated forms of deference, by yielding in minor arguments, by expressing more interest in the customer's personal affairs than the customer is expected to show in his, and by small personal services.
>
> 2. Under this ritual, it becomes essential that the habits of the customer be identified and protected. A strain is thus produced on the merchant to maintain nearly absolute consistency in his manners, his purchasing routines, and his hours of work. . . .
>
> The norms of deference imposed on the shopkeeper prevent him from displaying a distinctly higher status than his customers [in life style], while his aspirations toward the role of businessman impel him to do so.[3]

This picture is somewhat overdrawn, particularly if it is used to depict all retailer-customer relations. Certainly many of the most successful mass-retailers exhibit little of the deference suggested by the first "rule" cited above. And the smaller merchants who have succeeded without much servility are also numerous. But in spite of these and other criticisms of Caplow's picture, we must grant that a retailer in the typical American community today cannot long behave like the operator of a trading post on the Navaho reservation who says: "The important thing is to show the Indians who is boss."[4] Nor can he expect to take on the general role of social, eco-

[3] Theodore Caplow, *The Sociology of Work* (Minneapolis: University of Minnesota Press, 1954), pp. 118–19, 128–29. Caplow, it should be made clear, directs his remarks specifically to small shopkeepers.

[4] William Y. Adams, *Shonto: A Study of the Role of the Trader in a Modern Navaho Community*, Smithsonian Institution, Bureau of American Ethnology, Bulletin 188 (Washington: U.S. Government Printing Office, 1963), pp. 210–12, 287–90. The traders cited by Adams reverse every one of the rules of deference indicated above, and in order to discourage automobile ownership among the Indians, go so far as to deliberately create disorder and uncertainty in the marketing of gasoline.

nomic, financial, and technical advisor to the community, as did so many pioneer merchants of the Western frontier. In short, society has dictated the general limits of the retailer's role. It also dictates many of the details of his operation.

PRICING

As any one retailer faces his world, he finds that it tells him a number of things about what it considers appropriate pricing policies. Our society, for example, regards haggling and bargaining as permissible in some retail situations and improper in others. Automobile dealers are expected to bargain, haberdashers are not. Of course, the explanation can be offered that the size of the automobile transaction and the unstandardized condition of the trade-in are conducive to bargaining in the car dealership, while different conditions obtain in the haberdashery. This is perfectly reasonable, and true. But the point is that in other times, and at other places, haberdashers have been expected to bargain, while in our society they definitely are not expected to do so. Also, we generally feel that such professional men as architects and physicians, whose output is also unstandardized and sometimes of substantial size, should not bargain, although under some conditions they may discriminate between patrons.

Some patterns of discriminatory prices have become so widely accepted in the sale of some, *but not all*, goods and services that it requires a conscious effort of mind to appreciate that these patterns do, in fact, discriminate between customers. These conventional discriminations are often based upon age, and occasionally upon sex. Children's rates, lower than those for adults, are frequently offered in the sale of transportation, amusement, and other services. In cases such as the provision of restaurant meals and haircuts, it can properly be argued that the child receives a different, albeit perhaps more troublesome, service than the adult. This is not so in the case of many amusement and transportation services in which the child, charged the lower rate, receives exactly the same privileges as the higher rated adult. Some aspects of family-plan airline and railroad fares, and the free admission of women to baseball parks on Ladies' Day are examples of similar discriminations based upon sex.

Some discriminatory practices based on the patronage status of the purchaser seem to be of general acceptability. Special introductory rates for new subscribers are very frequently used in building magazine subscription lists. Department store private sales for the benefit of old customers cast the discriminatory advantage in the opposite direction. While magazine introductory rates usually are actually restricted to new subscribers, many so-called private sales are much less impregnable. In many stores the term is used to describe the practice of givng charge customers notice of approaching sales before the advertisements appear in the newspaper. Rational justifications can be offered for each of these discriminations. But again the point is that each of these sets of price differentials seems to be regarded as acceptable only within a particular context. Clothing merchants usually find that extra alteration charges are more readily accepted in the sale of women's clothing than in menswear. Generally however, commodity retailers, unlike service trade operators, usually do not think in terms of age or sex-based price differentials and the public doesn't seem to expect them to do so, although there is as much social justification for a child's discount on toothpaste as on movie admissions. A department store sale that was confined to noncustomers would engender waves of ill will, and no department store executive would dream of such a sale. Yet magazine publishers do it every day, with apparently very little criticism.

Another curious way in which public expectations, reinforced by retail practice, limit the retailer's freedom to select among competitive pricing alternatives is in the matter of "customary prices." This is the popular belief that only certain prices or price endings are appropriate for certain types of goods. The use of these prices has been condemned as a mechanism that forces price increases into unnecessarily large steps, and praised as a device that facilitates consumer comparisons. Whether desirable or not, most retailers feel that the public's expectation that these traditional price endings should be used is a very real force that must be considered in setting prices. Very few studies attempting to measure the strength of consumer attachment to customary prices have been reported. The best known one started with a hypothesis on the part of the researcher and his mail-order house sponsors that the whole thing was a myth. The only conclusion was that the dangers of testing outweighed the possible benefits of the test.[5] And finally the public often seems to have some vague sense of what it considers as unfair or fair prices. An experienced retailer puts it this way:

> It is generally accepted as poor policy to charge what the traffic will bear. Whenever an article is priced higher than eye-value would seem to justify, the retailer is at pains to explain that the fault is not his, but the high price of the manufacturer. Indeed, he may often shade his mark-on in order to avoid criticism.[6]

MERCHANDISE

The public also has some expectations as to the type and nature of the merchandise that each type of retailer will carry. Such expectations are in fact necessary, if shopping is not to be a matter of haphazard searching. The importance of these traditional expectations about merchandise offerings is denied to some extent by recent developments of "scrambled merchan-

[5] Eli Ginzberg, "Customary Prices," *American Economic Review*, XXVI (June 1936), 296.

[6] *Oswald Knauth*, "Considerations in the Setting of Retail Prices," *Journal of Marketing*, XIV (July 1949), 7.

dising," i.e., the sale of many types of goods in nontraditional outlets—for example, the introduction of nonfoods into grocery supermarkets. Yet it is interesting to note that some commodity lines, which the public apparently considers too different from the usual grocery stock, such as clothing accessories, have encountered considerable customer resistance in many supermarkets. On the other hand, soap is considered so traditional a grocery line that no one ever refers to it as a "nonfood," even though it is hardly edible; and consequently, no grocer would dare exclude it from his stocks.

A very different sort of public pressure arises if the retailer handles goods that come from sources that are objectionable to some portion of his public. The reaction may take the form of picketing, boycotts, or attempts to secure some type of controlling legislation. Most recently this sort of reaction has occurred in connection with the sale of goods originating in the communist-bloc countries. At various times, similar responses have been evoked by the sale of low-priced Japanese textiles, products made by firms that practice racial discrimination, prison-made and nonunion-made goods, and items from Nazi Germany and elsewhere.

And, of course, the public or a segment may protest if it considers the merchandise itself objectionable. Again, apparently, the reaction will often be directed with different strength against different types of retailers. At least one book distributor reports that the public seems to tolerate more lurid paperbacks in drugstores than it will in supermarkets.

SERVICES

When the Twentieth Century Fund sponsored its classic study of distribution costs a number of years ago, it also asked a distinguished panel to prepare recommendations on ways of reducing those costs. Among other things, the panel recommended that retailers separate the charge for each service rendered the customer from the basic price of the merchandise itself.[7] This suggestion was based upon the belief that the general practice of quoting a single price for the item and the attendant services leads many consumers to use more services than they really want or would be willing to pay for in a free market. The panel felt that many consumers would like the option of choosing between service and price savings. Also charging for services in proportion to use would be more equitable than the prevailing practice. The idea seems thoroughly reasonable. Yet many merchants, and especially the ones to whom this suggestion was particularly addressed, were, and to a great extent still are, extremely reluctant to adopt it.

Their reluctance has been based upon a strong feeling that the public associates a particular bundle of services with each type of store, and that

[7] Paul W. Stewart and J. Frederick Dewhurst, *Does Distribution Cost Too Much?* (New York: Twentieth Century Fund, 1939), pp. 351–52.

any attempt to reduce those bundles will create a sense of outrage. Again, the public expectations seem to have a differential impact. As a very perceptive analyst points out, what is considered appropriate will vary with the store's price policy and with the socioeconomic class it seeks to attract.[8] Department store operators claim that their comparatively long history as operators of full service institutions makes them subject to consumer expectations of expensive delivery, credit, exchange, return, and miscellaneous other privileges. Yet, they allege, the same consumers will patronize such competitive outlets as discount houses, chain stores, and mail-order house retail shops without demanding any of the services whose discontinuance by department stores would be vigorously resented. Undoubtedly the harshness of the situation is sometimes exaggerated by department store people as an excuse for poor profit performance, but nevertheless the problem does exist.

One aspect of retail services about which many people, including both customers and noncustomers, have strong feelings is the matter of store hours, and particularly the question of Sunday openings. In many areas local pharmacists' associations have detected some public dissatisfaction with the hours observed by drug stores and have formulated plans under which there will always be at least one pharmacy open in the community at any hour to handle emergency needs. In contrast, an increasing trend toward Sunday sales on the part of roadside clothing, hardware, furniture, general merchandise stores, and automobile dealers has induced a call for some type of control in many parts of the country. The issue is complicated by the varying economic interests of the retailers and the communities involved, the diverse desires of retail workers, and the thorny question of the proper position of government in matters that have religious overtones. But it is clear that a number of people in this country do believe that at least some types of stores should close on Sunday.

IMPACT OF SOCIAL PRESSURE

The strength of the social forces that we have just looked at can easily be overestimated. The merchants who are affected by these forces may be particularly likely to see more power than is actually there. Customs may persist, not because of any inherent vitality, but because of inertia and the absence of any strong incentive for change. Department store merchants who have been beset by discount house competition have found that they could, in many cases, move to self-service, to the elimination of some frills, and to separation of commodity and service charges. Possibly this increased freedom to compete has been due to changes in the consumer between

[8] W. T. Tucker, *The Social Context of Economic Behavior* (New York: Holt, Rinehart & Winston, Inc., 1964), pp. 73–81.

1935 and 1950 and 1964. Some of it probably is. But at least some of the change probably is a correction of an erroneous impression as to the amount of service the consumer really wanted. Katona mentions another instance of failure to judge what was permissible among the many apparel merchants who offered totally unneccessary seasonal reductions during the wartime shortage years of 1942 and early 1943.[9] Other such examples could be cited.

Yet in spite of all such instances, the fact remains that the retailer is in the business of dealing with the public, and so he must be responsive to the public's demands upon him. Frequently, as in the case of the mail-order firm that wanted to question the strength of customary pricing, attempts to test those demands involve risks of lost sales or of customer alienation. The risks are greatest, although sometimes the rewards also may be greatest, when an individual retailer tries to move independently, counter to the practices of his competitors. Thus, for example, two authors who generally favor independence and competitiveness in retailing, urge group action to reduce the returned goods rate:

> Although the individual store can do much to reduce its returns, group action of the retailers within a given shopping area is often necessary for best results. The group can afford to do many things which the individual store cannot do. Also, some of the steps the individual retailer might take would merely drive his customers to competitors, where they would still return as much merchandise, so that the returned-goods problem of the community would be as important as before. Group action, therefore, has the major advantage of making it easier to establish a sound educational program on the costliness of returns and of making it less difficult for individual stores to refuse returns because of the established "law" in the community governing such matters.
>
> Realizing the advantages of group action, merchants in such cities as Dallas, Los Angeles, Kansas City and Milwaukee have joined together to reduce returns. Such action usually involves agreement on one or more of the following points: establishing uniform time limits, setting up a standard policy of refusing to pick up certain merchandise for return, standardizing extra charges for return pickups, framing sanitary provisions and obtaining local ordinances involving sanitary considerations, activating educational campaigns and providing material for publicity drives, exchanging information about customers with records of excessive returns, and exchanging return-ratio data.[10]

Anyone who is dedicated to a classical "hard-core" antitrust position might question the propriety of some of the actions outlined above, although several of them are similar to recommendations of the Twentieth Century Fund's distribution cost panel. But they do also illustrate the difficulty of making individual changes in the established way of dealing with the public.

[9] George Katona, *Psychological Analysis of Economic Behavior* (New York: McGraw-Hill Book Company, Inc., 1951), p. 51. See also John K. Galbraith, *The Theory of Price Control* (Cambridge: Harvard University Press, 1952), p. 12.

[10] Delbert J. Duncan and Charles F. Phillips, *Retailing: Principles and Methods*, 6th ed. (Homewood, Illinois: Richard D. Irwin, Inc., 1963), pp. 591–92.

QUESTIONS

1. Compare the problem of discriminating among customers in a department store with the same problem in a self-service store.
2. What role does social pressure play in determining the prices a retailer charges and the merchandise he offers for sale?
3. Discuss some social pressures applied to retailers in your local community.

B. THE LAW

It has become increasingly evident that local, state, and federal laws have an effect on any action business decides to take. Retailing is certainly no exception. The various laws affect the buying, the selling, and the hiring practices, and the services offered. For example, in many cities, the retailer is not allowed to open his store on Sunday. In some areas he is not allowed to offer trading stamps. In others, he needs a license to conduct his business, e.g., liquor stores in New York State. Local laws usually involve licensing and store hour restrictions.

More important to the large retailer are the federal and state laws that impose pricing and buying restrictions. In addition, antitrust laws and certain amendments restrict the larger firms in their relationships with vendors and in the organization of their stores.

Two articles are presented in this section. The first article, by Roger Dickinson, "The Retail Buyer and the Robinson-Patman Act," describes the restrictions and many of the problems faced by the retailer in adhering to the law and at the same time making profitable purchases from vendors. In the second article, Donald Thompson sets forth some current interpretations of important cases which affect retailing and, in particular, the growing franchise field.

8

The Retail Buyer and the Robinson-Patman Act

Roger Dickinson

In 1936 the Robinson-Patman Act, designed primarily to curb the purchasing power of the large food chains, was passed by Congress. Since that time, both buyers and sellers have struggled with its provisions. Today, conformance with this statute remains a problem for almost all businessmen. In 1963, for example, a Robinson-Patman Act legal expert stated that ". . . the plain fact is that I expect now that there is no one business out of five thousand that is complying with the Robinson-Patman Act daily, and can."[1] In 1946 a judge maintained: "I doubt if any judge would assert that he knows exactly what does or does not amount to violation of the Robinson-Patman Act in any and all instances."[2] And in 1950 Justice Robert H. Jackson of the Supreme Court maintained that:

> I have difficulty in knowing where we are with this [the Robinson-Patman] Act, and I should think the people who are trying to do business would find it much more troublesome than we do, for it does not trouble me but once a term, but it must trouble them every day.[3]

It is against this background that the retail buyer must make his day-to-day decisions. Typical of his problems is the fact that the Federal Trade Commission has recently issued a complaint against Best and Company (a specialty store chain operating twenty-one units) alleging that its buyers had knowingly induced or received discriminatory advertising concessions from vendors.[4] Although the retail buyer is basically a citizen interested in obeying the law, he is aware that he will be evaluated against the performance of other buyers in the store—including his predecessor and suc-

Reprinted from California Management Review, Vol. 9, No. 3, pp. 47–54, by permission of The Regents of the University of California.

[1] Edgar Barton, Chairman of the Clayton Act Committee's Subcommittee on the Robinson-Patman Act of the American Bar Association, on April 4, 1963, as a panel participant in "Symposium: The Supreme Court and the Robinson-Patman Act," *Antitrust Bulletin*, IX: 1 (Jan.–Feb. 1964), 78.

[2] *United States* v. *New York Great Atlantic and Pacific Tea Co.*, 67 F. Supp. 626, 676–77 (E.P. Ill., 1946).

[3] *Standard Oil Co.* v. *FTC*, 340 U.S. 231 (1951), Transcript of Oral Argument, Oct. 9, 1950, p. 88.

[4] *Best and Co., Inc.*, Trade Reg. Rep. (FTC Complaints, Orders, Stipulations) para. 17,363 at 22,580 (1965). This action was brought under Sec. 5 of the Federal Trade Commission Act.

cessor[5]—as well as against the performance of buyers in other stores. In making this evaluation, his superiors often set up certain standards of performance, including a desired margin of profit.

This article is designed to present the Robinson-Patman Act from the point of view of the nonfood retail buyer. Sections are devoted to the Act, the nature of the buying problem, the sources of advice for the buyer, apparent broad alternatives open to the buyer, and the probable ramifications if the buyer disregards the Act. Food buying is excluded because the author knows little about this area and because this type of buying appears to be significantly different from other forms of buying.

PURPOSE OF THE ACT

The Robinson-Patman Act was passed as an amendment to the Clayton Act. Its principal purpose, according to Corwin Edwards, was to reduce the buying power of some organizations.[6] David Revzan maintains that the final version of the Act seems to restrict sellers more than buyers.[7]

In either case, the curbs on buying power were instituted directly in Section 2(c) (the brokerage provision which will not be considered in this article) and in Section 2(f). Section 2(f) states: "that it shall be unlawful for any person engaged in commerce, in the course of such commerce, knowingly to induce or receive a discrimination in price which is prohibited by this section." Notice that Section 2(f) only refers to price concessions. Thus, according to a literal interpretation of the statute, the buyer is only held responsible when seeking illegal price concessions.

Sections 2(d) and 2(e) refer only to the seller and insist that the seller distribute allowances, services, and facilities proportionately to all accounts. While nothing in the Act itself holds the buyer responsible for inducing concessions proscribed by sections 2(d) and 2(e), of late the inducement or receiving of discriminatory advertising allowances or services seems to constitute an unfair trade practice prohibited by Section 5 of the Federal Trade Commission Act.[8] The FTC apparently utilizes the FTC Act to pursue buyer practices which are beyond the technical confines of the Robinson-Patman Act but contrary to its spirit.

Most large retailers have some sort of power for a variety of reasons, and

[5] If the buyer remains in the store after leaving a given department, he will naturally be compared to his successor.

[6] Corwin D. Edwards, *The Price Discrimination Law* (Washington, D.C.: Brookings Institution, 1959), p. 626.

[7] David A. Revzan, *Wholesaling in Marketing Organization* (New York: John Wiley and Sons, Inc., 1961), p. 561.

[8] Wright Patman, *Complete Guide to the Robinson-Patman Act* (Englewood Cliffs, N.J.: Prentice-Hall, Inc., 1963), p. 163.

the retail buyers have many ways of utilizing this power, some undoubtedly quite legal. Many times, however, it is in the economic interest of both the vendor and the buyer to get together on concessions that might not be so clearly legal. The incentive for the buyer to bargain aggressively is increased by two factors:

1. *Many buyers in many industries have no way of finding out what other buyers pay for merchandise.* Buyers have indicated this lack of information to the author—both directly and indirectly—but it would also appear obvious for three reasons.

First, most sellers do not adhere rigidly to price lists and, indeed, many cannot afford this luxury. This is not to suggest that firms are legally supposed to adhere to a price list, or even to have a price list,[9] but once concessions are made from a price list perhaps a focal point has been broken, and there may be little confidence in any resting point.[10] In any event, a buyer will certainly not have confidence in a supplier's statement that the buyer is getting the most advantageous price when he knows that the price list is not being rigidly adhered to.

Second, nonsystematic differentials in the purchase price and allowances seem to exist among large buyers. The existence of differentials, however legal, may be inferred from the price evidence accumulated by the Commission.[11] Once a buyer for a large store finds that another large store is getting an item at a lower price, he is assured of getting the lower price also, unless the supplier is willing to run the risk of losing the account. Thus, to the extent that such discrepancies do exist among large accounts, it would appear that those stores paying the higher prices do not know that they are paying more.[12] In fact, it would appear that buyers in many industries simply have no way of finding out what others pay.

A third argument for the position that buyers do not know what prices others pay is that negotiation does occur. Indeed, as will be indicated later in this article, both academicians and the courts have maintained that buyers still have the right—and perhaps duty—to negotiate.

An additional point might be made here. Although it is much easier to estimate the quantities of merchandise purchased by a competitive firm than the price paid, securing even this information is not easy in most

[9] See Albert E. Sawyer, *Business Aspects of Pricing under the Robinson-Patman Act* (Boston, Mass.: Little Brown and Company, 1963), pp. 7–8.

[10] Thomas C. Schelling, *The Strategy of Conflict* (Cambridge, Mass.: Harvard University Press, 1963), pp. 111–115. A focal point is here considered a point that is prominent and conspicuous. Some qualitative characteristic or characteristics distinguish a focal point from the surrounding alternatives.

[11] For example, see *Admiral Corp.*, Trade Reg. Rep. (FTC Complaints, Orders, Stipulations) para. 17,230 at 22,308 (1965).

[12] There might be a few exceptions where a store will overpay on one model knowing that it is underpaying on other models. This would not, however, appear to be a regular practice.

retail stores. One cannot determine the sales volume that the store enjoys with a certain item or in a specific department from the over-all volume of the store.

2. *Another incentive for buyers to bargain hard is that discounts received may be large enough to be extremely worthwhile.* Thus, in the Automatic Canteen case, differentials as high as 33 percent were noted.[13] The final resting point may be related to specific economic factors such as marginal cost rather than to the original price list. In many instances, economic factors can create prices far below the price list of the supplier.

A buyer might desire answers to some questions relating to the Act. If he is permitted, for what may he negotiate? How aggressively can he negotiate? Can he be held in violation of the law if he does not bargain at all? Few buyers will want to ask these questions of the top management of the store because the answers would undoubtedly be ambiguous. In addition, this kind of inquiry on the part of the buyer would do little to enhance his image as a dynamic merchant.

INTERPRETATION OF THE ACT

Consulting a lawyer is a possibility, but few lawyers are skilled in the Robinson-Patman Act, and few buyers care to incur the expense. Also, a lawyer might tend to overemphasize legal considerations as opposed to business considerations. A buyer could consult other buyers, but the legal value of such advice might be questioned and, further, if a buyer feels that he might be doing something illegal, he would naturally hesitate to discuss it with others. A buyer might consult the FTC publications and opinions, but these do not appear to be geared to business reality. The FTC adopts extreme positions on the theory that, if it does not adopt these positions, questions will never be raised in the courts.[14] A buyer cannot afford to follow extreme views that will cost him profits. It would appear, therefore, that a buyer would rely primarily on academic sources and previous court cases.

Leading texbooks in retailing caution the buyer against negotiating too hard. Duncan and Phillips state that

> since the buyer who knowingly benefits from price discrimination is equally guilty with the vendor, the retailer must resist the temptation to bargain for a larger quantity discount than can be justified by a cost differential.[15]

Wingate and Friedlander maintain that the buyer should seek "the lowest prices given to competitors of his class."[16]

[13] *Automatic Canteen* v. *FTC,* 346 U.S. 61, 62 (1953).

[14] Barton, *op. cit.*, p. 40.

[15] Delbert J. Duncan and Charles F. Phillips, *Retailing: Principles and Methods* (Homewood, Ill.: Richard D. Irwin, 1963), p. 323.

[16] John W. Wingate and Joseph S. Friedlander, *The Management of Retail Buying* (Englewood Cliffs, N.J.: Prentice-Hall, Inc., 1963), p. 298.

Despite these cautions, textbooks insist that buyers still have the right to negotiate. Duncan and Phillips maintain that

> . . . despite the limitations placed on price bargaining by the Robinson-Patman Act, the buyer still has ample opportunity to negotiate for lower prices. There is nothing in the Act to prevent a buyer from buying at the lowest lawful prices that sellers are willing to offer or accept.[17]

Davidson and Brown state that, within the limits of the Robinson-Patman Act, ". . . considerable flexibility and opportunity for trading still exist."[18]

In the Standard Oil and Automatic Canteen decisions, the Supreme Court basically maintained that the buyer does have the right to bargain.[19] In 1953, in *Automatic Canteen Co. v. FTC*, Justice Felix Frankfurther held

> . . . that a buyer is not liable under Section 2(f) if the lower prices he induces are either within one of the seller's defenses such as cost justification or not known by him not to be one of those defenses.[20]

A buyer might feel relieved by the above statement, but Frankfurter went on to maintain that "trade experience in a particular situation can afford a sufficient degree of knowledge to provide a basis for prosecution."[21] In 1961, in *Mid-South Distribution, et al.*, v. *FTC*, it was held that some of the evidence was quite sufficient "to show the basis for inferences of buyer knowledge of seller nonjustifications."[22] Other court holdings will be alluded to later, but essentially the Court has not given clear guides—or at least if it has, the Commission has not followed them.

The fact that the courts and the Commission have not established effective, workable guidelines in the last thirty years for administering the Robinson-Patman Act is of little help to the buyer. The Act still exists, and the FTC obviously feels that the buyer is responsible for conforming to its provisions, as unclear as they may be. One unfortunate aspect of the Act is the extreme difficulty of defending an action against the FTC. One attorney, for example, has suggested to his colleagues: "Don't tell me whether you won or lost an antitrust case, you lost if you were in one."[23] Such cases have resulted in a severe drain on company funds and personnel. Moreover, in certain instances a store might face private, triple-damage suits which are burdensome and expensive to defend and which sometimes culminate in court injunctions that sharply reduce the company's flexibility.[24]

[17] Duncan and Phillips, *op. cit.*, p. 329.

[18] William R. Davidson and Paul Brown, *Retailing Management* (New York, N.Y.: The Ronald Press, 1960), p. 482.

[19] Jerrold Van Cise, former chairman of the Antitrust Section of the American Bar Association, panel participant on April 4, 1963, in "Symposium: The Supreme Court and the Robinson-Patman Act," *op. cit.*, p. 37.

[20] *Automatic Canteen Co.* v. *FTC*, 346 U.S. 61, 74 (1953).

[21] *Ibid.*, p. 79–80.

[22] *Mid-South Distributors, et al.*, v. *FTC*, 287 Fed. 2d 512 (5 Cir., 1961), 518.

[23] Jack I. Levy, "Doing Business Under the Antitrust Laws," *Antitrust Bulletin*, X: 3 (May–June 1964), 409.

[24] For the application of this to vendors, see footnotes 1 and 2 of Frederick M. Rowe, "Current Developments in Robinson-Patman Law," *Business Lawyer*, XXI: 2 (Jan. 1966), 499–514.

THE BUYER'S DECISION

Faced with these problems, a buyer would appear to have three general alternatives:

- A buyer might try to play the game with complete safety. He could decide *not to bargain at all.* Upon investigation of the law, however, he would realize that he could still be held liable because the Act holds it unlawful "knowingly to induce or receive a discrimination in price that is prohibited by this section." Thus, if the supplier offers a buyer a discriminatory concession, it is conceivable that upon acceptance the buyer might be held in violation of the Act. A buyer intent on playing the game with relative legal safety, however, might negotiate in certain instances. He might attempt to deal exclusively with suppliers who qualify as dealing only in intrastate commerce; he might deal with vendors who deal only with very large accounts; he might become the only account of a firm.

Although the above alternatives may be relatively safe from Robinson-Patman Act violations, there may be other legal risks involved. Solutions designed to insure safety against the Act might run the risk of violating various other statutes including Section 1 of the Sherman Act which holds that "Every contract, combination in the form of trust or otherwise, in restraint of trade or commerce among the several states, or with foreign nations, is hereby declared illegal." Thus, if a buyer becomes too zealous in protecting himself or the store from potential Robinson-Patman violations, he may end up in other types of legal trouble—perhaps more serious.

However, if a buyer only bargains occasionally and restricts these bargaining activities to what appear to be the more legal avenues, he will run a relatively small legal risk. From a business point of view, however, the risks may be quite large.

- Another alternative that a buyer might follow is to *bargain vigorously but in a manner that is likely to be considered legal.* In this instance, he would alter his patterns of negotiation. Such a buyer must be relatively knowledgeable of the Act. Some of the things he should know are outlined here, although again I am not necessarily claiming legal expertise.[25]

If good faith has been demonstrated, i.e., if the seller has demonstrated facts that would lead a reasonably prudent man to believe that he was responding to a lawful lower price of a competitor, the meeting of competition defense will be established.[26] Whether a supplier is permitted to meet competition only to retain old customers or, in addition, to gain new customers

[25] In this section it is assumed that all defenses available to the seller are also available to the buyer per the Automatic Canteen case.

[26] Daniel J. Baum, *The Robinson-Patman Act, Summary and Comment* (Syracuse, N.Y.: Syracuse University Press, 1964), pp. 35–36. The legality requirement has lately appeared to vanish. See Rowe, "Current Development in Robinson-Patman Law," *op. cit.*, p. 511.

as well has not been decided.[27] The meeting of competition applies to allowances, services, and facilities as well as to price.[28] The burden of proof is on the seller to show that he is within the exculpating provision of meeting competition.[29]

Several legal defenses are possible against a price discrimination complaint. The most famous defense is, of course, the cost defense which permits price differentials that are related to savings in manufacture, sale, or delivery. In addition, a price discrimination according to the Act must "... lessen competition or tend to create a monopoly in any line of commerce, or to injure and destroy or prevent competition. ..." Changing market conditions which affect the market generally or the marketability of the particular goods concerned may also be a defense. This last proviso of Section 2(a) of the Act does not apply to a raising or lowering of prices for a product or line of products in reponse to mere changes in market demand.[30] These defenses are particularly important if one accepts Rowe's point that Robinson-Patman Act proceedings proliferate with the ease of making a case.[31]

A discrimination in price refers only to goods of like grade and quality, although it is extremely difficult to establish what is a significant enough differential to quality for this.[32] A discrimination in allowances must also relate to goods of like grade and quality.[33] The FTC has consistently held that physical similarity was the important factor in determining like grade and quality, and this position was recently supported by the Supreme Court.[34] It would appear that a buyer is safe in bargaining for price concessions with merchandise that is significantly different in grade and quality, although a difficulty exists in being sure that a differential is significant in the eyes of the Commission or the courts. The FTC recently ruled that bath-

[27] It was ruled by the courts that Section 2(b) might be used defensively to keep an existing customer but not offensively to obtain a new customer, in *Standard Motor Prod., Inc.* v. *FTC*, 265 F. 2d 674–276 (2d Cir. 1959). This view was rejected in *Sunshine Biscuits, Inc.* v. *FTC*, 306 F. 2d 48 (7th Cir. 1962). The Commission has rejected the Circuit Court's view of the law in the Sunshine Biscuit case. See Baum, *op. cit.*, p. 35. Also, see Russell C. Dilks, "A Stepchild Gains Small Favor: The FTC and the Meeting Competition Defense Under the Robinson-Patman Act," *Business Lawyer*, XXI: 2 (Jan. 1966), 488, 489.

[28] *Exquisite Form Brassiere, Inc.* v. *FTC*, 301 F. 2d 499 (D.C. Cir. 1961), *Skueton, Inc.* v. *FTC*, 305 F. 2d 36 (7 Cir. 1963). See Russell C. Dilks, *op. cit.*, p. 482.

[29] *FTC* v. *Sun Oil Company*, 83 Sup. Ct. 358 (1963).

[30] See Cyrus Austin, *Price Discrimination and Related Problems under the Robinson-Patman Act* (Philadelphia, Pa.: American Law Institute, 1959), pp. 79, 80.

[31] Frederick M. Rowe, *Price Discrimination under the Robinson-Patman Act* (Boston, Mass.: Little, Brown and Company, 1962), p. 539.

[32] See Ralph Cassady, Jr., and E. T. Grether, "The Proper Interpretation of 'Like Grade and Quality' within the Meaning of Section 2(a) of the Robinson-Patman Act," *Southern California Law Review*, XXX: 3 (April 1957), 241–279.

[33] *Atlanta Trading Co.* v. *FTC*, 258 F. 2d 365 (2d Cir. 1958). The Commission apparently has accepted this position. See Baum. *op. cit.*, p. 56.

[34] *FTC* v. *The Borden Company*, Trade Reg. Rep. (New Court Decisions) para. 71,716 at 82,191 (1966).

tubs and other equipment of slightly different sizes and with slightly different features and design were not of like grade and quality.[35]

A buyer may not knowingly induce or receive disproportionate amounts of advertising, services, or facilities.[36] It is more difficult to legally defend against this type of complaint than to defend against price discriminations since fewer legal defenses are permitted. Advertising and other allowances are to be made available by suppliers on proportionately equal terms. The smaller number of legal defenses is particularly significant in light of the point made earlier that Act proceedings appear to proliferate with the ease with which the FTC can make a case.

A vendor may select his own customers. He is not forced to sell to small stores or other stores, providing he is not in restraint of trade.[37]

Under certain conditions, a supplier may continue a lower price forced upon him by competition. A Commission ruling indicated that a dairy company was justified in continuing its lower price for an indefinite period since the competitive vendor's offer was not a one-time offer but was expressly conditioned on the customer giving the competitor an exclusive status as a supplier.[38]

Special promotions can be legally hazardous. A buyer who

> instigates a special promotional campaign automatically possesses sufficient information to put him on notice that the allowances are probably not being offered on proportionately equal terms to competition. . . .[39]

The Commission has indicated that

> a buyer who induces a seller to depart from his customary pattern of allowances and grant a promotional payment two or three times greater than previously paid does so at his peril unless possessed of particular knowledge that the seller has been granting like concessions to others similarly situated.[40]

A store may not induce advertising for institutional promotional purposes above normal promotional allowances.[41]

A buyer desirous of using this second general approach would probably utilize certain types of behavior more than others. He might obtain many

[35] See Frederick M. Rowe, "Current Development in Robinson-Patman Law," *op. cit.*, p. 401. See also *Sears, Roebuck and Co.*, and *Universal-Rundle Corp.*, Trade Reg. Rep. (FTC Complaints, Orders, Stipulations), para. 16,644 at 16,644 (1963).

[36] *Grand Union Co.* v. *FTC*, 300 F. 2d 92 (2d Cir. 1962). This ruling was made under Section 5 of the FTC Act.

[37] Baum, *op. cit.*, p. 27.

[38] *Beatrice Foods Co., Inc.*, and *Eskay Dairy Co., Inc.*, Trade Reg. Rep. (FTC Complaints, Orders, Stipulations), Sec. 17,311 at 23,469 (1965).

[39] *Furr's Inc.*, Trade Reg. Rep. (FTC Complaints, Orders, Stipulations), Sec. 17,352 at 22,518 (1965).

[40] *American News Co.*, 58 FTC 27 (1961). This position was not commented upon in *American News Co.* and *Union News Co.* v. *FTC*, 300 F. 2d 104 (1962).

[41] *R. H. Macy and Co. Inc.* v. *FTC*, 326 Fed. 2d 445 (2d Cir. 1964).

offers from many vendors trying to get as broad a base as possible for meeting competition. A buyer for a low-price-oriented store might emphasize price concessions so that the defenses available under Section 2(a) might be utilized. A buyer for a quality operation might develop new products not of like grade and quality and, in his dealings for these new products, might emphasize price. The buyers in this group should know that FTC action will probably continue to be predicated on its ability to set up a case.

- As a third alternative a buyer might essentially *disregard the Act in an intelligent manner*. He is not deliberately violating the law, because he does not understand the law—nor does he consider such understanding a possibility. Such a buyer would not alter his patterns of negotiation to accommodate the Act, although he would negotiate with discretion.

A buyer utilizing this alternative probably accepts the position that supplier firms may be violating and perhaps must violate the Act. He probably feels that whether or not the supplier is violating the Act cannot be determined, because the buyer has no way of knowing what others pay for merchandise, the quantities in which they buy, or other factors relevant to a legal defense for the vendor. Therefore, such a buyer, in his opinion, would not be in violation of the letter of the law. He might argue that the buyer who selects the second alternative is just trying to avoid the law and that the buyers who resort to the second or third alternative are violating the spirit of the Act.

SELECTING A COURSE

The effects on society of the second and third alternatives would appear to be about the same. But the spirit of the Robinson-Patman Act is against the power of the buyer for a large organization. To live within this spirit, a large buyer would have to abrogate his power to the detriment of the management and the stockholders he represents. He would have to forego obvious legal loopholes to uphold the spirit of an Act that does not have general acceptance in the business community. He might feel that until Congress establishes a set of rules that all must adhere to—and this probably would permit the buyer to have access to the records of those vendors with whom he negotiates—he must negotiate to the best of his ability and intelligence. If he is violating any law, the chances of his being caught apparently are small. Out of thirty-seven FTC complaints under Section 2(f) between 1936 and 1963, only eleven concerned buyers connected with concerns of national prominence. Of those eleven, eight were dismissed, and three resulted in final orders.[42]

[42] Frederick M. Rowe, "The Federal Trade Commission's Administration of the Anti-Price Discrimination Law—A Paradox of Antitrust Policy," *Columbia Law Review*, LXIV: 3 (March 1964), 430.

Therefore, if a buyer buys for a large store in an intelligent manner, the chances of any legal repercussions are probably small. I am quite sympathetic to the third position, although, in certain industries, it might be more prudent for the buyer to adopt the second alternative.

EFFECTS OF THE ACT

If all buyers bargain as they choose, it can be argued that the Act will be rendered useless because, if buyers are permitted to negotiate in whatever manner they desire, the vendors—particularly small ones—are going to be hard pressed to uphold the Act. Since, in the first thirty years of the administration of the Act, buyers have been left pretty much alone, it might be well to make an estimate of what some effects of the Act have been. It should be recognized that these rather sweeping conclusions as to the effects of the Act are based on my observations and experience and only to a limited degree on interviews with merchandise executives. Many firms are reluctant to frankly discuss the Robinson-Patman Act for quite understandable reasons. In fact, I was denied certain interviews because of their possible legal ramifications.

THE LARGE VENDOR FIRM

The greatest effect of the Act, first, would appear to be that it has controlled the large supplier to some extent, particularly the supplier whose merchandise is not dependent upon a salesclerk to sell the final consumer. It has prevented such vendor firms from offering discounts that a large buyer might have induced them to make. Thus, smaller retailers buying from these "monopoly" sellers probably received lower prices relative to the large buyer than they would have received otherwise. An example where this effect has been felt is the toy industry.

A second result is that the large vendor firm may have been hurt because small vendor firms in most industries have felt relatively free from violations of the Act, despite the fact that actions of the Commission have often been against the small firm. Few small firms have been attacked by the Commission relative to the number of such firms. This feeling of comparative immunity means that the small vendor may cater more closely to the desires of his customers in price and other sensitive areas. Large buyers may be more interested in dealing with the small vendor for this reason.

A third effect of the Act is that certain large retail chains—particularly department store chains, such as Federated Department Stores, Inc., and R. H. Macy and Co., Inc.—have not centralized their buying to as great a degree as they might have done otherwise. If these large store chains could obtain huge discounts from the larger suppliers because of the additional power created by joint buying, there might have been greater incentive to centralize this power into stronger national buying groups. These firms have not centralized to such a degree because their individual buying systems have worked well. One of the contributing factors to this success is that, even legally, the small vendor firm has more latitude than the larger firm, i.e., fewer customers, fewer combinations of potential violations, etc.

With the help of the Act's effect on the large vendor, the relationship of the large local store to a small local supplier may permit the buyer for such a store to obtain more favorable arrangements than a strong central buying group might receive from large suppliers. A central buying group must generally deal with fairly large vendors because of the delivery constraints imposed upon it by its very size. The net effect of the policies of certain store chains to buy locally has been to aid substantially the small supplier.

A fourth effect of the Act is that larger vendor firms have been forced to advertise more nationally than they would have done otherwise. This national advertising has been required to support rigid price lists of certain large vendors and to prevent an erosion of their business to private brands. In food and other businesses, it seems evident that the growth of controlled brands of the large retail chains has been substantial,[43] partially as a result of the Robinson-Patman Act. Large vendors, even if they manufacture private brands, would generally prefer to sell their nationally branded merchandise because they will typically realize more profit on the incremental sale of this merchandise and because national brand business cannot be taken away from a vendor as easily as can private brand business. An executive for a food manufacturer readily admitted that one of the purposes of his firm's large advertising budget was to counteract the effect of private brands. This is also true of other industries.

A fifth effect of the Act is that vendor firms may have been induced to retain or set up independent wholesalers in certain industries. Thus, rather than themselves violating the Act, the larger vendor firms may have preferred to establish independent wholesalers over whom the manufacturers may have no direct control to violate the Act. Giving a profit to a wholesaler may be superior to adopting rigid business practices intended to cater to the act but not designed to meet the realities of the market.

SIDE EFFECTS

There have been other effects of the Act. Large buyers, if not possessing less power than formerly have become more sophisticated and careful in its use. The use of blatant requests (such as a demand for a 20 percent reduction in price or no business) is probably of less importance as a buying technique today than it was formerly. Another effect has probably been a decreasing

[43] See E. B. Weiss in *Advertising Age*, Jan. 24, 1966, p. 86.

respect on the part of the businessman for the law. Since many businessmen do and must violate the Act to exist, and a much larger number think that they might be violating the Act but are not sure, the business community may not have great respect for it. This lack of respect may carry into other facets of business, such as pricing. In my opinion, one of the effects of the Act does not appear to have been that of aiding the small retailer, considering both the Act's pluses and minuses.

These influences have occurred without substantial enforcement of its buying provisions. It is concluded, therefore, that lack of enforcement of the various buying sections does not make the Act sterile. Whether it would be more effective with the enforcement of the buyer provisions is another question.

CONCLUSIONS

Buyers for large retail enterprises have substantial leeway in the manner in which they may utilize their purchasing power. Some of the means they may employ are undoubtedly entirely legal. Until Congress passes extensive legislation designed to curb this power directly (and this may cause many problems), it will continue to be exercised by many retail buyers when the situation warrants.

A buyer is faced with three general alternatives in considering the Robinson-Patman Act: he may decide not to bargain at all; he may decide to bargain vigorously but in a manner very likely to be considered legal; or he may essentially disregard the Act in an intelligent manner, feeling that understanding the Act may not be a realistic alternative. None of these courses can be followed without risk. Alternatives that have small legal risks have large business risks, and, conversely, those with smaller business risks have larger legal risks. Unfortunately, the FTC can probably find ample grounds for charging violations against any individual or company at any time it chooses, regardless of the methods used by the buyer or his company.

QUESTIONS

1. Does the retail buyer have the freedom to bargain with a supplier under our present laws?
2. Are large and small manufacturers treated the same under the Robinson-Patman Act?

9

Franchise Operations and Antitrust Law

Donald N. Thompson

Franchise systems (and the contractually-integrated marketing systems of which they are a part) have grown more rapidly in recent years than any other form of distribution. This development may prove to be one of the most significant trends in marketing in the postwar period.

It is estimated that the franchise industry,[1] by the end of 1967, had reached $91 billion in annual sales, representing 12.0 percent of projected gross national product and 28.0 percent of projected retail sales in the United States for the year. Looking at another dimension, there are about 1,100 franchising companies and 400,000 franchised businesses in the United States, with new franchisees being added at a gross rate of 40,000 per year.[2]

TYPES OF FRANCHISING

It has become common to apply the term "franchising" to a variety of different economic and legal relationships. The relationship of interest in this paper is one in which an organization (the franchisor) with a pattern or formula for the manufacture and/or sale of a product or service, extends to other firms (the franchisees) the right to use the pattern or formula *subject to* a number of restrictions and controls.

There are two quite distinct classes of franchise systems: one involving a product or service, the other involving a trademark licensing arrangement. These two break down into six identifiable types, designated by the kinds

Reprinted from *Journal of Retailing*, Vol. 44, No. 4, Winter 1968–69, pp. 39–53.

[1] The term "franchise industry" suggests that a strong community of interest exists among franchisors despite their diversity of forms and backgrounds. According to Grant Mauk, President of the Duraclean Company, "I would say that we have more in common with other franchising firms, regardless of their industry, than we do with nonfranchising firms in our own industry. Our problems of motivation, training, business development of franchisee-franchisor relations are not shared by firms that simply sell their products to a totally independent operator or deal with employees in company-owned outlets." J. A. H. Curry and others, *Partners for Profit: A Study of Franchising* (New York: American Management Association, Inc., 1966), p. 12.

[2] Estimates on annual sales and number of franchisees are from a study of franchised business, by the writer, to be published in 1968. The study (and the research on which this article is based) was supported in part by a grant from the Marketing Science Institute, Philadelphia, and administered through Dr. E. T. Grether, University of California, Berkeley.

TABLE 1.

Types of Franchising	*Principal Industries Represented*
Product and Service Franchise Systems	
1. Manufacturer-retailer systems	Passenger car and truck dealers (Chevrolet); gasoline service stations (Standard); hearing aids (Beltone); swimming pools (Gold Medal); water conditioning systems (Culligan)
2. Manufacturer-wholesaler systems	Soft drink syrups (Coca Cola); beer (Falstaff)
3. Wholesaler-retailer systems	Food retailing (Independent Grocers Alliance); drug retailing (National Drug Cooperative); hardware retailing (Mr. Handyman); home and auto stores and automobile aftermarket (Western Auto); variety store retailing (Ben Franklin)
Trademark Licensing Franchise Systems	
4. T.M. franchisor-manufacturer systems	Fabricated textiles (Fruit of the Loom)
5. T.M. franchisor-wholesaler or retailer systems	Carpet and upholstery cleaning services (Duraclean); moving companies (Aero Mayflower); roadside food, beverage and soft ice cream restaurants (Howard Johnson's, Tastee Freez); hotels and motels (Holiday Inns); automobile, truck and trailer rental services (Hertz); coin-operated and regular laundry and dry-cleaning services (Arnold Palmer); tool and equipment rental (Abbey Rents)
6. T.M. franchisor-franchisee group on same level of distribution	Bread industry (Quality Bakers of America, Inc.); milk industry (Quality Chekd Dairy Products Association); mattress industry (Sealy Mattresses)

of market supplier and franchisee (*see* Table 1). Thus, a franchise agreement may exist between a manufacturer and retailers, between a manufacturer and wholesalers and between a wholesaler and retailers. A trademark franchisor may contract with manufacturers, with wholesalers or retailers or with franchisees on the same level of distribution as the franchisor.

In almost all the cases of significance, the franchisee operates using the franchisor's name as a trade name—A & W Root Beer, for example. It is very common for the franchisee to submerge his individual identity to the extent that the public is unaware it is doing business with an independent businessman. Many franchisors require their franchisees to maintain an establishment similar to, or identical in, physical appearance to those of other franchisees and to adhere to a standardized product or service as well as to a prescribed method of operation. In the extreme case, the franchisee is required to conduct every step of his operation in strict conformity with a manual furnished by the franchisor. The public is thus conditioned, by advertising and through personal exposure, to expect the same product or service from all establishments bearing the franchisor's trade name.

ANTITRUST—THE FRANCHISOR'S PARADOX

A central issue in franchising today is emphasized in the above definition which states that the right to carry on business under the franchisor's trade name and style of operation is granted to the franchisee "... *subject to* a number of restrictions and controls." Franchise contracts frequently require agreement by the franchisee to limit his sales to specified territories or to a stated group of customers; to use only that equipment or deal only in that merchandise furnished him by the franchisor or by a supplier named by the franchisor (a tying agreement); and to advertise, hire employees, keep records or landscape the premises only in accordance with the franchisor's rules and restrictions.

Because the antitrust laws limit the extent to which such controls may be enforced, the potential or existing franchisor faces a managerial paradox. A wholly-owned business enterprise is free to assign territories, select customers, fix prices and otherwise dictate any and all terms for the sale of its products. A firm with identical business interests which chooses to operate through a franchise system may find it difficult to compete against its wholly-owned competitors because it cannot invoke the same controls. The franchisor, especially the financially limited one, thus faces a dilemma. The unrestricted control of distribution afforded by directly owned outlets can involve prohibitive investment and management burdens. But the substantial cost savings available with franchising carry with them the disadvantage of relinquishing control over the marketing of goods once title to the product passes to the franchisee. In an era of extensive trademark branding, advertising and service and warranty obligations, the franchisor can find himself with continuing marketing obligations but with few legal rights that survive his surrender of title in the marketing of his products.

FOUR PIVOTAL CASES

Four recent Supreme Court decisions on the legality of various distribution controls handed down during the past two years[3] suggest the effect of antitrust on the operation and development of franchising in the United States. While the exact scope and total impact of these decisions is not completely clear, certain patterns have emerged. Before discussing the implications of these four cases, it is useful to review briefly the content of each one.

[3] *United States* v. *General Motors Corp.; Federal Trade Commission* v. *Brown Shoe Company; United States* v. *Arnold, Schwinn & Co.; United States* v. *Sealy, Inc.*

In the *General Motors* case,[4] the arrangement under challenge was a provision of the G.M. franchise agreement limiting the franchisee to a single business location. The contract did not restrict the territory within which a dealer could sell, but it prohibited dealers from establishing a new location or place of business without the prior written approval of G.M. This "one-place-of business" restriction is common to many franchise agreements, the usual argument being that a franchisee who opens additional outlets on the periphery of his exclusive territory thereby encroaches on and diminishes the value of the territories of adjacent franchisees.

Beginning in 1958, some franchised Chevrolet dealers in Los Angeles began supplying discount houses with new cars for resale at cut prices. In 1960, members of the Automobile Dealer Trade Association in the area agreed to bring the practice to the attention of General Motors' Los Angeles office. G.M. invoked its one-place provision to restrain sales through discount houses, arguing that such sales were equivalent to the establishment of an unauthorized sales outlet. Members of the Dealer Trade Association agreed to raise money to finance surveillance operations.

The Department of Justice brought suit on the basis that the restrictive contract provision and the way it was enforced both constituted unlawful restraints of trade in violation of Section I of the Sherman Act. The Supreme Court decided in favor of the government, but only on the narrow basis of a finding that there existed a "classic [horizontal] conspiracy in restraint of trade" between G.M. and its dealers.[5] Thus, the Court ruled against horizontal activity by dealers, in cooperation with a franchisor, to prevent resale of a franchised product to nonfranchised outlets. The decision is an application of the doctrine found in *Parke, Davis*[6] that a control, to qualify as truly vertical, must be free of any trace of horizontal origin, purpose or enforcement. G.M.'s policing of franchise customers was also viewed by the Courts as an unwarranted restriction on price competition, a goal which is unlawful *per se* when secured by combination or conspiracy.

The Court was explicit in stating that it did not consider the question of the legality of the location clause itself. The *Schwinn* case, discussed below, suggests that the one-place clause is probably unenforcible, and that a franchisor cannot act to squelch bootleg sales to discounters.

The Federal Trade Commission proceeding against the Brown Shoe Co.[7] was concerned with exclusive dealing.[8] Brown, the second largest shoe

[4] *United States* v. *General Motors*, 234 F. Supp. 85 (S.D. Cal. 1964); *reversed*, 384 U.S. 127 (1966).

[5] While many would scoff at the argument that a few dealers could compel General Motors to adopt a policy, the fact remains that the argument was considered and accepted by the Supreme Court.

[6] *United States* v. *Parke, Davis & Co.*, 362 U.S. 29 (1960).

[7] *Brown Shoe Co.* v. *F.T.C.*, 339 F. 2d 45 (6th Cir. 1964); *reversed* 384 U.S. 316 (1966).

[8] This is an agreement between supplier and dealer under which the franchisee agrees to deal exclusively with the franchisor. It is often confused with the terms "exclusive franchise" or "exclusive distributorship," which refer to the supplier's agreement with the dealer in a given geographical territory not to franchise any other dealer within that territory.

manufacturer in the country by dollar volume, had for years entered into franchise agreements with a number of independent shoe retailers. In exchange for such benefits as free signs, business forms and low-interest loans, each franchisee agreed to "concentrate" purchases of shoes in the "grades and price lines" manufactured by Brown, and to refrain from stocking or selling competitive shoes of equal grades and prices. Retailers who did not comply were denied these benefits. A number of other large shoe manufacturers had similar programs with retailers, so the arrangements did not involve the use of economic power in one market to restrain competition in another.

The F.T.C. charged, under Section 5 of the Federal Trade Commission Act, that Brown's franchise plan constituted an illegal tying arrangement, with the special benefits offered by Brown to franchised dealers serving as the tying product. The Supreme Court held that the leverage of these special benefits was used to secure exclusive patronage for Brown to the detriment of competition in the shoe manufacturing industry. While *Brown* is not strictly a trademark licensing case, it does show that the entire bundle of rights which a franchisor makes available to his franchisees may be viewed as separate from the franchisor's product, and may serve as a tying device.

A matter of further interest in *Brown Shoe* is related to the amount of competitive foreclosure necessary to invalidate an exclusionary program. Brown had tied up only 1 percent of total retail shoe outlets, and approximately 4 percent of the "choice" outlets for which the program was designed. The F.T.C. argued successfully that this degree of foreclosure, in the context of the shoe industry, was sufficient indication of probable competitive injury to warrant the issuance of an action against the company.

In the *Schwinn*[9] case, the central question was the degree to which a manufacturer may not only select the customers to whom he will sell, but also allocate territories for resale or restrict franchisees from selling to other retailers for resale. The restrictions were similar to those in *General Motors*, but without any findings of conspiracy.

Arnold, Schwinn & Company is a family-owned business manufacturing bicycles and a limited number of parts and accessories. In 1951, Schwinn had the largest share of the United States bicycle market, with 22.5 percent. By 1961 it had fallen to second, with a market share of 12.8 percent. The decline resulted from increased imports, and the growing share of market taken by the Murray Ohio Company, a private label manufacturer.

Schwinn sold 85 percent of its bicycles directly to franchised retailers under the "Schwinn Plan." Under the Plan, bicycles were ordered through one of twenty-two franchised wholesalers. Schwinn extended credit, shipped bicycles directly to the retailer and paid a commission to the wholesaler

[9] *United States* v. *Arnold, Schwinn & Co.*, 35 U.S. Law Week 4536 (decided June 12, 1967). Schwinn provides an extreme example of the time and expense involved in a modern antitrust defense. The investigation, trial and appeals extended over a decade in time, sent a 22,000 page record to the Supreme Court and cost the family-owned company an estimated $1 million.

who had taken the order. The wholesaler acted as a manufacturer's representative, and normally carried no responsibility for warehousing, billing or credit.[10]

Franchised wholesalers were instructed to distribute only to franchised Schwinn retailers in their respective territories. The retailer, in turn, was authorized to purchase only from or through the distributor to whom his area was assigned, to sell only at one designated location and only to ultimate users—not to nonfranchised retailers, particularly discount houses. Sales to nonfranchised retailers such as discount houses were grounds for franchise cancellation. Unlike Brown Shoe, Schwinn did not restrict either wholesalers or retailers from carrying other makes of bicycles as long as they gave Schwinn products at least equal prominence with other brands in display and promotion.

The *Schwinn* case went to the Supreme Court solely on the issue of territorial restrictions. There was no question of restraint on interbrand competition, or of price fixing. In its decision, the Court upheld a District Court finding that "where a manufacturer sells products to its distributor subject to territorial restrictions upon resale, a *per se* violation of the Sherman Act results."[11] The same *per se* illegality was found to apply "to restrictions of outlets with which distributors may deal and to restraints upon retailers to whom the goods are sold."[12]

However, the Court did not find all vertical territorial restrictions to be *per se* illegal. In the case of agency or consignment sales, where title and risk of loss remain with the franchisor, the validity of these restrictions is subject to test under the rule of reasonableness. This requires that there be adequate interbrand competition, that dealers be free to handle competing products, and that there be no element of price fixing involved. These requirements probably exclude many larger companies, notably General Electric, whose lamp consignment marketing structure is already under Justice Department attack.

Essentially, the majority decision in *Schwinn* seemed to say that separate standards would be applied in judging the legality of sales on the one hand, and of alternative methods of distribution on the other. A franchisor cannot limit either the territory or the customers of his franchisees for those products which the franchisee *purchases*. The franchisor can restrict territories and customers if he retains title and risk, and if the effect of the restriction is not unreasonably restrictive of competition.[13]

[10] Wholesalers did maintain warehouses where they stocked small inventories to supply retailer's replacement needs on an emergency basis. About 15 percent of Schwinn sales were made directly to wholesalers in this way.

[11] *United States* v. *Arnold, Schwinn & Co.*, *op. cit.* at 4566.

[12] *Ibid.*

[13] *Schwinn* did not indicate what was left of the "newcomer" or "failing company" defenses for territorial restraints that had been established in the earlier *United States* v. *White Motor Co.*, 372 U.S. 253 (1963).

It is notable that the Court rejected a defense argument by Schwinn that it had adopted the challenged practices to enable it and its small, independent franchisees to compete more effectively with giants like Montgomery Ward and Sears, Roebuck.

Finally, the Court indicated that it would treat other postsale controls on product use in exactly the same way. Thus, the ruling seems to apply, at least in principle, to *any* restrictions on the franchisee, however nominal, if they curtail the freedom of that franchisee to do as he wishes with the product. Whether this ruling will be applied as firmly against smaller firms as against larger ones with market dominance is, of course, uncertain, but historical patterns of antitrust enforcement suggest it will not.

In the *Sealy* case,[14] decided by the Supreme Court on the same day it handed down the *Schwinn* decision, the arrangement under challenge involved an agreement between Sealy, a trademark owner, and thirty trademark franchisees, under which the prices of trademarked bedding products and the territories in which franchisees would operate were agreed upon. The Court concluded that because the franchisees controlled Sealy, Inc., the controls imposed were really horizontal and not vertical in nature and, therefore, were in violation of Section I of the Sherman Act. The existence of a price-fixing clause nullified Sealy's arguments for the need to protect its trademark, and led the Court to refuse to consider arguments on the business or economic justification, or the reasonableness of the controls involved.

The Court did not answer the question of what might have happened had market division not been part of an "aggregation of trade restraints" which included price fixing. It thus seems to have reserved opinion on the legality of a territorial allocation among small concerns which is incidental to use of a joint trade name and common advertising plan, and which does not include price fixing.

IMPACT OF PIVOTAL CASES

In its decisions on these four cases, the Supreme Court has made it clear that there is nothing illegal, as such, in a company choosing to distribute products or services through a selective distribution system such as franchising, so long as the franchisor does not dominate his industry. The Court emphasized that the mere use of the term "franchise" with an agreement has no impact on the legal considerations applicable to that agreement. In general, the legality of a franchisor's enforcement of territorial restrictions or tying agreements on franchisees depends on whether the franchisee is in the relation of a vendee, or an agent, or consignee.

Notably, the Court demonstrated its continuing hostility to price fixing in any form, and to any distribution controls imposed, either along with price

[14] *United States* v. *Sealy, Inc.*, 35 U.S. Law Week 4571 (decided June 12, 1967).

fixing or with the purpose of facilitating it. In *General Motors* and in *Sealy* the presence of price-fixing clauses made it irrelevant as to whether the agreements being considered, or the franchise systems as a whole, were either "lawful or economically desirable."[15]

As well as reiterating, in *Sealy*, its opposition to distribution controls imposed horizontally by franchisors, the Court took a strong position with respect to certain nonprice restrictions imposed vertically on franchisees. *General Motors*, *Brown Shoe* and *Schwinn* indicate that such vertical restrictions are almost, although not quite *per se*, illegal. Thus, before concluding that Schwinn's territorial controls were totally invalid, the Court pointed out that Schwinn was neither a new company nor a failing one. It is possible to interpret the test of reasonableness of vertical controls applied in *Schwinn* to permit a franchisor to establish, first, that he is unable to finance an effective agency or consignment arrangement, and, second, that he could not obtain franchisees willing to handle his products without granting some territorial protection.[16]

Several managerial problems arise from the new emphasis placed on the use of agency or consignment arrangements. Although such arrangements do much to allay franchisee reluctance to handle high-risk products, and provide a strong inducement to potential franchisees unable to finance costly inventories, they do have negative aspects. Many franchisors may be unable to afford the additional costs involved in an agency or consignment system. Many franchisors are concerned that consignment arrangements will cause tax problems and labor pressure for unionization of franchisee employees. Also, these forms of distribution remove some of the franchisee's sense of independence and personal motivation, often the principal reasons for franchising in the first place.[17]

While it is still too early to assess other long-range effects of the "agency or consignment" loopholes in *Schwinn*, it is possible to predict the general areas in which adjustments of marketing practices are likely to take place.[18]

[15] *United States* v. *General Motors Corp.*, *op. cit.*, at 142.

[16] The inability to obtain franchisees was successfully offered as a defense several years earlier in *Sandura Co.* v. *F.T.C.*, 339 F. 2d 847 (6th Cir. 1964). Sandura, a manufacturer of floor coverings, had great financial problems, and franchisee-retailers were expected to take on primary responsibility for sales promotion and merchandising. Sandura offered its franchisees closed territories, within each of which the designated franchisee had the exclusive right to sell Sandura products to retail dealers. On appeal from an F.T.C. ruling, the court of appeals pointed out that "closed territories made for the health and vigor of Sandura, increasing the competitive good that flows from interbrand competition without any showing of detriment to intrabrand competition." *Ibid.*, at 858.

[17] J. A. H. Curry, *et al.*, *Partners for Profit: A Study of Franchising*, *op. cit.*, p. 24; Robert L. Grover, *Statement* before United States Congress, Senate, Subcommittee on Antitrust and Monopoly, Committee on the Judiciary, *Distribution Problems Affecting Small Business—Part I*, 89th Congress, 1st Session (1965), p. 63.

[18] See Betty Bock, *Antitrust Issues in Restricting Sales Territories and Outlets* (N.I.C.B. Studies in Business Economics No. 98), New York: National Industrial Conference Board (October 1967), esp. pp. 31–39.

Where a franchisor wishes to retain territorial restrictions on his franchised dealers, a shift backward in the location of riskbearing (and particularly in responsibility for inventories and warehousing) is probable. Thus, the impact of changes in profit and loss falls more heavily on the franchisor. If the shift in riskbearing is sufficiently large, and requires substantial capital outlays, then direct distribution (bypassing wholesalers) or even vertical ownership integration of distribution units will become more attractive than it was prior to *Schwinn.*

Where a franchisor does *not* wish to retain territorial restrictions on his franchised dealers, and is willing to allow intrabrand competition among wholesalers or retailers, he can sell the franchised product outright and be freed of subsequent responsibilities in its distribution. In lessening the closeness of his relations with franchisees, the franchisor may also reduce their incentives to promote his product. Also, if the location of risk-bearing is shifted forward to franchisees, the franchised product will have to be strongly supported and promoted by the franchisor so that franchisees can continue to handle it in competition with dealers who are subsidized, in part, by other manufacturers.[19]

It is not clear that the Court intended its rulings in these four cases to apply across the board to all six types of franchising mentioned above. In particular, it is not clear that the decisions apply to the situation where a trademark franchisor contracts with wholesalers or retailers—Avis, or MacDonald's hamburgers, for example. In these situations, unlike the four cases discussed, the franchisor does not sell a product, but rather licenses only the use of his name and the method of doing business.

There are a number of considerations unique to such trademark franchising. Notably, the franchisor-licensor has an obligation to protect the identity of origin, uniformity, quality and public image of his trademarked product or service, or risk the diminution or loss of the trademark itself. It is possible in trademark franchisor cases that the validity of the controls imposed will continue to rest, in the first instance, on whether these controls are necessary to protect the trademark.[20] Thus, trademark franchising, the fastest-growing segment of franchised business, may find itself exempted from the most binding of the Court's pronouncements.

One aspect of the Court's opinion in *Brown Shoe* and *General Motors* is worthy of mention. The Court found that Brown's restriction on franchisee handling of competitive shoe lines was a restraint on the franchisee's freedom to deal, as well as being a restriction on competitor's access to the market. There is an emerging concept in these and other recent antitrust cases[21]

[19] *Ibid.*, p. 35.

[20] See James K. Eckmann, "Antitrust Problems in Trademark Franchising," *Stanford Law Review*, 17 (May 1965), 926–41. The issues are set out in *Denison Mattress Factory* v. *Spring Air Company*, 308 F. 2d 403 (5th Cir. 1962), and *Engbrecht, et al.* v. *Dairy Queen Company*, 203 F. Supp. 714 (D. Kan. 1962).

[21] *Simpson* v. *Union Oil*, 337 U.S. 13 (1964); *Klor's Inc.* v. *Broadway-Hale*, 359 U.S. 207 (1959).

that the individual businessman has a right to complete freedom in making his own business decisions, and that any unreasonable restriction of this right will give rise to antitrust action.

With these several qualifications, the four Supreme Court decisions lay out fairly clearly the present antitrust approach to horizontal and vertical controls found in what the Court refers to as "usual and ordinary franchise systems."

RELATIONSHIP BETWEEN FRANCHISOR AND FRANCHISEE

A final significant antitrust issue concerns the treatment of franchisees by the franchisor, particularly in a situation where market leverage may exist. In the recent *Simpson* and *Atlantic Refining* cases,[22] the Supreme Court took note of the great difference in bargaining power held by franchisor over franchisee in judging whether controls in the franchise contract were, in fact, accepted "voluntarily" by franchisees.

The experience of the automobile manufacturers provides a case history of what happened in one industry where franchisors were accused of using coercion, intimidation and arbitrary franchise cancellation to evoke franchisee compliance with arbitrary demands. After extensive hearings in 1956, Congress enacted the so-called Auto Dealer Day in Court Act.[23] The Act permits automobile franchisees to sue in Federal Courts for damages caused by failure of the franchisor to ". . . act in good faith in performing or complying with any of the terms or provisions of the franchise, or in terminating, cancelling, or in reviewing the franchise of said dealer."[24] A comprehensive review by Stewart Macaulay of the first ten years of the Act suggests that the legislation has forced an improvement in relationships between automobile franchisors and their franchisees.[25]

The discontent that culminated in the "Auto Dealer Day in Court Act" is not limited to the automobile industry. The business press today carries an increasing number of reports of private lawsuits filed by franchisees against franchisors on issues of contract enforcement, and particularly on franchisee termination.[26] Discontent is sufficiently widespread to have caused the introduction, in the last two Congresses, of bills that would extend coverage of the Act to all franchisees.[27] The message is fairly clear—franchisors

[22] *Simpson* v. *Union Oil*, *op. cit.*; *Atlantic Refining Co.* v. *F.T.C.*, 381 U.S. 357 (1965). The former involved Section 1 of the Sherman Act; the latter, Section 5 of the F.T.C. Act.

[23] 15 U.S.C.A. 1221 et seq. (1958).

[24] 15 U.S.C.A. at 1222.

[25] Stewart Macaulay, "Law and Society—Changing a Continuing Relationship Between a Large Corporation and Those Who Deal With It: Automobile Manufacturers, Their Dealers, and the Legal System," *Wisconsin Law Review*, Part I (Summer 1965), 483; Part II (Fall 1965), 740.

[26] For example, *Rawlins, et al.* v. *American Oil Company*, C89–67 (D. Utah, May 29, 1967).

[27] H.R. 11972, 89th Cong. 2d Sess. 1966; H.R. 2818, 90th Cong., 2d Sess. 1967.

have a responsibility to continuously reevaluate whether their controls serve legitimate business purposes, whether contract enforcement with franchisees is being carried on in good faith, and whether there are less restrictive means of accomplishing the results being sought.

The relationship between franchisor and franchisees in the development of new controls also deserves attention. In particular, the use of franchise advisory committees to recommend or approve controls entails serious problems. While a franchisor may act in good faith in seeking the counsel of his franchisees, controls originating in a franchisor-franchisee committee might easily be interpreted, as they were in *General Motors*, as a conspiracy to restrain competition in violation of Section I of the Sherman Act, or as an unfair method of competition under Section 5 of the F.T.C. Act.

CONCLUSION

The constraints imposed by recent antitrust decisions may affect the direction of growth, but should not affect either the continued viability or legality of any of the six types of franchise organization. Franchising, as part of the subset of systems utilizing selective distribution, has been specifically sustained by the Court as a way of doing business.[28] However, the recent decisions may weigh more heavily on those franchise systems involving a product or service than on those which revolve around a trademark licensing arrangement.

The decisions all point to the fact that in the future a much higher standard of proof is to be required of franchisors of the reasonableness of their controls over franchisees and of the absence of less restrictive means to achieve the same ends. The Supreme Court, in *Schwinn*, said that it is not even *sufficient* to demonstrate sound business reason and intent on the part of a franchisor who would impose controls. Assuming nonpredatory motives and business purposes, it is also necessary to demonstrate that the impact of the control in the marketplace is precompetitive.

The decisions suggest that the more restrictive the control, the more persuasive the proof must be. The case of customer or territorial restrictions probably requires the highest degree of proof, both that the restriction is desirable and that, without it, the franchisor's ability to compete would be impaired. In addition, it may be necessary to show that the franchisor is either a new company or a failing one (or that an agency or consignment arrangement is in effect), that adequate interbrand competition exists, and that there is no element of price fixing involved.

Tying agreements—the requirement that the franchisee purchase the franchisor's equipment or products—are probably as hard as territorial restrictions to justify. The justification required for controls on advertising,

[28] *United States* v. *Sealy, Inc.*, slip opinion, p. 10.

hiring and record keeping is probably not as demanding as the above, but even these areas will certainly be judged at least on the bases of reasonableness and the absence of less restrictive ways of maintaining the franchisor-franchisee relationship.

QUESTIONS

1. Identify the various types of franchising. What kinds exist in your city?
2. What was the significance of the Schwinn case?

C. THE CONSUMER

In both manufacturing and marketing the consumer is the major uncontrollable factor in the firm's environment. Since the consumer, at least in retailing, has free choice in the outlets he patronizes and in the quality and varieties of goods he purchases, management's interpretation of the consumer's tastes and trends becomes the basis for all decisions that are made. Thus, for example, the judgment that women will start wearing longer skirts would cause an immediate adjustment in the types of goods being purchased and perhaps a change as well in the vendors who are contacted. In addition such a change may cause other departments to adjust accordingly.

Shifts in the spending patterns of consumers also cause changes in retail offerings. Population movements can affect the choice of location regionally (in the case of national chains) and/or within a metropolitan area. The first article, "Plenty of People . . . but More Competition for the Food Dollar," presents some of the statistics that are of major interest to retail firms.

An important concept which has been slow in developing, but is now finding support in the interpretation of consumer research, is that of market segmentation. As used in retailing this refers to the view that different markets can be identified on the basis of different sets of criteria, e.g., by statistical means such as income, or by some sociological or psychological characteristic (such as the blue-collar consumer). In his article, A. C. Samli actually develops a Segmentation Index based on the buying behavior of a number of purchasers of carpeting. His index is composed of many of the usual consumer characteristics, such as income, occupation, and education.

The article by James McNeal, concerning the reactions of consumers and retailers to a rumored discount house, brings out clearly the preconceived notions of consumers on this subject. In McNeal's second article, on the child consumer, a specific segment of the market is identified and its obvious ramifications for the retailer are spelled out. The last article, by Gregory Stone, develops the thesis that all consumers have certain social profiles and that they can be identified through the use of proper research techniques.

10

Plenty of People . . . but More Competition for the Food Dollar

At least one thing seems certain for the future: The 1970s should see no shortage of people. Although the birth rate is declining, the United States population is expected to total approximately 213.2 million by 1975. This represents an increase over today's total population of some 14 million—the equivalent of the present population now residing in the combined metropolitan areas of Boston, Washington, D.C., Pittsburgh, St. Louis and San Francisco.

And this is only the beginning! By 1980, the grocery industry must be prepared to serve the needs of an estimated 225 million persons. That's 26.7 million more than 1969's total. To more graphically visualize this increase: this added number of potential supermarket customers equals the total combined population living today in the states of Montana, Wyoming, Colorado, North Dakota, South Dakota, Nebraska, Kansas, Minnesota, Iowa, Missouri, Wisconsin and Illinois!

POPULATION SHIFTING SOUTH AND WEST

Another consideration of importance to the food industry's planning for the 1970s is the gradual migration of population to the South and West. In the aggregate, population by 1975 will have increased approximately 7 percent. But only the Middle Atlantic states of the eastern area and the Southern and Western states will exceed this average growth percentage. In these areas, population gains will range from 9 percent in the Middle Atlantic to as high as 18 percent in the Southern California-Los Angeles area.

Within these population shifts, there is evidence that the urbanization of our population will continue. Of the twenty-six million increase in popu-

Reprinted from *Progressive Grocer*, 2nd Annual Report on Grocery Product Movement, July 1969, pp. 54–57.

lation predicted for 1980, approximately twenty million will live in metropolitan areas. This movement intensifies the possibility of the growth of super city concentrations within this century between such urban areas as Boston, New York and Washington, D.C. and Los Angeles and San Francisco.

DISPOSABLE INCOME ON THE RISE

With the surge of population growth, there's going to be more spending money in the customer's pockets, too. Today, United States disposable income, which includes all earnings after taxes, totals $588 billion. By 1975, it is anticipated that there will be an additional $282 billion available, bringing the disposable income level to $870 billion. If this growth rate seems extraordinarily high, a glance at recent history shows that this is not an exorbitant estimate. In the period from 1960 to 1968, for example, disposable income in the United States jumped nearly 75 percent.

Putting these figures into a perspective of per capita and per household, this is the disposable income situation today: $3,431 per capita and $11,346 per household. By 1975, these amounts are expected to reach levels of $4,669 per capita and $14,668 per household. All indications are that this more-money-in-the-pocket trend will continue throughout the 70s with the emergence of the 1980s witnessing a per capita disposable income of $5,760 and $17,471 average per family.

FOOD STORE'S SHARE DWINDLING

These figures may make the food retailer's mouth water but there are some negatives which tend to dull the bright prospects. While the consumer will continue to spend more on food products, the food store's share of that dollar is gradually diminishing.

Today, with expenditures for food at some $101 billion, food stores are missing out on about $23 billion of that total. By 1980, while the totals will continue to increase, it is estimated that this difference between what the food stores' registers will ring up and the total amount spent on food will have grown to $51 billion.

DRIVE-INS AND CONVENIENCE FOODS ANSWER NEED

This trend of consumers turning to other forms of retailing outlets to satisfy their food needs reflects the tempo and character of the times. The increased affluence of the average American, the growing numbers of working housewives and the abundance of leisure time has broadened the interests and activities of the family. Everyone in the family is tending to have his own schedule of working, playing and eating. As a result, the traditional big meal, with all members of the family sitting down together, is gradually disappearing from the American scene.

In its place, there is more eating on the run with an emphasis on easy, quick-to-fix convenience foods at home. But perhaps most significant for the food retailing business is another answer to this eating trend which is drawing more and more food dollars outside the supermarket—the food drive-ins and the quick-stop, take-out food restaurants. The rapid growth of the MacDonalds, the Colonel Sanders, the Shakey's and the proliferation of new names in this food retailing field is no accident. These companies are dovetailing their merchandising effort with the eating needs of the customer and beating the supermarket to the selling punch.

SUPERMARKETS ANSWER DRIVE-IN CHALLENGE

But forward-looking supermarket planners are not ignoring this challenge by the drive-in and quick food restaurants. Rather, this selling invasion is being answered with increasing numbers of delicatessens and take-out food departments being installed in new and remodeled food stores. But the supermarket is going to have to intensify these efforts and augment them with new merchandising ideas in the 70s if the drive-in threat is to be answered effectively.

One of the most imaginative approaches is now on the drawing boards at Ralphs Grocery Co. in Los Angeles. In addition to offering customers the wide selection and variety of products in its supermarket design, the new Ralphs will also have attached satellite stores—one a restaurant and the other a convenience store. Each of these units will be open during regular store hours and will remain open after the supermarket section has closed at night.

With a concerted effort by food retailers in these special and new selling areas, the food store's dwindling percentage of the food dollar logically might tend to decrease less than is now predicted. As of 1968, approximately 12.1 percent of disposable income was spent in food stores. Unless food retailers do something unusual to reverse this trend, the percentage, according to predictions, will have been reduced to 10.6 percent by 1980.

AREAS OF PRODUCT CATEGORY GROWTH

In supplying the demands of the supermarket shopper of the 70s, the A. C. Nielsen Co. reports that tonnage of all packaged grocery commodities is expected to increase approximately 22 percent above that in 1968.

The growth, however, will not be across-the-board but will vary with different product categories. For example, except for new product development or substantially changed marketing programs, fats and oils, canned goods, cereal products and basic ingredient items seem slated for below average growth.

Equaling the average growth figures are such product classifications as beverages, condiments, sweeteners and household supplies. Higher than average growth, Nielsen reports, can be expected from paper products, pet foods and "new or speciality" items. . . .

A CHANGING CUSTOMER CONFIGURATION

But the average supermarket shopper is changing in more ways than in total numbers and in the amount of spendable money available. Since the beginnings of the supermarket, the store design and its merchandising appeals, in varying degrees, have been directed at the adult female shopper. Shopping was a traditional assignment of the housewife and she accepted it without too much question. But times are changing.

The supermarket of the 1970s will see a gradual dilution of this adult housewife pattern. Due to the rapid growth of the below-34 age brackets in the next few years there will be an increasing number of younger shoppers, teenagers, and more male participation in supermarket buying with the steady increase in numbers of working wives. Each of these changes will present special challenges to the supermarket in areas of merchandising, display and services.

INEXPERIENCED SHOPPER GROWING IN IMPORTANCE

In both the younger shopper and the male shopper the supermarket is facing an educational problem. At a time when many stores are looking for a way to cut personnel costs, these customers are going to need someone to answer their questions about foods and menu planning, to advise them on how to buy and where to find products in the store, to offer methods of preparing fresh meats and produce and to alert them to new items.

Some stores are attempting to answer this need with such devices as information phones located at strategic points throughout the store, through printed recipe and menu planning sheets handed out in related departments free of charge, and through the use of a store hostess who offers serving suggestions and assists customers in shopping. In the future, these services may have to be augmented with consumer schools.

In addition to educational efforts, the store of the 70s will also have to become more aware of the special wants of this younger group, and become better acquainted with the vagaries of male buying habits.

POPULATION TRENDS

(In millions; Source: Dept. of Commerce)

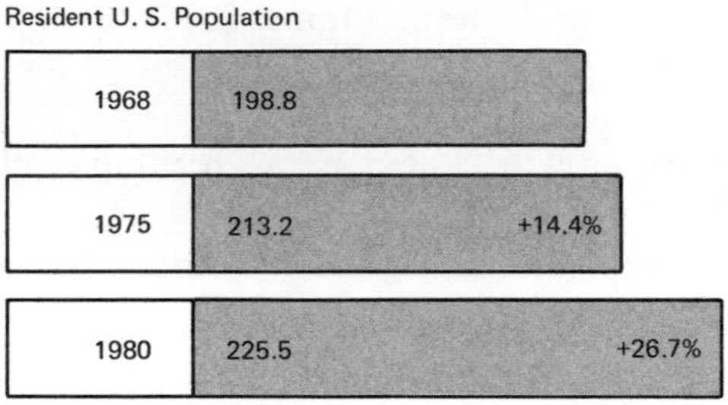

Growth of population to 1980 levels will witness dramatic changes in size of various age groups with the 20 to 34 age group showing the greatest increase.

POPULATION RELOCATION IN 70s

(In millions; Source: Dept. of Commerce, A. C. Nielsen)

Change from 1968 to	–1975	–1980
National	+ 7%	+13%
New England	+ 5%	+10%
New York	+ 5%	+ 8%
Middle Atlantic	+ 9%	+15%
East Central	+ 3%	+ 7%
Chicago	+ 6%	+12%
West Central	+ 4%	+ 7%
Southeast	+ 9%	+15%
Southwest	+ 8%	+14%
Los Angeles	+18%	+32%
Remaining Pacific	+14%	+25%

As the population grows it will also be shifting to the south and west with such areas as the Los Angeles region scheduled to increase by 32% over 1968 totals.

POPULATION URBANIZATION CONTINUES

(In millions: Source: Dept. of Commerce)

	1968	1975	% Increase	1980	% Increase
Total Population	198.8	213.2	+7.2	225.4	+5.7
Metro	125.2	135.7	+8.4	144.7	+6.6
Non-Metro	73.6	77.5	+5.3	80.7	+4.1

Indications are that more and more of the population will move to urban areas during the 70's with over 60% of total U.S. population living there by 1980.

PROJECTION PERSONAL INCOME TRENDS

(Source: Dept. of Commerce, A. C. Nielsen)

	1968	1970	1975	1980
Per Capita	$ 3,431	$ 3,767	$ 4,669	$ 5,760
		% Gain +9.8	% Gain +23.9	% Gain +23.4
Per Household	$11,346	$12,306 +8.5	$14,668 +19.2	$17,471 +19.1

Disposable income will continue to rise in next decade with a U.S. total of over a trillion dollars by 1980. By then, per capita income will be double that of 1968.

FOOD EXPENDITURE TRENDS

(Source: Dept. of Commerce, A. C. Nielsen, Predicasts)

☐ Personal Consumption Expenditures Food (Billions)　■ Food Store Sales (Billions)

$71.9 | $101.3 | +35.3% $97.3 | +38.4% $140.2 | +23.9% $120.6 | +26.0% $176.7

1968　1975　1980

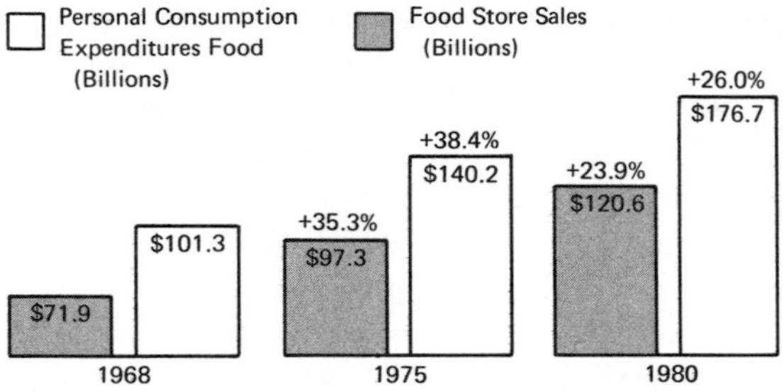

The A. C. Nielsen Co. predicts that although the total amount spent on food will increase, the food store's share will not increase proportionately in the 1970's.

EXPENDITURES FOR FOOD AS A PERCENT OF INCOME

(Source: Dept. of Commerce, A. C. Nielsen, Predicasts)

% income allocated to:	1968	1975	1980
All food personal consumption expenditures	17.2%	16.1%	15.6%
In food stores	12.1%	11.2%	10.6%

Growing competition from drive-ins and fast-food restaurants is expected to cut into the food store's share of food expenditures—reaching low of 10.6% in 1980.

CUSTOMERS WILL STILL BE HUMAN

Inherent to all of these customer opinions and desires for the supermarket of the 1970s is the underlying fear of the cold, unfriendly, dehumanized store. Shopper sensitiveness to this prospect should alert food industry planners to an important consideration about the future: No matter how automated and efficient the supermarket becomes, the customer still is going to be human, with much the same wants, needs and desires as today's supermarket shopper.

In the 1970s, customers will still want to shop where they can pick, choose and handle the store's merchandise; where a large selection and variety of products is available; where they can have their shopping and food preparation questions answered by store personnel; where they will feel that their patronage is appreciated and where shopping remains a pleasant social activity.

In the face of a growing challenge for the customer's dollar from other types of food retailing establishments and with the seemingly inevitable and necessary growth of the store in size and efficiency, it is going to be competitively more important than ever for the supermarket to answer the consumer's demands. The store must continue to offer courteous service, imaginative merchandising, well-trained personnel, and a demographically fitted merchandise mix.

The tools for more efficient operations are within the food industry's grasp but these computer and automated opportunities must not be allowed to overshadow old-fashioned humanism. Success for the supermarket in the 1970s will still depend on customer satisfaction. . . .

QUESTIONS

1. What is the significance of population growth to grocery retailing?
2. Though disposable income is rising, the food stores' share of consumer expenditures is declining. Why?
3. What action can the grocery chain take to offset this trend?

11

Interrelationship Between the Market Segments and the Buyer Behavior

A. Coskun Samli

Perhaps the most important aspect of modern markets is their heterogeneity. While some consumers need rain tires, the others may be in need of snow tires, heavy duty tires, and the like. Coping with this heterogeneity is the greatest challenge for today's marketing practitioners. No one firm can cater to all segments of the market simultaneously and be fully successful. A market, be it for automobiles, for appliances, or for carpeting, is not homogeneous. It is composed of many different groups with different incomes, tastes, values, and motives. In a competitive market system, the firms that understand the characteristics of their markets and try to satisfy the particular needs and wants prevailing in these markets increase their probability of success.

Components or segments of a market can be identified on the basis of different sets of criteria. A component or a segment "is any subsection of a total market that is worth cultivating."[1] Different behavior patterns prevail in various segments of the consumer market. The existing possibilities of stratification of the market provide a basis for the marketing practitioner to identify his own market segments. A marketing strategy of segmentation (which is simply dealing with different components of the market differently)[2] enables the practitioner to be selective and concentrate on more feasible segments. It is, however, still open for discussion whether or not segmentation is wise,[3] and if so on what basis it should prevail.

Instead of answering these questions directly an inductive approach is presented in this paper. This approach involves the following stages: The detailed discussion of a study which attempted to identify different market

Talk delivered before the X ESOMAR Seminar held at Lucerne, November 2–5, 1969. An earlier and shorter version of this paper appeared in the Summer 1968 issue of the *Journal of Retailing* under the title "Segmentation and Carving a Niche in the Market Place."

[1] Alan A. Roberts, "Applying the Strategy of Market Segmentation," *Business Horizons* (Fall 1961), p. 65. Also see A. Coskun Samli, "Market Segments—A Key to Marketing Strategy Development," *Business Perspectives* (Winter 1966), pp. 21–26.

[2] Wendell R. Smith, "Product Differentiation and Market Segmentation as Alternative Marketing Strategies," *Journal of Marketing* (July 1956), pp. 3–8.

[3] For a strong argument against segmentation see William Reynolds, "More Sense about Market Segmentation," *Harvard Business Review* (September-October 1965), pp. 107–14.

segments to which four separate retail establishments have been catering; the construction of what is termed a *segmentation index;* the analysis of universality of the segmentation index; and finally the construction of a logical flow model as a guideline for development of a segmentation index.

The largest section of this paper which is the detailed discussion of an empirical study is based on an analysis of the characteristics of typical customers of four retail stores in buying wall-to-wall carpeting. The present article offers a brief discussion of the criteria that can be used for segmentation, the findings of a field study are presented, and finally, an attempt is made to measure the segments on the basis of an index and to focus upon the role of segmentation in the struggle for survival.

BASIS FOR SEGMENTATION

Although the contributions of Joan Robinson and Edward Chamberlin have been significant in bringing imperfect market systems into focus as more realistic models for study, it was sociologists like Lloyd Warner who have provided a workable path for marketing practitioners. Warner and his associates analyzed the heterogeneous markets in terms of Index of Status Characteristics (ISC) and concluded that there are five socioeconomic categories. Following this pattern, students of marketing, like Pierre Martineau, have delved into specific consumption behavior of each category.[4] Such analyses pave the way for what has come to be known as market segmentation. Perhaps because they were more tangible and easy to identify, earlier attempts to segment the market were all based on demographic characteristics. In addition to ISC's age, sex, income distribution, geographic location, educational and occupational background, and, finally, the stage in the life cycle are all utilized as the basis for segmentation. Indeed, any one of these variables or a combination thereof has been very useful in many marketing decisions.

More recently, however, it has been asserted that demography is not the best way of looking at markets. Rather, markets should be scrutinized, as Daniel Yankelovich contends, "for important differences in buyer attitudes, motivations, values, usage patterns, aesthetic preferences, or degree of susceptibility."[5]

This is so because, as he further asserts, "we are not dealing with different types of people, but with differences in people's values." Morris J. Gottlieb, among others, looked at compulsiveness or punitiveness as factors to segment

[4] Pierre Martineau, "Social Classes and Spending Behavior," *Journal of Marketing* (October 1958), pp. 121–30. A more sophisticated statistical analysis of socioeconomic variables is presented in: Frank M. Bass, Douglas J. Tigert and Ronald T. Lonsdale, "Market Segmentation: Group Versus Individual Behavior," *Journal of Marketing Research*, August 1968, pp. 264–76.

[5] Daniel Yankelovich, "New Criteria for Market Segmentation," *Harvard Business Review* (March-April 1964), pp. 83–90.

the market for antacid-analgesics.[6] It follows that a man who may be driving an expensive car may prefer cheap whiskey, or a woman who shops at White Front may wish to have dinner occasionally at the Brown Derby.

Other scholars have tried to analyze market segments on the basis of demand elasticities attributable to different groups. Reaction of different consumer groups to changes in prices is used to group them into somewhat distinguishable segments.[7] John G. Myers used price quality relationships in segmenting the market for a group of private brands.[8]

This controversy of demographic versus nondemographic criteria for segmentation stems, at least partially, from the fact that attempts are often made to classify people somewhat arbitarily. However, if the consumers of certain products or customers of certain businesses were to be analyzed and categorized *after the fact*, segmentation is expected to be more realistic. The users or consumers of certain products do have common characteristics; to the extent that these characteristics can be detected and measured segmentation is achieved. If, for instance, on the average, Cadillac owners are between the ages of 35–55 and belong to the upper-upper socioeconomic category, it may be possible to develop, change, or continue the marketing strategy for Cadillacs accordingly. All the aspects of market potential, estimates, pricing, promotion, product characteristics, and distribution can be planned along similar lines.

In the case of retailing, especially for specialty stores, demographic characteristics of the immediate market appear to be of great significance, since these characteristics are determinable and somewhat quantifiable. Although there is always some degree of heterogeneity in its markets, a high-status apparel specialty store such as I. Magnin's appeals primarily to an identifiable and quantifiable market. This quantification lends itself more readily to demographic criteria. In such cases it is more important to determine the segments that the retail outlets appeal to rather than to identify the market segments most suitable for each product or product line.

PRELIMINARY CONSIDERATIONS AND THE METHOD USED

Three basic decisions on the part of the consumer must be made when shopping for carpeting. The first of them is the style the consumer likes best, the color and texture best suited for the home. The second is choosing the best quality, and the last one is the price the consumer can best afford.

In a market where speciality stores are competitively pressured by

[6] Morris J. Gottlieb, "Segmentation by Personality Types," in Lynn H. Stockman (ed.) *Advancing of Marketing Efficiency* (Chicago: American Marketing Association, 1958), pp. 148–58.

[7] Ronald E. Frank and William F. Massy, "Market Segmentation and the Effectiveness of a Brand's Price and Dealing Policies," *The Journal of Business* (April 1965), pp. 186–200.

[8] John G. Myers, "Determinants of Private Brand Attitude," *Journal of Marketing Research* (February 1967), pp. 73–81.

department and discount stores, the speciality carpet store has to convince the prospective consumer that his store is the place where all three of these basic decisions can be made effectively. The discount carpeting stores on the other hand emphasize price and bargain aspects and expect this factor to be of prime importance in buying carpeting. Both of these approaches are efforts to appeal to different consumer groups and hence to survive and prosper.

The data for this study were obtained through a survey of 294 families in a large western metropolitan area. In selecting the sample, random lists of the customers of a discount carpeting speciality store and an exclusive carpeting speciality stóre were utilized. In addition, lists of recently completed homes in the area, telephone solicitations for prospective respondents, and door to door canvassing for families that had recently purchased carpeting were utilized to develop a random list of customers who purchased carpeting during the past two years.

Four different retail stores were involved in the study. The first one (Store A) is a discount specialty carpeting store. The second is a high-status speciality carpeting store (Store B). The next one (Store C) is a high-status department store, and finally the last one (Store D) is a middle-class department store.

SOCIOECONOMIC ANALYSES

An analysis of the income distribution of the respondents indicated a significant difference in the incomes of the clients of the four stores. As shown in Table 1, Store A had the smallest percentage of customers in the upper three income categories ($7,500–$9,999, $10,000–$14,999, and over $15,000). Especially, in the highest income category Store A was the lowest.

Table 2 depicts the educational background of the respondents according to stores patronized. It can be noted that Store A customers have had rela-

TABLE 1.

Income Level Distribution

Income	*Store A Percent respondents*	*Store B Percent respondents*	*Store C Percent respondents*	*Store D Percent respondents*
Under $3,000	6.2	—	2.8	2.4
3,000–3,999	6.2	4.2	2.8	—
4,000–4,999	8.6	4.2	8.3	7.1
5,000–5,999	11.1	4.2	—	4.8
6,000–7,499	16.0	8.3	11.1	19.0
7,500–9,999	28.3	29.1	30.6	28.6
10,000–14,999	22.1	41.6	36.1	26.2
Over $15,000	1.2	8.3	8.0	11.9

TABLE 2.

Education of the Respondents*

Education Level	*Store A Percent respondents*	*Store B Percent respondents*	*Store C Percent respondents*	*Store D Percent respondents*
Less than eight years	4.9	—	—	2.4
Eight to twelve years	49.2	29.1	41.7	31.7
Some college	32.0	41.6	38.9	43.9
Bachelor's degree	8.6	16.6	16.6	14.6
Beyond bachelor's	2.5	8.3	2.8	5.0
Master's degree	2.5	4.2	—	2.4

*Man of the house only.

tively less education than the customers of other stores. The highest level of education prevailed among the customers of Store B (high-status specialty carpeting store).

Occupational characteristics of the customers were also consistent with education and income. As indicated in Table 3, customers of Store A were more heavily composed of skilled workers and government employees, as opposed to a substantially greater concentration of white collar, supervisory, and professional workers for Store B. Store C also showed a significant deviation from Store A in the occupational makeup of its customers.

TABLE 3.

Occupation of the Respondents*

Occupation	*Store A Percent respondents*	*Store B Percent respondents*	*Store C Percent respondents*	*Store D Percent respondents*
Supervisory	8.6	14.3	20.0	12.0
Clerical	2.5	—	5.7	—
Other white collar	13.5	33.3	20.0	12.0
Professional	11.1	14.3	11.4	24.0
Skilled workers	24.6	4.8	14.3	14.4
Unskilled workers	7.4	4.8	—	7.2
Government employees	17.2	4.8	8.6	12.0
Self-employed	7.4	14.3	5.7	4.8
Retired-unemployed	7.4	9.5	14.3	7.2

*Man of the house only.

The monthly payments of the Store A customers for their homes also show a slight tendency of being lower as seen in Table 4. The average monthly payment for this group is $106 as opposed to $112 for the Store B and $114

TABLE 4.

Monthly House Payments of the Respondents

Monthly Payments	*Store A Percent respondents*	*Store B Percent respondents*	*Store C Percent respondents*	*Store D Percent respondents*
Below $60	8.2	—	—	2.4
$61–80	14.1	7.1	13.9	14.3
81–100	16.5	21.4	30.6	23.8
101–120	24.7	35.8	13.9	23.8
121–140	21.2	17.9	19.4	9.5
141–160	4.7	7.1	13.9	9.5
Over $160	4.7	3.6	—	14.3
House paid for	5.9	7.1	8.3	2.4

for Store D customers. Home ownership also indicated that payments of Store A customers were less than those of Stores B and C.

Survey findings indicated that Store A customers live in homes that are, on the average, nine and one-half years old and they have lived in them a little over five years. In contrast, Store B customers live in newer houses (about six and one-half years old) and have lived in their homes about 4.1 years. The size of the home and the number of rooms having wall-to-wall carpeting did not show any significant difference among customers of the various stores.

Ownership of luxuries can also be used as indicative of socioeconomic class. For the purpose of this study, four products were singled out as luxury items: color television, stereo phonographs, boats, and air conditioning. Table 5 depicts that relatively fewer Store A customers owned these luxuries.

TABLE 5.

Ownership of Various Luxury Items

Item	*Store A Percent respondents*	*Store B Percent respondents*	*Store C Percent respondents*	*Store D Percent respondents*
Color television	9.3	21.4	11.1	9.5
Stereo	54.1	70.4	55.5	66.7
Boat	14.0	25.0	14.9	11.9
Air conditioning	61.9	75.0	63.9	66.7

This observation is true of all the items considered.

Finally, a few comments can be made about car ownership by the respondents as indicative of socioeconomic class membership. Store A customers owned more cars than other carpet buyers; 13.2 percent had three cars as opposed to about 4 percent in other groups. This is consistent with the fact that more wives in this group worked (26 percent in contrast with 21 percent of Store B customer wives), and thus more cars were needed. An analysis of cars according to price ranges showed that Store A customers owned relatively lower priced cars (Table 6).

TABLE 6.

Car Ownership by Price Ranges

Price Range	*Store A Percent respondents*	*Store B Percent respondents*	*Other Percent respondents*
High	3.5	12.5	7.3
Medium	28.3	37.5	36.2
Low	68.0	50.0	57.6

SEGMENTATION INDEX

By using weights for each category, it was possible to develop an index indicating segmentation, called Segmentation Index (SI). Appendix A illustrates the criteria and the weighting scale used for SI. Table 7 displays

TABLE 7.

Segmentation Index*

Socioeconomic criteria	*Store A*	*Store B*	*Store C*	*Store D*
Income level distribution	502.9	611.5	589.1	588.1
Education of respondents	261.2	216.1	280.5	295.3
Occupation of the respondents	151.3	200.1	182.8	177.6
Monthly house payment of respondents	351.8	378.9	355.6	399.8
Ownership of luxury items	393.3	571.8	413.5	431.0
Car ownership by price ranges	170.4	225.0	202.7	202.7†
Total	1830.9	2303.4	2024.2	2094.5

*Points are arrived at by multiplying the assigned weights for each category with the percent distribution figures presented in Tables I through VI.

†Since Stores B and D are somewhat closer, the same figure was used for this category because the available data were for both of these stores combined.

total points for each one of the four stores for each socioeconomic category as well as the total points.

As can be seen, in all items but one, Store A had the lowest, and Store B had the highest scores. If the SI for Store A is assumed to be 100, then SI's of Stores B, C, and D are 125.8, 110.5, and 114.4, respectively. As evidenced by these figures, significant difference in SI's prevailed especially between Stores A and B.

Thus it can be seen that the customers of the discount specialty store were mainly of a relatively lower socioeconomic group. It is therefore necessary to analyze the buying behavior of this group in order to determine the merchandising, pricing, and advertising policies that would improve the image of this store, as well as the services rendered by this company, to improve the image of its marketing performance.

THE BUYING BEHAVIOR OF STORE A CUSTOMERS

The following analyses of the buying behavior of this group indicate also what can be done with the customer groups of the Stores B, C, or D if one were to be interested in marketing performance of these firms also.

In analyzing the occasions that prompted the purchase of carpeting, the total survey results showed that refurnishing and moving were important. However, in the case of Store A, refurnishing was by far the most important of these two (27.1 percent). As shown in Table 8, the customers of Store B on the other hand stated that the major occasion was moving (50.0 percent). It seems from the table that most of the carpeting sold by the discount specialty store is of the replacement type rather than those that were purchased

TABLE 8.

On What Occasion Did Respondents Buy Carpet?

Occasion	*Store A Percent respondents*	*Store B Percent respondents*	*Store C Percent respondents*	*Store D Percent respondents*
Moving	15.3	50.0	25.0	38.1
Remodeling	14.1	17.9	8.3	7.1
Refurnishing	27.1	17.9	19.4	28.6
Family event	1.2	—	5.6	—
Purchasing new furniture	1.2	3.6	2.8	2.4
Deciding to buy carpet	14.1	—	8.3	9.5
Replacing old carpet	12.9	10.7	13.9	4.8
Other	14.1	—	16.7	9.5

for the first time for a new home. Shopping before the purchases was not very common among the customers of Store A. Overall, the largest proportion of the respondents in this group did the least shopping, as can be detected in Table 9. This may indicate that they consider the choice of stores rather limited, or they have made up their minds before shopping. Further evidence indicated that the latter assertion is correct.

TABLE 9.

Shopping Before the Purchase

Customers of	*Did not shop around*	*Shopped one stores*	*Shopped two stores*	*Shopped three stores*
Store A	54.1%	12.9%	17.6%	16.4%
Store C	55.6	5.6	16.7	22.2
Store B	32.1	14.2	21.4	32.1
Store D	52.0	20.0	28.0	—
Total survey results	44.8%	14.0%	21.4%	19.8%

TABLE 10.

Where Respondents First Heard About Store

Sources	*Store A Percent respondents*	*Store B Percent respondents*	*Store C Percent respondents*	*Store D Percent respondents*
Recommendation—friends	11.3	30.4	40.0	9.1
Recommendation—relative	3.8	4.4	—	9.1
New store	1.3	—	—	—
Saw the store	13.8	26.0	20.0	27.3
Newspaper advertisement	63.0	17.4	40.0	27.3
Friend worked there	6.0	—	—	—
Radio	—	4.3	—	—
Other	3.8	2.5	—	27.3

The survey established that advertising plays a very important role in communicating the name of Store A to the market. A great majority of its customers (63.0 percent) said that they first heard of this store through newspaper advertisements (Table 10). On the other hand, for Stores B and C, word-of-mouth advertising or reputation played a more important role, which is evidenced by the fact that 30.4 percent and 40.0 percent of their respective customer respondents indicated hearing about the store upon the recommendation of friends.

Another important aspect of buying behavior involves the reasons for preferring a store. Significant differences were detected when the reasons for customers buying at one particular store were analyzed (Table 11).

TABLE 11.

Factors That Made Customers Decide to Buy at One Particular Location*

Factors	*Store A Percent respondents' preference*	*Store B Percent respondents' preference*	*Store C Percent respondents' preference*	*Store D Percent respondents' preference*
Reasonable price	8	5	7	6
Good selection	3	1	3	4
Close to home	7	6	9	7
Newspaper advertising	5	11	9	10
Advertising	9	6	9	10
Right price	2	6	7	2
Best buy available	4	6	2	4
Recommendation of friend	6	2	9	7
Recommendation of relative	9	6	9	10
Sales	1	11	5	1
Good guarantee	12	11	5	10
Good reputation	9	3	1	2
Better service	12	4	4	7

*Same numbers indicate similar weights in rating.

Although price orientation can be detected easily among the customers of the discount specialty store, the customers of the exclusive specialty store paid more attention to selection, reputation, and work-of-mouth advertising, as indicated by heavy emphasis on the recommendation of friends.

Analysis showed that the method of buying also differed among the customers of different stores. It was noted that a greater percentage of Store A clients visited the store than did the patrons of Store B (Table 12). Evidently the lower socioeconomic class customers preferred to go to the store personally rather than to ask the salesmen to visit them at home.

TABLE 12.

How Did the Customers Buy?

Method of buying	*Store A Percent respondents*	*Store B Percent respondents*	*Store C Percent respondents*	*Store D Percent respondents*
Visited the store	83.0	65.8	75.0	64.7
Had salesman come to home	11.0	23.7	13.9	20.5
Both	6.0	10.5	11.1	7.3

The customer purchase satisfaction was examined by asking the respondents whether or not they would recommend the store to others. Table 13 shows that the high-status department store (Store C) had the greatest pop-

TABLE 13.

Would the Respondents Recommend the Store?

Store	*Percentage*
Store A	88.1
Store B	92.9
Store C	94.4
Store D	83.3

ularity in this respect. Store loyalty can also be tested by learning whether or not the respondents would go back to the same store. Table 14 depicts the survey findings on this aspect. Once again loyalty was the highest toward Store C, for a greater percent of its customer respondents said they would go back to the same store again.

TABLE 14.

Would the Respondents Go to the Same Store Again?

Store	*Percentage*
Store A	46.5
Store B	53.5
Store C	63.9
Store D	29.3

Although the customers of the specialty discount store did not shop around much, when they were asked where they would choose to shop, the exclusive specialty store was the most popular place, as indicated in Table 15.

TABLE 15.

Where Would the Respondents Shop?

Customers	*Store A Percent respondents*	*Store B Percent respondents*	*Store C Percent respondents*	*Store D Percent respondents*
Store A	—	6.7	22.2	16.1
Store E	—	13.3	5.6	—
Store C	50.0	60.0	—	61.0
Store D	4.3	6.7	11.1	10.5
Store F	4.3	—	—	—
Store G	8.7	—	5.6	—
Store B	2.2	—	22.2	—
Store H	2.2	6.7	11.1	—
Store I	6.5	—	—	—
Others	21.7	6.7	22.2	16.1

According to the analyses of buying behavior in relation to socioeconomic classifications, different motives and different points of emphasis prevail in buying carpeting; as a result, consumers patronize retail establishments that are distinctly identifiable.

The typical customer of Store A belongs to a relatively lower socioeconomic group. However, the buying behavior seems to be consistent with the socioeconomic status. This group of respondents are more price-oriented. They did not shop around very much before the purchase. They went to the store to buy rather than have the salesman come to their home. They paid more attention to advertisements than to reputation or word-of-mouth advertising. They are economy minded, practical people who make up their minds and then act accordingly.

CONSIDERATIONS FOR POLICY DECISIONS

After looking at the socioeconomic groups and buying behavior, it can be stated that Store A is a successful concern in terms of identifying its segment on the basis of socioeconomic criteria and dealing with it effectively. As a discount specialty carpeting store, the firm has emphasized price and variety rather than trying to establish a status image. It has utilized mainly factual and promotional advertising, with heavy emphasis on price and sales; there has been virtually no emphasis on institutional appeal.

This type of approach evidently appealed to the store's present market. Its customers, being more price-and-economy minded, were attracted mainly by newspaper advertising. They purchased mainly wall-to-wall carpeting for redecoration of the house; hence price and economy appeals were stronger to them than high status, image, and reputation.

However, the fact that customers of the store were hesitant to go back to it or recommend it to friends and relatives indicates a need for a change in emphasis. Some institutional appeal could be useful in advertising to create a better name for the store. There also may be a danger of having an inadequate image caused by an overall company policy of treating the present sales as a one-shot proposition. In this case the possibility of future repeat sales are not considered as an important goal. A change in this attitude means emphasizing the fact that within a few years these customers will come back either for replacement or, more important, for additional carpeting for the rest of the home. Most important, word-of-mouth advertising is still one of the cheapest and most effective types of promotion. Even though the sales to customer (A) may be a one-shot proposition, if (A) is not satisfied he may influence the thinking of (B), (C), and (D), who otherwise would be potential customers for Store A.

In developing a strategy for the future, Store A has basically three alternatives. It may try to appeal to a slightly higher socioeconomic group without endangering its present business. This is desirable because a slight upgrading in the image would allow the store to gain further esteem of the present clientele to the point where they will start a word-of-mouth campaign. Also, some higher socioeconomic customers may start patronizing the store. Some effort in slightly more institutionalized advertising may, at least partially, fulfill this objective. The second alternative is to maintain the *status quo*. Although the store has been successful, this is no assurance for the future; lack of loyalty may become a significant bottleneck in later years. The last, but the least feasible, alternative is to change the image completely and try to appeal to a higher socioeconomic group. This will mean direct competition with Stores B and C.

The success of Store A rests on meeting the needs of its well-defined market. The discount specialty store managed to carve a niche in the market by identifying a socioeconomic group and satisfying its desires effectively. Its success in the future will depend also on the continuation of the present situation.[9]

CONDITIONS FOR GENERAL APPLICABILITY

Although only one major product line has been analyzed in this paper, the method used and results are applicable to a wide variety of products and retail stores. It is quite likely that only in shopping goods will a segmentation index be significant and shopper behavior readily identifiable. Although a store's image is identifiable and significantly different in retail establishments dealing primarily with convenience goods, e.g. grocery stores or drug stores, buyer behavior is not substantially different than those buying shopping goods. In this study the relative status of each one of the four stores was known beforehand. Otherwise it would have been necessary to determine the image of the store in question. Once the image is known, it is appropriate to consider a change in the strategy in terms of appealing to the same segment or changing it.

Upon establishing the image a segmentation index must be developed. The method displayed here for the construction of such a tool is by no means fixed. Factors used in the index can be changed as well as their relative weights. It is the construction of an index which is sensitive enough to distinguish our store from those of competitors which is the important point. Proper usage of this index necessitates having knowledge of consumer purchase behavior. A sensitive segmentation index is not important where buyer behavior and segments cannot be related to each other.

In matching market segments and buyer behavior, it must be realized that this match applies only to the business in question. Therefore we are concerned with the purchase behavior of customers of say Store A who as a group also have distinguishing characteristics which help to identify them.

[9] W. R. Smith, *op. cit.*

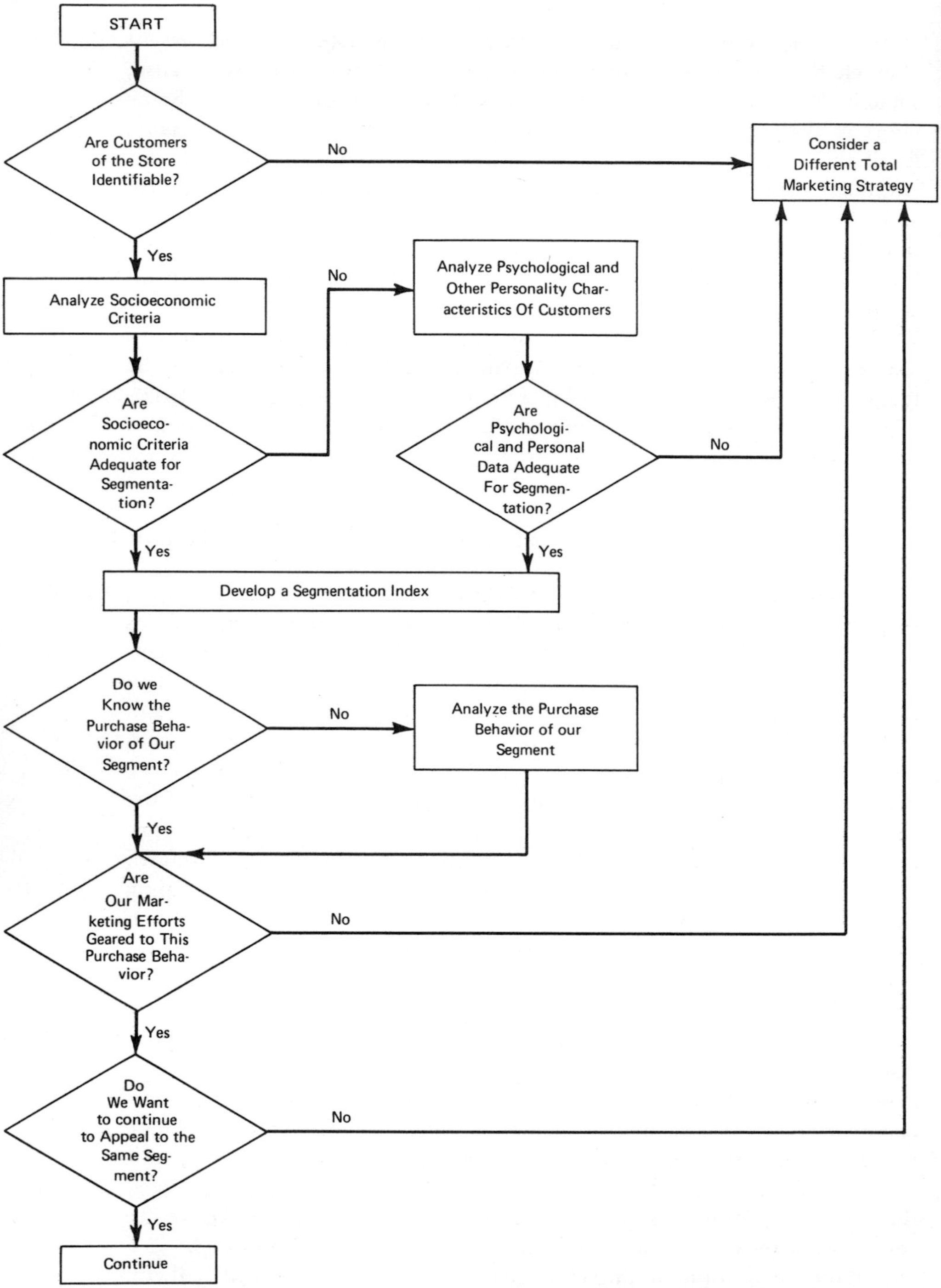

FIGURE 1. A logical flow chart of segmentation activity of a retail establishment

These characteristics may be lost if we were to study the wall-to-wall carpeting buying habits of a very large subsector in the economy, e.g. senior citizens. Thus the firm by matching the segment and buyer behavior can carve its niche in the market place.

Figure 1 illustrates a logical flow chart for the firm's segmentation efforts. It is applicable to manufacturers as well as retail stores. Many of the details as to what the factors are and how the Segmentation Index is developed are omitted. Two types of steps are distinguished: questions and necessary actions. Proper sequencing provides a logical order for the strategy development. Furthermore, such models can be used in computer simulator studies.

The model here implies the existence of a going concern. It then makes provisions for a logical exploration of the prevailing strategy. Similar models can be developed for different product lines as well as different establishments. For a beginning firm or a new product line a somewhat different model is likely to be utilized. In such cases since the image of the firm or the product is not known, activities will be geared to a special market segment somewhat arbitrarily. However in time as it becomes possible to establish and change the firm's appeal in the market place, the proposed model is likely to become necessary for survival and success.

A STRATEGY FOR SURVIVAL

The data presented in this article show that, with some effort, the marketing practitioner can identify his market. Such identification is necessitated by the lack of homogeneous demand caused by different customs, desire for variety, or desire for exclusiveness, or from basic differences in user needs; that is, by socioeconomic differences. This identification of his immediate market enables the merchant to understand his customers better. Hence he is able to formulate more effective policies by matching his segmentation efforts and the buyer behavior in his segment. The end result of this endeavor is mutual satisfaction on the part of both the marketing practitioner and his market.

This practice of identifying the market and catering to it adequately is the process of carving a niche in the market. The end impact on the economy as a whole is the minimization of waste, of resources and marketing effort, and stimulation of welfare; these can be considered as the basic goals of a market economy.

Just like individuals or species, a firm survives because there is a place for it in the existing external structure. As our research shows, the existing conditions in the environment offer an opportunity which, if explored properly, enable the firm to survive and prosper. It is not the total environment as much as one of its well-defined components that is the key for the firm's survival.

This well-defined slice which can be called a segment, niche, a foothold, or a footing[10] can be analyzed effectively according to its socioeconomic characteristics. Once the segment is identified, its characteristics may be further analyzed on the basis of nonsocioeconomic criteria. Identification of the segment for a going concern, particularly for specialty stores, appears to be especially possible on the basis of these criteria. The identification and careful definition of this phenomenon can at least guide the firm partially to establish the right pattern of behavior. The rest of this right pattern of behavior is dependent upon considerations other than the characteristics of the segment. The objectives of the firm and its ability to utilize the tools that it has in its possession, such as advertising, product, price, capital, etc., are among these considerations. They enable the firm to carve its niche either deep and well-defined or superficial and blurred. Dealing with a well-defined market segment and capitalizing on it by carving a niche, however, is not the *only* way to survive. It is one of many different ways of surviving and prospering,[11] but it is a very important one.

APPENDIX A

Criteria and Weights Used in Segmentation Index

Categories	*Weighted by*	*Categories*	*Weighted by*
Income	1–8	Stereo	3
Education	1–6	Color television	4
Monthly house payment	1–7	Boat	5
Profession:		Car ownership:	
White collar	3	High-Priced Car	5
Blue collar	1	Medium-Priced Car	3
		Low-Priced Car	1
Luxury Items:			
Air Conditioning	2		

QUESTIONS

1. Why is segmentation of a market an important concept to the businessman?
2. Describe Store A's customer.
3. Describe the buying behavior of Store A's customer.

[10] Wroe Alderson, *Marketing Behavior and Executive Action* (Homewood, Illinois: Richard D. Irwin, 1957), p. 55.
[11] *Ibid.*, pp. 54–56.

12

Reactions of a Small Town to a Rumored Discount House

James U. McNeal

Discounting, or low-margin retailing, is a merchandising concept that has had phenomenal growth in the past decade. Because it is believed that discounting requires a large reservoir of potential customers, discount houses typically have located in cities or shopping areas containing at least 100,000 people.

Currently, there are indications that some discounters are modifying their strategy and attempting also to locate in small communities. Such is the case of the Tempo Discount Centers (Gamble-Skogmo) which recently located its 26th unit in a small town and plans more in other small towns.[1]

This paper reports the attitudes of a small town toward the discount house concept. The attitudes discussed are about the *concept* of discount house rather than about a specific discounter because the study was based on a rumor—a rumor that a discount house of some sort was to locate in town.

The town discussed in this report was a relatively small Southwestern community (25,000 people), slightly rural in nature. While it was located within an hour's drive to either of two large cities, it was commonly described as "out of the way." The town essentially had no industry and depended upon a state university for its existence.

The rumor that a discount house might locate in this town developed in the latter part of 1964 and immediately intensified. An examination of the rumor divulged the following information:

(1) The rumor was widespread within the town.
(2) The rumor usually did not contain the name of the discount house but suggested that it would be an independent.
(3) The rumor contained the belief that the discount house would locate immediately.

It was decided that the rumor afforded a good opportunity to conduct an attitudinal survey of a small town toward discounting since interests were high. It was believed that under these circumstances responses would be easier to obtain and more representative of an individual's feelings about the subject. Further, it was felt that a study conducted *before* the discount

Reprinted from *Southern Journal of Business*, Vol. 1, No. 2, April 1966, Proceedings of the Annual Meetings, Miami Beach, November 11–13, 1965, pp. 189–96.

[1] See "Small Town Greets the Discounters," *Business Week* (Oct. 3, 1964), pp. 90, 94, 96.

house located would more nearly define the feelings of the community toward discounting in general.

A follow-up study is planned after a discount house is established in the community. This later study will allow a measure of the actual impact of a specific discounter on the town, and it also will show any changes in the community's attitudes toward discounting brought about by the discounter.

1. THE STUDY

For purposes of the study the town was defined as consisting of potential consumers (households) and businessmen (stores). An area sample of 270 households was selected to represent consumers. The household interviews were held in the home and only female adult residents were interviewed.

Every business that could be construed as viewing a discount house as a competitor was included in the sample of businessmen. The result was a group of ninety-one retail outlets, both chain and independent, that included grocery stores but excluded service retailers such as barber shops. These interviews were directed to the store owners or the store managers in the case of a chain.

The interviews with both groups of respondents ranged from ten to thirty minutes in length. After introductory remarks, each respondent was asked three questions to which an affirmative or negative answer could be given. After the initial response the interviewee was asked to explain his answer. The responses were recorded on an interviewer guide during the interview. Where responses of consumers indicated no knowledge of discounting, the resulting data sheets (6) were omitted from the analysis.

The three questions asked of each group are set out in Table 1. Question 1, which was the same for both consumers and retailers, was designed to elicit any attitudes about discount houses possessed by the respondents. Question 2 was supposed to determine any changes in behavior patterns that would be caused by the actual location of a discount house in the community.

TABLE 1.

Question	*Consumers*	*Retailers*
1	It has been rumored that a discount house of some sort may begin operation in town. Assuming that it does, how do you feel about it?	It has been rumored that a discount house of some sort may begin operation in town. Assuming that it does, how do you feel about it?
2	If the discount house is established, will it cause you to change any of your shopping behavior?	If the discount house is established, will it cause you to change any of your business practices?
3	How do you think the merchants in town will feel about it?	How do you think most consumers in town will feel about it?

In the case of the consumers the question was concerned with shopping behavior; for the businessmen, competitive behavior. The third question was included to see how each group of respondents viewed the others attitudes toward a discount house. It also was expected that this question, when directed to consumers, would indicate their views of the competitive nature of discounters relative to town merchants.

2. RESPONSES OF RETAILERS

Attitudes Toward Discount Houses

Sixty percent of the retailers displayed negative feelings toward the proposed discount house, 30 percent offered favorable reactions, and 10 percent made both negative and positive comments. Of those retailers opposed to the discount house, over 50 percent reasoned that it would injure their business. One druggist stated it this way: "Man, I can't compete with the way those guys [discounters] operate." The remaining 50 percent of those opposed to the discount house believed that, in various ways, it would hurt the community. Some of the reasoning of this group is expressed in these statements: "They [discounters] practice questionable merchandising techniques that people don't like." "They take advantage of people." "They take money out of town."

As for the 30 percent of the retailers who said that they favored the idea of a discount house locating in town, over one-third believed that it would attract additional trade from other communities and consequently give the present retailers a chance at more business. The remaining two-thirds of this group of retailers saw the discount house as a boon to the community. They thought that it generally would stimulate buying, offer more jobs for people, and make a sizeable contribution in taxes.

Of the 10 percent of the retailers that expressed both positive and negative reactions, the majority recognized the competitive force of the discount house but believed that it would be a contribution to the community. "Sure, it'll hurt me, but in the long run it'll be good for the town," one of these retailers said.

Influence on Competitive Behavior

About 70 percent of the businessmen said that they anticipate no change in their business practices if a discount house is established. The main reasons for this viewpoint were either that this group saw its product offering as different from that of a discounter (52 percent) or its customers were loyal and would not shop elsewhere (20 percent). One hardware dealer said, "You're not gonna get the kind of customer I have in a discount house." The remainder of the group that foresaw no change in business practices said either that they were already adjusted to any new competition (15 percent) or there was simply nothing they could do (12 percent).

The 30 percent of the retailers that stated that it would undertake some competitive action if a discounter entered town was split equally between two strategies. Half said that they would readjust their prices in order to place themselves in a more competitive position. One retailer stated it this way: "As long as I offer the services I do and come close to meeting their [discounters'] prices, I'll do all right." The other half of this group said that they either would adjust their product offering so as to be competitive with the discounter or adjust it so that they would not be in direct competition with him. Adjusting product offering to be more competitive is exemplified by this statement: "I'll simply put in some cheaper lines of merchandise." Adjusting product offering to avoid competition, according to one retailer, is possible "by not handling lines the discounter will handle."

Retailers' View of Consumers' Attitudes Toward Discounter

Eighty-five percent of the retailers felt that the town's people would welcome a discount house. Most (70 percent) of these retailers believed that consumers would be attracted to the discounter's low prices. Twenty percent said that the people would like the discount house because of its novelty. The remaining 10 percent said that the town's people would be attracted to the discounter's wide selection of merchandise.

Of the small number (15 percent) of retailers that felt that the community would not welcome a discount house, almost all said that people knew discounters were unethical. By "unethical" was meant either selling poor quality merchandise or pricing fictitiously. One appliance dealer said it this way: "They [discounters] fool the people into thinking their prices are lower when they're not. And most people know this."

Discussion

In general the retailers viewed the discount house as a very potent competitive force. Most of them were against its entrance and most of them believed the town's people would welcome it. Even those (30 percent) that said that they were in favor of the discounter's arrival did not actually state that they were immune from the discounter's competitive actions.

The retailers interviewed definitely viewed discounting as a distinct type of retailing. This is evidenced by the fact that most of them assumed the rumored discount house to be a strong competitor even though they had not yet observed it in operation. This behavior implied that the retailers were generalizing about all discount houses.

Viewing discounters as unethical merchandisers was a practice of a significant number of retailers in the sample. Such behavior cannot be supported; thus it must be either a form of rationalization or an indication that many conventional retailers do not understand the discounter's operation.

It is interesting to note that a number of those retailers who were against the entrance of a discounter considered it from a social, or community, point of view rather than from that of an individual. This behavior might be expected in a smaller town where people are often community-centered as compared to large city dwellers who often act independently of the city. On the other hand, such a response might have been offered in order to answer in a socially desirable tone.[2]

As noted, around 70 percent of the retailers said that they would make no changes in their business methods if a discounter did enter the field. An analysis of this data showed that over 80 percent of this group also answered that they believed the town's people would welcome a discounter. These two statements have a hint of contradicition to them. Most of the members of this latter group, however, said that they did not view themselves in competition with discounters because of their unique product offering or the loyalty of their customers.[3] While this thinking demonstrates a good deal of confidence, it also implies refined understanding of one's customers. Such detailed knowledge is usually considered a rare situation in small retailing.

Over two-thirds of those retailers who said that they would make no competitive adjustments for the incoming discount house answered in Question 1 that they were against the discount house because of its competitive nature. Again, there appears to be inconsistency in answers. Some of it is explained away, however, by the fact that a number of these retailers believed that they already had made all the competitive adjustments possible. The remaining retailers, though, apparently did offer inconsistent responses to Questions 1 and 2. In effect they said that a discount house would be serious competition for them but they intended no changes in business practices to cope with it. It is possible that they may have had competitive measures in mind but did not wish to disclose them.[4]

Fourteen of the 91 retailers interviewed were chain stores. Analysis of the chain retailers' responses revealed no significant differences from those of independent retailers.

3. RESPONSES OF CONSUMERS

Approximately 85 percent of the households stated that they were in favor of a discounter locating in their town. Most (60 percent) of the re-

[2] It is socially desirable for businessmen to view competition as a healthy situation. It is well known, though, that privately, competition usually is viewed by the businessman as his major deterrent to success.

[3] Gross notes that among department stores it is typical of them to first reject innovations such as discounting on the basis that they more or less have a captive market. This appears to be occurring among the group of retailers in this study. See Walter Gross, "Strategies Used by Major Department Stores to Compete with Low-Margin Retailers," *Journal of Retailing* (Summer, 1964), pp. 11–18.

[4] They were told, however, that the interviewer would hold all answers in strictest confidence and only generalizations were wanted; not specific competitive moves.

spondents said that the discount house would save them money by providing goods at lower selling prices. About 20 percent of this group said that the discount house would add pleasure to the shopping task. One housewife said this: "I'm for it [the discount house]. It'll sure make shopping a lot more enjoyable." The remainder of households that favored the discount house viewed it from a community orientation. They said it would be good for the community because it would offer employment and tax income and aid low-income groups.

Of the 15 percent of households that were against the discount house coming to their town, 45 percent felt that it would severely hurt other merchants.[5] Another 35 percent said that the merchandise stocked by discounters was usually poor quality.[6] Fifteen percent of the informants said that a discount house would take money out of the community. For example, one housewife said, "You spend money in a discount house and it ends up in New York." The remaining five percent of this group felt that the discount house would bring undersirable people to the town.

Influence on Shopping Behavior

Slightly over 70 percent of the households interviewed said that the discount house, if it came, would change some of their shopping behavior. Fifty percent of these respondents believed that they would purchase a major portion of their needs at the coming discount house if possible.[7] A housewife, for example, said, "I'll buy everything there I can if they have it." Over 25 percent of this group reported that they would buy anything at the discount house that was priced lower than that of other stores. Slightly less than 25 percent of these informants said that they would occasionally "take a shopping spree" at the discount house with friends and buy "anything on special."

Twenty percent of those who indicated that they would shop at the rumored discount house said that it should minimize their out-of-town shopping. Over 30 percent of the would-be shoppers commented that they would be more price conscious after the discounter arrived. (The implication was that prices are presently fairly rigid but that the discount house would stimulate price competition.)

About 30 percent of the households believed that the discount house would not influence their shopping behavior.[8] Of this 30 percent, about one-

[5] All of these respondents were directly associated with retail stores that could be interpreted as being in competition with the typical discount house.

[6] A small portion (20 percent) of these households also were directly associated with retail stores that could be interpreted as being in competition with the typical discount house.

[7] This type of consumer is typically described as "the economic shopper." See Gregory P. Stone, "City Shoppers and Urban Identification: Observations on the Social Psychology of City Life," *The American Journal of Sociology* (July, 1964), pp. 36–45.

[8] About half of this group consisted of those respondents who stated in Question 1 that they were against the rumored discount house.

third stated that they preferred to continue shopping with merchants with whom they are familiar.[9] Another 18 percent said that they thought it was wrong to shop with any but local merchants.[10] The remaining 52 percent of these consumers said in various ways that the discount house was not a good place to shop. Some statements were: "They're too crowded"; "There is no one there to help you"; "Parking is usually a problem at a discount house."

Consumers' Views of Retailers' Attitudes Toward Discounting

More than 90 percent of the households interviewed believed that the town's merchants would be opposed to the entrance of a discount house because of its competitive nature. As one housewife stated, "Have you ever seen anyone welcome a kick in the shins?" When the respondents spoke of the competitive nature of the discounter they always refer to pricing, but, additionally, they spoke of wide selection, parking, and evening openings.

The remaining respondents (about 10 percent) believed that merchants would welcome the arrival of a discount house. These housewives reasoned that discounters are inevitable and that one located in the town would be easier to compete with than the ones located in nearby large cities.

Social Class and Attitudes Toward Discounting

Believing that social class would influence responses about discounting, data were obtained during the interviews in order to determine a measure of social class for each household.[11] Preferences for a discount house (as expressed in Question 1) were considered in terms of social class scores. The results are illustrated in Table 2 below.

TABLE 2.

Social class	*n*	*For discount house*	*Against discount house*
upper	20	15 (75%)	5 (25%)
upper-middle	81	67 (82.5%)	14 (17.5%)
lower-middle	106	88 (83%)	18 (17%)
upper-lower	38	34 (89%)	4 (11%)
lower-lower	25	25 (100%)	0 (0%)
Total	270	229 (85%)	41 (15%)

[9] Stone terms this type of shopper, "the personalizing consumer." See Stone, *op. cit.*, p. 38.

[10] This is "the ethical consumer" according to Stone. See Stone, *ibid.*

[11] An index of social status was computed through an adaptation of the McGuire-White system. See Carson McGuire and George D. White, *The Measurement of Social Status*, Austin: Department of Educational Psychology, The University of Texas, March, 1955. (Mimeographed)

All social classes overwhelmingly favored the coming discount house. There was an indication of an inverse relationship between preferences and class; the lower the class the greater the percentage of members favoring the introduction of the discount house. Examination of those social class members stating that they were against the discount house, however, indicated that about half of them were associated with business and might be expected to answer in this manner. After accounting for this latter group, then, the data indicated that preferences for a discount house were equally strong among the five social classes.[12]

Discussion

The responses of the households in this study indicate the following:

(1) Most of the members of the community felt that the discount house was a powerful type of competition and that its main competitive weapon was price.
(2) Most members of the community, regardless of social class, indicated a desire for a discount house because they believed it would provide savings in their purchases.[13]
(3) Those community members not favoring the rumored discount house typically were concerned with the welfare of the present merchants. This is understandable since the heads of these households were owners or employees of retail stores that could be considered competitors of a typical discounter.
(4) There was a segment of the community, although relatively small, that felt that discount houses handled inferior merchandise.[14]

4. GENERAL COMMENTS

The responses discussed here were in terms of discount houses in general rather than of a specific discount house. The statements by consumers, no doubt, were flavored by previous experiences with discount house in major cities. The responses of the retailers surely were influenced by materials that they had read and by discussions they had held with suppliers and other retailers. Because of these factors, the attitudes expressed here may not be adequate to predict the actual behavior of the town's people toward a discount house should one locate in their community.

[12] This does not mean that these social class members would shop at a specific discount house. It would depend on its image. This information does imply, though, that all social classes were receptive to the discount house concept.

[13] A recent study also showed that low price was the most important factor in attracting customers to the discount house. See Frank J. Devlin, *Public Reaction to Discount Stores* (Cleveland: John Carroll University School of Business, 1965).

[14] This finding differs somewhat from the John Carroll University study which found a very significant portion of respondents feeling discounters handled inferior goods. It is interesting to note that the J.C.U. study was with people who had had considerable experience with discounters. An implication of the two studies is that many consumers lose confidence in the product offering of discounters as they gain experience in shopping in these outlets.

At least three findings of the study are of significance to a discounter who may be considering locating in the community under study. First, the households, in general, would welcome a new, different shopping facility—one that would add some excitement to shopping. Certainly, an outlet that promises these things plus money savings should receive a warm welcome.

Second, the study indicates that initial competitive reaction by present retailers to a new shopping facility probably would be slight and disorganized. As noted earlier from the report by Gross, initial reaction to the discounter by conventional retailers has been that of rejection, that is, they simply do not believe that the discounter can harm their business. Gross implies further that some time may pass before the conventional retailer starts competitive measures directly aimed at the discounter.[15]

Third, and on the negative side, there is a segment of this community, and probably of most communities its size, that may resist the entrance of a discount house. This group consists of (1) those people associated with already existing retail stores, (2) those who believe that discounters handle inferior merchandise, and (3) those who think that a discounter would take money out of the community. While this group is small, it is probably a relatively high income group. Further, even though the group is small, it may contain opinion leaders who can influence the purchase patterns of many other community members.

A follow-up study has been planned and will be conducted after a discount house locates in this community. The resulting report will provide a check on the attitudes and implied behavior reported here.

QUESTIONS

1. Is a discounter a threat to all retailers? Explain.
2. Do you agree with the retailers' statement—"They [discounters] fool the people into thinking their prices are lower when they're not."?
3. Table II indicates that there is an inverse ratio between preferences for a discount house and social class. Aside from price savings, what other aspects of consumer behavior can account for this fact?

[15] Gross, *op. cit.*, p. 14.

13

The Child Consumer: A New Market

James U. McNeal

Marketers—retailers and manufacturers—employ a variety of demand factors to define markets. They commonly use income, size, location, education and many other criteria. For years one important means of segmenting markets has been the concept of life-cycle. Essentially, the markets were divided into the following categories: (*a*) young single adults, (*b*) newly married couples with no children, (*c*) young married couples with young children, (*d*) married couples with adolescent children, (*e*) married couples whose children have moved from home.[1]

However, in recent years some marketers began to realize that the life-cycle as a criterion for market definition was omitting an increasingly important market segment; namely, the youth market. Seemingly overnight, the marketer became aware that youth, in addition to adults, had desires for goods and money to back them up.

The result of this realization was a flurry of activities aimed at what was termed the "teen market."[2] Companies, and divisions of companies, cropped up to make products for the teens, advertisements to teens proliferated (often from a special division in an advertising agency concerned only with teens), and retail stores started setting aside areas termed such things as "teen-land" and junior shops.

Today, the teen market is a truism among marketers. There are copious facts and figures about it. And hundreds, perhaps thousands, of marketers are striving hard for their share of the 10–12 billion dollars spent annually by the nearly twenty million teens.

Now, the perceptive marketer is discovering still another new age-graded market even younger than the teen market—*the child market*. There has always been an awareness in modern marketing of the influence of the child on household purchases. And aggressive marketers capitalize on this relationship, for example, with numerous advertisements that tell the child to encourage the *family* to buy cereals, soft drinks and even automobiles.

Reprinted From *Journal of Retailing*, Vol. 45, No. 2, Summer 1969, pp. 15–22, 84.

[1] For a discussion of life-cycle as a base for market segmentation, see William D. Wells and George Gubar, "The Life-Cycle Concept in Marketing Research," *Journal of Marketing Research*, 3 (November 1966), 355–63.

[2] See, for example, "Do Ad Men Understand Teen-Agers?" in James U. McNeal (ed.), *Dimensions of Consumer Behavior* (New York: Appleton-Century-Crofts, 1965), pp. 210–17.

The new child market referred to here, however, does not mean the children that influence parental purchases. Neither does it mean items purchased by the child for the household such as milk and bread. And, neither does it include the billions of dollars spent on children by parents.

The term, child market, as employed here, refers to that group of children between the ages of 5 and 13 (roughly the elementary school age children) that make purchases of goods and services for personal use and satisfaction.

There have always been children just as there have always been teenagers. But definitively speaking, in order for a group to be termed a market, it must be sizable, it must have desire and it must have ability to buy. As our affluence has grown it has backed down through the teen level and finally to the children. Consequently, there is now a large number of children in the United States with many desires and money to fulfill them.

In the case of children there is an additional requisite for being a market. There must be an understanding of money and the purchase act. As Reisman *et al.*, have noted, however, affluent Americans tend to give their children consumer training at a very early age.[3] Typically, an American youngster makes his first independent purchase around age five.[4] During at least a year prior to the solo, the parents were training him diligently in the art of consumption. This training included such things as letting the youngster give the money to the supermarket cashier or retrieve a box of cereal from the shelf, and showing him how to give the squeeze-test to a loaf of bread.

Probably the consumer training was intensified after the solo act in order that the child might eventually relieve the parent of more menial purchase tasks such as the "bread and milk runs" or the returning of some product for exchange.

SIZE OF CHILD MARKET

To measure the child market we need to ask two questions. How many children are there? How much money do they have to spend? The individual marketer, of course, wishes to know what portion of this total market wants his product and how much of it the youngsters will buy.

In 1967, there were an estimated 36,732,000 children in the United States ranging from age 5 to age 13.[5] By 1985 this group is forecasted to have a minimum growth of 17 percent (to 40,447,000) and a possible growth of

[3] David Riesman, Nathan Glazer and Reuel Denny, *The Lonely Crowd* (New York: Doubleday and Company, 1953).

[4] James U. McNeal, "An Exploratory Study of the Consumer Behavior of Children," in James U. McNeal (ed.), *Dimensions of Consumer Behavior* (New York: Appleton-Century-Crofts, 1965), pp. 190–209.

[5] *Current Population Reports*, Series P-25, No. 286 (Washington D.C.: Department of Commerce, July 1964), p. 6.

53 percent (to 52,719,000).[6] There is today an almost equal number of girls and boys among the 36.7 million children, and they are distributed among approximately 20,000,000 families.

Stating how much money these youngsters have to spend is difficult. Their sources of purchasing power are numerous. They include earned income from odd-jobs, paper routes, etc., gifts from parents and relatives (particularly grandparents) and allowances which generally are perceived as a combination of earnings and gifts.

Yet those organizations that normally gather income data (government agencies, trade associations and universities) have not concerned themselves with this market, or in most cases, even recognized it as a market. Consequently, income data for this group is unavailable and only can be roughly estimated.

Even if income data were available, little is known about the children's saving habits. Lack of this information makes it still more difficult to estimate their expenditures.

With the assistance of some interested faculty members of the University of Georgia, an average weekly expenditure of $1.10 was determined.[7] It is believed that this is a conservative figure. Further, it is believed that this figure would not vary significantly over large numbers of children from most income groups but would vary directly with the age of the child.

If this "guesstimate" can be accepted, it means that this market has a value of approximately 2 billion dollars annually. This value is in agreement with verbal estimates made by some advertising agencies and businessmen.

While the $2 billion figure may seem small when compared with the expenditure of other age groups, it is a very significant amount when viewed in terms of various products such as gum, candy and frozen desserts. For example, assume that each member of this group chews two pieces of gum per week or approximately 100 pieces per year. This means consumption of 3,673,200,000 pieces of gum or approximately $36,700,000 in expenditures for this one product.

DEMANDS OF THE CHILD MARKET

Basically the child consumer is no different from any other consumer—he wants things that satisfy his needs.[8] For this new consumer, the purchase act provides two levels of satisfaction. First, the obvious satisfaction is produced by the items purchased, consisting normally of a wide array of sweets and a few inexpensive toys. The second dimension of satisfaction stems from the purchase *act* rather than from *what* is purchased. In effect, the purchase

[6] *Ibid.*

[7] This figure consists of an estimated *average* of 50 cents per week received from parents and 60 cents per week from gifts and earnings.

[8] Much of the material in this section and the following sections is adapted from McNeal, *op. cit.*

act is evidence of "grown-upness." And, surely, at the top of the youngster's hierarchy of needs is the need to be considered mature by adults.[9]

Gradually the inherent value of the consumption act declines with maturity. The first type of satisfaction, that produced by possession and use of products, becomes increasingly important. This change in the value of the purchase act normally occurs between ages 5 and 12. Thus, this span of time might aptly be termed the apprenticeship period of consuming.

From the viewpoint of the two types of satisfaction, the new child consumer demands products, mostly sweets, to satisfy his present needs, and demands to obtain them in an independent manner.[10] He wants such items as candy, ice cream and gum constantly. He is inconsistent in his purchase habits at first, seemingly having little brand, or even product, preference. At one time he may spend minutes trying to make a candy purchase decision; yet, the next time he may purchase on impulse.

He usually disregards future needs, spending only for the present. Thus, saving money usually means saving it until he again is in a place of purchase. He gives no consideration to the source of funds. His demands are endless, and he expects money to be likewise. On the other hand, since he is just learning to understand the concept of money, he fortunately thinks in terms of pennies and nickels rather than dollars. And more fortunately, by the time he concerns himself with "dollar" purchases, he usually has learned respect for the source of funds and is willing to work for them.

As mentioned above, the child quickly seeks independence in his purchase behavior. He wants to give the money personally to the "store-man," put the coins in the vending machine and retrieve the products from their shelves and cases. And one of his greatest childhood thrills is his first trip to the store by himself. What an expression of independence! It is exciting, mysterious and self-rewarding. Usually he is quite nervous while he is in the store, particularly during the actual exchange. This uneasiness typically accompanies the trip back home, and he welcomes the sight of his house. Once home, there is a feeling of both relief and accomplishment. Henceforth, he demands to make the trip frequently, and his parents are usually willing to permit him to do so because he can also perform the "milk and bread run." Thus, there is recognition by both youngster and parents that he is now truly a consumer.

DEVELOPMENT OF CONSUMER BEHAVIOR PATTERNS

By age seven the child consumer has "soloed," and begins to perfect his consuming skills. He achieves this refinement in a variety of ways. Mainly, he copies the consumer behavior patterns of his parents. Bandura has noted

[9] Arnold Gesell and Frances Ilg, *The Child from Five to Ten* (New York: Harper and Brothers, 1946).

[10] The degree of independence desired in the purchasing process appears to vary directly with ages. McNeal, *op. cit.*, pp. 195–96.

that the child copies not only the general patterns of behavior but also "the mannerisms, voice inflections, and attitudes which the parents have never directly attempted to teach."[11] The youngster applies these patterns of behavior at every opportunity. He asks to make trips to the store, and during in-store shopping with his parents, he attempts to assist them.

At the same time that the child is copying parental behavioral patterns, the parents are usually trying to teach the child the procedures of purchasing. If the child cannot immediately implement some newly learned behavior, he often pretends to do so in his play. As one youngster stated, "I play store all the time."

The child also copies the consumer behavioral patterns of his peers and seeks advice from them about consumption. This peer influence usually becomes strong at age seven. The nature of the influence typically consists of recommendations about flavors and brands of sweets.

The child also learns a great deal about consumer behavior from advertising, particularly that on television. From advertising the child learns about brands, types of stores and pricing. And even though there may be a dislike for television advertising that increases with age, the child readily admits that the advertising does influence his consumer behavior.

By the time the child reaches age nine or ten, he has a simple understanding of the marketing process. He can discuss the functions of stores, the sources of products and even the concept of profit. He even discusses such matters as sales, bargains and trading stamps. Some of this knowledge is acquired in the classroom under such terms as "social studies" and "the environment we live in."

By age nine the glow of the shopping process is wearing off, and if permitted, the child may show discrimination in making shopping trips. This reduction of interest in consumption can be expected as shopping begins to lose its problem character and the youngster develops a feeling of competence in it. By ritualizing those activities in which he has developed competence, he can achieve freedom to meet new zones of experience.[12]

By the time the child reaches his last year of elementary school, his consumer behavioral patterns are much like those of an adult. He is assigning social value to many products, participating in family discussions about major purchases and is on a first-name basis with a number of "store people."

MARKETING TO THE CHILD CONSUMER

The fact that there is a child market cannot be denied. The most obvious evidence is the large amount of marketing effort aimed at this market.

[11] Albert Bandura, "Social Learning Through Imitation," in Marshall R. Jones (ed.), *Nebraska Symposium on Motivation* (Lincoln, Neb.: University of Nebraska Press, 1962), pp. 214–15.

[12] John E. Anderson, "The Development of Behavior and Personality," in Eli Ginzberg (ed.), *The Nation's Children*, II (New York: Columbia University Press, 1960), 57.

It is true, for example, that much advertising to children is attempting to get them to influence the purchases of their parents. But, increasingly, marketers are seeing children as a market, and are devoting attention to them from this viewpoint. Instead of saying, "ask your mother to buy so-and-so," advertisements to children often simply say, "buy so-and-so."

In supermarkets, for instance, products that appeal to children are placed at lower levels for their convenience. Only a few years ago these same products were displayed at a higher level so they could *not* reach them. These same supermarkets often have smaller shopping carts for the children as well as racks for parking bicycles. One supermarket chain, with the advice of a number of outstanding behavioral scientists, conducted studies of children's shopping behavior.[13] The study not only provided a wealth of information on children's attitudes toward shopping, but also furnished a great deal of insight into their actual purchase behavior patterns.

Manufacturers have been quick to recognize the potential of the child market and have provided it with a wide array of products ranging from fashions[14] to candies.[15] These same manufacturers heavily promote these products directly to children via television programs for children, comic books, the backsides of cereal packages and other media. Producers of children's products have even entered the school environment in order to promote the goods. They give the teachers such items as pencils and book covers which are, in turn, given to the children. In some cases the manufacturers are even furnishing books containing advertisements of their products.[16] One producer of food goods has developed a coloring book that can be purchased from magazine racks in supermarkets.[17] It appears to be an ordinary coloring book except that it contains some pictures of the manufacturer's products.

Marketing to children is not without its problems, however. To some parents the idea of selling to children conjures up visions of exploitation of the innocent and unknowing.[18] Consequently, marketers must be careful when "courting" the child consumer so as not to offend the parent.

Catering to children can be troublesome for the retailer. He frequently claims that children damage goods or fixtures and make shopping unpleasant for adults.

Finally, there is the problem of finding adequate media through which to advertise directly to children. The marketer is normally limited to a few

[13] "A Study of the Child as a Consumer" (Cincinnati: The Kroger Food Foundation, 1954). (Mimeographed.)

[14] "Kid Stuff Swings to a Grownup Look," *Business Week* (April 17, 1965), pp. 66 ff.

[15] *The Avisco Candy Study* (Philadelphia: FMC Corporation, 1964).

[16] The author's daughter used a supplementary geography book during the fifth grade which was furnished by a bakery. The bakery's bread was generously advertised throughout the book.

[17] *Grocery Store Coloring Book,* Bozell and Jacobs, Inc., and Skinner Macaroni Co., 1965.

[18] Roy G. Francis, "Some Sociological Implications of Demographic Change," in William A. Mindak, *Proceedings of the 8th Biennial Marketing Institute of the Minnesota Chapter* (Chicago: American Marketing Association, 1961), p. II-y.

television programs, a small number of radio programs, and comic books. Usually he is not allowed, for example, to place cards on school buses or sign boards near the schools.

CONCLUSIONS

A child market definitely exists in the United States. Like the teenager and adults, the child has wants and the means to satisfy them.

The specific desires of the child market differ from those of older consumers. Therefore, this new market must be treated differently by marketers who wish to serve it. Special advertisements in special advertising media must be employed. Merchandising at the retail level must take the nature of the child into consideration.

Marketing to this young group is difficult and troublesome. But the rewards may be great. Not only can marketers benefit profitably by serving this market now, but they may be ensuring themselves for future marketing as the youngster grows. If the child is served correctly in his early consumer years, he probably will develop store and brand loyalties that will remain throughout his life. Such a marketing strategy might be termed "growing customers for future use."

QUESTIONS

1. What retail outlets can realistically consider the child as a consumer?
2. Discuss the ethical problems faced by both the retailer *and* the manufacturer in appealing to this market.
3. What means can a retailer use to reach this market?

14

City Shoppers and Urban Identification: Observations on the Social Psychology of City Life[1]

Gregory P. Stone

A growing body of evidence seems to be signifying a change in the focus of urban sociology away from the study of urbanism as a *way* of life toward the study of urbanism as a way of *life*. Until recently the view of urbanism as the polar antithesis of the personal, familistic, sacred, and consensual life of the isolated tradition-bound community has imbued most sociological investigations of the city.[2] Recent research suggests theoretical possibilities for explaining how, in the impersonal and anonymous milieu of the city, the individual can establish the requisite social identification for distinguishing himself as a person. Many studies imply the hypothesis that typical social relationships characterized by primacy (or at least a quasi-primacy"),[3] in Cooley's sense, have arisen to provide such a matrix of identifications.[4]

Reprinted from *American Journal of Sociology*, Vol. 60, No. 1, July 1954, pp. 36–45.

[1] The author wishes to express his gratitude to his wife, Margaret, who assisted in the field work, provided helpful criticisms, and otherwise assisted; also to his colleague, William H. Form, for a critical reading. Some of the observations made here appear in greater detail in Gregory P. Stone, "Sociological Aspects of Consumer Purchasing in a Northwest Side Chicago Community" (unpublished Master's thesis, University of Chicago, 1952).

[2] In Durkheim, Maine, and Tönnies the "polarities" proposed are not so antithetical as they have sometimes been construed. It seems quite clear that Tönnies, especially, did not propose *Gemeinschaft* and *Gesellschaft* merely as antithetical categories but also as elements of an antinomy such that any tendency toward one form of social relationship evokes countertendencies (see Ferdinand Tönnies, *Fundamental Concepts of Sociology*, trans. and supplemented by Charles P. Loomis [New York: American Book Co., 1940], esp. pp. 221–22).

[3] They are not primary in the sense of encompassing the lives and aspirations of the participants or secondary in being antithetical to the primary group. Schmalenbach has proposed *Bund* as a category to fill the conceptual lacuna. However, it is not the purpose of this article to make a conceptual contribution, and the gap has been filled by a loose interpretation of the concept "primary group" (see Herman Schmalenbach, "Die Soziologische Kategorie des Bundes," *Die Dioskuren: Jahrbuch für Geistenswissenschaften*, I [1922], 35–105).

[4] Early observations relevant to this hypothesis may be found in Schmalenbach, *ibid.*; more recently, in Harry C. Harmsworth, "Primary Group Relationships in Modern Society," *Sociology and Social Research*, XXXI (March–April, 1947), 291–96; and in Robert E. L. Faris, "Development of the Small Group Research Movement," in Muzafer Sherif and M. O. Wilson (eds.), *Group Relations at the Crossroads* (New York: Harper & Bros., 1953), pp. 155–84. Empirical studies bearing on the hypothesis include William F. Whyte, *Street Corner Society* (Chicago: University of Chicago Press, 1943); Morris Janowitz, *The Community Press in an Urban Setting* (Glencoe, Ill.: Free Press, 1952); and "The Imagery of the Urban Community Press," in Paul K. Hatt and Albert J. Reiss, Jr. (eds.), *Reader in Urban Sociology* (Glencoe,

These observations are the more theoretically strategic because most refer to contexts where life is supposedly impersonal and anonymous.

This article is an attempt to supplement such findings with data on shopping. Few treatises on the sociology of the city fail to designate the market place as the epitome of those "impersonal," "segmentalized," "secondary," "categoric," and "rational" contacts said to characterize human relations in the city. Yet the study reported here points to the possibility that some urbanites, as a consequence of the relationships they establish with the personnel of retail stores, manage to form identifications which bind them to the larger community.

PROCEDURE

Some time ago the writer was engaged by a private research agency to study popular reactions to the establishment of a large chain department store in an outlying business district on Chicago's Northwest Side. One of the techniques was a schedule administered to 150 adult female residents[5] of the area surrounding the business district. Their responses to certain questions indicated disparate definitions of shopping situations and markedly different orientations to stores in general. The latter were implicit in the criteria by which the housewives said they evaluated stores in the area and in the expectations they had of store personnel as they encountered them in shopping. Particularly striking, in contrast to customary sociological notions, was their recurrent statement that market relationships were often personal.

This suggested a typology of shopping orientations as a basis for a more intensive analysis of the anomalies. The procedure for its construction and application consisted of four steps: (1) a fourfold classification of the *responses* to one particularly discerning question, called here the "filter" question; (2) a similar classification of *informants* as consumer types on the basis of demonstrated consistencies between their responses to the filter question and a number of other questions termed "indicator" question; (3) a schematization of the consumer types as *empirical models;* and (4) the construction of *social profiles* based on the patterns of social characteristics associated with the consumer types. These procedures revealed further anomalies which are analyzed in the concluding section of the article.

Ill.: Free Press, 1951), pp. 532–41; Erwin O. Smigel, "Unemployed Veterans in New York City" (unpublished doctoral dissertation, New York University, 1948), pp. 134–39. An extensive bibliography on the study of primary groups is available in Edward A. Shils, "The Study of the Primary Group," in Daniel Lerner and Harold D. Lasswell (eds.), *The Policy Sciences* (Stanford University: Stanford University Press, 1951), pp. 44–70.

[5] Because marital status was a variable which might have distorted the findings of the study, 26 single, widowed, or divorced subjects were eliminated from the original 150 informants. Housewives were originally selected as informants because they do most of the buying, but it seems that this situation is changing.

ORIENTATIONS TO SHOPPING

Responses to the question, "Why would you rather do business with local independent merchants (or large chain stores, depending on a prior choice)?" persistently revealed markedly different orientations to different kinds of stores as well as diverse definitions of shopping. Because of the discriminating power of the question, it was used as a "filtering" device for achieving a preliminary classification of the consumers on the basis of their orientation to shopping.[6]

Replies to the filter question were grouped into five empirical categories of criteria housewives used to evaluate stores: (1) economic, (2) personalizing, (3) ethical, (4) apathetic, and (5) a residual category of unique or indeterminate criteria. As may be seen, some statements did not fall precisely into single categories. When a response included multiple orientations, it was coded for each category.

The Economic Category

Remarks coded in this category clearly indicated that the informant regarded shopping as primarily buying, her behavior being unambiguously directed to the purchase of goods. The criteria applied to the evaluation of stores included: an appraisal of the store's merchandise in terms of price, quality, and variety; a favorable evaluation of store practices that maximize the efficient distribution of goods; conversely, an unfavorable evaluation of practices and relationships with personnel which impede the quick efficient sale of merchandise; and a favorable rating of conditions which maximized independence of customer choice. The following four responses are typical of this category:

> I prefer large department stores. They give you better service. Their prices are more reasonable. . . . There's a wider selection of goods.
>
> I prefer big chains. They have cheaper stuff. It's too expensive in small stores. Then, too, I like the idea of helping yourself. Nobody talks you into anything. You can buy what you please.
>
> I suppose I should help the smaller stores, but I can do best at the chains. Local merchants are too nosey—too personal—and their prices are higher. The prices in chains are good, and you get self-service in chains.
>
> I like to shop in local independently owned stores. You can get better grade materials and better service there. If anything goes wrong with the

[6] Merton distinguishes orientation from role: "The social orientation differs from the social role. Role refers to the manner in which the rights and duties inherent in a social position are put into practice; orientation . . . refers to the theme underlying the complex of social roles performed by an individual. It is the (tacit or explicit) theme which finds expression in each of the complex of social roles in which the individual is implicated" (Robert K. Merton, "Patterns of Influence," in Paul F. Lazarsfeld and Frank Stanton [eds.], *Communications Research 1948–1949* [New York: Harper & Bros., 1949], p. 187).

> material, you always have a chance to go back and make a complaint. They'll make it good for you. They have more time. You're more familiar with that kind of store and can find what you want in a hurry. Some of them allow you stamps on their budget plan, and that saves you a lot of money.

The Personalizing Category

In this category were placed responses defining shopping as fundamentally and positively interpersonal. Such informants expressed a tendency to personalize and individualize the customer role in the store and rated stores in terms of closeness of relationships between the customer and personnel. Consequently, "purely" economic criteria, such as price, quality, selection of merchandise, and highly rationalized retailing techniques were of lesser importance. These four remarks exemplify the category:

> I prefer local merchants. They're friendlier and not quite so big. . . . Although prices are higher in small stores, when you trade with local merchants you have a better chance to be a good customer. They get to know you. People in smaller stores greet you cordially when you come in. They get to know you, and make an effort to please you.

> I'd rather trade at my own store than a public store. That's why I prefer local merchants. They're more personal. They get to know your name. They take more interest in you as a human being.

> Local merchants give you better service. They get so they know you. The chains are impersonal. They don't try so hard to please you. The customer doesn't mean anything to the clerk in the big chain stores, because it's not his business.

> I shop at independents if they have the merchandise. They usually know you by name and try to please you. In the big store no one knows you. . . . Maybe it's because I feel at home in the smaller store. When you're in them, you feel more wanted. You feel lost in a big store.

The Ethical Category

Responses in this category signified that the informants feel a moral obligation to patronize specific types of stores. They perceive shopping in the light of a larger set of values rather than of specific values and more immediately relevant norms. Store patronage was appraised in anticipation of such moral consequences. The following excerpts express it:

> It would be better if they were all neighborhood stores. The chains put people out of work because the people have to wait on themselves. But that's what happens in a machine age. They set up everything like a factory. If there's another depression, the chains will put people out of work, because they are set up on a self-help system. So, if you let the chains run the little business out, they will be wrecking their own chances for jobs, if times get too bad.

> I prefer the local independents. I think that the chain store is taking too much business away from the little fellow.

> I prefer local merchants if they have the variety and a large selection of

> goods. You know, they're making a living and you want to help them out. The chain stores are making a living too—a damn good one!
>
> You have to give the independent merchant a chance to earn his bread and butter. The chain stores grab it all. The big chain store has no heart or soul.

The Apathetic Category

Included in this category are responses showing that the informant was not interested in shopping and did not discriminate kinds of stores. They emphasize the minimizing of effort in purchasing. Illustrations are:

> I don't know. I guess there's not much difference.
>
> Local merchants are O.K. It depends on where you happen to be. Whichever store is the closest is O.K. with me.
>
> It depends on which is the closest.
>
> Chain stores. You can get everything there in one trip. There's nothing particular to like about either kind of store.

Questions on the consumer's image of a good clerk and good store manager, unpleasant and pleasant shopping experiences, and price, quality, and service satisfactions were used as "indicators" to test the consistency with which the orientations elicited by the filter question were maintained. Responses to these questions lent themselves, with some exceptions,[7] to a classification like that set forth above.

After replies to the filter and indicator questions were coded as described, the interviews were again examined, and the coding of answers tabulated for each interview. Informants were placed in exclusive categories when the tabulation of the relevant coded responses demonstrated consistent orientations to the shopping situation. The essential criterion of consistency in this case was met by the requirement that the *majority* of coded "indicator" responses must coincide with a coded "filter" response.

A TYPOLOGY OF CONSUMERS

The final classification of housewives yielded four consumer types: (1) economic, (2) personalizing, (3) ethical, and (4) apathetic. Brief sketches of these types were constructed to summarize the characteristics of each as expressed in clustering and interrelated responses to the "filter" and "indicator" questions. These sketches are *empirical models* of the types; they are not designed as concepts for the formulation of propositions to be directly incorporated into a theoretical system.

The empirical models of the consumer types are presented here with the caveat that probably no single consumer was adequately described by any

[7] E.g., the questions directed toward the informant's satisfaction with price, quality, and service in stores forced her thinking into an "economic" frame of reference. Thus, these more structured questions were used as indicators only when "economic" and "apathetic" orientations had been signified in response to the "filter" question.

of the models. The models represent composites of actual consumers and their characteristic role orientations.[8]

The Economic Consumer

Here was the closest approximation to the "economic man" of the classical economist. This type of shopper expressed a sense of responsibility for her household purchasing duties: she was extremely sensitive to price, quality, and assortment of merchandise, all of which entered into the calculus of her behavior on the market. She was interested in shopping. Clerical personnel and the store were, for her, merely the instruments of her purchase of goods. Thus, efficiency or inefficiency of sales personnel, as well as the relative commensurateness of prices, quality, or the selection of merchandise, were decisive in leaving her with a pleasant or unpleasant impression of the store. The quality she demanded of a "good" clerk was efficiency.

The Personalizing Consumer

This type of consumer shopped "where they know my name." It was important that she shop at her store rather than "public" stores.[9] Strong personal attachments were formed with store personnel, and this personal relationship, often approaching intimacy, was crucial to her patronage of a store. She was highly sensitized to her experiences on the market; obviously they were an important part of her life. It followed that she was responsive to both pleasant and unpleasant experiences in stores. Her conception of a "good" clerk was one who treated her in a personal, relatively intimate manner.

The Ethical Consumer

This type of shopper shopped where she "ought" to. She was willing to sacrifice lower prices or a wider selection of goods "to help the little guy out" or because "the chain store has no heart or soul." Consequently, strong attachments were sometimes formed with personnel and store owners or with

[8] Nevertheless, a *post hoc* attempt to "verify" the typology met with some success. Specifically, a number of items dealing with shopping behavior but not included in the construction of the typology were significantly associated with variations in consumer type in logically compatible directions: number of shopping trips to the downtown central shopping district ($p < .02$; $T = .18$), patronage of women's department stores and specialty shops for women's clothing ($p < .05$; $T = .16$), acquaintance with salesclerks ($p < .01$; $T = .21$), chain store versus independent store patronage ($p < .001$; $T = .35$).

[9] The personal pronouns "I," "me," and "my" found their way frequently into the interviews, one indication of the extent to which they built up strong identifications with the stores they patronized. Therefore, their relationships with store personnel are referred to later as "primary" or "quasi-primary," for the store has become incorporated into the social self of the consumer. As Cooley put it, "The social self is simply any idea, or system of ideas, drawn from the communicative life, that the mind cherishes as its own." Hence the store may be seen as a part of the social self of the personalizing type of consumer (see Charles Horton Cooley, *Human Nature and the Social Order* [New York: Charles Scribner's Sons, 1902], p. 147).

"stores" in the abstract. These mediated the impressions she had of stores, left pleasant impressions in her memory, and forced unpleasant impressions out. Since store personnel did not enter in primarily as instrumentalities but rather with reference to other, more ultimate ends, she had no clear conception of a "good" clerk.

The Apathetic Consumer

This type of consumer shopped because she "had" to. Shopping for her was an onerous task. She shopped "to get it over with." Ideally, the criterion of convenient location was crucial to her selection of a store, as opposed to price, quality of goods, relationships with store personnel, or ethics. She was not interested in shopping and minimized her expenditure of effort in purchasing goods. Experiences in stores were not sufficiently important to leave any lasting impression on her. She knew few of the personnel and had no notion of a "good" clerk.

The distribution of these types in the sample is shown in Table 1.

TABLE 1.

Distribution of Consumer Types

Type of Consumer	*Number*	*Per Cent*
Economic	41	33
Personalizing	35	28
Ethical	22	18
Apathetic	21	17
Indeterminate	5	4
Total	124	100

SOCIAL PROFILES OF THE CONSUMER TYPES

As found in writings on urbanism and the mass society, a city—an area characterized by the absence of many traditional controls, a predominance of segmented depersonalized relationships, and the proliferation of alternative activities—is a place where the consumption of goods is presumably structured as either a highly rational and rationalized activity, the relationship between the consumer and the sales clerk being instrumental, with minimal emotional involvement on the part of either; or an onerous task performed reluctantly by consumers eager to complete their transaction as easily and quickly as possible. Lynd's observations have emphasized the latter consequence, while Simmel has treated both consequences.[10]

[10] Robert S. Lynd, "The People as Consumers," in the *Report of the President's Research Committee on Social Trends: Recent Social Trends* (New York: McGraw-Hill Book Co., 1933), p. 242; Georg Simmel, *The Sociology of Georg Simmel*, trans. with an introduction by Kurt H. Wolff (Glencoe, Ill.: Free Press, 1950), pp. 414–17.

Certainly one cannot deduce from the conventional propositions of urban sociology that buyer-seller relationships would take on quasi-primary characteristics. The ethical type of shopper isolated in this study also presents a paradox. Neither type—the personalizing consumer nor the ethical consumer—fits into the perspective of conventional urban social psychology.[11]

The most obvious and, in the light of conventional urban sociology, the most plausible hypothesis explaining the personalization of market relationships in the city as well as the "moralization" of such relationships is that these processes merely manifest a carry-over of rural or "small-town" shopping habits to the metropolitan market place.[12] We would expect, then, that personalizing and ethical consumers are predominantly housewives who learned to shop in nonurban environments. But the data offered no support for this hypothesis, in so far as the types of consumers studied were not significantly differentiated by place of birth.[13] As a matter of fact, the majority of consumers classified in each type were native-born Chicagoans. Although the types were significantly associated with parental place of birth, this was because ethical consumers—presumably not to be thought of as a characteristically urban type—included proportionately and significantly more *third-generation* Chicagoans than any other type. These data suggest that the orientations to shopping typical of both ethical and personalizing consumers did not originate in an atmosphere foreign to metropolitan life but precisely in the context of the metropolitan milieu.

On the basis of this general hypothesis, relationships between specific social and economic variables and variations in consumer type were subjected to statistical tests of significance. Significant associations were found for number of children, membership in voluntary associations, and social class.[14]

[11] Cf. Tönnies' statement: "In the *Gesellschaft*, as contrasted with the *Gemeinschaft*, we find no actions that can be derived from an *a priori* and necessarily existing unity; no actions, therefore, which manifest the will and the spirit of the unity even if performed by the individual; no actions, which, insofar as they are performed by the individual, take place on behalf of those united with them" (*op. cit.*, p. 74). Yet, in the metropolis, we find the consumer who patronizes a particular store with the best interest of the owner in mind—the ethical consumer—and the consumer who enters the market place with the "will" to build unity out of her relationship with the seller—the personalizing consumer.

[12] "To a greater or lesser degree, therefore, our social life bears the imprint of an earlier folk society. . . . The population of the city itself is in large measure recruited from the countryside, where a mode of life reminiscent of the earlier form of existence persists." (Louis Wirth, "Urbanism as a Way of Life," *American Journal of Sociology*, XLIV [July, 1938], p. 3).

[13] The chi-square test was used as a measure of the significance of all associations reported here, and, where necessary, T has been used to determine the degree of association. A probability of .05 or less was used as an acceptable indication that the association between two variables could not be attributed to chance variations.

[14] Social class was determined from the application of the "Index of Status Characteristics" described in W. Lloyd Warner, Marchia Meeker, and Kenneth Eels, *Social Class in America* (Chicago: Science Research Associates, 1949). Other results not accepted as statistically significant included associations with age ($p < .20$); officerships in associations ($p < .95$); religious denomination ($p < .70$); occupational status of head of consumer's household ($p < .20$); education of consumer ($p < .20$); education of head of consumer's household ($p < .10$); and ethnic status ($p < .20$).

Explanations of the above relationships always required taking into account the participation of the consumer in the larger social life of her community and suggested that personal involvements in various phases of the social structure of the Northwest Side also played a part in determining her role orientation in the market. On the assumption that variations in personal involvement could be measured by objective and subjective indexes of community identification, further associations were subjected to statistical tests of significance. The results disclosed significant association between variations in consumer type and locus of last place of residence, residence of friends, and the consumer's desire to remain in or leave the Northwest Side.[15]

A qualitative analysis of the above associations suggested that each consumer type was characterized by a distinctive patterning of social position and community identification. To spell out with statistical precision the entire complex of variables identifying each type and assess their relative weights was, at best, extremely difficult and rendered unfeasible by the small number of cases and the consequent impossibility of holding variables constant. To circumvent these difficulties, a "social profile" was drawn up for each type of shopper, none of which was intended directly to represent the empirical data. Rather they represent *some* social condition which the clustering of relationships point to as *probably* shaping orientations.

The Economic Consumer

Youth, aspiration, and economic disadvantage, when they described lower-middle class housewives, set the stage for the formulation of an economic orientation to shopping. The physical requirements of the economic role were exacting and could best be performed by the young. Economic consumers were socially mobile and seldom loath to instrumentalize the customer-clerk relationship as the orientation required. Many were just passing through the Northwest Side on their way to more highly esteemed residences farther out on the metropolitan periphery. Their mobility aspirations, however, were seriously qualified by the presence of children who demanded care and cost money at a period in their married life when funds were already low and by subordinate ethnic status in the local area. These qualifications demanded the exercise of caution on the market and the adoption of an economic definition of shopping. Unattached to the local area and free of

[15] Except for homeownership, all the other indexes used—length of residence in current dwelling place, length of residence in the Northwest Side, age moved into the community, and subjective evaluation of the residential area—were associated at more than the .05 level but less than the .10 level. This clustering of community identification indexes adumbrates the principal point of this article elaborated in the final section. In the Northwest Side, homeownership was structured in such a way that it had to be rejected as a valid index of community identification. Specifically, there were negative associations with education, length of residence, residence of friends, and previous residence; and positive associations with age when the informant moved into the area. Probably that variable reflected the postwar housing shortage more than anything else.

encumbering allegiances, the economic consumer was able to participate in the market in a detached, interested, and alert manner.

The Personalizing Consumer

Without access to either formal or informal channels of social participation, because of her lower social status, her very few or very many children, and the fact that she had spent the early years of her married life outside the local area, this type of consumer established quasi-primary relationships with the personnel of local independent retail institutions. In a sense, her selection of local independent merchants coerced her into a personalizing orientation to shopping. For, given her status equality with store personnel and the fact that she was a newcomer the adoption of a different definition of shopping could have eventuated only in disharmony and friction which would have been difficult to absorb without other available primary relationships to take up the shock. Even so, this coercion was hardly disadvantageous to such a consumer. The quasi-primary relationships she was forced to develop on the market compensated for her larger social losses, for, although she had recently moved into the area leaving most of her old friends behind, she attached positive value to living in the Northwest Side and expressed no desire to leave it.[16]

The Ethical Consumer

Relatively high social status, long residence in the Northwest Side, and an unfavorable response to the "social deterioration" accompanying the rapid business growth of the area were prime requisites for the development of an ethical orientation to the market. The "ethic" is an alignment with the symbols of small business against the big business that menaced the housewives' way of life. Patronage of local independent merchants more concretely realized the alliance. In addition, it maintained social distance between the higher-status customer and the lower-status clerk in a shopping situation where social distance was difficult to maintain but, at the same time, necessary to protect the established status of the customer in the larger community.

The Apathetic Consumer

Characteristically, apathetic consumers sought to minimize effort in shopping, and this characterized the older women. Either downward mobility or a lack of success in attempts at upward mobility[17] constricted the aspira-

[16] The social characteristics of the personalizing consumer resemble those of the "substitute gratification" readers of the urban community press reported in Morris Janowitz, "The Imagery of the Urban Community Press," *op. cit.*, p. 540.

[17] A greater proportion of the husbands of apathetic shoppers had completed their secondary-school education or gone on to college than in any other consumer type. Yet, the husbands of the majority of apathetic consumers belonged to lower social strata. When the social class of the 57 informants whose husbands had either completed high school or attended

tions of apathetic consumers and confined them to local neighborhood life. Long residence in the Northwest Side begun at an early age, and a strong positive local identification promoted strong bonds with others in the community. The market, in any case, was too far beyond the horizon of experience of the typical apathetic consumer to warrant much attention or interest.

The four profiles described above permit some speculation about the temporal allocation of shopping orientations. Apparently, economic and personalizing orientations were more often adopted by housewives who had recently moved into the area, and ethical and apathetic orientations by those who had lived in the area for relatively long periods of time. Aspiration, marginality, and success are perhaps the crucial intervening variables. This suggests the hypotheses: (1) the higher the level of aspiration among newcomers to a residential area, the greater the likelihood that they will adopt economic orientations to shopping; (2) the lower the level of aspiration and the greater the marginality of newcomers, the greater the likelihood that they will adopt personalizing orientations; (3) the greater the success long-time residents of a residential area have enjoyed, the greater the likelihood that they will adopt ethical orientations to shopping; and (4), conversely, the less the success, the greater the likelihood of consumer apathy among long-time residents.

What remains to be discussed and explained is the place of the personalizing role orientation in resolving the disparity between the apparent subjective indications of positive identification with the Northwest Side offered by personalizing consumers and the fact that objective indexes of community identification did not point to the likelihood that they would develop a sense of community belonging. Objectively, personalizing consumers were not integrated with the Northwest Side; subjectively, they were.

URBAN SOLIDARITY AND THE PERSONALIZATION OF MARKET RELATIONSHIPS

Despite the fact that certain objective conditions for community identification were absent among many personalizing consumers,[18] a clear majority of the informants concerned expressed no desire to leave the community

college was examined, the results showed that 23.8 percent of the 21 apathetic consumers were included in the higher educational group and could be placed in the upper-middle or lower-middle social classes, while 33.7 percent had been recruited from the upper-lower social class. In contrast, 38.1 percent of the remaining 98 informants were included in both the higher educational group and the middle social classes, while 11.1 percent had completed their secondary education or attended college and were, at the same time, members of the lower status levels. The significance of these relationships was established by the application of the chi-square test; thus a significant proportion of the husbands of apathetic consumers had been educated "above" their social status.

[18] Many had lived a short period of time in their current residences and in the community at large; a majority said that most of their friends lived outside the Northwest Side, and most had moved into the area at a relatively late age.

and, at the same time, evaluated it favorably. In short, without objective basis, personalizing consumers seemed typically to have identified themselves with the Northwest Side.

A hypothesis was advanced to explain the discrepancy: *Among the 119 housewives subjective identification of some with the area in which they lived was a latent function*[19] *of their personalization of market relations.* These consumers usually implied that strong social bonds tied them to the personnel of the stores they patronized. In the absence of other neighborhood ties, such a bond was apparently strong enough to provide the basis for the consumer's attachment. It follows that, if personalizing consumers, *in contrast to the other types,* identified themselves subjectively with the locality when objective indexes of local community identification did not suggest that likelihood, the hypothesis stated above could not be rejected.

To test the hypothesis, all informants who had indicated subjective identification with the community either by expressing a preference for continued residence there or by evaluating the community in positive terms were singled out for analysis. In addition, four objective indexes of local community identification were controlled: (1) length of residence in the Northwest Side; (2) age of the informant when she moved to the Northwest Side; (3) location of last place of residence; and (4) location of most of her friends. Those members of the selected group of "subjectively identified" informants who had lived in the Northwest Side six years or less, moved into the area at twenty-nine years of age or more and into their present residences from outside the Northwest Side, and said that most of their friends lived outside the community, were interpreted as having formed subjective identifications with the Northwest Side with *no apparent basis.* Informants characterized by three of the above criteria were said to have formed subjective attachments with *little apparent basis.* Those to whom two of the criteria applied were regarded as having become identified with *some apparent basis.* Finally, informants for whom only one criterion applied were interpreted as having formed a sense of community belonging with *apparent basis.* If personalizing consumers in the selected group of subjectively identified informants were found to have established community identifications without or with little apparent basis more often than the other consumer types, the hypohtesis, it is contended, could not be eliminated.[20] Tables 2 and 3 summarize the results of the test.

Collapsing the first and second rows of Table 2 and 3 and comparing

[19] "*Functions* are those observed consequences [of social acts] which make for the adaptation or adjustment of a given system . . . *latent functions* being those which are neither intended or recognized [by the social actor or actors]" (Robert K. Merton, *Social Theory and Social Structure* [Glencoe, Ill.: Free Press, 1949], pp. 50–51).

[20] The data placed severe limitations upon the achievement of any more satisfactory test, largely owing to the fact that the entire range of findings reported here was unanticipated at the inception of the research. For a discussion of the adequacy of the criteria used and the test itself see Stone, *op. cit.*, pp. 124–28.

TABLE 2.

Basis for the Identification of Consumers Preferring to Live in Chicago's Northwest Side

Objective Basis for Community Identification	*Type of Consumers*				
	Economic	*Personalizing*	*Ethical*	*Apathetic*	*Total*
No apparent basis	2	4			6
Little apparent basis	3	6		2	11
Some apparent basis	4	5	6	5	20
Apparent basis	3	2	2	4	11
Total	12	17	8	11	48

TABLE 3.

Basis for the Identification of Consumers Favorably Disposed to Chicago's Northwest Side

Objective Basis for Community Identification	*Type of Consumers*				
	Economic	*Personalizing*	*Ethical*	*Apathetic*	*Total*
No apparent basis	2	3			5
Little apparent basis	3	6		2	11
Some apparent basis	2	5	7	4	18
Apparent basis	3	2	2	4	11
Total	10	16	9	10	45

the personalizing consumers with the other types taken as a whole permitted the application of the chi-square test of significance to the ensuing fourfold distributions. The results allow the conclusion that a *significantly larger proportion of personalizing consumers had established subjective identifications with the Northwest Side without or with little apparent basis than had consumers of the other three types taken together.*[21] Consequently, the hypothesis was retained.

The hypothesis has important implications for urban social psychology. That field has perhaps been concerned too long with the disintegrative effects or the dysfunctions of urbanism. Urban sociologists have documented with an admirable meticulousness the difficulties accompanying urban living and the obstacles in the path of achieving moral consensus in the metropolis. But they have failed to explain the obvious fact that people in goodly numbers

[21] The level of significance and degree of association for the two distributions are ($p < .02$; $T = .36$) and ($p < .05$; $T = .32$) respectively—a relatively high degree of significance and association for such a small number of cases.

do manage to live and survive in urban environments and that, among many of them, there is a patent sense of identification with the metropolis.

Durkheim observed long ago that the family was being replaced by occupational groupings as the seat of moral consensus in the organically solidary society.[22] However, it may be more sagacious not to single out any one nexus of human relations and attribute to it the function of generating consensus in the mass society. Instead, one might observe that life in the metropolis is largely routinized and that relationships bearing many of the qualities that Cooley spoke of as primary in nature may be established in any area of life where communication is frequent and regular. Such relationships can have the function of integrating the person with the larger society in which he lives.

QUESTIONS

1. Demonstrate how each of the four types of shoppers would approach the purchase of a television set.
2. Describe the ethical consumer's profile.
3. Present suggestions on how retail management might use the information found in this article.

[22] Émile Durkheim, *The Division of Labor in Society*, trans. George Simpson (Glencoe, Ill.: Free Press, 1947), Preface to the second edition, pp. 1–31.

PART III

THE INTERNAL ORGANIZATIONAL MIX

A. CONSUMER FEEDBACK

B. GOODS AND SERVICES

C. PHYSICAL DISTRIBUTION

D. COMMUNICATION

A. CONSUMER FEEDBACK

By its very nature, the retail firm receives prompt and continuous feedback in the form of stock fluctuations, which indicate what the consumer is buying. By simply standing around in a store and listening, the retailer is bound to learn something about the consumer. However, with the proliferation of stores and the addition of merchandise lines, the large retail organization is increasingly turning to formal research for feedback information, which can be used to guide management in making decisions.

In the articles by Frank Mayans and Benjamin Engel, the research function as performed in the retail firm is described and several applications are presented. In the last reading, Stuart Rich and Subhash Jain demonstrate a social research technique (Warner's) used to classify shoppers.

15

Research in Retailing

Frank Mayans

We at Federated Department Stores feel that research is part and parcel of management's decision-making process.

First, a word about Federated. Federated Department Stores reached a pre-tax income of 10.3 percent of sales in 1964. We probably did as well or better in fiscal 1965. We do not think it is as good as it might be, and we should be reaching for 12 percent, 15

Reprinted from *Retail Control*, Vol. 34, No. 9, May 1966. © 1966 by Controllers Congress, National Retail Merchants Association.

percent or more pre-tax income on sales. Research, and I am now referring to the Federated home office research department, intends to do what it can to help reach these goals.

NEW MANAGEMENT METHODS NEEDED

Federated has thirteen divisions, each run by very smart management. Years ago a typical store owner-manager was so close to the store, customer and community that he was closely attuned to the intimate needs of the business. He did not need a huge, expensive research study to tell him what the customers thought about the store. If he was any good, he would have been aware of it and taken action before a decent research study could even be designed. He controlled the business with a sure touch.

But life complicates. Department stores now have branches, selling in many subcommunities. Management must now engage in many ancillary community activities. The size of the business has grown. The old way of doing things is no longer possible.

One thing certainly has not changed, and that is the axiom that our operating franchise in any community depends completely upon how people feel about our store, its merchandise and services, and how the store fits in with their own needs and aspirations.

FUNCTION OF RESEARCH

Today management needs answers which must come through formal research, since they can no longer go out and find the answers themselves. Perhaps even more important, management has less time than ever to ask the stimulating questions. The Federated research department is designed to help provide answers, and to raise basic questions.

Mr. Herbert Landsman, Executive Vice President of Federated, recently spoke before the NRMA on the obligation of research to come up with provocative questions. His major point was that research had an unparalleled opportunity to expose these important questions to management, questions that might lead to the great innovations we need in retailing.

At Federated we have an economic research department, an area research department, marketing research, and electronics research. All of these groups are actively engaged in helping our stores plan and operate.

FUNCTION OF RESEARCH DEPARTMENTS

All retailers operate in an economic climate. When the economy in a particular market is strong and vigorous, the opportunity opens up for added business. If things look as if they are going to slow down in six months or so, the pie shrinks and we need to be extra careful in the day-to-day operations. Our economist and his staff spend full time on trying to predict this future, by market, both short- and long-range. We buy the best talent we can afford to help us construct this economic picture of the future.

They do a highly sophisticated job. They have developed extremely reliable sales forecasting techniques that have been instrumental in Federated's profit performance. We think it is no coincidence that some of our most impressive results have come in periods of relatively lean sales growth. Accurate forecasting has helped our merchants to plan close to the vest, to hold down on inventory investment, to control costs in periods when the general economy was sluggish.

LONG-RANGE PLAN SHOULD INCLUDE CONSUMER MARKET STUDY

When it comes to long-range planning, stores have found it advantageous to use both economic research and marketing research in setting their objectives. Our stores develop ten-year plans, and a consumer market study can be a critical part of these. An example is a recent study conducted for one of our Eastern divisions. Some of the major questions were:

1. What is the present customer mix (income, age, occupation)? What should this mix be in ten years?
2. If the division wants to increase its share of market among important market segments (women working downtown, higher price line customers, blue collar customers, etc.), what does it need to do?

The division was found to have its strongest appeal with the upper-middle income families, an income group expected to grow tremendously in the next decade. We were able to compute how much added business the store would have simply on the basis of the customer mix of the future as people's income rose. We were able to show that the market was moving into the store's major strengths.

BLUE COLLAR FAMILIES DISSATISFIED

There was a problem largely unrelated to income, and this had to do with blue collar families. They will continue to be an important part of the market, and as their incomes rise, certainly will be a group with high potential sales. Traditional department stores have not been as successful with this group as they have with white collar groups.

What did these blue collar customers think of the store? They felt the store was the fashion leader, selling the very highest quality merchandise. The problem basically was that the blue collar group was less pleased with the salespeople, the credit or other services. We need to do a better job in this division developing this segment of the market.

STORE PRICE STRUCTURE AND BUYING HABITS OF CUSTOMERS

This market study I am referring to also reviewed the store's price structure and related it to the buying habits of its customers. In some of the branches, there seemed to be an opportunity for better-priced business that was going to the specialty stores. There also were a significant number of customers who shopped the store but were buying budget men's furnishings and intimate apparel in other department stores.

A cynic might say that if the store had any feel for the market they would have known such things. This, I believe, would be missing the point. Any merchant knows which departments are doing well in sales without looking at the figures. They can sense the activity, they hear comments from the buyer and the customer, and they see the merchandise move through the department.

This does not mean that we do not need sales figures. If we are to make judgements on sound objective information, these things must be measured as precisely as possible. Formal consumer studies can help do some of this measuring.

HANDLING THE UNIQUE MARKET

Sometimes it is necessary to plan a store's objectives in a unique market. One such market is Miami Beach which is as odd as they come. Our market studies, which included summer and winter interviews, laid out the dimensions of an ever shifting population which provides the background against which the store must do its planning. The study helped this division plan its efforts in this very complex market.

HANDLING DAY-TO-DAY STORE BUSINESS

Our research department is also active in helping the stores, when they need such help, in running their day-to-day business. Our stores operate with seasonal plans, and an integral part of our operation is a planning meeting at which the previous six months' results are evaluated statistically. From this analysis arise challenges for the next season.

While the basic part of the evaluation covers such things as return-on-investment, profit and loss analysis, evaluation of gross margin factors, sales by department, and so on, we will cover during these planning meetings subjects that have been of interest to stores. These will range from such things as "Is Santa Claus Important to Downtown" (we think he is), to a review of restaurant operations.

ANALYSIS OF FOOD OPERATIONS

We are now undertaking a detailed analysis of food operations. The major problem revolves around our restaurant facilities, particularly in branch stores. This study will become part of our seasonal planning meeting with each store.

Besides research related to long-range planning and seasonal planning, we engage in a substantial number of special projects that are done at either divisional or Federated management request. Some have to do with new businesses our stores might want to go into, or an evaluation of an advertising slogan. One store asked us to find out about their restaurant—why was it not successful? I wish I could report to you that we uncovered deep psychological reasons for this snubbing of our little restaurant in our very successful branch. The problem was that a large portion of customers did not even know it existed.

STUDY OF CUSTOMER RESPONSE TO DISCOUNT OFFERS

Discounters set off a flurry of activity for us. Many of our stores needed to know how customers responded to discounter offerings versus what we were selling. One such study was done for a division which had a leading discount store right across the street from its downtown store. There was no question that the discount store had the low price image. Most everything else went our way: quality, fashion, service, and so on.

We asked customers how much they expected to pay for a series of items in specific department stores and specific discount stores. We then related this expected price to their reported buying behavior on similar items.

It turned out that a good majority of our department store customers will still buy at the department store if they feel the price differential is not too great. As the price differential widens, more and more swing to the discount stores. I am sure most merchants recognize that a department store with a sound customer franchise is offering more to the customers than simply a T.V. set or a Broadway show album. They are providing service, credit, fine treatment in the handling of the transaction, and guaranteed satisfaction, that a customer is willing to pay for.

A customer was willing to pay a proportional amount more when buying a brand item in our department stores, depending on the price range involved.

PHONOGRAPH RECORDS THE EXCEPTION

One category of merchandise was an exception. The discount store did an outstanding job in attracting customers in phonograph records. The answer in this case was not price. The discount store department was extremely well laid out, with a tremendously wide selection and excellent service. In short, they had a good department, and this counted more than price.

CUSTOMER REACTION TO STORE BILLING METHODS

One of our divisions went from country club to descriptive billing, and one must in all honesty say that there was less than universal customer endorsement.

Questions by the store management:

1. What was the extent of the customer dissatisfaction?
2. Why were those who did not like it dissatisfied?
3. Was there a risk of reduced sales?

A major consumer study was undertaken and you might be interested in our answers:

1. The customers believed the store's billing to be basically error free. Better acceptance could reasonably be anticipated with time.
2. Descriptions of certain departments were confusing and certain modifications were made.
3. Regular charge customers who spent a great deal of money at the store showed the greatest dissatisfaction. A special effort was made to service these customers when they called with complaints.
4. Some customers did not realize that sales checks were microfilmed and could easily be recovered if needed. The continued existence and recoverability of sales checks was vigorously publicized.

AREA RESEARCH—OR SITE LOCATION

Besides the economic research which provides the climate in which our stores operate, and the marketing and statistical studies that help the stores plan and operate their business, we have a large professional group concentrating on site locations.

Area research on site location has become a highly specialized phase of the retail research efforts. Our objective is to locate and build branch stores for immediate profit and long-range growth potential. Obviously, this is one of the big decisions in our business involving large capital investment and a long-term commitment to operate at the elected site.

CHOOSING A SITE LOCATION IN SUBURBIA

Most of this work at Federated and other retailing organizations has dealt with the burgeoning suburbs of the great American metropolitan complexes. The growth of the suburban market was so obvious that almost all retailers joined the rush to suburbia.

But simply to be in the suburbs is not enough. We consider in great detail all the population and economic factors and trends which might apply, the highway systems and public transportation, the vitality of the downtown parent store, and many other elements.

FUTURE EXPANSION MUST BE CONSIDERED

Our experience has been that strategic errors are possible unless the total market configuration is carefully thought out in advance.

If a division tries to put a branch store in the best spot available, without consideration of where it will put other branches that it will need in the future, it may find that that one branch has eliminated two or three branch sites which would have produced a better net result by giving up the one best site.

SHAPE OF CITY IS IMPORTANT

Many factors enter into final decisions about a site. It is interesting that this detailed analysis often begins with a simple study of the configuration of the city complex. Cities generally have clearly defined shapes; a diamond, a square, an elongated rectangle. The shape of a city often is dictated by natural barriers; rivers, oceans, lakes, hills, ravines—or by the lack of such barriers. These geographical factors, combined with transportation facilities, affect the way a city grows, and the way a customer-oriented business such as retailing can profitably expand.

One of our major cities, Cincinnati, is diamond-shaped with the central business district near a major river and at the southern point of the diamond. Hills rise steeply from the river, and a highly industrialized valley splits the city into two triangular halves. This, combined with the extremely slow development of modern expressways, has led to the development of clearly defined regional shopping areas. The key to continuing growth in this instance was the location of major branches at the western, northern and eastern points of the diamond.

OTHER FACTORS

Strategic examinations of trading areas are in every case followed by detailed analyses of other factors; existing and potential competition, the probable drain on business at the downtown parent store, and the extent of newspaper coverage to name but a few. Not many managements today would risk a decision as to branch store location without the detailed, hard facts that a professional research operation can provide.

Talking to the professionals in this area is fascinating. You quickly learn there is more to this art than meets the eye. Such things as micro-climate (fog will hang over a small area, and it will generally be clear a short distance away), garbage dumps (the odor ruins the garments), shifting land (the cost of building zooms), and visibility (a great site, but it cannot be seen from the access roads) are sure ways to disaster.

PSYCHOLOGICAL CONSIDERATIONS

We may find that a majority of shoppers travel ten to fifteen minutes to shop a particular regional center. However, if a modern expressway were available, the same people might very well be willing to travel not only longer distances, but for a longer period of time.

Conversely, we have found that psychological barriers sometimes exist in geographic areas where natural barriers have been eliminated. Take the case of three contiguous southern cities. If you were to drive around, your impression would be that they form a single trading area. Nevertheless, a large majority of the residents in each city perceive the other two cities as separate places.

One of the cities, which is connected to the other two by a modern causeway over a body of water, is rarely or never visited by the residents of the other two cities for any purpose whatsoever. And while there is greater contact between the two cities directly contiguous, there is only a minimum of movement between the two. Obviously, it will take more than one store to service this area.

RESEARCH AND EDP

Federated is very heavily involved in EDP as we seek to find a proper place for it in our operations. There is hardly an area of our business where we are not seeking applications, if appropriate, for this exciting development.

Our present concentration is in stock maintenance systems. We feel this has tremendous pay-off and is worth the massive effort we are putting behind it.

We are beginning to use the computer more and more for a sophisticated mathematical analysis. Many illustrations of projects I gave previously, from consumer research to site location projects, have made use of the capabilities of electronics. We conceive of its use not of a different kind, but an integral part of our data processing and information systems.

CONCLUSION

I think it safe to say that research has made some big and valuable contributions to the art or science of retailing goods and services. With a growing body of knowledge, better tools, and a keener awareness of its potentials, research should make even greater contributions to retailing.

We should do some things much better than we do now. We need to do a better public relations job, within retailing and within our own organizations, concerning our functions, our objectives, our methods and how we can be of help.

We should also be more creative in our approach. We should ask and answer more of the fundamental questions about where our business should be going and how we can get it there quickly, efficiently and profitably. These things are our common concerns, and I believe retail research is now of sufficient maturity to join in the quest.

QUESTIONS

1. Why is research so much more important today in retailing than twenty years ago?
2. Discuss five projects a research department may engage in on behalf of the management of a department store.
3. If the sales of a handbag department have continued to increase at a rate of 7 per cent a year over the past ten years, is it true that research is unnecessary?

16

Research Is Vital—But Application Is the Payoff

Benjamin Engel

Vast amounts of information are being accumulated on markets, on customers, and on channels of distribution. The information grows increasingly detailed and progressively more refined.

The professional analyst, of course, is perpetually dissatisfied with the amount and quality of the data made available to him, or which he obtains by primary research. And this is as it should be. The dissatisfaction is inherent in the professional attitude itself.

Yet it is questionable that business now benefits to the extent that it might from full utilization of the existing stock of information and of methodological know-how for the development of volume and the improvement of profit.

Reprinted from *Marketing Precision and Executive Action*, Proceedings of the Forty-Fifth National Conference of the American Marketing Association, June 20, 21, 22, 1962. Edited by Charles H. Hindersman, published by the American Management Association, pp. 580–603.

From a management point of view, the payoff on research is in its contribution to insight, judgment and decision.

What can be done to realize a greater return on the investment which has been made and continues to be made in research? I shall address myself to this question by sketching some examples of research which has contributed to business judgments or decisions. The studies from which these examples are drawn varied considerably in complexity and scope. I cite them for one of two reasons, or both: their substantive bearing upon problems of distribution, or their methodological interest.

CASE #1

Somehow, "research" conjures up an image of complexity, long duration, and great expense. Yet the insights we seek sometimes are almost absurdly easy to achieve—not always, certainly, but often.

In January, 1957, or more than five years ago, an analyst of Federal Reserve figures on departmental sales of department stores pointed to the soft-goods opportunities of which so-called discount houses were to make such good use—although he then saw the competitive threat coming from another direction.

The analyst noticed how much more quickly sales in certain Basement departments were growing than in their Main Store counterparts, or other Basement departments (see Table 1). The stores reporting the figures he cited did not include Sears, Ward, or Penney units.

TABLE 1.

Department Store Sales, Selected Departments Percent Change from 1947-49 Average to 1956*

	Basement	*Main Store*
Women's & Misses' Sportswear	33%	39%
Girls' Wear	33	38
Boys' Wear	35	18
Infants' Wear	27	19
Men's Clothing	27	8
Men's Furnishings	22	13
All departments, including others	7	11

*The 1956 data were partially estimated at the time this table was prepared.
Source: Federal Reserve System for basic data.

> In the Basement, as in the Main Store (he said at a private meeting of a department store group), Sportswear and Girls' Wear have done exceptionally well. Infants' Wear has done better in the Basement than Upstairs and . . . so has Basement Boys' Wear.

> This difference between Upstairs and Basement performance of some Children's . . . departments is a point well worth noting. It's perfectly true that consumers have been trading up. Wanting as many goods as they do, something has to give. They seem to be less willing, judging by these figures, to spend on certain types of Children's Wear than on other types of goods.

Are we quite certain that some of our stores without Basements, in their enthusiasm to trade up, are not handing over some of our potential volume to the Sears and the Penneys?

He drew the conclusion that different parts of the store might have to go in different directions to satisfy the customer.

> By all means let's trade up to the customer's level, but let's not forego available volume in lower price-lines if that's where the customer wants to trade in a particular department.

Department stores were wide open to low-end competition in soft goods at the time this analysis was made. The significant point here is that their own figures were signaling the danger. They had only to heed them.

There is good reason to conjecture that if suburban branch stores which rarely had Basement departments had been designed to include them, the growth of discount houses might have been much more limited than it actually has been.

CASE #2

"Give the lady what she wants" is a long established retailing maxim. It is not always easy to tell what the lady wants, however, and some of us experience greater difficulty than others in finding ways to motivate her.

A merchant we know once was in charge of the grocery and bakeshop operations of an eastern department store. Part of the responsibility he delegated to his assistant was the preparation of copy for signs pointing up promotional displays.

Dissatisfied with his assistant's rather unimaginative efforts, the department manager urged him to find something to say which would appeal to the customer. The sign which appeared over the Danish pastry next morning said, "Good for breakfast," and named the price.

This was not quite what he had in mind, the long suffering but still patient department manager told his assistant. If he could think of nothing himself, he might examine the copy appearing on packages or containers for selling points that would appeal to the customer.

Not long afterward, the department manager made an excellent buy. Imported canned hams of fine quality were offered to the store's customers at an extraordinarily low price. When he checked the sign, the department manager discovered that his assistant had taken to heart the advice he had received. In letters bold and clear, the sign said, "Perishable. Must be refrigerated."

The story happens to be true. One shudders to think what the assistant might have written if he had read about Vance Packard's "hidden persuaders"—or worse yet, the Oedipus complex.

CASE #3

The department store analyst we quoted earlier drew his conclusions from publicly available statistics. A company's own figures and published data always are the first sources to check. Frequently, however, neither can answer an important marketing question. An interview type of consumer or dealer survey then may be in order.

Parenthetically, it may be of interest to consumer goods manufacturing companies represented here to note that dealer surveys usually cost less than consumer surveys, and, in our experience, in the fields of investigation open to both, never have failed to indicate exactly the same marketing conclusions as consumer surveys. In the case we are about to cite, a consumer survey was needed.

A manufacturer wanted to determine how best to exploit the youth market for his product. For purposes of making the problem concrete, let us suppose that the company in question was a major producer of small transistor radios, although this was not the actual product.

It was thought that a major portion of the young people who acquired small transistor radios received them as gifts. Among other promotions, therefore, each year's advertising program included a substantial effort to push them as high school graduation gifts.

TABLE 2.

Ownership of Small Transistor Radios* and Others Portables by High School Students in an Eastern Seaboard State

Age at Last Birthday	*Percent of Total Interviewed* Own Small Transistor Radio†	Own Other Portable Radio‡	Do Not Own Portable Radio	Total	Number Interviewed
Under 15	7.1	14.3	78.6	100.0	84
15	17.1	30.5	52.4	100.0	164
16	28.0	51.5	20.5	100.0	200
17	35.4	57.0	7.6	100.0	237
18 and over	26.8	67.6	5.6	100.0	71
Total	25.5	46.1	28.4	100.0	756

*Product which was subject of actual survey was not small transistor radio.
†Including owners and non-owners of other portable radios.
‡Excluding owners of small transistor radios.
Source: Survey by author.

A survey of high schoold students in an eastern seaboard state was designed to include information on ownership and methods of acquiring the instruments. Of the students questioned who owned small transistors, 95 percent had, in fact, received them as gifts. As Table 2 shows, however, almost all of the students interviewed already had acquired a portable radio of some kind by the time they graduated. Late spring and early summer might be a good time to promote the instruments, but the years preceding graduation were the most important by far.

CASE #4

Business analysis has been greatly influenced in the postwar years by a number of academic disciplines. The development of high-speed computers has made the application of complicated mathematical models to the solution of business problems a practical enterprise, at least for large companies. For better or for worse, depth psychologies and their complex and problematic techniques have been adapted to market research needs. Yet some of the simplest analytical approaches continue to yield the volume and profit results they always have yielded when properly applied.

A large credit jewelry store in a southern city had engaged in heavy direct-mail promotion for many years, particularly during the Christmas season. For reasons of cost, the number of mailers each Christmas was fixed. The mailing lists used were supplied by a company engaged in that business. The objective was to allocate the mail pieces among the many areas of the city and its suburbs so as to maximize sales and the number of accounts.

In the past, circulars had been distributed to occupants of all dwelling units in those parts of the store's trading area where it had the greatest numbers of accounts. When the accounts were classified by mailing area, however, and compared with numbers of dwelling units, it was found that the proportion of customers to residents was exceptionally small in some of the very areas in which the store had the greatest absolute number of accounts.

The mailing areas were arrayed in order of the ratio of store accounts to dwelling units. The areas of the store's greatest relative strength received all of the mailed pieces. Irrespective of the absolute number, the areas of least relative strength received none, except, of course, for actual accounts.

This simple and essentially mechanical procedure was modified by only one judgment factor. Management of this credit jewelry operation was convinced that high-income families were poor sales prospects. The one or two high-income areas which showed great relative strength were eliminated from the mailing list. Whatever the reasons may have been for their good showing, it was judged to be a statistical "fluke."

A more refined approach obviously was possible, but time was pressing. Admittedly, too, this technique contributed nothing to the development of business in the areas of weakness. But it did produce a sharp increase in sales and the number of new accounts opened, and these were the immediate objectives.

CASE #5

The professional analyst naturally prefers to dwell upon the successes he or his colleagues have achieved. Sometimes, however, research is misdirected. At best, the results then are trivial.

An attempt once was made to determine the reasons for success or failure of a major recording company's pop records. A woman who had had considerable musical training secluded herself for weeks with a stack of records, a phonograph, and a huge work sheet with almost all conceivable characteristics and circumstances of record issuance as column headings, and a listing of the names of records (and their sales) on the many many lines.

After prolonged study of the correlations disclosed by this work sheet, the disheartened musician and her research associates were forced to the conclusion that the most significant factors of success were (a) the performers, and (b) the response of consumers to the specific configurations of melodies, lyrics, and arrangements. The mountain had labored . . .

A learned appendix on Gestalt psychology might have provided elegant cover for the retreat. The researchers had the good taste to forego this opportunity, and "payola" had not yet entered the language.

CASE #6

The most elementary media research can help greatly in directing advertising to the desired audience at minimal cost. While the case about to be cited is drawn from the field of industrial marketing, analogous problems of media selection by manufacturers, distributors, and retailers of consumer goods readily suggest themselves.

A machine-tool manufacturing company and its advertising agency wanted to determine the best trade magazines in which to advertise a general purpose tool. The available data included the distribution of the manufacturer's sales and of the several trade books' circulation, by industry—the Standard Industrial Classification in general use. In addition, circulation breakdowns were available by types of readership and by size of plant.

This instance of media research is of particular interest because of the manner in which judgments were employed where there were gaps in the data. The company knew whom it wanted to reach. The purpose of the research was to determine how best to reach these people.

A formula first was devised to favor the publications whose circulation, by industry, matched the manufacturer's sales most closely. The best prospects were likely to be companies like those to which the manufacturer had sold in the past.

Because the product was a general-purpose tool, smaller plants were deemed better prospects than larger ones which generally employ a greater proportion of special-purpose tools. This judgment was based upon experience, and was embodied in specific numerical weights attached to copies circulated in plants of various sizes. In effect, a discount was taken on large-plant circulation.

Similarly, in accordance with the interpreted experience of the actual process by which the manufacturer's customers reached their buying decisions, only four types of executive functions were considered in "qualifying" the circulation. Copies going to production management were given full weight. Progressively greater discounts were taken on copies going to corporate management, engineering departments, and purchasing agents. School, library, and all other circulation was discounted completely. The readers the company wanted primarily were the works managers and the shop foremen—not the occupants of executive suites. Finally, the formula for rating the several magazines took account of the cost per black-and-white page.

The result was that some of the trade books of greatest prestige in the metal fabricating industries received the lowest ratings, and were dropped from the company's advertising program. The less prestigious books got the business because they had the readers the machine-tool manufacturer wanted. The conclusions drawn from the analysis were not airtight, but full use had been made of all available data, both statistical and experiential, to arrive at the decision.

CASE #7

Whether you know New York City or not, it would require no elaborate investigation to determine that it was inadvisable for a single hot dog stand in Coney Island to advertise in *The New York Times*. But what of the manufacturing company which ran a doubletruck ad in a national magazine when it barely had achieved an organization which was adequate for regional distribution?

While we are on the subject of media, we may as well take note of an advertising syndrome long familiar to marketing clinicians. Its most flagrant symptom is an overwhelming concentration of space or linage in publications of greatest circulation. Unfortunately, while it rarely is fatal to the carriers, this pathological condition sometimes contributes to the terminal illness of secondary media.

There are fewer and fewer daily newspapers, and many of those which continue publication are in financial difficulties. The irony is that the secondary newspapers' rates frequently overdiscount for their lesser circulation.

A study was made of all ads for specific items run by a midwestern department store during a six-month period. Space costs were compared with sales of the advertised items in the three days following the appearance of each ad. In most instances, the ratios of sales to space costs were *greater* for ads run in the paper of *lesser* circulation than in the paper of greater circulation. The ads in the secondary paper continued to show greater sales productivity when the results in the various departmental groupings were compared.

Additional findings of this study are of general interest. Within each broad grouping of departments, comparisons were made of the sales productivity of store-paid ads and those ads paid for, in whole or in part, by manufacturers. Sales of merchandise promoted in co-op ads were significantly *less*, in proportion to *gross* space costs, than sales of merchandise for whose advertising the store alone had paid. On a *net* basis, however, the productivity of the co-op ads was greater. Manufacturers' ad allowances made the difference.

CASE #8

There are other occasions when research turns up data which are both unexpected and of paramount importance. The largest men's clothing store in a Great Lakes city had just been completely remodeled. To its consternation, management noted that what it termed "the common man," particularly the young man of moderate means, was, if anything, a less frequent customer than before. Had the new elegance of the decor frightened him into buying from stores of the plain-pipe-rack variety? Should the store drop a notch or two in its price-line emphasis and in its volume promotions?

A consumer survey established that the store was, in fact, losing some of the business of younger men. They thought no less well of the store than before. There had been no shift to other stores because they concentrated on cheaper merchandise. The problem arose, however, at a time when suburban shopping centers were just beginning to develop in the area. There were no truly regional centers, so management of the men's clothing store simply had underestimated the rate at which business was being diverted from downtown. The heads of young families, of course, were the customers being diverted most often.

Conclusion: suburban branch expansion—and not an attempt to change the store's character—was what was needed. The store had been saved from a costly error. Had it moved into lower price-lines, it would have damaged, perhaps irremediably, its standing with the middle and high-income customers who made it the dominant men's store in the city. Almost assuredly, its gains in cheaper merchandise would not have been adequate compensation. And it might have lost sight completely of the major reason for attrition of its volume, i.e., diversion to the suburbs.

CASE #9

A set of figures derived from a survey does not automatically produce a successful strategy. Interpretation of the data and the actions predicated upon them require sound judgment.

In a phone survey of the residents of a suburb of a major metropolitan area, the housewives interviewed were asked where they last had bought a number of types of merchandise (see Table 3). Their responses made it plain that a shopping center, including a department store, located in the same suburb was a satisfactory source of children's wear, nylon hosiery, men's sport shirts, and similar items of a "convenience" nature. A major purchase, however, such as furniture or a coat, was one for which they were much more inclined to shop in the downtown areas of two nearby cities.

Theoretically, these shopping habits might reflect poor merchandising in the shopping center, but there was no sign of exceptional deficiency. A more plausible explanation was that the assortments of the downtown

TABLE 3.

Shopping Area in Which Residents of One Suburb Last Bought Selected Items of Merchandise

	Percent Naming Shopping Area					
		Large nearby cities				
	Shopping center in same suburb	*Major city*	*Secondary city*	*All other*	*Total*	*Don't know, no answer**
Item of children's wear	80.3	9.4	1.7	8.6	100.0	25.3
Nylon hosiery	78.9	8.6	2.5	10.0	100.0	48.7
Man's sport shirt	75.8	11.4	0.0	12.8	100.0	50.0
Draperies or curtains	71.9	15.2	1.8	11.1	100.0	66.5
Woman's dress shoes	68.4	14.2	6.6	10.8	100.0	24.1
Street dress	53.5	21.2	11.0	14.3	100.0	25.3
Article of furniture	45.7	27.8	15.3	11.2	100.0	54.3
Woman's coat, full—length, untrimmed	19.7	37.6	11.1	31.6	100.0	26.0

*Respondents not naming shopping area as percent of total interviewed. Total interviewed was 158.
Source: Survey by author.

shopping area—far superior to those which were possible in a shopping center of this size—would draw the residents of this suburb whenever they were shopping for items of high unit value, or whose styling was a paramount consideration. If this were so, it probably would be fruitless for the stores in the center to attempt to sell the so-called better goods in large quantity.

A breakdown of most recent purchases, by shopping area by price-range, and including residents of all suburbs in the trading area, strengthened this view. For example, as Table 4 shows, 16½ percent of all coats purchased whose prices were reported cost more than $90. But over 24 percent of the coats bought in the largest nearby city were in this highest price-range.

Similarly (the table does not appear here), 17 percent of all the most recent purchases of women's dress shoes, that is, excluding play shoes and casuals, were in price-lines over $14.00. But 31½ percent of the shoes bought in the major nearby city were in this highest price-range. If it was unlikely that the shopping center could develop a big business in the highest price-lines of coats, it appeared equally unlikely that it could do so in shoes.

As Table 5 shows, the two were related. Women who bought the expensive coats also bought the better shoes. Moreover, a series of similar cross-tabulations showed similar price-range relationships, even between wholly unrelated classifications of goods, for example, between women's street dresses and men's sport shirts.

TABLE 4.

Shopping Area and Price Paid for Most Recently Purchased Woman's Full-Length Untrimmed Cloth Coat by Residents of Trading Area of a Suburban Shopping Center

	Percent reporting specified price						
	$35.00 or less	*$35.01 to $50.00*	*$50.01 to $70.00*	*$70.01 to $90.00*	*Over $90.00*	*Total*	*Number reporting price*
Suburban shopping center							
Department store	34.5	44.8	6.9	6.9	6.9	100.0	29
All other stores	63.2	21.0	10.5	0.0	5.3	100.0	19
Large nearby cities							
Major city	12.6	28.6	20.2	14.3	24.3	100.0	119
Secondary city	12.7	33.8	19.7	16.9	16.9	100.0	71
All other*	32.7	24.0	17.3	13.5	12.5	100.0	104
Total	23.4	29.3	17.5	13.2	16.6	100.0	342

*Including "don't know" and "no answer."
Source: Survey by author.

These price-line relationships, of course, were related to fundamental factors of income and social status. Their merchandising significance was that one could not simply trade up in a single classification or department, but probably would have to do so in a broad array of goods to make the effort effective.

Furthermore, as Table 6 demonstrates, more of the store's customers wanted increased offerings in moderate and low-priced goods than in the

TABLE 5.

Prices Paid for Most Recently Purchased Women's Shoes and Women's Coats by Residents of Trading Area of a Suburban Shopping Center

Price of Shoes†	*Price of coat.**						
	$35.00 or Less	*$35.01 to $50.00*	*$50.01 to $70.00*	*$70.01 to $90.00*	*Over $90.00*	*Total*	*Number reporting both prices*
$6.00 or less	44.9	27.6	17.2	6.9	3.4	100.0	58
$6.01 to $9.00	32.3	32.3	14.5	11.3	9.6	100.0	62
$9.01 to $11.00	16.1	33.9	25.0	14.3	10.7	100.0	56
$11.01 to $14.00	13.0	35.1	16.7	14.8	20.4	100.0	54
Over $14.00	6.4	10.6	21.3	21.3	30.4	100.0	47
Total	23.5	28.5	18.8	13.4	15.8	100.0	277

*Woman's full-length untrimmed cloth coat.
†Woman's dress shoes, not play or casual.
Source: Survey by author.

TABLE 6.

Opinions of a Department Store's Assortments at Various Price Levels

	Percent of total interviewed		
	Lower-priced goods	*Moderate-priced goods*	*More Expensive or "better" goods*
Too small	18.0	15.3	8.7
About right	69.3	79.3	75.3
Too large	1.7	1.8	12.5
Cannot generalize, varies by department	6.0	1.1	1.3
Don't know, no answer	5.0	2.5	2.2
Total*	100.0	100.0	100.0

*Total interviewed was 818.
Source: Survey by author

higher price-lines. Their dissatisfaction with the store's pricing was made even plainer, as Table 7 shows, by comparing their rating of the store in this respect with their rating of the quality and variety of its merchandise, or the services it offered.

TABLE 7.

Consumer Ratings of Department Store in Shopping Center Compared with "Average" of Other Department Stores and Larger Specialty Stores in Which They Shop

In Order of Increasing Disapproval

	Percent of respondents				
	Poorer	*About the same*	*Better*	*Total*	*Don't know, no answer**
Quality of merchandise	2.8	65.0	32.2	100.0	1.2
Liberality of credit and collection policy	3.6	84.5	11.9	100.0	12.7
Speed with which new fashions are offered	5.7	73.0	21.3	100.0	15.6
Variety of assortment	9.8	54.7	35.5	100.0	0.5
Delivery speed and adherence to promises	10.1	73.4	16.5	100.0	52.7
Ease of returns and adjustments	11.2	74.3	14.5	100.0	43.3
Salespeople's service	14.0	66.6	19.4	100.0	2.3
Prices of merchandise of equal quality†	42.5	56.1	1.4	100.0	1.6

*Maximum possible number of respondents is 818, the total sample. Percentage distribution of respondents excludes "don't know" and "no answer." Proportion of latter group to total sample shown in last column.

†Question asked was: "For equal quality of merchandise, do you think ______'s prices generally are about the same, higher, or lower than in other department and larger specialty stores in which you shop?" Replies of "higher" are classified as "poorer"; replies of "lower" are classified as "better."

Source: Survey of author.

CASE #10

Practical considerations of space and inventory investment, plus a realization of where the bulk of the volume originated clinched the argument against trading up. The report summarized a portion of the survey data in these terms:

> (The store's) principal strength lies with those who buy merchandise in medium and medium-high price-lines. It is weaker with medium-low and low-end customers, and weakest with the buyers of . . . better merchandise. The store's principal competitors for low-end business are in

its immediate shopping area. The competition of (the largest nearby city) and (secondary city) stores is most effective in higher price-lines.

There appears to have been a falling-off of traffic at both (this store) and other stores in the . . . Shopping Center. There is some evidence that unfavorable economic developments have contributed to these declines, but there is explicit criticism of some aspects of (this store's) merchandising and price policies. Transportation difficulties also may be playing an important role. . . .

(The store's) charge account customers think well of the quality of the merchandise it offers. They are less well satisfied with salespeople's service. They are most critical of the store's prices. These evaluations are made in terms of comparisons with other stores in which they shop.

In spite of criticism of (the store's) prices and of (its) price-line emphasis, comparative data on departmental average sales checks indicate that customers are mistaken in their impression. These comparisons, however, have been made only in terms of other stores' Main Floor or Upstairs departments.

The store may very well be missing the volume other stores get in their Basements. It is suggested that management first check the accuracy of many customers' unfortunate impressions of the store's pricing . . . particularly in key departments of heavy traffic and repeat business. It is suggested, further, that it carefully examine its present emphasis upon special value promotions, clearance sales, and similar devices which serve to establish a reputation for good values before attempting to set up Basement-type sections or full-scale operations. But no approach to the problem, it must be stressed, can be permitted to alienate present customers by "cheapening" the store.

While the results of our surveys are of principal value in connection with matters of broad store policy, indications of specific departmental strengths and weaknesses merit management attention. The importance of Dresses, Sportswear, and Children's . . . departments cannot be over-emphasized.

A portion of this highly detailed study has been summarized because of four of its characteristics: (a) it addressed itself to vital merchandising questions; (b) the techniques employed demonstrably were both strong and subtle enough to elicit the required data; (c) mere statistics were not enough, the data had to be interpreted with care to arrive at the necessary judgments; and (d) firm recommendations could be made and were made on the basis of clearly established facts.

CASE #11

The survey described was based upon two wholly separate, but related samples. One was drawn from telephone listings of the trading area, the other from the charge accounts of the department store in the shopping center. Comparison of percentage distributions of the two samples by area yielded a minor byproduct, a rough relative measure of the store's market penetration in each area.

Analysis of the sample of charge accounts itself brought some useful information to light. It was learned that, on the average, revolving charge accounts produced substantially more business per account than regular charge accounts. Breaking down all accounts by the ages of eldest children, it was found that purchases per account climbed steadily as the family matured, reaching a peak when the eldest child was of junior-high age, then dropping rapidly. Increased mobility of women with older children was presumed to be one of the operative factors.

As was to be expected, residents of the closest suburb were the store's best customers. Accounts of residents of more distant areas were more likely to be delinquent than were those living close to the shopping center. Accounts of families who had moved into their present homes within the past two years were most likely to be delinquent.

The point here is not so much the intrinsic interest of the findings themselves as it is that every business can develop information of considerable value by sampling of its own records. If the raw data themselves are overabundant, any other course frequently is impossible. For purposes of insight and policy, an analysis need not necessarily meet the stringent standards of accuracy and completeness required, say, for a P & L. How many firms could reduce their paper work by either periodic or spotcheck samplings for vital information? How many more companies would learn quickly and act promptly on both the problems and the opportunities disclosed?

CASE #12

Careful consideration of tomorrow's customers in tomorrow's stores is a necessity. Products, markets, and channels of distribution undergo constant change, and the rate of change itself quickens with almost every passing year. It nevertheless is a safe guess that nine-tenths of the companies represented at this conference will make nine-tenths of their profits in the next five years, or the next decade, not by their more radical innovations, but by doing well, or doing better the very things they best know how to do.

While we gaze starry-eyed into the future, billions of dollars of business each year walk right out of some stores and into others—not because customers prefer the others, but because the stores they first enter do not satisfy their needs. The figures in Table 8 may not be typical of America's department stores, but they are enough to give pause to anybody concerned with the efficacy and the costs of distribution, particularly at the point of sale to the consumer.

Shoppers were interviewed for one complete week at each of the seven department stores whose survey results are summarized in the table. Over 40 percent of the 9,100 people interviewed as they left these stores had not spent a nickel. The seven-store range of failure was 28 percent to 51 percent.

Abstruse questions of "image" are not the issue here, just plain-as-apple-pie old-fashioned merchandising and selling.

Some of these people, one might think, were not shopping seriously, so the situation in these stores may not be as bad as it seems. But the figures tell us otherwise. Seven out of ten shoppers said they had one or more specific purchases in mind when coming to the stores. In the course of these "exit surveys," the interviewers ascertained exactly what the shoppers had come to buy, whether they had in fact bought it, and, if not, why not. It would carry us too far afield to examine why they had not. The point here is that the experience was fresh in their minds, and there is little reason to doubt that a reported failure to buy represented the frustration of an actual intent to buy.

Of the shoppers who planned to buy one or more items, 39 percent failed to buy any of them. The seven-store range of failure was 27 percent to 46 percent.

It is of more than passing interest to note that the customer who succeeds

TABLE 8.

Planned and Actual Purchases of Shoppers Leaving Seven Department Stores

	Per-cent "Yes"	*Number Interviewed*		*Percent "Yes": range among seven stores*	
		"Yes"	*Total*	*High*	*Low*
1. Did you buy anything in the store today?	59.8%	5,428	9,077	72.1%	49.1%
2. Had you planned to buy anything specific today?	70.3	6,378	9,077	76.0	62.5
3. If planned specific purchase(s): Did you make any?	61.3	3,907	6,378	72.9	54.2
a. If "Yes": Did you make any unplanned purchase?	34.1	1,333	3,907	43.7	24.9
b. If "No": Did you buy anything else?	26.8	663	2,471	43.3	13.5
4. If did not plan any specific purchase: Did you buy anything?	31.8	858	2,699	43.4	18.9

Source: Surveys by author.

in the primary purpose of a shopping trip is more likely also to make an unplanned purchase than the customer who fails in this purpose is to buy anything at all. Had information been collected on the sequence in which departments were shopped, it is safe to guess, the disparity between the two groups' impulse purchases would be even more apparent. Each department in a store is partially dependent upon every other.

The role of advertising in creating customer traffic at all seven stores was checked. No storewide promotional event was in progress during any of the survey periods. It was found that in these stores, about $14\frac{1}{2}$ percent of the planned item-purchases represented advertised merchandise. The seven-store range was 8 percent to 20 percent. A note on technique: shoppers were asked to identify ads by newspaper, the day the ad had appeared, price advertised, etc., and a judgment of the accuracy of recall was made in terms of criteria developed for the purpose.

Was the merchandise which had been advertised, and which customers wanted to buy actually sold? In all four of the stores in which this was checked, approximately 70 percent of the items sought actually were bought. In other words, 30 percent of the theoretically available direct sales benefit of advertising was wiped out while the customer was in the store.

If only half the people who walked out of the stores had bought something, the number of customers buying would have been one-third greater. If only half the advertised items sought but not bought actually had been purchased, the number of advertised items sold would have been one-fifth greater. How many new products would it take to offer the stores in question as great a volume opportunity as this? How many painful cost reductions would it take to equal as great a profit opportunity as this?

QUESTIONS

1. What in-store sources of research information does a department store have? What are the advantages and disadvantages of using such data?
2. What major types of information should a store management be concerned with?
3. What kind of research study could you recommend to a men's wear retailer situated in downtown Cleveland?

17

Social Class and Life Cycle as Predictors of Shopping Behavior

Stuart U. Rich and Subhash C. Jain

This article is concerned with application of concepts of social class and life cycle to consumer shopping behavior for the purposes of segmenting the market. That these concepts help in understanding the consumer is generally accepted. As Martineau said,

> The friends we choose, the neighborhoods we live in, the way we spend and save our money, the educational plans we have for our children are determined in large degree along social class lines. A rich man is not just a poor man with more money. He probably has different ideals, different personality forces, different church membership, and many different notions of right and wrong, all largely stemming from social class differentials. With its disciplinary pressures of approval and disapproval, belonging versus ostracism, social class is a major factor shaping the individual's style of life [16].

Thus for a marketing program to be effective, it must be designed to reach the social class that fits one's product or service. Similarly, life cycle has been used as an independent variable in analyzing housing needs and uses, income, finances, and the purchase of a standard package of items to be consumed at each stage in life [3].

However, recent changes in social and economic circumstances of consumers—such as increase in discretionary income, leisure time, opportunities for higher education, increasing social benefits, movements to suburbia—have raised some doubts about the effectiveness of social class and life cycle to explain consumer behavior. Several articles [6, 15, 19, 26, 27] in academic and professional journals indicate how people supposedly of different classes tend to resemble each other in the market place. This was also reflected in the *Wall Street Journal*.

> It is no news that blue-collar pay is rising. It's not even particularly news that blue-collar workers have been raising their pay somewhat faster than white-collar workers. The extent to which these blue-collar increases have been creating what is in effect a new class blending traditional blue-

Reprinted from *Journal of Marketing Research*, Vol. 5, No. 1, American Management Association, February 1968, pp. 41–49.

> collar and white-collar spending habits, social customs and ways of thinking, is perhaps not so well realized. But recently this has become the most striking of all blue-collar trends [14, p. 1].

A similar trend has been noted about life cycle. As a J. C. Penney's executive said,

> The youth market is influenced by the population explosion, education which teaches reason rather than memorization, sweeping changes in social attitudes. Young people have a "no depression complex," a refreshing honesty and self-effacing humor. They also have a higher level of "taste achievement" which they have acquired themselves. The youth market is witty, worldly, and has money to spend. This market has influence on all the other markets (parents, young adults, older people who respond to youth) [7].

In summary, the traditional distinctions between the various social classes and stages in the family life cycle seem to be quickly diminishing. The main objective of this article is to report the findings of a study done to test the usefulness of social class and life cycle in understanding consumer behavior during changing socioeconomic conditions.[1] In presenting our findings, other studies, and certain statements, and assertions will be referred to which our empirical findings support or refute.

METHOD

The data used in this study were originally collected by one of the authors for a comprehensive work in 1963 on shopping behavior of department store customers [22]. The data consisted of about 4,000 personal and telephone interviews in Cleveland and New York. For this article part of the data was reanalyzed, namely the results of 1,056 personal interviews with a probability sample representing all women 20 years of age and older residing in the Cleveland standard metropolitan statistical area. In collecting the original data, a random procedure divided this Cleveland area into 19 zones and selected a sample of places—one place in each zone. This random procedure was repeated and a second, independent sample was drawn, providing a replicated probability sample.[2]

The two major variables used here were social class and family life cycle. Social class was stratified by a multiple-item index, Warner's Index of Status Characteristics [28] widely used in social research.[3] In this index Warner had four variables, source of income, occupation, dwelling area, and house type. This index was modified and source of income and house type were replaced

[1] This study was done for a doctoral dissertation [10].

[2] For a step-by-step description of the research procedure used, including sample design, see "Technical Appendix on Research Methodology" [22].

[3] For a full discussion of different methods of social stratification and how and why we used Warner's Index, see Chapter 2 [10].

with the amount of income and education of family head. Warner originally used source of income only because of the difficulty in obtaining income amount. It has been found that house type, which is mainly a reflection of house value is mainly dependent on occupation. If house type and occupation were used, occupation would have been weighed very heavily. Therefore, education—also an important determinant of social class—was substituted for house type.

To measure life cycle, the following breakdown was used: under 40 without children, under 40 with children, 40 and over without children, 40 and over with children. This gave a measure of the effects of age, married status, and children in the household—all important determinants of shopping behavior. Using 40 as the dividing point for age indicated whether there were preschool children in the household, another important factor influencing shopping habits [22].

Highlights of the differences in shopping behavior of women in various social classes and stages in the life cycle are described here. Chi-square tests were used to ascertain which of these differences were significant at the .05 level and to determine, for instance, whether social class affected women's interest in fashion and choice of shopping companions.

FACTORS AFFECTING SHOPPING

Interest in Fashion

If traditional distinctions between the women in various social classes and stages of the life cycle are disappearing an indication would be expected in women's interest in fashion. Respondents' interest in fashion was measured from these five statements, each printed on a separate card and handed to the respondent. She was asked to state her preferences, which were noted by the interviewer.

1. I read the fashion news regularly and try to keep my wardrobe up to date with fashion trends.
2. I keep up to date on all fashion changes although I don't always attempt to dress according to these changes.
3. I check to see what is currently fashionable only when I need to buy some new clothes.
4. I don't pay much attention to fashion trends unless a major change takes place.
5. I am not at all interested in fashion trends.

In Table 1, the fashion interests of the women belonging to various social classes are compared. Fashion plays an important part in the lives of all women regardless of class. Except for the lower-lower class, in which a slightly higher percentage of women than in other classes showed no interest in fashion at all, very small percentages of women among all other classes found fashion uninteresting.

King made essentially the same point, emphasizing the broad appeal of fashion [13]. This finding supports Weiss's remark "Fashion today is the prerogative of a substantial majority of our population—men, women and children" [29, p. 104]. However, these findings do not entirely agree with the traditional research of Barber and Lobel who found that social class differences determined the definition of women's fashion [1]. Although this was true for knowing fashion changes, it did not apply to keeping the wardrobe up to date, which concerned all women.

The present survey also showed that women in different stages of the life cycle did not vary significantly in their fashion interests. For instance, 48 percent of women 40 or over with children either read the fashion news regularly or kept up to date on all fashion trends compared with 50 percent of women under 40 with children. Katz and Lazarsfeld, however, found that interest in fashion declined with the life cycle [12].

Table 2 summarizes the methods that women in various social classes used for following fashion trends. Except for watching television and listening to the radio, where the differences between social classes were not significant, the helpfulness of the various methods shown in keeping women up to date on fashion changes increased with social class level. The rate of increase varied, however, with different methods. For example, in the category "discussing fashion with others," there was relatively little difference between the lower and middle classes. In "looking at newspaper ads," there was

TABLE 1.

Interest in Women's Fashions by Cleveland Women Shoppers, by Social Class

Statement on degree of interest	*Social class*					
	L-L	*U-L*	*L-M*	*U-M*	*L-U*	*U-U*[a]
Read news regularly and keep wardrobe up to date	14%	8%	9%	10%	19%	9%
Keep abreast of changes but not always follow	19	29	42	50	47	64
Check what is fashionable only if buy new clothes	15	22	15	17	17	9
Only pay attention to major fashion changes	22	23	19	14	14	18
Not at all interested in fashion trends	24	16	12	9	3	—[b]
Don't know	6	2	3	—	—	—
Total	100%	100%	100%	100%	100%	100%
Number of cases	132	346	265	206	36	11

[a]In this and subsequent tables, *L* = lower, *M* = middle and *U* = upper.
[b]In this and subsequent tables, a dash represents less than .5 percent.

a sharp rise in helpfulness from the lower-lower class to the upper-lower class, but the difference is not particularly significant until the upper-upper class. In summary, the traditional view of greater fashion interest for higher social classes generally holds true for particular methods used to keep informed of fashion although the increase in interest is seldom in any direct proportion to the increase in social level.

Unlike social class, life cycle did not affect fashion interest. There were no significant differences in the methods used by women in various stages of the family life cycle for being informed of fashion changes.

TABLE 2.

Methods Helpful to Cleveland Women on Fashion Trends, by Social Class

Method	Social Class					
	L-L	U-L	L-M	U-M	L-U	U-U
Going to fashion shows	5%	3%	7%	9%	22%	18%
Reading fashion magazines	14	13	11	23	36	27
Reading other magazines	17	18	26	31	28	46
Reading fashion articles in papers	22	34	46	45	56	64
Looking at newspaper ads	39	57	60	68	67	91
Going shopping	36	50	53	63	75	73
Discussing fashion with others	21	22	29	34	36	46
Observing what others wear	22	36	81	51	58	55
Watching television	32	28	25	26	25	46
Listening to the radio	2	5	5	2	8	—
Don't know	3	1	1	—	—	—
No interest in fashion	30	18	14	10	3	—
Total[a]	243%	285%	358%	362%	414%	466%
Number of cases	132	346	265	206	36	11

[a]Total exceeds 100 percent because of multiple responses.

Sources of Shopper Information

Newspaper ads are an important source of shoppers' information. The degree of helpfulness which women attributed to newspaper advertising was analyzed. Women in various social classes seemed to find newspaper ads helpful to about the same degree, except a slightly greater percentage of women in the lower-lower class found them somewhat more helpful.

Another measure used to study the importance of newspaper ads was to analyze the regularity with which women in different social classes looked at newspaper ads. Here again, women of different status groups showed no significant differences in the regularity of their looking at newspaper ads. These results agreed with findings of a recent study reported in *Editor and Publisher:*

> The daily newspaper's coverage of the market place on the average day is nearly universal. Almost every household, 87%, gets a newspaper. . . . The mass exposure opportunity represented by this high percentage of page opening is remarkably consistent for men and women of all ages, incomes, educational attainments and geographical locations [25].

Carman has reported a similar finding about the importance of newspaper ads as a source of information for members of different social classes [2, p. 29].

Among women in the various stages of the family life cycle, those with children considered the newspaper ads more helpful. For instance, 88 percent of the women 40 and over with children found ads helpful compared with 73 percent of those without children. Among the women under 40 with and without children, the percentages were 81 and 70, respectively. Further analysis showed that women with children looked at newspaper ads more often than those without children. Age itself had little effect on either the regularity of looking at ads in newspapers or the helpfulness attributed to these ads.

This finding about life cycle differs from what Miller pointed out in 1954,

> The younger housewives are easier to educate to an awareness of product and brand; it is easier to get across to the younger housewives the reasons why they should try it or buy it; and the younger housewives are less fixed in their buying habits and brand loyalty, and will be more inclined to change their buying patterns in response to advertising [17, p. 65].

Again we note that some of the traditional distinctions among the social classes and stages in the family life cycle may be disappearing.

Interpersonal Influences in Shopping

Interpersonal influences play an important part in shopping decisions. For practical application to marketing, it is necessary to know who these influencers are for each segment of the market. The traditional view has been that upper classes interacted more with members of the immediate family and put great emphasis on lineage. The middle class, though, was generally considered self-directing, had initiative, and was dependent on themselves and their friends more than on relatives. Like the upper classes, the lower classes depended on relatives and family members more often [8, p. 286]. Our findings differed in some respects from this view.

Table 3 and 4 present data on the impact of interpersonal influences on shopping decisions under two categories, helpfulness attributed to discussing shopping with others and persons with whom respondents usually shopped. In both categories, women in various social classes showed no significant difference in the influence of friends on shopping. The husband was slightly more important as a shopping influence for the middle and upper classes than for the lower classes, and children were more likely to be taken on shopping trips by the middle and upper classes. However, mother and other family members were not mentioned to any large extent by the lower classes as traditional research would indicate.

Note also in Table 3 that the proportion of women who attributed no help to discussing shopping with others was not significantly different for the three classes. This does not agree with what Rainwater, Coleman, and Handel said, "the working class largely depended on word-of-mouth recommendation before making major purchases" [21, p. 210].

TABLE 3.

Discussion of Shopping with Others, Cleveland Women, by Social Class

Consider it helpful with	*Social class*[a]		
	Lower	*Middle*	*Upper*
Friends	34%	37%	50%
Husband	13	18	24
Mother	5	5	6
Other family members	20	14	18
No one	36	39	32
Total[b]	108%	113%	130%
Number of cases	478	471	47

[a]Significant differences were noted even when we divided the respondents into six social classes. However, to save space here in some instances only three classes are shown.
[b]Total exceeds 100 percent because of multiple responses.

TABLE 4.

Persons with Whom Cleveland Women Usually Shop, by Social Class

Usually shop with	*Social class*					
	L-L	*U-L*	*L-M*	*U-M*	*L-U*	*U-U*
Friends	32%	31%	26%	34%	39%	46%
Husband	20	25	32	35	33	9
Mother	5	7	9	9	3	—
Children	10	15	22	23	28	—
Other family members	21	23	16	10	8	18
No one in particular	26	20	17	22	17	36
Never shops with others	—	2	1	2	—	—
Total[a]	114%	123%	123%	135%	128%	109%
Number of cases	132	346	265	206	36	11

[a]Total exceeds 100 percent because of multiple responses.

Shopping Enjoyment

Most women enjoyed shopping regardless of their social class. However, women in different social classes had varying reasons for enjoying shopping. Some reasons—such as the recreational and social aspects of shopping, seeing new things and getting new ideas, and bargain hunting and comparing merchandise—were mentioned by all social classes without any significant difference. Another reason, namely acquiring new clothes or household things, was more enjoyable for the two lower classes. However, a pleasant store atmosphere, display, and excitement were specified as reasons for enjoying shopping by a greater proportion of the women in the upper-middle, lower-upper, and upper-upper classes. Stone and Form found that enjoyment in shopping was not a function of social status [24]. This was in accord with our general finding on shopping enjoyment although, as just noted, the reasons for enjoyment sometimes varied among social classes.

Life cycle did not have any effect on the enjoyment of shopping for clothing and household items. For instance, 38 percent of the women over 40 with children enjoyed shopping for such reasons as pleasant store atmosphere, displays, and excitement compared with 36 percent in this age group without children. For women under 40 without children, the percentages were 37 and 41, respectively.

Stone and Form claimed that younger women with children enjoyed shopping more than other women. In this study, neither age nor the presence of children in the family seemed to make any difference for women in their enjoyment of shopping.

Shopping Frequency

The frequency with which women shopped during the year was significantly associated with social class. For example, 38 percent of the women in the upper class and 34 percent in the middle class shopped 52 or more times a year compared with 24 percent in the lower class. These findings do not match those of Stone and Form. According to them, women in either the upper or the middle class shopped less often than women in the lower or working class.

Younger women shopped more often than older women, but presence of children did not make any significant difference within the two age groups (Table 5). Stone and Form found the frequency of shopping trips mainly dependent on children in the family.

Importance of Shopping Quickly

The higher the social status of a woman, the more she considered it important to shop quickly. Thus 39 percent of upper class women regarded it important to always shop quickly though only 30 percent in the lower class and 34 percent in the middle class did. Only 10 percent of upper class women

TABLE 5.

Frequency of Shopping Trips of Cleveland Women, by Life Cycle

Times per year	*Stage in life cycle*			
	Under 40		*40 and over*	
	No child	*Child*	*No child*	*Child*
52 or more	30%	30%	25%	31%
24 to 51	33	25	17	20
12 to 23	23	28	18	21
6 to 11	2	4	6	7
1 to 5	12	12	27	21
Less than once	—	—	2	—
Never	—	—	1	—
Don't know	—	1	4	—
Total	100%	100%	100%	100%
Number of cases	66	474	240	276

felt it was not important to shop quickly compared with 19 percent and 29 percent in the middle and lower classes, respectively. According to Stone and Form, however, the upper and lower classes spent more time shopping than did the middle class. Huff found that women of high social status spent the most time on an average shopping trip [9].

For life cycle, Stone and Form found that women in their forties felt most hurried, and women in their twenties were divided evenly between those who felt they had adequate time and those who did not. In their study age was found to be the determining factor of the importance of shopping quickly. In this study, women under and over 40 with children put more stress on quick shopping than those without children. These findings thus show different behavior patterns about the importance of shopping quickly.

Browsing

Tendency to browse without buying anything was more prominent among the upper-lower (41 percent), lower-middle (44 percent), and upper-middle (42 percent) classes. Yet women in the lower-lower, lower-upper, and upper-upper classes mentioned it less often (Table 6). Stone and Form discovered that lower class women did more browsing than middle and upper class women, a finding obviously different from this study's.

Further, women under 40 with or without children, browsed more (24 percent and 22 percent, respectively) than women 40 and over (12 percent for those with and without children); but Stone and Form did not find the life cycle to have any relationship here. Again, traditional distinctions among the various social classes and stages in the family life cycle may be changing.

TABLE 6.

Browsing of Cleveland Women, by Social Class

Regularity of occurrence	*Social Class*					
	L-L	*U-L*	*L-M*	*U-M*	*L-U*	*U-U*
Regularly or fairly often	29%	41%	44%	42%	22%	18%
Once in a while	30	37	35	36	31	27
Never	40	21	20	22	44	55
Don't know	1	1	1	—	3	—
Total	100%	100%	100%	100%	100%	100%
Number of cases	132	346	265	206	36	11

Downtown Shopping

Several authors have reported how the continued expansion of the shopping centers has challenged the traditional role of the downtown area [5, 11, 23]. In this study, the lower the social status, the greater the proportion of downtown shopping (Table 7). Sixty-eight percent of lower-lower class women were designated as high downtown shoppers, only 22 percent of the lower-upper class and 18 percent of the upper-upper class were considered to be so. This finding is different from that reported in *Workingman's Wife*, "A comparison between the shopping of middle class women and working class women shows the provinciality of the latter. Fewer working class than middle class women classify themselves as 'regular shoppers' in the central business districts" [21, p. 21]. Thus there is a change in downtown clientele. Once the upper class shopped downtown more often; now it may be the lower classes who patronize downtown more.

This also suggests that suburban shopping centers are becoming increasingly more important for the upper classes. This has been noted in

TABLE 7.

Shopping Done Downtown by Cleveland Women, by Social Class

Proportion of downtown shopping[a]	*Social class*					
	L-L	*U-L*	*L-M*	*U-M*	*L-U*	*U-U*
High	68%	50%	42%	33%	22%	18%
Low	19	33	37	50	59	64
None	11	15	19	15	16	18
Don't know	2	2	2	2	3	—
Total	100%	100%	100%	100%	100%	100%
Number of cases	132	346	265	206	36	11

[a]High downtown shoppers shop downtown half or more of the time; Low downtown shoppers, one-quarter or less of the time; None means women who do not shop downtown.

Women's Wear Daily, "It is a mistake to promote just $25 dresses in a suburban store. . . . We have found, from experience, that higher price clothes do sell in depth in the suburbs" [20, p. 40].

Cross tabulations by life cycle showed a tendency for young people to patronize shopping centers more than older people, as suggested by other findings.

No significant differences on downtown shopping existed among the women in the various social classes living in the city. However, among the suburbanites, social class was inversely related to downtown shopping. For instance, among the city dwellers about 60 percent of the women in the two lower and two middle classes were ranked as high downtown shoppers. Yet, among the out-of-city residents 43 percent of lower-lower class women and 37 percent of upper-lower class were considered high in-town shoppers; only 32 percent in the lower-middle and 27 percent in the upper-middle class were high downtown shoppers. The percentages for the two upper classes further decreased to 22 percent and 18 percent, respectively.

In contrast, about 70 percent of the women in the two upper classes (living in the suburbs) were low downtown shoppers though the same percentage was 29 percent for the lower-lower class and 40 percent for the upper-lower class. However, when the high and low categories were considered together and compared with the "none" group, downtown shopping by suburbanites increased in each higher social class.

In general, a greater proportion of higher class women shop downtown, but women in the lower classes appear to shop more intensively in the central business district.

Type of Store Preferred

As seen in Table 8, higher class women more often named the regular department store as their favorite. The department store maintained a broad image as a favorite store since 51 percent of the lower-lower class women and 60 percent of the upper-lower class designated it their favorite store. A greater percentage of lower-lower (14 percent) and upper-lower (11 percent) women favored the discount store than did women in either the middle or upper classes.

Several writers have emphasized that women in various social classes differ in the department stores they patronize and have different expectations about each store [4, 16, 18]. Therefore, the authors looked at the particular stores which women named as their favorites among the different regular department stores. Three department stores in Cleveland were mentioned far more often than others, and these were called a high fashion, a price appeal, or a broad appeal store.

As shown in Table 9, the high fashion store became more important for each higher class. But, the price appeal store was inversely related to social class. The broad appeal store was mentioned by the two middle classes more often. These findings generally agreed with what Martineau discovered:

> the blue collar individual, as his family income goes up, proceeds from cars to appliances to home ownership to apparel. He and his family are candidates for almost any store, and the most successful stores which would traditionally appeal to them have held them by steadily trading up, both in merchandise, store facilities and their image. . . . The point again is that this person has changed. He is not the same guy. He has long since satisfied his needs and wants and now he is interested in satisfying his wishes [15, p. 56].

The high preference of the lower class shoppers for the regular department stores is therefore not surprising.

The kind of department store women in the various social classes mentioned most often was also analyzed for the following kinds of merchandise:

TABLE 8.

Kind of Favorite Store of Cleveland Women, by Social Class

Kind of store	*Social class*					
	L-L	*U-L*	*L-M*	*U-M*	*L-U*	*U-U*
Regular department	51%	60%	77%	83%	88%	91%
Discount department	14	11	6	2	—	9
Variety and junior department	2	6	6	5	—	—
Mail order	9	14	5	2	3	—
Medium to low specialty	2	2	1	—	6	—
Neighborhood	11	2	1	1	3	—
Others	11	5	4	7	—	—
Total	100%	100%	100%	100%	100%	100%
Number of cases	132	346	265	206	36	11

TABLE 9.

Kind of Department Store Favored by Cleveland Women

Kind of department store	*Social class*					
	L-L	*U-L*	*L-M*	*U-M*	*L-U*	*U-U*
High fashion store	4%	7%	22%	34%	70%	67%
Price appeal store	74	63	36	24	19	18
Broad appeal store	22	30	42	42	11	15
Total	100%	100%	100%	100%	100%	100%
Number of cases	67	208	204	71	32	10

women's better dresses; house dresses and underwear; children's clothing; men's socks and shirts; furniture; large appliances; towels, sheets, blankets and spreads; and small electrical appliances and kitchen utensils. Here again the two upper classes specified the high fashion store as their favorite for the first five of these eight kinds of merchandise. Women in the two lower classes shopped at the price appeal store most of the time for all items.

Analysis of the favorite store of women in various stages of the life cycle showed that the regular department store ranked high among all women except that younger women with children showed somewhat less preference for it. Table 10 shows that 57 percent of the younger women with children and 65 percent of the younger women without children mentioned the regular department store as their favorite. Discount stores were preferred by the younger women a little more than by the older ones. No significant differences were revealed between the types of stores favored by women in various stages of the family life cycle for the eight kinds of merchandise individually.

TABLE 10.

Kind of Favorite Store of Cleveland Women, by Life Cycle

Kind of favorite store	*Stage in life cycle*			
	Under 40		*40 and over*	
	No child	*Child*	*No child*	*Child*
Department	65%	57%	83%	79%
Discount	9	13	2	2
Mail order	5	11	2	7
All others	21	19	13	12
Total	100%	100%	100%	100%
Number of cases	66	474	240	276

CONCLUSION

Socioeconomic changes in income, education, leisure time, and movement to suburbia cut across traditional class lines and various stages in the life cycle. Some authors like Rainwater, Coleman, and Handel have found social class a significant factor in determining consumer behavior [21]. However recent writings seem to indicate that social class distinctions have been obscured by rising incomes and educational levels [14, 15].

Our empirical findings tend to support the second viewpoint. The random sampling procedure used assured every Cleveland woman 20 years of age or older an equal chance of being selected, and interviewer bias was closely controlled. Hence we are able to generalize about shopping behavior in Cleveland. Admittedly, all findings cannot be applied to women in other cities. However in the original study, which included Cleverland and New York-northeastern New Jersey metropolitan areas, many patterns of shopping behavior for women in particular income or life cycle categories were almost identical in the two areas despite the contrasting patterns of size, geographical location, demography, and kinds of stores found in these two cities [22].

Spot checks made of Cleveland and New York women in the present study again produced similar results. For instance, among women under 40 with children in Cleveland, 30 percent shopped 52 or more times per year compared with 34 percent for this group in New York. For women 40 and over with children, the percentages were 31 and 30 for the two cities. On the importance of being able to shop quickly, 30 percent of the lower social class women in Cleveland felt this was always important, as did 34 percent of the middle class women and 39 percent of the upper class women. In New York these percentages were 29, 36, and 39, respectively. In other words, there seems to be evidence that many of the shopping behavior patterns of Cleveland women exist in other cities.

The findings thus question the usefulness of life cycle and social class concepts in understanding consumer behavior in view of recent changes in income, education, leisure time, movement to suburbia, and other factors. Students of marketing and store executives may need to reconsider how far these sociological concepts should be used for segmentation purposes and what their probable impact will be on marketing policies and programs.

References

1. Bernard Barber and Lyle S. Lobel, "Fashion in Women's Clothes and the American Social System," *Social Forces*, 31 (December 1952), 124–31.
2. James M. Carman, *The Application of Social Class in Market Segmentation*, Berkeley, Calif.: University of California, 1965.
3. Lincoln Clark, ed., *The Life Cycle and Consumer Behavior*, Vol. 2, New York: New York University Press, 1955.
4. Richard P. Coleman, "The Significance of Social Stratification in Selling," in Martin L. Bell, ed., *Marketing: A Maturing Discipline*, Chicago: American Marketing Association, December 1960, 177.
5. Thomas Lea Davidson, *Some Effects of the Growth of Planned and Controlled Shopping Centers on Small Retailers*, Washington, D.C.: Small Business Administration, 1960.
6. Editors of *Fortune*, *Market for the Sixties*, New York: Harper and Row, 1960.
7. "Experts Set Youth Market Guidelines," *Women's Wear Daily*, 113 (October 18, 1966), 19.

8. August B. Hollingshead, "Class Differences in Family Stability," in Reinhard Bendix and Seymour Martin Lipset, eds., *Class, Status and Power*, New York: The Free Press, 1965.
9. David L. Huff, "Geographical Aspects of Consumer Behavior," *University of Washington Business Review*, 18 (June 1959), 27–35.
10. Subhash Jain, "A Critical Analysis of Life Cycle and Social Class Concepts in Understanding Consumer Shopping Behavior," Unpublished doctoral dissertation, University of Oregon, 1966.
11. C. T. Johanssen, *The Shopping Center Versus Downtown*, Columbus, Ohio: The Ohio State University, 1955.
12. Elihu Katz and Paul F. Lazarsfeld, *Personal Influence*, Glencoe, Ill.: The Free Press, 1955, 263–8.
13. Charles W. King, "Fashion Adoption: A Rebuttal to the Trickle Down Theory," *Proceedings*, Summer Conference, American Marketing Association, June 1964, 108–25.
14. Frederick C. Klein, "Rising Pay Lifts More Blue Collar Men into a New Affluent Class," *The Wall Street Journal*, 165 (April 5, 1965).
15. Pierre Martineau, "Customer Shopping Center Habits Change Retailing," *Editor & Publisher*, 96 (October 26, 1963), 16, 56.
16. *Motivation in Advertising*, New York: McGraw-Hill Book Company, 1957, 166–7.
17. Donald L. Miller, "The Life Cycle and the Importance of Advertising," in Lincoln Clark, ed., *The Life Cycle and Consumer Behavior*, Vol. 2, New York: New York University Press, 1955.
18. Vance Packard, *The Status Seekers*, New York: Pocket Books, Inc., 1961, 113.
19. Peter G. Peterson, "Conventional Wisdom and the Sixties," *Journal of Marketing*, 26 (April 1962), 63–5.
20. Trudy Prokop, "Jack Weiss: No Gambler, But a Man of Decision," *Women's Wear Daily*, 113 (November 28, 1966), 40.
21. Lee Rainwater, Richard Coleman, and Gerald Handel, *Workingman's Wife*, New York: MacFadden-Bartell Corp., 1962.
22. Stuart U. Rich, *Shopping Behavior of Department Store Customers*, Boston, Mass.: Division of Research, Graduate School of Business Administration, Harvard University, 1963.
23. George Sternlieb, *The Future of the Downtown Department Store*, Cambridge, Mass.: Harvard University, 1962.
24. Gregory P. Stone and William H. Form, *The Local Community Clothing Market: A Study of the Social and Social Psychological Contexts of Shopping*, East Lansing, Mich.: Michigan State University, 1957, 20.
25. "Survey Proves High Exposure for Ads on Newspaper Pages," *Editor & Publisher*, 97 (October 3, 1964), 17–8.
26. Thayer C. Taylor, "Selling Where the Money Is," *Sales Management*, 91 (October 18, 1963), 37–41, 122, 124, 126.
27. ——, "The I AM ME Consumer," *Business Week* (December 23, 1961), 38–39.
28. Lloyd W. Warner, M. Meeker, and K. Eells, *Social Class in America*, Chicago: Social Research, Inc., 1949.
29. Edward B. Weiss, "The Revolution in Fashion Distribution," *Advertisting Age*, 34 (June 24, 1963), 104–5.

QUESTIONS

1. What techniques did the author use to segment those surveyed?
2. Why is life cycle considered to be a useful technique for segmenting those surveyed in conducting retail research?
3. Do you agree with the authors that social class distinctions have been obscured by rising incomes and educational levels? Support your argument.

B. GOODS AND SERVICES

This section falls into two major parts. The first contains readings on decisions affecting the choice of goods and services; the second, readings on all aspects of pricing these same goods and services.

The article by Harold Hoffman, entitled "The Myths and Folklore of Vendor Relations," points out the areas of conflict between the retail buyer and the manufacturer. In the next one, E. L. Salkin is concerned with recent approaches to making the proper decision on a specific problem: how many skirts a department buyer should purchase; he shows the application of linear programming in making this decision. The final article, by William Reagan, discusses in the first half the pros and cons of reducing the services offered consumers.

The first article on pricing is by Stanley Hollander, "The 'One-Price' System—Fact or Fiction?" in which he discusses the many variations in prices and discounts available from traditional and discount type outlets. Benson Shapiro, discusses the many facets of pricing, noting especially the psychological effects prices have on the consumer. In "Estimating Price Elasticity," Douglas Dalrymple indicates, through simple correlation, that the elasticity of lines of merchandise can be estimated. The last article, by Eugene Beem, discusses the role of the food discount store, and concludes that though these stores are growing at a rapid rate, they will not dominate the industry in spite of their emphases on low prices.

18

The Myths and Folklore of Vendor Relations

Harold Hoffman

The nature of buyer-seller relationships has long been a subject of debate and a source of irritation in the efficient functioning of the wholesale markets. It has resulted in all kinds of misunderstandings as to motives, practices, and basic rationale between manufacturers on the one hand and their retailer customers on the other.

Through the years, there has developed an increasing degree of egocentrism on the part of these two key marketing groups. They have come to view the marketing function as a two part affair, not necessarily related to a common purpose or goal. Buying and selling are looked upon as a battle; and one from which both participants frequently emerge bloody with losses and failure. Distrust of each other's motives, ignorance of each other's problems and goals are much in evidence as one examines this situation in depth. The result is a loss in the effectiveness of the marketing programs of both stores and their suppliers.

BUYERS AND SELLERS EFFICIENT BUT HOSTILE

One curious aspect of this phenomenon is that both groups are highly efficient technicians. They have demonstrated their mastery at producing and selling larger and larger quantities of varied consumer goods at a profit. Yet a most vital part of their function is performed in a milieu of hostility and isolation. One must speculate on the intriguing possibilities of what could be done in the market place if buyers and sellers viewed marketing as a joint enterprise.

It is high time that we give some attention and analysis to this block in the funnel of a free flowing distribution complex. It is now urgent that we identify the reasons for the persistence of the tradition of "buyer vs. seller." To think clearly and objectively about this problem we must be willing to abandon usual partisan emotionalism and consider that marketing is in fact a continuum with manufacturers at one end, retailers at the midpoint and both pumping goods toward the ultimate consumer at the other end. With

Reprinted from *New York Retailer,* April 1962, pp. 2–5.

this theory as our guide, we may now proceed to examine the functioning of our markets as a sociological problem.

Even a casual look at our wholesale markets will reveal that the sources of conflict lie in the kinds of interpersonal relationships that prevail. There exists here a well established system of norms and sanctions firmly imbedded in the behavior patterns of both buyers and sellers. The basis of the system is the mutually cherished though insistently denied tradition of Caveat Emptor. The whole culture perpetuates itself with a carefully nurtured system of commercial folklore and mythology.

One can observe a merchandise manager introducing a neophyte buyer to the market with a series of warnings, cautions and statements all built around the idea of mayhem in the market place. Equally as illustrative is the picture of the sales manager "breaking in" the beginning salesman with inside information on how to deal with the whims and fancies of his buyers and their stores. In both cases the key words for success are "dazzle, confuse, entertain, threaten, cajole and bargain." A sorry spectacle indeed in a society oriented to efficiency!

A STUDY OF BUYER AND SELLER ATTITUDES TOWARD EACH OTHER

While our markets are not places where one should expect to find sweetness and lyrical joy, what we do find is literally a jungle of misunderstanding and a morass of hostility. The key to how this social subsystem works (of the concepts held by its members) was the object of an informal study undertaken by the writer. He asked respondents to state "off the cuff" reactions regarding their opposite number in the market place:

Buyers were asked to state their candid opinions of manufacturers and their representatives. They responded as follows:

Manufacturers and salesman are:

> . . . Unaware of store problems, functions and requirements.
> Users of ancient methods of manufacturing and merchandising.
> Afraid to carry inventory, manufacturing only after they sell.
> People who do not honor order commitments.
> And a variety of other choice descriptions: "dumb, slick, smooth, crooked, parasitic, etc."

The same kind of question was put to manufacturers and their salesmen, and the following kinds of answers were obtained.

Buyers are:

> . . . Representatives of mammoth retailing combines in a conspiracy against legitimate profits by manufacturers.
> Generally ignorant of the problems of manufacturing.
> Time wasters who spend their market periods in inaccessible meetings. . . .
> And a variety of other choice adjectives: "smart, dumb, slick, smooth, crooked, parasitic, etc."

While the data from such an informal study cannot be accepted as conclusive, it is certainly an indication of a situation highly dangerous to the smooth functioning of a highly complex market. The astonishing similarity of the replies further serves to accent the degree of isolation and the lack of communication between these two key groups. The pressure system of conflict and mistaken image of each other is in no small way responsible for the high turnover of suppliers on the part of retailers, and the equally short lived relationships with customers on the part of manufacturers.

SOME WELL ESTABLISHED MYTHS

The fact that buyers and sellers take such very similar views of each other must lead one to the conclusion that these ideas have a common heritage, a common source. It is the thesis of this paper that all the foregoing has as its source a philosophy stemming from a tradition of commercial folk lore and a well established mythology. Let us examine some of these notions to see how they affect the conduct of buyers and sellers as agents of their particular phases of marketing.

The price myth: A widely held view is that all prices quoted by vendors are negotiable. This, in turn, leads to the next.

The bulk purchase myth: Buyers should and can become as expert as manufacturers for the purpose of setting prices. Technical production background can easily be acquired.

Personal friendship myth: A good buyer or salesman can perform miracles providing they have the "right" friends.

The secret deal myth: This one holds that special favors or price allowances can be kept secret on an "only for you" arrangement.

The advertising allowance myth: Advertising moneys allocated to stores come from "special funds" and do not affect the quality/price relationship of the merchandise being purchased.

The finished deal myth: This notion widely held by manufacturers holds to the idea that once goods are shipped, the manufacturer has fully discharged his end of the deal.

The closed meeting myth: This theorem explains that market decisions are best made in splendid isolation. Buyers get the best opportunity to make efficient marketing decisions in meetings restricted to retailers only.

The mutual ignorance myth: Manufacturers know nothing about retailing and retailers know little of prime marketing. A corollary to this one is that neither can be expected to know.

The consignment myth: Holds that retailers cannot be expected to assume responsibility for the ultimate sale of goods. They are merely the vehicles through which manufacturers may reach the consumer.

The commonality myth: Buyers and sellers have nothing in common except their obligation to meet in the market place and negotiate from carefully devised positions of strength.

Many readers will be moved to argue that these are not myths, but rather the way things are or should be. This kind of reaction (which the writer has experienced) is further proof of the extent to which the myths are embedded in the patterns of our commercial life. What proves them to be myths is the number of successful exceptions to the buyer vs. seller concept.

THE NEED FOR OUTSTANDING AND MUTUAL RESPECT

In case after case both retailers and their vendors have established the fact that they have a vested interest together in the total marketing task. Many stores pride themselves on the degree of long term relationships with their vendors. Likewise many vendors have adopted marketing programs which have been successful in spite of the fact that those programs violate every one of the themes of the precious myths. Many instances of joint planning, and open merchandise meetings with vendors, devoted and close working together by buyers and salesmen, further substantiate the mythological basis of current folklore.

What is more important, however, is that recognition of the need for communication and understanding in the market place is essential. The economy of the country is largely dependent upon the degree of efficiency with which buyers and sellers operate. A key to that efficiency lies in opening up channels of communication in the already established channels of distribution. A first step in that direction might well be the identification of the aforementioned mythology and its replacement with a sound system of mutual respect and joint effort in building profitable business.

QUESTIONS

1. Which of the myths, as outlined in the article, do you think comes closest to the truth?
2. Comment on the following: Since retailers and manufacturers have the same goal (profits), there is little reason for conflict.

19

Linear Programming for Merchandising Decisions

E. Lawrence Salkin

The maturation of the computer as a standard tool for use in business has resulted in the concomitant growth of a new technique for management decision making known as management science. Management science, in

Reprinted from *Journal of Retailing*, Vol. 40, No. 4, Winter 1964–65, pp. 37–41, 58–59.

the main, is based upon the application of mathematical theories that before the development of the computer were regarded as mere mathematical curiosities. This was true because of the vast number of calculations required to solve the problems. With a computer, the application of these mathematical theories becomes practical and a tremendous aid to the decision-maker. Such problems as inventory control, allocation of personnel, capital and expense budgeting, marketing plans, can be solved more logically through the use of the various techniques of management science.

Retailing is a highly complicated business operation, and retailing executives can profitably make use of many of the techniques mentioned above to chart a course through the complex maze of decisions required to cut costs and increase profits. At this point, most computer installations in retail companies are being used as workhorses, processing accounts receivable, accounts payable, payrolls, and merchandise information. As the problems arising from putting these functions on a computer are solved, it is conceivable that computer time will be made available for the scientific applications required for the mathematical analyses of management science. Looking forward to this development, the enlightened retail executive should familiarize himself with the techniques for scientific decision-making.

It is the purpose of this paper to illustrate just one of the many ways a scientific approach to decision making can be implemented. The case cited herein is hypothetical and simplified, since no computer was available for calculations required for a more expanded situation; however, it is felt that the problem stated is a valid one, and, by expanding the mathematical model herein presented, can be effectively used in real situations with the aid of a computer. The mathematics used is based upon linear programming theory, and the approach and techniques used have been adapted from *Executive Decisions and Operations Research*, 2nd ed., by David W. Miller and Martin K. Starr (Englewood Cliffs, N.J.: Prentice-Hall, Inc., 1969).

THE PROBLEM

Let us imagine a buyer of a budget skirt department with the bulk of his volume achieved by two price lines: $4.00 and $7.00. The buyer, contemplating no change in his current price lines, wishes to maximize gross margin for these two price lines combined for the coming season within the framework of certain predetermined goals. To do this, the buyer must plan to have sold a certain number of units of the $4.00 and $7.00 skirts by the end of the season. Though he has past unit sales records to guide him, he does not wish to rely on his empirical judgment alone to make the decision. The buyer decides that with the data available he can use a linear programming model to help determine the optimum number of skirts in each of the two price lines that should move through his department during the season. The data to be used is shown in Table 1, including the algebraic symbols that will be used for the formulas.

Four factors have been selected: Cost of Sales, Turnover, Average Age, and Average Income of Customers. Cost of Sales has been selected since it is reduced from initial markon to arrive at gross margin. The gross margin is the figure arrived at after accounting for markdowns, shortages, etc. Turnover is selected since it determines the amount of average inventory investment required to attain the desired volume. As turnover is increased the investment required is correspondingly lowered. Customer Age and Income are selected since these factors are basic in determining the character of the department.

Other factors, such as sales per square foot, average gross sales, markon, etc., could have been selected. However, care should be taken to use those factors that are most relevant to the problem. The use of too many factors complicates considerably the computations required for a solution.

COMPILATION OF DATA

The buyer has compiled the data used from various sources:

Gross Margin, Cost of Sales, and Turnover, listed in columns A and B, are estimated from past figures attained by the department for each classification.

Family Income and Age Level, listed in columns A and B, are supplied by the Market Research Department from a recent research study of customer habits.

Average Planned Goals per unit for both skirts combined are listed in column C. In effect, these figures are the quantification of management's merchandising policy for this department. For example, management desires to concentrate most of its promotional activity toward the $7,000-and-over income level, with an age level of 27 years and over; therefore these goals are listed as averages per unit to be attained for the coming season.

TABLE 1.

Planned Goals for Season Sales of $4.00 and $7.00 Skirts

	A		*B*		*C*
	Symbol	*$4.00 Skirt**	*Symbol*	*$7.00 Skirt**	*Planned Goals*
Gross margin per unit (in dollars)	P_1	$1.50	P_2	$2.70	Maximum
Cost of sales per unit	C_1	$ .45	C_2	$ .65	$ .60
Turnover for the season	T_1	4.0	T_2	3.0	3.2
Average family income (in thousands) purchasing each type skirt	I_1	$5.5	I_2	$7.8	$7.0
Average age level purchasing each type skirt	A_1	22	A_2	30	27

*The symbol for the $4.00 skirt is S_1 and the symbol for the $7.00 skirt is S_2.

Gross Margin, Cost of Sales, Turnover, Income and Age Level form the boundaries within which the optimal number of skirts to be carried will be found. Any combination of skirts carried that does not equal or surpass the planned goals listed in Table 1 are not acceptable as a solution. The problem is to select the combination of skirts that achieves all the planned goals and, at the same time, maximizes gross margin. In this problem, the combination that maximizes gross margin with cost of sales equal to or less than \$.60, turnover equal to or better than 3.2, income equal to or better than \$7,000, and age equal to or better than 27 years is the best solution to be found. It is this solution that the buyer will use to plan for the coming season.

THE FORMULAS

The formulas for this particular linear programming model are shown in Table 2, with the customary use of such symbols as $\geq$ and $\leq$ meaning "equal to or greater than" and "equal to or less than," respectively. This form is used because, as explained previously, the buyer wishes to equal or improve on the planned goals, not *merely* equal them. Inequations 1., 2., 3., 4., 5., 6., and 7. form boundaries comprising all the goals desired. In technical terms, these are called the "constraints" or "restraints" of the linear programming problem. Inequations 6. and 7. are included as constraints since the solution to the problem must result in a zero or positive value for each skirt in order to be implemented. It is impossible to merchandise a negative number of skirts. Equation 5. is known as the objective function, which, in this case, means that gross margin is to be maximized within the boundaries desired.

TABLE 2.

Inequations for the Linear Programming Solution

1. $C_1S_1 + C_2S_2 \leq \bar{C} \geq C$ Minimum	5. $P_1S_1 + P_2S_2 =$ Maximum
2. $T_1S_1 + T_2S_2 \geq \bar{T} \leq T$ Maximum	6. $S_1 \geq 0$
3. $I_1S_1 + I_2S_2 \geq \bar{I} \leq I$ Maximum	7. $S_2 \geq 0$
4. $A_1S_1 + A_2S_2 \geq \bar{A} \leq A$ Maximum	

Note: $\bar{C}$, $\bar{T}$, $\bar{I}$, and $\bar{A}$ indicate planned figures, as shown in Column C, Table I.

The right hand side of the inequations ($\leq \bar{C} \geq C$ Minimum: $\geq \bar{T} \leq T$ Maximum, etc.) are written in this form to further delineate the area within which the optimal solutions must be found. To illustrate, when we substitute the values found in Table 1 into inequation No. 1. of Table 2 we have the following:

$$.45S_1 + .65S_2 \leq .60 \geq .45$$

This means that the average cost of sales in the final or optimal solution must be equal to or less than .65 and equal to or greater than .45. It is obvious that it would be impossible to have an average cost of sales of less than the minimum of .45, and any average cost of sales over .60 is unacceptable as it exceeds the boundaries for this factor. This is true for the remaining inequations, except that the maximum values would be considered impossible.

COMPUTATION OF THE OPTIMAL SOLUTION

The computations required for arriving at a solution to this problem involve no more than simple algebra. It is the large number of computations required that complicates matters. The number of computations in the method presented here increase considerably as the number of variables and constraints are increased. Other computational methods, such as the Simplex Method, can be used for expanded problems but are too unwieldy for this comparatively simple algebraic approach.

As for the solution itself, the data listed in Table 1 is substituted into the inequations listed in Table 2. The inequations with the values substituted are shown in Table 3.

TABLE 3.

Inequations to be Solved for the Optimal Solution

1. $.45S_1 + .65S_2 \leq .60 \geq .45$	5. $1.50S_1 + 2.70S_2 = \text{Maximum}$
2. $4.00S_1 + 3.00S_2 \geq 3.20 \leq 4.00$	6. $S_1 \geq 0$
3. $5.50S_1 + 7.80S_2 \geq 7.00 \leq 7.80$	7. $S_2 \geq 0$
4. $22.00S_1 + 30.00S_2 \geq 27.00 \leq 30.00$	

Each combination of two of the above inequations is solved simultaneously as linear equations.[1] If there were three skirt classifications considered, each combination of three inequations would be solved simultaneously as equations, etc. The values obtained for each skirt classification from each solution are substituted back into inequations 1 through 5 to find a total value for each factor. In order to determine the optimal solution, all that do not fall within the values listed on the right hand side of the inequations are eliminated from consideration.

[1] For example, equations 1–2 would be solved as follows:

$$.45S_1 + .65S_2 = .60$$
$$4.00S_1 + 3.00S_2 = 3.20$$

with the solution resulting in $S_1 = .224$ and $S_2 = .768$. This, by coincidence, is the optimal solution.

After eliminating all the combined solutions that do not satisfy all the constraints, we then look for the solution that satisfies all constraints and will yield the highest gross margin. All solutions with factors that fall outside the boundaries are italicized in Table 4. As can be seen, the values computed from equation 1–2 yielding an average gross margin of $2.41 are the optimal solution.

All other values, except for those of equations 2–3, fall outside the boundary. For example, equation number six yields a gross margin of 2.49, but one of the tabulations is outisde of our boundary limits. In this table all figures listed in italics represent figures outside our boundary limits.

The S_1 and S_2 values for equation 1–2 are converted into percentages of 22.6 percent and 77.4 percent respectively. These percentages are applied to the planned sales for the season, in this case $100,000. Thus the opti-

TABLE 4.

Solutions for Combined Equations

Equations	*Values* S_1	S_2	*Equation 1*	*Equation 2*	*Equation 3*	*Equation 4*	*Average Gross Margin Per Unit**
1-2	.224	.768	$.60	3.20	7.30	28.00	$2.41
1-3	−2.000	2.308	.60	—	7.00	—	—
1-4	− .563	1.313	.60	—	—	27.00	—
1-6	0	.923	.60	*2.77*	7.20	27.70	*2.49*
1-7	1.333	0	.60	*5.32*	7.30	29.30	*2.00*
2-3	.269	.708	.58	3.20	7.00	27.20	2.32
2-4	.278	.697	.58	3.20	*6.97*	27.00	2.30
2-6	0	1.067	*.69*	3.20	*8.32*	*32.00*	*2.88*
2-7	.800	0	.36	3.20	*4.40*	*17.60*	*1.20*
3-4	.091	.833	.58	*2.86*	7.00	27.00	*2.39*
3-6	0	.897	.58	*2.69*	7.00	*26.90*	*2.42*
3-7	1.272	0	.57	*5.10*	7.00	28.00	*3.43*
4-6	0	.900	.59	*2.70*	7.02	27.00	*2.43*
4-7	1.227	0	.55	*4.90*	*6.75*	27.00	*1.84*

*All figures listed in italics are outside our boundary limits. That is why the figure $2.41 is considered the largest gross margin per unit.

TABLE 4(A).

Optimal Solution Converted to Total Units Based on $100,00 Planned Sales

	$4.00 Skirt	*$7.00 Skirt*
Value from equation 1–2	.224	.768
Proportional percent	22.6%	77.4%
Proportional sales	$22,600	$77,400
Number of units order	5,650	11,057
Gross margin	(for both skirts)	$38,328.90

mum sales that would maximize gross margin for both skirts would be $22,600 for the $4.00 skirt and $77,400 for the $7.00 skirt. These sales are converted to 5,650 and 11,057 units respectively with a resulting total gross margin of $38,328.90.

No other combination of $4.00 and $7.00 skirts within the constraints set up would yield a greater gross margin.

CONCLUSION

At first reading, this approach to decision making might seem ponderous and complicated. In reality, the theory and implementation are fairly simple. The data to be used for the solution are usually easy to obtain and the availability of a computer makes the large number of computations involved in expanded applications of the linear programming model a routine matter.

Analyses of this nature can be used for any period of time desired, and, in conjunction with the open-to-buy, are useful in developing merchandising plans as the season progresses.

The advantages of this mathematical approach to decision-making over empirical judgments are considerable:

1. The decision maker is required to approach the problem in an orderly, logical manner, and remove all extraneous factors from consideration.
2. The ultimate goal in the problem is the maximization of profit, which is the ultimate goal of any business endeavor.
3. The merchandising policies of the department are more clearly defined, and help to pinpoint those merchandise lines that contribute most to the department's merchandising image with the greatest profit.

In closing, this scientific approach to solving retailing problems in no way impinges upon the artistic aspects of merchandising; taste and fashion sense are still required in selecting the best sellers within each price range. The day-to-day operational problems within each department would still have to be solved without recourse to mathematics. However, the scientific approach is most useful in reducing the number of decisions to be made, and allows the merchant to concentrate on those problems that require his most creative attention.

QUESTIONS

1. How has the computer brought about interest in mathematical decision making?
2. Without the aid of linear programming, how would the buyer ordinarily solve this problem?

20

Full Cycle for Self-Service?

William J. Reagan

Managements of most stores have faced and continue to face unremitting pressures to adopt increasing degrees of self-service or impersonal selling. These pressures may be classified into three types:

1) Self-service orientations of ancillary interests
2) Expectations and preferences of customers
3) Increased competition of self-service stores

Self-Service Orientations of Ancillary Interests

Manufacturers of display fixtures, lighting equipment, cash-register equipment, packaging materials, and most consumer commodities have accepted the concept of impersonal selling and have designed their products accordingly. Advertising agencies and the publishers of trade periodicals have continuously pointed out the impact of advertising in pre-selling goods and the processes of self-service techniques.

As a consequence, fixtures have been designed emphasizing the cubic dimensions, compartmentalization, and flexibility necessary to implement self-service. Cash-register systems have been devised to simplify the payment procedure for both charging and cash-paying customers. Packaging manufacturers have designed their services to maximize the promotional and protective benefits of packaging and to minimize retail repackaging requirements and customer pilferage. Product manufacturers themselves have designed their products to capitalize upon these changing conditions.

These efforts to help direct the retailing process are independently conceived and promoted. Their advantages must be sold to retailers who decide what elements will be co-ordinated in their store systems.

Expectations and Preferences of Customers

Rising standards of living and changing living patterns have helped to change the attitudes with which consumers regard goods. One scholar has advanced five criteria as means to determine the aggregate-characteristics profile of any goods which changes over time. They are: (1) the rate at which

Reprinted from *Journal of Marketing* ,Vol. 25, No. 4. April 1961, American Marketing Association, pp. 15–21.

a product is purchased and consumed; (2) the gross margin of the product; (3) an adjustment factor representing the amount of services applied to goods to meet needs of consumers; (4) time of consumption during which the product gives up the utility desired; and (5) searching time or the measure of average time and distance from the retail store.[1]

Mere listing of these criteria is sufficient to make it clear that the mass-characteristics profile for each product changes through time. The general trend in the United States has probably been to modify luxury and "near-luxury" goods in the direction of semi-necessity and necessity classifications.

This ungrading in consumption patterns has altered the set of product characteristics for each product in consumers' minds. Distribution channels and store-merchandising practices have also changed in the attempt to distribute goods more economically. Self-service has become an important way to retail goods, especially those with a relatively high replacement rate, and relatively low values for gross margin, adjustment, time of consumption, and searching time.

Merchandise made for mass market is typically widely advertised and highly standardized. It is designed for customers who want utility, dependable performance, and acceptable or "modern" styling. Much of the merchandise in the nondurable, repetitively purchased category can often be sold by the effective display, full accessibility, and explanation techniques of the well-integrated impersonal selling program. Even much of the durable goods designed for the mass market requires little personal sales assistance beyond competent credit-extension clerks when the goods have been largely pre-sold and are well-presented for self-service appraisal. Indeed, William H. Whyte, Jr., asserts that the consumer, by selling himself on "big-ticket" items has earned a price cut, and that ". . . whether manufacturers like it or not, he is going to get it."[2]

Increased customer familiarity with goods of all descriptions has tended to make a widening variety of goods eligible for self-service attention. Thus, in stores aiming at the mass markets, traditional store merchandise assortments have been reoriented in response to the more compelling classification criterion of "self-service salability." Customers support this change of assortment character whenever they feel that a better combination of convenience, other services, and price are offered.

Modern supermarkets, drug stores, and discount department stores have proved that the range of items that customers consider "complementary in purchase" is far wider than assortments that are "complementary in use."[3] By maintaining the traditional assortment emphasis upon merchandise

[1] Leo Aspinwall, "The Characteristics of Goods and Parallel Systems Theories," in *Managerial Marketing: Perspectives and Viewpoints*, Eugene J. Kelley and William Lazer, editors (Homewood, Illinois: Richard D. Irwin, Inc., 1958), pp. 437–41.

[2] William H. Whyte, Jr., *The Organization Man* (Garden City, New York: Doubleday and Company, Inc., 1956), pp. 348–49, footnote.

[3] F. E. Balderston, "Assortment Choice in Wholesale and Retail Marketing," *Journal of Marketing*, 21 (October, 1956), 175–83.

items that are complementary in use, some stores deny themselves whatever advantages are inherent in assortments that are complementary in purchase and capable of being sold on a more impersonal basis. In some large department and departmentized specialty stores, departmental inter-selling is only a partial remedy to overcome the big inconvenience to consumers of too frequent financial accountings. These transactions bear the correlative risk of psychologically and physically tiring the customer by: (1) repetitively reminding her that she is spending money, (2) loading her with bulky packages unless she requests delivery, and (3) distracting her from concentration upon solving the problems of her household and family.

To a considerable extent, consumers act as "pollinizing agents" in transferring their preferences from one store to another. What they find and like in one retail store they want to find in other stores. Consumers in practically all economic groups have been exposed to self-service buying in supermarkets. They have taken with them some of the characteristics of self-service buying when patronizing other stores, such as increased initiative in finding items wanted, greater willingness to read signs and labels, and closer merchandise inspection. Most stores have responded to such aggressive tactics by evolving toward more open accessible displays, toward more specification-differentiated fixturing, toward more complete merchandise signing, etc.

Increased Competition of Self-Service Stores

The trend toward increased impersonalization in retailing has received considerable impetus from the apparent successes of those stores which have adopted self-service. Indeed, the trend toward the adoption of self-service borders on the revolutionary.

In 1948, 75 percent of grocery-store volume was clerk-serviced, whereas in 1958 some 84 percent was done on a self-service basis.[4] The 1959 Directory of Drug Chains showed over 60 percent of chain drug stores in the United States to be operated with some form of self-service, compared to 55 percent in the 1958 Directory and 49 percent in 1957.[5] Nearly two-thirds of new chain drug stores opened since 1954 have been self-service outlets equipped with checkout lanes.[6] Experience in variety stores is similar with all the major chains engaged in conversion to self-service programs.

Limited-service department and specialty stores of all types have also embraced self-service. This includes the "Quick Service" program of Sears, Roebuck and Company and the practices of most latter-day "discount" or "progressive" department stores. Hardware, stationery, toy, and other type stores have also engaged in self-service to an increasing degree.

Stores retaining personal clerk service and the traditional store layout,

[4] *25th Annual Nielsen Review of Retail Grocery Store Trends*, 1959, p. 15.
[5] *Chain Store Age*, Vol. 34 (December, 1958), p. 10.
[6] *25th Annual Review of Retail Drug and Proprietary Store Trends*, 1959, p. 18.

fixturing, display, etc., thus have been faced with an aggressive enterprise differentiation form of competition in self-service. In addition to this competition in service, price competition has been accentuated.

The service policy of most self-service stores is based upon providing only competitively desirable or necessary services above the common service of assortment assembly. When additional services such as credit or delivery are added, the attempt is usually made to offset these costs by charging for them as directly as is competitively possible. Lower personal selling costs engendered by self-service enables them to enhance an already favorable price spread when compared with stores committed to absorbing more of the traditional retailing amenities. As a result, clerk-service stores are faced with increasing price competition for the merchandise items that both types of stores carry and perhaps increasing difficulty in retaining exclusive lines.[7]

REASONS FOR PREFERRING PERSONALIZED SERVICE

Against the mounting pressure from these fronts, some store managements hesitate to adopt self-service where possible for the following reasons:

1) Honest doubts that self-service is wanted or that it can reduce expenses
2) Inability of self-service to satisfy all customers
3) Difficulties of applying self-service to all merchandise items
4) Possible aversion to competitive practices that self-service evokes
5) Other reasons for resistance to self-service

Doubts That Self-Service Is Wanted or Able to Reduce Expenses

Most store managements probably recognize that, for the great bulk of consumer goods, the range of necessary selling service has shifted noticeably on the continuum from personalized service toward more impersonal service or self-service. Nevertheless, the managements of many prestige department and departmentalized specialty stores, the remaining strong bastion of individual selling attention, believe that more lasting and profitable enterprise differentiation can be achieved by fighting the impersonalization of retailing which supermarkets have nearly made their trademark.

With the view that customers want more intimate personal relationships with stores, some take the position that better and more personal salesmanship is needed, not the abolition of it. These managements tend to accept only peripheral features of impersonal selling programs and consciously work to assimilate as much of the cost-reduction features as possible without compromising the character of their full and individualized services.

Other managements regard self-service more favorably but doubt that it

[7] Victor Lebow, "The Crisis in Retailing," *Journal of Retailing*, Vol. 33 (Spring, 1957), pp. 17–26, 55.

can substantially reduce costs in their operations. They agree that perhaps staple stock will sell, but fear that the newer styles, "ensemble," and impulse purchases will not; that customers will consistently buy the lowest-priced goods; that pilferage will increase; that salespeople will have to be replaced by equally expensive stockpeople.

Cost comparisons with self-service operations usually begin with a direct item-for-item examination of comparative selling costs. The next step may be realization that other costs, such as training, pilferage, returned goods, credit, and delivery may also be affected. Conjecture as to the relative change that self-service might induce in these expenses is further complicated by the possibility of changing sales levels.

Perhaps not widely recognized yet is the notion that regrouping of departments according to relative degrees of item self-serviceability may contribute to increased economies through a larger average departmental scale of operation. That is, departmentalization by function rather than by merchandise purpose may permit an increase in the number of items serviced by the same or only slightly increased departmental input effort.

Something like this seems to have taken place in food distribution where the number of items carried in the average modern supermarket has grown from about 1,000 items in 1933 to about 6,000 items in 1956 and where average sales per store in 1934 were $42,000 compared to $893,000 in 1956.[8] According to the same authority, food chains have reduced their margins from $22\frac{1}{2}$ percent to 18 percent on the sales dollar in the 21 years prior to 1957 ". . . because of self-service innovations and the development of modern supermarkets where increased volume has made practical the introduction of time- and cost-saving machinery."[9] It was during this period also that meats and produce became "undepartmentized" from the customer's viewpoint and joined the swelling of both food and non-food items in being available on a self-service basis.

Inability of Self-Service to Satisfy All Customers

Competition and the drive to be successful have encouraged retailers to strive for yearly increases in sales and profits. To achieve these increases, many clerk-service stores have expanded beyond the prestige market that they were orginally designed to serve and now straddle two markets: the prestige or "class" market, and the volume or "mass" market. In this position, they need to stock and sell enough goods in the mass market to reach their rising break-even points, and yet carry the proper merchandise and personalized services to retain the exclusive atmosphere acceptable to the class market.

[8] National Association of Food Chains, *Progress in Food Distribution*, a statement by John A. Logan, President, National Association of Food Chains, to the Consumers Study Subcommittee of the Committee on Agriculture, House of Representatives, May 8, 1957, pp. 15, 24.

[9] Same reference as footnote 10.

Many full-service managements recognize that self-service for the mass market and personal sales service for the prestige market would be desirable. However, they resist changing their operational set-ups to provide sales service compatible to the merchandise and customer needs of both markets. Having spent thousands of dollars and many years in the patient development of full-service reputations, most managements hesitate to jeopardize these reputations with innovations that are associated with limited-service stores.

Difficulties of Applying Self-Service to All Merchandise Items

Supermarkets are able to apply self-service exclusively to all items in their assortments. This is because the items sold are typically in the relatively scrutable, repetitively purchased, lower-priced category. Much of the merchandise sold in department and specialty stores has opposite characteristics. In addition, some merchandise has a large number of variable specifications such as styles, sizes, colors, or price lines which make full exposure of goods for customer accessibility difficult.

For example, in a recent year one manufacturer of men's shirts made 42 different collar-and-cuff styles in the white shirt alone. The company made 51 different collar styles and sleeve-length combinations. This combination of collar styles and sizes alone made a total of more than 2,000 different shirt specifications. In addition to this basic white-shirt stock, other shirts were made in different fabrics, stripes, patterns, and solid colors. Most men's furnishings departments and stores carry selections from several different manufacturers' lines and often one under their own label. Clearly it would be uneconomical, if not impossible, to display in open arrangement such a wide variety of shirts. Stores emphasizing wide selections, the new or novel in merchandise, and custom-fitting items have additional problems in the implementation of self-service.

Possible Aversion to Competitive Practices That Self-Service Evokes

It is probable that the continued impersonalization of selling in retail stores and especially supermarkets has contributed to a weakening in customers' institutional loyalty. Part of the strong patronage accorded trading stamps, premium plans, etc. may be explained in the transference of customer loyalty from the retail institution *per se* to the merchandising attraction or appendage that accompanies purchase of goods.

In lieu of traditional store services, supermarkets have tended to compete by offering differential trading-stamp plans, premium offers, coupon plans, lotteries, and other variations for which external product differentiation has been suggested as a classification.[10] Whether many store managements that resist impersonal selling do so partly in order to protect themselves from

[10] E. T. Grether, "External Product and Enterprise Differentiation and Consumer Behavior," *Consumer Behavior and Motivation*, Robert H. Cole, editor (Urbana, Illinois: Bureau of Economic and Business Research, The University of Illinois, 1955).

the possibility of engaging in this kind of competition is doubtful. It is also questionable whether they fully appreciate the magnitude of the market that they are losing to trading stamp and premium redemption plans. In some cases at least it is conceivable that neither the stamp-dispensing retailer nor the consumer is paying for the stamp operation but that would-be retailers of premium merchandise are supporting it by allowing their normal markons to be given away.

Other Reasons for Resistance to Self-Service

Several other reasons support those managements which prefer clerk service. In some cases, stores have experimented with self-service and received adverse results. Although the quality of these experiments has varied widely, adequate tests to provide "before" and "after" comparative results have been nearly impossible to design. Large, multi-unit chains like Sears have an advantage in this respect in that they can judge an innovation in well-designed test stores before applying it to all. According to a Sears official, self-service was initially installed in "about 125" stores in 1953 to determine its effectiveness.[11]

In other cases, managements may be unusually sensitive to the feelings or preferences of salespeople who naturally fear the inroads of impersonal selling upon their livelihoods. This paternalism for their employees in some cases may be an influence combining with others to make self-service less desirable. In still other cases, store managements committed to the personal selling approach prefer to wait and see how effective their suburban department or specialty stores are before submitting to further degrees of self-service. In these newer suburban stores, fixtures incorporating full exposure and open accessibility of goods have been widely used. The commonly experienced peaking of sales in many branch stores might encourage further experimentation with impersonal selling in time.

INCREASED IMPERSONALITY IN RETAILING

Despite these very real objections and difficulties in accepting further degrees of self-service, evidence of increased acceptance in full-service stores is not hard to find. Under a host of modified titles, such as "self-selection," "selective open selling, or SOS," "simplified selling," "open selling," "display merchandising," self-service or impersonal selling is being applied to ever more heterogeneous assortments.

Increasing degrees of self-selection are employed in many departments of these stores, such as notions, stationery, housewares, records, drugs and

[11] Personal letter from G. R. Berger, Manager, Research and Development Division, Sears, Roebuck and Company, Chicago, Illinois, May 15, 1957.

cosmetics, toys, and others. Indeed, some full-service department stores have successfully tried the supermarket version of self-service in such departments as toys, greeting card and trimming supplies, and books at peak-selling periods such as Christmas. Macy's in New York uses it for stationery and greeting cards, books, garden supplies, hardware and paints on a regular basis.

Other influences affecting the impersonality trend should be mentioned. The increased encouragement that customers receive to use automatic vending machines, mail-order catalogs and Christmas supplements, newspaper order coupons, and telephone ordering facilities is presumably based on the interpretation that more customers might want this more impersonal service. It is also quite possible that today's face-to-face personal selling in stores lacks some of the warmth or genuine concern that it possessed in days when "regular customers" were more common.

Realization that self-service in full-service stores need not and cannot parallel exactly the development in supermarkets has caused the institution of modified checkout systems in some cases. This modified checkout system offers customers the option of buying goods either through conveniently located cashier checkout stations or through salespeople. There are some control problems in this dual approach. However, offering customers the option of sales service or self-service might be considered the addition of another service. Moreover, it sets up a choice situation in which customers can decide the issue so well phrased in *The Lonely Crowd:* ". . . how much the slow progress toward automation in the tertiary trades is due to . . . consumer demand to buy personalization along with a product, and how much to the needs of the work force itself to personalize . . . whether the customer asks for it or not."[12]

THE SOURCE OF RETAIL INNOVATIONS

Since self-service originated in food retailing, it is easy to understand why full-service managements emphasizing personal sales attention might consider it dubiously. Most of these managements regard it as antithetical to their own more personalized services. This is the customary reception accorded a marketing innovation that has been introduced and successful at the opposite-service level.

Retailing innovations have usually entered the marketplace from two levels: (1) the prestige or full-service level where new conceptions of service are usually emphasized, and (2) the minimum service level where new cost-cutting concepts yielding ultimate price benefits to customers are emphasized. After suitable test periods, the dynamics of enterprise differentiation compel tests on other retail-service levels. Thus, credit plans were introduced on the

[12] David Riesman, Nathan Glazer, and Reuel Denney, *The Lonely Crowd* (Garden City, New York: Doubleday and Company, Inc., 1950), pp. 310–11.

upper-service levels, proved acceptable to growing numbers of consumers, and eventually were added to the service components of many limited-service stores. Just as the stronger full-service stores hesitate to accept self-service which they consider to be a service of an unwanted nature, limited-service stores hesitate to accept innovations that they consider to be of a service character. The J. C. Penney Company, for instance, has just in recent years been converting its stores to credit.

Self-service gained its acceptance as a price-reducing innovation. It is now in the "dressing-up" or adaptive stage where variations on the basic theme are being devised to make it more suitable for appropriate merchandise in stores on higher-service levels. Diversity in retail service patterns will surely continue. Some merchandise items may always need personalized sales attention and it is to be hoped that some stores will continue to serve this need.

It seems clear, however, that the range of selling service applied to consumer goods generally has shifted perceptibly in the direction of increased impersonality. Store managements should continue to be alert to the significance of this shift.

QUESTIONS

1. What are the major objections of customers to self-service?
2. What types of goods lend themselves to self-service selling?
3. Why has self-service increased in retailing?

21

The "One-Price" System—Fact or Fiction?

Stanley C. Hollander

One of our more cherished beliefs holds that American retailing is characterized by almost universal adherence to a one-price policy. As generally used, the phrase "one-price system" sums up the feeling that retail sales in this country are made in stores that (1) have abolished haggling and bargaining, charging all customers, at any one time, the same price for the same merchandise; (2) are open to any and all retail shoppers; and (3) observe the fixed prices placed by manufacturers upon "fair-traded" merchandise.

Reprinted from Journal of Retailing, Vol. 31, No. 3, Fall 1955, pp. 127–44.

The consumer who speaks of "getting a discount," or of "getting it wholesale," usually means that a purchase has been made under conditions deviating from one or more of these beliefs—and we will use the same general meaning here. "Discount sales" are those made contrary to one or more of the above three postulates.

Typical of our cherished belief in the "one-price" system are two quotations from speeches delivered at American Economic Association meetings, one in 1915 and the other in 1950. R. K. Bowker, in discussing price maintenance, said, "A. T. Stewart, pioneer in the department store business . . . did the community the great service of replacing with fixed retail price the old system of bargaining and haggling which wasted the time of lady shoppers and salespeople when I was a boy."[1] Senator Ralph E. Flanders, in discussing "How Top Executive Decisions Are Made," described how, many years ago, "John Wanamaker started the practice of marking the price clearly on all the goods in his store. This did away with dickering between customer and salesman. . . . Customer satisfaction soon showed in a preference for dealing at Wanamaker's, and this preference animated a general movement towards plain and definite pricing."[2]

More important than speeches, however, are the ways in which the belief in a one-price system has influenced our actions. For example, in retail education, with two exceptions,[3] we have tended to avoid any real discussion of whether bargaining or some other form of price discrimination may prove advantageous for the storekeeper. Certainly, as a general rule, we do not discuss how or when to bargain or discriminate.

Legislative Action

A belief in the one-price system as both the norm and the goal of the retail economy has characterized many of the agencies through which business is subjected to social control. Among the manifestations of this belief, we can find a vast body of legislation, including especially resale price maintenance laws, designed to show up the one-price system. We can also find many judicial rulings expressing the same normative view. In one important case, for example, the presiding justice ruled that a considerable body of evidence indicating widespread price-cutting of electrical appliance prices in the New York market did not indicate a breakdown of resale price maintenance except among "those favored groups having access to discount houses."[4]

[1] R. K. Bowker, "Price Maintenance—Discussion," *American Economic Review,* March 1916, p. 208.

[2] Senator Ralph E. Flanders, "How Top Executive Decisions Are Made," *American Economic Review* (Supplement), May 1951, p. 96.

[3] The two exceptions are John W. Wingate and Elmer O. Schaller, *Techniques of Retail Merchandising* (Englewood Cliffs, N.J.: Prentice-Hall, Inc., 1952), pp. 184–85; and Clarence Henry McGregor, *Retail Management Problems* (Homewood, Ill.: Richard D. Irwin Co., 1953), pp. 92–94.

[4] Decision, *General Electric Company* v. *R. H. Macy & Co., Inc.,* New York Supreme Court, New York County, No. 5881 (1950).

The assumption that the "average" or "normal" New York City consumer did not have access to discount purchases clearly underlay the decisions in this case. Similarly, while the Better Business Bureaus and other co-operative groups for business self-regulation tend to avoid any official position on discount selling, we sometimes encounter statements such as the following: "Because of a very strong, very active Better Business Bureau in Dallas, which polices and guards the rights of newspaper, radio and television advertisers, the discount houses are primarily underground."[5] Many forms of discounting have flourished because of strong economic motivations, in spite of a vast congerie of administrative, legislative, and judicial restrictions.

Danger of Unrealistic Views of the One-Price System

Although businessmen are likely to have more realistic views of discounting than educators or jurists, their judgment also can be clouded by faulty perception of the deviations from the one-price system. There is a tendency, for example, to consider present-day discount selling of appliances and furniture as a shocking aberration from normal business practice. Some businessmen seem to agree with the *Life* reporter who wrote recently, "Before World War II, there were only a handful of discount houses in the U.S."[6] This belief—that discount selling is a sudden and striking innovation of the postwar economy—may trap a merchant in one of two ways.

If the merchant sees such competition as new, and perhaps transitory, he may feel capable of adjusting to it—*and* controlling it—by adopting utterly ineffective measures. Many appliance retailers and their local associations have acted as though discount selling could be curbed through advertising campaigns directed at consumers, through pledges of allegiance to the "one-price system," through campaigns for serial number registration, and other such devices. Such approaches were used widely in an equally futile attempt to curb discounting before the war. In view of the strong economic motives for discount selling, there can be no thought of controlling it by mild and easy measures (if, indeed, it can or should be curbed at all). Proof of the great difficulty of stopping discount selling may be seen in the recent history of the Magnavox Company, manufacturers of radio and television receivers. In July 1953, this firm, which enjoys a considerable reputation in the trade for its vigorous price maintenance efforts, advertised widely, "Why You Can't Buy a Magnavox at a Discount."[7] Yet by August 1954 the company felt that the price situation had deteriorated to a point requiring the cancellation of all existing dealer franchises, subject to a highly selective renewal policy.

[5] Bobbye L. Hughes, "Dallas Merchants Hit by Discount Operators," *Retailing Daily*, April 2, 1953, p. 26.

[6] Herbert Brean, "Discount Houses Stir Up a $5 Billion Fuss," *Life*, August 9, 1954, p. 52.

[7] See, for example, *Time*, July 20, 1953, p. 10.

The other danger is that discount selling, if not viewed in perspective, may be credited with undue importance. One example of such overemphasis is the speech of Louis Goldblatt, in which discounting is viewed as a horrible menace, "taking American Business back to the Dark Ages of Merchandising."[8]

Another example may be found in a recent report of the National Distribution Panel, which estimated discount sales at over $25 billion annually, and rising. Though the panel did not define the term "discount sales," the general nature of the report seems to indicate that the reference was to sales by rather irregular retailers, such as discount houses, differing in important ways from "regular" or "normal" retailers. There were frequent references to "discount channels," "certain types of competitors," and "how we will meet such competition."[9] Sales of over $25 billion (about as much as total United States purchases of appliances and automobiles in 1953, or about 40 percent of all nonfood purchases) by unconventional outlets would indeed indicate a dire outlook for retailing as we know it. The department store, for one, would appear in great peril.

How "Discounting" Threats Have Been Overestimated

In actuality, there is no need for such alarm. A $25 billion figure for discount sales may be quite reasonable, but only if we accept the broad definition of such sales used by the present writer: "all sales deviating from one or more of the three postulates of the one-price system." Such a definition, for example, embraces practically all automobile sales, since almost every dealer will bargain, in normal times, over trade-in allowances and thus discriminate between customers. Defining discounting in this way is useful in measuring the extent to which we, as a nation, do or do not have a one-price system. It is not useful in measuring the threat to "regular" established dealers. Bargaining over trade-in allowances is not a threat to the conventional automobile dealer; it is the convention of his trade.

If, continuing the automobile example, we consider only the "bootleg" or "used-new car" dealer (that is, the unfranchised dealers) as representative of discount activity, which seems to be what the National Distribution Panel has done, we come up with a different answer. Discount selling, quantitatively, becomes rather unimportant. The "bootleg" dealer may be significant as a nuisance to the franchised dealer, or as an outlet for the franchised man's surplus cars, or as a reminder to the consumer to bargain sharply. But simple observation indicates that bootleg dealers are moving only a small fraction of the nation's total automotive production.

Similarly, while there have been many "discount houses" (in the original

[8] Speech, Louis Goldblatt (Goldblatt's, Inc.), Chicago Merchandising Executives Club, as summarized in *Advertising Age*, September 27, 1954, p. 37.

[9] National Distribution Panel, *Discount Selling Report* (Washington, D.C.: Domestic Distribution Department, Chamber of Commerce of the United States, 1954), p. 4.

sense of secluded shops to which admission could be had only upon presentation of introductory cards) such stores have been the source of only a small portion of all discount purchases. Whether one goes to Tallman's 1938 study of Boston consumers or to Heidingsfield's 1951 study of Philadelphia families,[10] one finds the same answer: most discount buyers receive their discounts from "conventional" or "regular" retailers and wholesalers. A recent study[11] of the Syracuse, New York, appliance market implies much the same thing. It reports two thirds of all sales of major appliances as having been made "with some price inducement," but it also indicates that regular, stock-carrying dealers were responsible for the bulk of all sales. A study of 1952–1953 appliance purchases in the Chicago metropolitan area, long considered a center of discounting, revealed much the same condition. Only between 9 and 10 percent of all the purchases studied were made by such price-conscious, semiself-service retailers as Sears, Roebuck and Polk Brothers.[12]

Discounting Likely to Persist

The lesson of our price history seems to be that deviations from the one-price system have been important elements in the economy, in the past as well as today, and that such deviations are likely to persist. These have included rather consistent selling of appliances and hard lines at less than list prices, alongside of and as a part of conventional retailing. But these elements do not involve a fatal threat to conventional retailers who are willing to operate efficiently, offer desired customer services, and price realistically.

The threat may be more dangerous to retailers unwilling to make such adjustments. The persistence of discounting and the uneven enforcement of supposedly maintained prices has imposed a special handicap upon law-abiding retailers, and perhaps history does prove that they should have been more vigorous in opposing resale price maintenance. Recent department store reactions to discount selling seem to indicate that a more realistic view is prevailing.

PART II

A brief review of persistent deviations from the one-price system may be helpful in pointing up some of these views.

Some consumer discounts are obtained in "regular" retail establish-

[10] Gerald B. Tallman, "When Consumers Buy at 'Wholesale'," *Harvard Business Review*, Spring 1939; Myron S. Heidingsfield, "The Penetration of Discount Buying Among Philadelphia Families," *Economics and Business Bulletin of Temple University*, December 1951.

[11] Alfred W. Swinyard, *Metropolitan Syracuse Appliance Dealer Survey* (Business Research Center of Syracuse University, in co-operation with Collegiate Associates for Market Measurement, 1954).

[12] "Polk Brothers—Discount House or Supermarket?" *Advertising Age*, November 1, 1954, p. 56.

ments, that is, sellers openly and ostensibly carrying on a retail business with all comers, while other discounts result from transactions in places supposedly closed to the retail customer. The discounts may result from bargaining and haggling, they may be offered on a systematic basis, or there may be some rather individualistic price discrimination without particular system. The deviations from the "one-price system" in particular lines may have become so widespread that they are accepted as the conventional way of doing business, or they may be considered abnormalities. But they add up to a rather major exception to the commonly accepted view of the American retail economy. Most of the illustrations of these deviations cited below have been taken from prewar sources, as evidence of the extent to which these practices have some considerable history. However, no perceptive retailer should have difficulty in locating modern counterparts.[13]

Individualistic Discrimination in Conventional Retail Institutions

If we look at "regular" retail sellers, we will find that some stores do not meet the one-price test of charging all customers the same price at the same time, because of discriminations determined on an individual basis. As Appel has pointed out, these include stores in which bargaining and haggling are tolerated or even encouraged. Some such stores are located at the extremes of the retail social scale; dealers in rare books and *objets d'art*, on one hand, and secondhand dealers on the other. Appel adds, "There remains . . . a small fringe of shops of this type, haggling or 'two-price' stores either in some swanky shops in large cities, or in low-grade stores."[14]

More intermediate are the New York hat shops reported using the quoted price "as the point of departure for bargaining"; the furniture stores in which the customers are passed along from turnover man to turnover man and "forced to haggle for their purchases as their grandfathers did"; the independent gasoline stations willing to charge favored customers a few cents less than posted prices; and the neighborhood liquor dealers willing to make rather similar proportionate reductions under like conditions.[15]

The extent to which bargaining elements are, and have been, involved in automobile sales is too well known to require documentation. Bargaining may also center around other concessions, rather than focus upon the base price itself. The Wingate and Schaller discussion of bargaining cited above,

[13] An excellent summary of contemporary manifestations appeared in the E. B. Weiss series, "The 'Off-List' Revolution," *Advertising Age*, August 16, 23, 30, and September 6, 1954.

[14] Joseph H. Appel, *Growing up with Advertising* (New York: The Business Course, 1940), p. 55.

[15] Irene Till, "The Fiction of the Quoted Price," *Law and Contemporary Problems*, June 1937, p. 368; A. F. Williams, "The Problems of the Furniture Retailer," *Harvard Business Review*, July 1930, p. 463; Edmund F. Learned, "Pricing of Gasoline, A Case Study," *Harvard Business Review*, November 1948, p. 742; "Little Fellow Breaks His Pet Law, and Gets Away with It," *Retailing* (Executive Edition), January 24, 1938, p. 3.

for example, looks particularly at the problem of when to provide the obdurate customer with free alteration services.

Parallel in Professional Services

A somewhat similar example of individualistic price discrimination may be found in the marketing of professional services. In fact, physicians and attorneys regard the practice of tailoring fees to the client's "ability to pay" as one of the hallmarks of their high professional development. It is interesting to speculate, although the present writer has no direct information on the subject, on the extent to which various types of craftsmen, journeymen, and repairmen practice a somewhat similar individual price discrimination in retailing their services. In a sense, the true action sale (used to some extent in retail selling, although of course much more common in wholesale transaction) is a pure example of individual discrimination, since each price is determined separately.

Conventional Discrimination in Conventional Retail Institutions

In spite of all the exceptions, however, bargaining over price appears to be the exception rather than the rule in most retail transactions. When conventional retailers discriminate between customers, they usually do so on some systematic basis.

In fact, it is sometimes assumed that the large store cannot discriminate at all unless some way is found to routinize its discounts. Actually, this is not true. Instances in whch department store people have taken a sudden markdown to close the sale of an expensive fur coat, carpet, piece of furniture, or appliance are not unknown. The general merchandise manager of one large appliance and sporting goods chain has been quoted testifying as follows, "Mr. Smith drew chuckles when he said a chain doesn't expect to get $299 when it advertises a [television] set for that price. He said they are prepared to sell it lower than the advertised price."[16]

The whole discounting process is made easier, however, when salespeople or billing clerks can tell, almost automatically, who is and who is not entitled to the discount. Highly systematic methods of discrimination meet this test. Some such discounts have become so widespread that they are regarded as the conventional, or normal, way of doing business. These include discounts based upon age, sex, or patronage status. Children's rates, lower than those for adults, are frequently offered in the sale of transportation, amusement, and other services. (Minnesota movie operators, in fact, quote three rates: children, junior, and adult.) "Ladies' Days" at ball parks are examples of discounts based upon sex. Many magazines offer new subscribers especially low subscription rates. On the other hand, some stores conduct

[16] "Tells Monarch-Saphin Company Hearing of Davega Prices," *Retailing Daily,* April 27, 1953, p. 58.

"private sales," restricted to old customers, although these usually can be penetrated by new buyers. All of these practices have been, and are, so customary that only a minute's reflection is required to realize that all are deviations from a one-price policy.

Retail Employee Discounts

Less conventional, but widespread, are discounts based upon the employment status of the shopper. The discount to store employees is a very common practice in department and dry goods stores, as well as in many other retail institutions. Chute,[17] studying a group of Ohio department and dry goods stores in 1932, reported that all but one of the stores studied granted such discounts. In many cases, the employee's discount is available to relatives and friends of employees, and to former employees. Many stores place rigid curbs on the use of the discount, but others are fairly lax about the matter. One drug chain was reported, during the 1920's, as being concerned if any employee's discount purchases were too small. Since the chain's employee prices could not be matched elsewhere, failure to take advantage of the discount was considered prima-facie evidence of pilferage.[18]

Professional Discounts

Outsiders often qualify for discounts because of their profession, although there are grounds for believing that such professional discounts were more common before the war than they are today. Even so stanch an advocate of the one-price system as John Wanamaker gave, at least as late as 1899, a 10 percent discount to ministers, a 6 percent discount to dressmakers, and even a special discount "to customers who set themselves up as 'purchasing agents' for friends."[19] A company history, issued in 1922, commented with some amazement that R. H. Macy and Company gave special discounts only to its own employees and not to teachers, clergymen, professional shoppers, and others.[20]

During the late 1930's and early 1940's, the National Retail Furniture Association was active in a campaign for the elimination of such professional discounts. The manager of the association's eastern office wrote, on November 17, 1941, to a friend engaged in similar work in Philadelphia, reporting that several leading specialty shops were seriously considering dropping their discounts, but that the major department stores "have

[17] A. Hamilton Chute, *Employee Discounts and Vacations in Ohio Department and Dry Goods Stores* (Columbus: Bureau of Business Research, The Ohio State University, 1932), p. 51.

[18] Doris J. Mirrieless, "Keeping Employee Purchases Within Bounds," *Chain Store Age* (Administration Edition), September 1928, p. 32.

[19] Ralph M. Hower, *History of Macy's of New York* (Cambridge: Harvard University Press, 1946), pp. 430–31, n. 29.

[20] Edward Hungerford, *The Romance of a Great Store* (New York: Robert M. McBride and Co., 1922), p. 95.

definitely not taken this step as yet."[21] Four days later, however, he was able to report more success. Druggists still extend professional discounts in that "practicing physicians have always been accorded special discounts by pharmacists on purchases of pharmaceuticals and supplies for their personal use or for dispensing."[22]

Group Discounts

Discounts based upon the purchaser's group affiliations are, and have been, fairly common. Employees of various firms (a classification somewhat akin to the professional one cited above), members of automobile clubs, brethren in various lodges—all these have qualified for some retail discounts. Seligman and Love noted the discount to other firms' employees as a growing practice in 1932.[23] In 1940, the president of the Pennsylvania Bell Telephone Company wrote the Philadelphia Trade Relations Council, outlining the steps his firm had taken to stop discount solicitation of its employees, as well as the limitations of such action:

> Some years ago there were Philadelphia wholesalers and retailers who carried advertising in our official telephone directory inviting patronage of our employees at a discount. We stopped this. They then circularized our people and encouraged the designation of key people who would direct prospective buyers to sources of supply at a discount. So far as this is done on our company premises or with official telephones or on company time, we several years ago directed that all such activity should cease. . . .
>
> I cannot guarantee that there is no one in the organization who knows of the availability of discounts and passes the word along.[24]

As early as 1924 automobile clubs were seeking discounts for their members,[25] and in 1942 a representative of the Automobile Club of New York testified that not only had some 750 retailers agreed to give discounts to the club's members but that similar plans were operated by "the larger automobile clubs all over the country."[26]

Many lodges sought similar arrangements for their members. An example might be found in the United Fraternal Buyers, a currently operating Philadelphia organization, formed in 1926 to co-ordinate discount buying for the

[21] *In re National Retail Furniture Association et al.*, United States Federal Trade Commission, Docket 5324, Exhibit 865, Exhibit 866.

[22] Trade Relations Committee, Pennsylvania Pharmaceutical Association, "Pharmacy's Current Economic Problems," mimeographed, July 20, 1953.

[23] Edwin R. Seligman and R. A. Love, *Price Cutting and Price Maintenance* (New York: Harper & Bros., 1932), p. 107.

[24] *In re National Retail Furniture Association et al.*, Exhibit 791.

[25] Richard H. Lee, "Serving the Motorist—The Work of the National Motorists Association," *Annals of the American Academy of Political and Social Science*, November 1924, p. 268.

[26] Testimony of John T. Gren, Public Hearing on Senate Bill 2058, Int. No. 1646, New York State Senate Committee on the Judiciary, Albany, April 9, 1942, transcript, pp. 50ff. The American Automobile Association now reports that the survival of such plans in New York City and Washington, D.C., are exceptions to the general rule (letter, June 30, 1953).

local chapters of such organizations as the Moose, the Eagles, the Shriners, the Elks, the Red Men, Knights of Pythias, and Veterans of Foreign Wars. Organized at the suggestion of James J. Davis, former United States Secretary of Labor and then chief officer of the Loyal Order of Moose, United Fraternal Buyers distributed at one time 85,000 membership cards.[27]

Buyers' Leagues

Very similar to the above groups are the many co-operatives and associations formed solely for the purpose of securing discounts for their members. These organizations do not, like true co-operatives, distribute merchandise themselves. Instead, they act as agents, directing their members to other retailers and wholesalers who will sell on a discount basis. Quite often such leagues receive commissions from the sellers as well as dues from the members. Instead of sharing in residual profits through dividends at the end of the accounting periods, the members receive flat discounts at the time of purchase.

An example may be found in the Exhibitors' House Cooperative Association of Philadelphia. It claims 12,000 direct members of the association, each of whom pays annual dues of one dollar. The organization's facilities are also made available to members of about 170 affiliated groups. Space in the headquarters establishment is rented to discount vendors, but much of the annual volume is done on a referral basis.[28]

The buying leagues that Los Angeles retailers consider more important than the city's 60 admitted discount houses and the approximately 150 federal employee buying organizations cited by the District of Columbia Business Practices Council are also examples of this type of co-operative.[29]

Such buyers' leagues are not new. Very shortly after World War I, considerable attention was attracted by the Association of Army and Navy Stores, Inc., which even Secretary Stimson and General Pershing joined. The association drew its buyer-membership from veterans and military personnel who, in return for a small membership fee, became entitled to discounts from cooperating stores. As late as 1942, it was claimed that the association could get its members discounts in many leading New York specialty stores.[30]

[27] Testimony of Raymond R. Walsh, *In re National Retail Furniture Association et al.*, transcript, p. 46–75ff.

[28] Interview with Raymond K. Barcklow, president, May 29, 1953.

[29] "Army PX's Win a Round," *Business Week*, August 22, 1953, p. 61; Lester Gilbert, "Consumer Buyer Leagues Held Throttling Los Angeles Retailers," *Retailing Daily*, February 2, 1950, p. 8.

[30] "A Buying Public's Union," *The New York Times*, July 11, 1920, Section VI, p. 1; and Abraham Lowenthal, *Memorandum Submitted by a Committee of Retailers in Opposition to the Feinberg-Delaney Bill*, (Public Hearing, New York State Senate Committee on the Judiciary, Senate Bill Int. No. 1646, pr. No. 2058), p. 17.

Open and Avowed Price Cutting

Some discounting today takes the form of openly and widely flaunting manufacturers' established prices, either by outright price cutting or by special "premium" deals of one sort or another. In one sense, such discounting could not be so classified, by definition, until resale price maintenance became legalized. The avowed, open price cutter, such as John Schwegmann or "Doc" Webb, could not be called a discounter until the manufacturer's price he reduced had the sanction of "fair trade" behind it.

But there is no need to prove that such sellers existed prior to 1937, or prior to the war. The mere fact that a resale price maintenance bill was introduced in every session of Congress from 1918 on is sufficient evidence that there were even then many retailers who would not observe manufacturers' suggested prices. During the 1920's and the 1930's, appliance retailers complained bitterly that this was the role played by public utility companies. It was claimed that the utility companies, seeking to build up their load factors, were selling appliances at "discount" prices, thereby forcing appliance retailers to the wall.[31] The appliance dealers sought rather vigorously for legislative restrictions on such sales, but only Oklahoma (1936) and Kansas (1935) responded. State courts held the Kansas law unconstitutional, and the Oklahoma act never received court test.[32]

Trading Stamps

One way of openly violating manufacturers' established minimum prices on sales to all customers without actually reducing the nominal price tag is through giving a premium or gift. The giving of trading stamps is an old, and once highly controversial, version of such premium operations.[33] The courts have split on the question of whether the gift of trading stamps with fair-traded merchandise constitutes a violation of the minimum price agreements. In two important cases, Pennsylvania held it to be permissible, while New York ruled otherwise.[34] In view of the low actual cash value of the trading stamps, one is tempted to agree with the Minnesota attorney general asked to rule upon the same question. He dismissed the matter, saying "the law does not concern itself with trifles."[35]

[31] Two very thorough discussions of the problem, although with perhaps something of a pro-utility point of view, appeared in the *Journal of Land and Public Utility Economics:* Warren Wright, "Appliance Merchandising by Public Utility," November 1931; and Richard A. Harvill, "The Opposition to Public Utility Appliance Merchandising, August 1932.

[32] Edith N. Cook, "Legislative Restrictions on Marketing Integration," *Law and Contemporary Problems*, Spring 1941, p. 276.

[33] Cf. Frank Waggoner, "Discount Stamps: Half a Century Old and Still Going Strong," *Sales Management*, March 15, 1949, p. 87.

[34] *Bristol-Myers Co.* v. *Lit Brothers, Inc.* (Penna. Sup. Ct. 1939) 336 Pa. 81, 6 Atl. 843, and *Bristol-Myers Co.* v. *Picker* (N.Y. Ct. of App., 1950), 96 N.E. (2nd) 177.

[35] Opinion of the Attorney General of Minnesota (December 27, 1947) 1948–1949 *Trade Cases*, Part. 62, 214.

Club Plans

The premium becomes of great significance, however, in the operation of club plans, such as currently attract attention in the marketing of both appliances and soft lines. Under these plans, a woman acting as "secretary" sells appliances and other merchandise, often including "fair-traded" goods, to her friends on a dollar-a-week basis, accumulating the orders for delivery from club headquarters. Each purchaser receives, in addition to the items bought, the privilege of selecting free gifts having a retail value of about 20 percent or more of her purchase. *Retailing Daily* has reported rumors that one such plan alone did a $30 million business in 1952.[36] The age of the many clubs presently operating successfully is not known to the present writer, but one appliance manufacturer has defended sales to several clubs, declaring that their merchandising methods are of long standing and acceptance in the trade.[37] The Larkin Company of Buffalo, New York, developed a similar plan for the sale of soap in 1890, and had thirty years of success with it.[38]

The Amusement Field

Apparently during the prewar period deviations from the one-price policy were especially common in such service industries as amusements and resort hotel operation. Such deviations were not really different in kind from the other discounting activities discussed herein, but they seem to have been especially important. A fascinating history of Broadway entertainment indicates the volume such activities reached at times:

> Cut-rate admissions gradually developed into a big business of its own. In 1915, the largest handler of cut-rate theatre tickets . . . was Joe Leblang, who also sold tickets for hits at speculators' prices . . .
>
> To compete with Leblang, many managers issued their own cutrate tickets at half-price, under subterfuges like "People's League Tickets" and "Special Playgoer's Voucher." But Leblang was unchallenged king of cut-rate (or "cut throat" as some embittered managers declared). In 1916 Leblang admitted in a courtroom that he earned $320,000 a year on cut-rate tickets alone. *Variety*, in later years, observed that many a Broadway weakie "went over with a Leblang, for he kept many a legit show running."[39]

Very similar to the cut-price ticket was the "two-fer," a voucher entitling the possessor to purchase "two tickets for the price of one." These were

[36] Bob Okell, "Club Plans, Tea & Coffee Co.'s Move Goods," *Retailing Daily*, December 3, 1952, p. 27.

[37] Reply affidavit of William J. O'Brien, Secretary, Landers, Frary & Clark, April 29, 1953, *Landers, Frary & Clark* v. *International Solgo, Inc.*, New York State Sup. Ct., New York County, No. 4039—1953.

[38] Mildred B. Schei, "The Larkin Company: A History" (unpublished Master's thesis, University of Buffalo, 1932), p. 22.

[39] Abel Green and Joe Laurie, Jr. *Show Biz* (New York: Henry Holt and Co., 1952), p. 193.

sometimes passed out indiscriminately on the street or on the counters of co-operating cigar stores; at other times they were distributed by direct mail or through various groups such as employee associations and fraternal orders. *Business Week* has reported a revival of the practice, and a drama critic for the *Chicago Tribune* recently described a touring production shown in that city as being one for which "only the incurable sucker buys less than two tickets for the purported price of one."[40]

Other popular devices during the period were the "fun book" (a set of coupons, sold at a very low price, entitling the holder to free or reduced rate admissions to a considerable number of attractions) and the "due bill" (a prepaid order for hotel or restaurant services, sold at a discount). There has been some revival of the fun book, but Green reports that the due bill is virtually unknown today.[41] This contrasts with its rather wide use during the 1930's, when specialized brokers sprang up to engage in the purchase and sale of these orders.

PART III

The sellers described above might be considered as "regular retailers" in that, by and large, they operated openly and ostensibly as retailers, doing business with all comers. But there are (and were) many firms which, besides selling below list price and/or offering various other types of price concessions, operated in such a way as to impress their customers that they would not sell the merchandise in question to everyone. Some of these "irregular" or "unconventional" sellers actually do (and did) restrict their patronage, while others pay little attention to the supposed limitations upon patronage. These institutions are discussed below.

Discount Houses

Among these unconventional sellers are various types of "closed" retail establishments: stores having a "private" or "restricted" group of customers. In this group we find the institution that has attracted so much attention recently, the discount house: "a cut rate establishment, handling general merchandise, featuring national brands, and catering to a private clientele."[42] A 1944 report of the Federal Trade Commission summarized the role of such houses as follows:

> Another irregular type of outlet consisted of the so-called discount houses which, with inconspicuous headquarters and display rooms, undertook to supply advertised brands of many commodities at substantial discounts from usual retail prices. These dealers did no public

[40] Claudia Cassidy, "On the Aisle," *Chicago Tribune*, November 30, 1954, Pt. IV, p. 7.
[41] Abel Green, editor, *Variety*, letter of Feb. 16, 1953.
[42] Frances M. Lehman, "The Discount House," *Journal of Retailing*, February 1943, p. 19.

advertising except to the extent of circularizing by mail selected lists of former buyers and recommended prospects. Located in populous centers, they depended largely on word-of-mouth transmission of information about their low prices for cash. Some of these outlets were reported to attain total sales, for all commodities handled, running into millions of dollars a year. At their place of business well-known electrical appliances often could be bought at marked reductions.[43]

"Open" Showrooms

A somewhat similar institution, found in the history of the furniture industry, has been the "open showroom." Showrooms are operated in the furniture field, both by manufacturers and independent middlemen, to provide centralized display and stock facilities for the smaller retailers, interior decorators, and others who cannot possibly display full assortments. Conventionally, consumers are admitted to the showroom only upon introduction by a recognized retailer or decorator who is then credited with any subsequent sales made to those customers. In practice, some showroom operators will do business directly with consumers who thereby believe (with or without justification in various cases) that price concessions are being offered. Some other showroom operators fall into a somewhat intermediate position, requiring a sponsor before the consumer is admitted, but accepting as sponsors various agents and "merchandise brokers" not generally recognized as "regular" retailers by established merchants.

In December 1937, *Retailing* published a list of the leading discount houses and open showrooms in New York City.[44] One of the firms listed was then over thirty years old. With relatively little effort, through the use of the telephone directory and a few leads from other discount sellers, the present writer was able to locate eighteen of the twenty-six listed firms, still operating in New York City in June 1951. One of these eighteen had diminished to the point of a token existence, its name and corporate entity being carried by a group of accountants for some sideline activities. A few of the furniture showrooms had become relatively minor figures in the trade. But most of the eighteen had flourished over the years. One additional discount seller on the original list was reported as operating a very successful discount house in Los Angeles.

Industrial Discounts

We have already noted the deviations from the one-price system involved in the customary retail employee's discount. But retail workers are not the only ones to receive such benefits from their employers. Many wholesale,

[43] *Report of Distribution Methods and Costs* (Washington, D.C.: Government Printing Office, 1944), Pt. IV, p. 149.

[44] Earl Lifshey, "They Can Get It for You Wholesale," *Retailing* (Home Furnishings Edition), December 20, 1937, p. 2.

manufacturing, service, and commercial organizations also provide discount privileges for all or some on their staff.

Quite commonly manufacturers allow employees to buy their own merchandise at a discount, subject to varying degrees of control over leakage to outsiders. Discount sales of the firm's own goods have been described as "standard operating procedure . . . generally considered a legitimate employee benefit."[45] There is nothing new involved in the extension of such privileges; they were, for example, reported as customarily granted to salaried employees in the meat-packing industry in 1928.[46] The volume involved can be substantial; the General Electric Company has advertised that its employees and pensioners received discounts amounting to $5,000,000 on purchases of GE merchandise in 1951.[47]

But many employers go beyond this and actually procure merchandise for their employees from outsiders at a discount. *Printers' Ink* found that about 15 percent of the manufacturers it studied had some arrangement for the discount purchase of goods for employees. Professor Gilchrist, after studying discount buying in Los Angeles, reported that discounters there believed the practice was growing.[48] The Army Post Exchange Service, of course, provides an extreme example of this type of activity, but it is also well grounded in private industry.

Hackett[49] has traced the practice back to the period immediately after World War I, when apparently many manufacturers became interested in the operation of company stores to help employees meet inflationary conditions. All during the 1930's, the topic of "industrial buying," as this practice was called, was one of the more controversial issues in retailing and in personnel relations. *Business Week* estimated that between seven and ten thousand United States firms furnished their employees with the names of discount houses where cut prices were available. Tallman reported,[50] through the National Association of Purchasing Agents, that some 80 percent of the New England firms he studied had some facilities for assisting their employees with discount purchases. A Toledo, Ohio, gasoline retailers association complained that at least 46 firms in that area alone bought gasoline and accessories for their employees at a discount. Finally, a campaign to curb industrial buying was spearheaded by the National Retail Furniture Association, which claimed that at least 1,800 firms in New York City, 1,100 in

[45] Nathan Kelne, "Should Discount Buying Be Tolerated at the Home Office," *Printers' Ink*, April 10, 1953, p. 30.

[46] A. H. Garver, *Personnel and Labor Practices in the Packing Industry* (Chicago: The University of Chicago Press, 1928), pp. 198–201.

[47] Advertisement, *Philadelphia Evening Bulletin*, August 15, 1952, p. 5.

[48] Kelne, *loc. cit.;* and Franklin W. Gilchrist, "The Discount House," *Journal of Marketing*, January 1953, p. 268.

[49] J. D. Hackett, *Labor Management* (New York: Appleton-Century-Crofts, Inc. 1929), pp. 624–28.

[50] *Op. cit.*

Chicago, and 600 in Detroit bought for their employees.[51] Laws prohibiting such purchases were obtained in some states, and a number of department stores agreed to stop giving such discounts. But the evidence cited above indicates that the campaign was less then completely and permanently successful.

"Backdoor" Sales

Another means by which consumers "get it wholesale" is by doing exactly what the term implies: buying from wholesalers and manufacturers who ostensibly do not make such sales. This old and well-established practice is said to have been tolerated by even such an ardent exponent of the one-price system as Marshall Field himself: Wendt and Kogan describe Mr. Field's practices as follows:

> In each department [of the wholesale establishment, about 1880] was a city buyer whose task it was to fill orders with items not regularly carried by Fields. . . . Many of their customers took advantage of their service to get articles for relatives and friends at wholesale rates. But when department chiefs, tracing some such sharpster, complained to Field, he waved them off. This chicanery, he emphasized, cost little when compared with the overall profits derived from the service.[52]

Agents of the Greater Detroit Jeweler's Association, posing as consumers, went shopping for silverware at nine wholesale jewelry establishments in 1928. Only one of the nine refused to sell to the shoppers, and only three charged full retail price. In 1937, the National Association of Master Plumbers complained that over one fourth of all plumbing wholesalers in the United States were willing to make consumer sales at the going prices for contractor business. By 1950, the association's president was willing to take an even stronger position, claiming that most wholesalers would sell direct. In 1946, the Federal Trade Commission stated "retail hardware dealers were being deprived of sales . . . because of the practice of some wholesalers selling hardware store items direct to consumers at wholesale prices.[53] Many similar complaints, coming from present-day retailers as well as those of several decades ago, could be cited.

[51] "Wack 'Wholesalers'," *Business Week*, June 18, 1938, p. 27; *N.A.P.A. Handbook of Purchasing Policies and Procedures*, I (New York: The National Association of Purchasing Agents, 1939); "Toledo Retailers Find Means to Combat Employee Discounts," *National Petroleum News*, April 14, 1937, p. 51; Lester B. Colby, "Retailers Open Fight on Company Purchases at Wholesale for Employees," *Sales Management*, March 15, 1936, p. 358.

[52] Lloyd Wendt and Herman Kogan, *Give the Lady What She Wants* (Chicago: Rand McNally and Co., 1952), pp. 196–97.

[53] "Detroit Retailers Begin Fight on Retailing by Wholesalers," *Sales Management*, October 27, 1928, p. 77; "Some Do—and Some Don't," *Domestic Engineering*, July 1937, p. 79; George O. Toepfer, "Every Plumber Must Have a Store," *Modern Trends in Plumbing and Heating Retailing* ("Plumbing and Heating Business Series") (New York, *ca.* 1950), p. 1; Federal Trade Commission, *Report on Retail Price Maintenance* (Washington, D. C.: Government Printing Office, 1945), pp. 490–91.

Catalogue Jewelry Trade

Discount retailing bearing the guise of wholesaling is perhaps epitomized by the catalogue jewelry industry. The members of this industry issue catalogues covering a wide range of jewelry, gift, and (in some cases) appliance, luggage, and sporting goods items. Some of these catalogues are distributed to small retailers, particularly agents and brokers of the sort described below, who use the illustrations in lieu of stock for sales purposes. Thus these catalogue firms are, in a sense, wholesalers. However, most of the catalogues are sent to industrial concerns, co-operative buying bureaus, state and local government offices, and buying clubs, where they are used for purchases by employees and members.

In a Federal Trade Commission action[54] involving a leading firm in this industry, Dr. Theodore Beckman testified that at least 60 percent of the company's business would have to be classified as retail trade. Prewar volume in this industry has been estimated at about $200 million.[55] There are some grounds for believing that its present volume may be considerably greater. Besides the postwar inflation of prices in the lines handled by these houses, there are reports of the deep penetration of their catalogues into markets throughout the country. As Weinberg wrote in 1952 in *Retailing Daily*, "Practically every purchasing agent of large industrial companies has these discount catalogues on his desk and is able to get 'pots and pans' at 20 to 30 percent off for company personnel. There is nothing secretive about it."[56]

Such comments merely echo the complaints heard over fifty years ago (at a time when at least two of the present leading firms had already entered the business).

Agents and Brokers

In the history of discounting, some transactions at least, have involved the use of an agent or broker—that is, someone who knows where, and is willing, to obtain the item in question "at wholesale" for the customer. Sometimes it is a retailer in another line who is willing "to pick up the merchandise." Sometimes it is a craftsman or contractor who has access to various supply houses. Gilchrist,[57] for example, reported that many Los Angeles repairmen

[54] *In re L. & C. Mayers, Inc.*, Federal Trade Commission, 1932, Docket No. 2038, Defendant's stipulations, May 10, 1933, and transcript of testimony, p. 1587, as corrected by order of the hearing examiner, April 5, 1934, and decision on appeal, United States Circuit Court of Appeals, June 9, 1938. Also see, *In re Bennett Brothers Company*, Federal Trade Commission, Docket No. 4640.

[55] Federal Trade Commission, *Trade Practice Rules for the Catalog Jewelry and Giftware Industry* (Washington, D.C.: The Commission, 1943), p. 1.

[56] Art Weinberg, "Industrial Sales Making Inroads in Regular Chicago Area Volume," *Retailing Daily*, December 8, 1952, p. 46.

[57] Gilchrist, *loc. cit.*

could "get if for you at cost plus ten percent."[58] In other instances, it may be someone who specializes in discount buying and selling. Thus Gross noted that the curbstone broker, "an interior decorator of little or no training who 'carries his office in his hat,'"[58] was a concomitant of open showroom operations. One writer in 1936 noted that her town, "a fairly large but conservative one," had at least three "merchandising organizations" that carried no stock but sent their patrons to discount suppliers.[59] And the merchants of Tampa, Florida, became so irritated at sideline retailing in 1940 that they persuaded the city government to adopt

> an ordinance to license [under a prohibitive fee] the privilege of selling goods, wares, and merchandise which are not of the same general description as those usually produced or carried in stock by those offering same for sale and which are sold at a price represented to be less than the current retail price of said goods, wares, and merchandise.[60]

The classifications of discount selling set forth above are not intended as rigid and exclusive categories. There is considerable blending and overlapping between the groups. Sometimes two or more forms of discounting are involved in one transaction; thus an employer might direct a discount-seeking worker to a broker or agent of some sort who procures the goods through a retail storekeeper willing to grant concessions. The close resemblance of some types of discount sellers to each other, and their interrelationships, are indicated by a cautiously worded New York State legislative report:

> "Industrial selling" started shortly after World War I. It began as a paternalistic effort on the part of a few banking institutions to obtain scarce food products for their employees. Gradually it spread to other establishments, and in time some of the larger establishments created special departments within their organizations to purchase goods at savings to their employees. Where the purchasing power of a large establishment was used, it did effect savings to employees on certain goods. In many cases, these savings were in lieu of salary increases.
>
> In the course of time, a number of concerns opened outlets which catered to the employees of these establishments. They set themselves up in the guise of wholesalers, discount houses, cooperatives, brokers, and other descriptions.[61]

But the classification does indicate some of the varieties of discounting presently having an impact upon the economy, as well as those of interest before the war.

[58] Alfred Gross, "The Marketing of Household Furniture" (unpublished Doctor's dissertation, New York University, 1946), p. 208.

[59] Hannah Lees, "Only Saps Pay Retail Prices," *The American Mercury*, December 1936.

[60] Ordinance No. 754–A, passed August 13, 1940.

[61] New York State, Joint Legislative Committee on Unfair Trade Practices, *Report*, Legislative Document No. 51. (1950) (Albany, N.Y.: William Press, Inc., 1950), pp. 11–12.

PART IV

It is relatively easy to amass such anecdotal evidence of discounting and, if space permitted, many more cases, complaints, and accounts of deviations from the one-price system could be presented. However, such evidence, even though it is highly suggestive, does not answer the question: Do we have more, or less, of a one-price system today than we had at any given time in the past—say 1900 or 1930?

There are many reasons why we do not have an answer. The total volume of consumer sales, both per capita and *in toto*, both in monetary and real terms, has increased so much during our brief history that any sort of comparative analysis is likely to go astray. Moreover, the problem is complicated by the fact that the product-mix, as well as the total volume, has changed during the period. The short span of most of our statistical series does much to hamper research in American retailing. The Bureau of the Census, for example, did not begin its annual estimates of total retail sales for the country until 1935. Most of our retail information is grouped according to stores classified in terms of their principal or nominal merchandise lines (food stores, hardware stores, etc.) instead of by any kind of business or by price policy. Most of the figures on discounting that have been published have emanated from extremely partisan sources. A retailer's statement that "millions of dollars' worth of business is being done by people less legitimate than me" does not constitute particularly creditable evidence without considerable substantiation, usually lacking. Even though some people may be proud of their ability to buy at a discount, consumer studies of discounting are hampered by the fact that many others are inclined to be rather secretive about it. No two students of discounting seem to have agreed upon definitions. Some are concerned only with sales by "irregular" dealers, others are interested in at least some of the deviations of conventional dealers.

The definition problem also arises in another extremely important sense. The General Electric Company has announced, as of December 1954, that it will no longer issue or declare list prices for its major appliances. Should a researcher regard one sale of a GE appliance taking place in November 1954 for less than list as a discount sale, and another sale of the same appliance, at the same price, in January 1955, as not a discount transaction? Time after time we get caught up on the paradoxical question: If discounting goes on to the point of a complete breakdown of the price structure, do we then have anything that can really be called discounting?

In the light of all these difficulties, we may still agree with the 1937 comment, "To secure accurate information on the total sales to consumers at so-called 'wholesale' prices is an impossible task."[62] Tallman did develop, on the

[62] Henry D. Taylor, "Wholesale Buying by Consumers," *Journal of Marketing*, October 1937, p. 113.

basis of a careful study of New England consumers, an estimate that about 6 percent of all retail sales in the Boston area, apart from the food, general merchandise, drug, and restaurant categories, were made on a discount basis.[63] However, Tallman's figure could not be used as a statement of the total deviations from the one-price system in that area at that time, since he does not seem to have been interested in problems of trade-in allowances, conventional discounts, open and avowed cutting of list prices, haggling, etc. Heidingsfield found that discount-buying habits had become at least somewhat entrenched among 46 percent of the Philadelphia families he studied.[64] But again, a highly restrictive definition of discounting was used. Consequently, while some light is shed by such studies our question remains unanswered.

However, this much is clear—and it is the important thing. Deviations from the one-price system have been significant enough to be of concern to businessmen all during the twentieth century. There is even evidence of discount sales of appliances during the height of the World War II sellers' market.[65] Many of the deviations from the one-price system are rooted in sharply entrenched habits. The economic motives for discounting are equally strong. Many consumers, for obvious reasons, are interested in buying for less than full retail. Many retailers and wholesalers find such business profitable. Some full-price retailers find the discount retailer a useful outlet for excess stocks. Many manufacturers, relying on the assumption of an elastic demand, are delighted by price cutting at the retail level. Many others may disapprove, but consider the benefits to be obtained by policing prices not worth the costs of such activity. Some employers and unions consider discount buying for staffs and members as a relatively low-cost way of improving welfare.

Given all these factors, can any retailer reasonably expect to live in an economic world in which deviations from the one-price system are not practiced?

QUESTIONS

1. In what types of "legitimate" outlets (both service and retail) can a consumer expect to receive a discount?
2. Discuss some of the discounts that are available to you or members of your family. What are the purposes of such price reductions?

[63] Tallman, *op. cit.*, pp. 340–41.
[64] Heidingsfield, *op. cit.*, p. 6.
[65] "Yet during ten years of merchandise shortages of varying degrees of severity . . . the discount house grew." *Grey Matter* (Chain Store Edition), Grey Advertising Agency, New York, April 1952, p. 2.

22

The Psychology of Pricing

Benson P. Shapiro

Pricing is an area of primary importance in marketing. It is central to the profitable operation of a business, and to much of economic theory. In spite of its importance, however, it has been an area of little theoretical understanding and even less operating precision; business thinking about pricing has been referred to as "superstitious," "fuzzy," and "riddled with black magic."[1]

One pricing concept which has been almost universally accepted by economists and businessmen is the negatively sloped demand curve. Such curves, stating that as price rises demand decreases, and vice versa, form the basis for the economic theory of the market mechanism and for the pricing policy of businessmen. The emphasis has characteristically been on such questions as: "How much will unit volume increase if we cut the price?" and "If we raise the price, will the additional revenue per unit more than compensate for the loss in unit volume?" This kind of thinking, originally developed for undifferentiated agricultural commodities in a nineteenth-century economy devoted to the fulfillment of basic needs, leaves little room for the insights of modern behavioral science. Of particular importance, the *psychology* of pricing has been neglected almost completely.

Some businessmen and academicians, however, *are* aware of certain psychological aspects of pricing. Many retailers, for example, consider a price of $2.99 much more attractive than one of $3.00; on the other hand, they know that consumers see little difference between $2.98 and $2.99. And Andre Gabor and C.W.J. Granger, both of the University of Nottingham in England, who are probably the most successful and extensive researchers in this area, have studied the connotations of prices for cost and quality.[2] What we do know about the subject may be meager, compared to the literature available on other aspects of marketing, but the evidence indicates

Reprinted from *Harvard Business Review,* Vol. 46, No. 4, July-August 1968, pp. 14–25, 160.

[1] See respectively, Richard T. Sampson, "Sense and Sensitivity in Pricing," HBR November-December 1964, p. 99; Alfred R. Oxenfeldt. "Multi-Stage Approach to Pricing," HBR July-August 1960, p. 125; and W. A. Dimma, "Pricing Practices That Work," *Business Management*, February 1965, p. 57.

[2] "On the Price Consciousness of Consumers," *Applied Statistics,* November 1961, p. 170.

that consumers are not so simply motivated as the economists' demand curve implies.

The literature of marketing and economics includes several significant studies of the psychology of pricing, and I shall review them in this article. I shall place most of the emphasis on the role of price as an indicator of quality to the consumer, because this has been a very neglected concept that may prove quite useful to retailers and manufacturers.

PRICE CONSCIOUSNESS

Determining the level of consumer price knowledge is an important part of determining the meaning of price. Two studies, one by an industry group and the other by two scholars, are helpful here. They tell us something about the number of people who remember price variations, the relation of such price knowledge to social class, and other factors.

The *Progressive Grocer* study (performed in conjunction with Colonial Stores) covered 60 frequently advertised and highly price-competitive brand items.[3] Several thousand customers were shown these items and asked to state the price of each. In addition, each customer was asked if he or she used each item, and to supply information about his or her age, income, and size of family. Price consciousness was found to be quite high for *some* products but varied greatly. For instance:

The correct price of Coca-Cola six-packs was remembered by 86 percent of the respondents, and 91 percent named a price that was not more than 5 percent off the right figures.

On the other hand, only 2 percent could recall the exact price of a shortening; 34 percent were within 5 percent of the right figure.

The median items were Ivory bar soap, with 17 percent exact recall and 32 percent in the plus-or-minus 5 percent range, and Scott towels, with 16 percent exact recall and 24 percent in the 5 percent range.

In this study, the sex, age, and income of respondents appeared to make little difference.

A rigorous experiment by Andre Gabor and C.W.J. Granger casts more light on the question of price consciousness.[4] A sample of 640 English housewives was chosen at random within stratified areas. Only 15 commodities were used, and the respondents were interviewed by 44 University of Nottingham volunteers who were given careful oral and written instructions. The students successfully completed 428 interviews.

In addition to demonstrating, as the *Progressive Grocer* study does, that price consciousness is quite high for some products, the Gabor-Granger research suggests a relationship between social class and price consciousness.

[3] "How Much Do Customers Know About Retail Prices?" *Progressive Grocer*, February 1964, pp. c104–c106.

[4] Andre Gabor and C.W.J. Granger, op. cit.

Housewives in the highest social class were more willing than housewives in lower classes to *name* a price for a commodity, whether the price was correct or not; but the percent of correct prices recalled tended to be greater the lower the social class of the respondent. For the seven commodities for which prices were stable over time and consistent between stores, 51 percent of all respondents knew the correct price, 28 percent guessed incorrectly, and 21 percent did not name a price at all. (To indicate the range: in the case of tea, 79 percent of the answers were correct; in the case of breakfast cereals, only 35 percent were correct.)

CONNOTATIONS OF QUALITY

Now let us turn to the role of price as an indicator of the quality of a product. Here is where we begin to find very practical (and sometimes surprising) implications for manufacturers and retailers.

Two studies deserve our attention—one done in 1954 by Harold J. Leavitt, and the other in 1966 by Gabor and Granger, the same scholars who conducted the research on price consciousness described earlier. Both studies conclusively show that customers *do* use price as an indicator of quality, and that the strength of this phenomenon varies with socioeconomic class, product type, and retail outlet.

New Correlation

The Leavitt study, "A Note on Some Experimental Findings About the Meaning of Price," dealt with four products: floor wax, razor blades, moth flakes, and cooking sherry.[5] Leavitt used 60 subjects—30 Air Force officers (majors and lieutenant colonels) and 30 male and female graduate students, most of them in their thirties and forties. Two brands of each product were offered, and four sets of prices were developed for each product pair. (For instance, Brands A and B of one product were priced at 68 cents and 72 cents, 66 cents and 74 cents, 62 cents, and 78 cents, and 52 cents and 88 cents; similarly, four pairs of prices were given for each of the other three products.)

The choice situations were on paper; no physical product or brand was presented. The price combinations (one for each product) were distributed among the subjects in no special order. A subject had to choose Brand A or Brand B for each product. He also was asked to answer a question regarding satisfaction with the choice, and to rate the product in terms of quality differences he believed to exist among brands based on his previous experience.

The subjects often chose the higher-priced products. Leavitt reports:

> When faced with choices between two brands of floor wax, 57 per cent of our subjects selected the higher-priced brand [all pairs of prices are

[5] *Journal of Business*, July 1954, p. 205.

> pooled here]; 30 percent of the subjects chose the higher-priced razor blades; 24 percent the higher-priced moth flakes; and 21 percent the higher-priced cooking sherry. [Page 208].

The question on satisfaction yielded another interesting result: when the subject believed that there was a difference in the quality between brands, he felt a psychological conflict. Leavitt observed that the subjects tended to have more doubts when they chose the lower-priced brands than when they chose the higher-priced brands. Further, the greater the perceived quality difference, the greater the uncertainty about a choice. Thus, the competing brands of floor wax were believed to have the greatest difference in quality (the cooking sherries had the least difference); many more of the subjects indicated doubt about their selection in this product category than any of the others, and the percentage of doubt was greater among those choosing the lower-priced floor wax than those choosing the higher-priced one.

Leavitt sums up his findings by emphasizing that increased price may cause increased demand:

> These findings suggest that demand curves may not invariably be negatively sloped, that price itself may have more than one meaning to a consumer, and that a higher price may sometimes increase, rather than decrease, his readiness to buy. One might guess that a high price may be an attracting instead of a repelling force for particular brands of many different brands of items. [Page 210.]

The Leavitt work can, I believe, be criticized on two obvious points. First, his sample is small and not very broad; also, the subjects appear to be similar in age, education, and social class. Second, and more important, the simulated purchase procedure is quite contrived—the subject does not have to spend his money. This would, of course, bias the results in favor of the higher-priced product.

The results, however, seem so strong that these shortcomings do not detract from the conclusion that some consumers judge the quality of some products by their prices. The question of *which* consumers and *which* products will be considered later, but let me observe now that the number of consumers using price as an indicator of quality may be substantial.

"Reverse" Demand Curve

In 1966, Gabor and Granger reported on another study of price perception.[6] The study was detailed, complex, and mathematically rigorous. The experimental work was based on a simulated purchase situation using six different products. Essentially, the investigators probed to determine the consumer's "too cheap" and "too expensive" curves, and, from those, the buy-response curve. Two methods of questioning were used. Gabor and Granger found that "considerable proportions of the subjects trusted price rather more than the evidence of their senses." The authors observed:

[6] "Price as an Indicator of Quality," *Economica*, February 1966, p. 43.

> What is interesting is not so much the fact that consumers exist who would not be deterred by a very low price for a given article, but rather that this phenomenon is not ubiquitous. . . . We felt that [price would be an indicator of quality for] a wide range of commodities, such as textile products, simply because their quality cannot be ascertained by sight and, owing to constant changes in technology and fashion, past experience is of little use in this respect. The reputation of the manufacturer, the brand and the shop do, of course, matter, but it would be difficult to deny that a reputation for high quality and high price generally go together. [Page 50.]

Although this careful study has the weakness of dealing with a simulated purchase situation in which the customer "buys" at no cost to himself, it is of great significance because it provides (1) a concept of the meaning of price and its effect in the purchase decision, and (2) a means for quantifying data in this are—a kind of framework on which to hang numbers. This work will, if applied adroitly, provide a base for marketers and market researchers to use the concept of price as an indicator of quality. The "reverse" demand curve can be quantified, and the normal demand curve can be better understood (and possibly better quantified at the level of the individual consumer). Although many of the conclusions are tentative, the thinking is a starting point for further rigorous analysis.

Some marketers are already using the concept of price as an indicator of quality. Alfred R. Oxenfeldt's "Multi-Stage Approach to Pricing" provides several examples. He writes:

> Among producers one finds Patou boasting that its Joy perfume is the most expensive, and Chock Full of Nuts implying much the same thing about its coffee. Without being explicit, some retailers seem to claim that no store charges more than they—and, strangely, this image is a source of strength.[7]

One of the best examples of the strength of psychological pricing comes from an article by Oswald Knauth:

> In one case a retailer was able to purchase hosiery, having a normal market value of $2.00 per pair, for about 65 cents a pair, and offered it at $1.00. A mere handful of customers responded. Why? Reasons were searched; the values were unquestioned, the advertising forceful, the day fair. But the price of $1.00 suggested just that value, as this is a normal price for medium-grade hosiery. Two weeks later, the same goods were advertised at $1.14, which suggested higher value, with an enormous response.[8]

CUSTOMARY PRICES

Prices set by custom, tradition, assumed consumer psychology, and other nonobjective means are termed "customary prices." In the article just cited, Knauth writes:

[7] Oxenfeldt, op. cit., p. 129.

[8] "Considerations in the Setting of Retail Prices," *The Journal of Marketing*, July 1949, p. 8.

> Odd prices are greatly in vogue, on the theory that price just under a round number suggests to the customer a saving. . . . Such prices were first named in order to suggest a saving and later became woven into the pattern of custom. [Page 10.]

(An executive of a large Midwestern department store chain told me that his store had found it had higher volume when it priced its merchandise at "odd ball" prices. In one case, many items of clothing had moved faster at $1.77 than at $1.69 in spite of the higher price.)

In a more recent article, Stanley C. Hollander states:

> Psychological prices take three forms or, more precisely, three degrees of rigidity. One is a belief that prices ending with certain numbers are proper while other endings are not. . . . A second somewhat more confining form of psychological pricing controls the entire figure instead of just the ending. This is illustrated by the prevalence of highly specific price lines in the women's dress trade, at both wholesale and retail. . . . The third type of psychological pricing, an extreme form of price lining, eliminates all options except a single price point. The five cent candy bar was once . . . the prime example of a prevailing price point.[9]

Gabor and Granger, in *Economica*, suggest that the most common type of psychological pricing, i.e., pricing just below the round number, is a circular process, with the stores acclimating the customer to expect it, and the customer responding over time so that the stores continue that mode of pricing. The authors offer several examples, such as nylon stockings sold at prices ending in eleven pence. When offered stockings at a price ending in ten pence, some customers could not accept that as a "real" price. It is interesting to note that consumer awareness of psychological prices caused some unusual aberrations in the Gabor and Granger data, making them more difficult to analyze.

The prevalence of customary prices shows that the consumer, in many cases, perceives price in a noneconomic manner. Price, thus, is a powerful piece of information for the consumer. Let us examine the reasons.

JUDGING QUALITY BY PRICE

The important role of price in indicating the quality of many products can be explained in four ways.

1. *Ease of measurement* In a paper delivered to the American Marketing Association, Donald F. Cox offers a useful way to look at pricing. He views a product "as an array of cues" and states that the "consumer's task in evaluating a product is to use cues [information] from the array as the basis for making judgments about the product." A cue can be evaluated on two dimensions: predictive value and confidence value. Cox states:

> Predictive value is a measure of the probability with which a cue seems associated with [i.e., predicts] a specific product attribute. . . . Con-

[9] "Customary Prices," *Business Topics*, Summer 1966, p. 47.

> fidence value is a measure of how *certain* the consumer is that the *cue* is what she thinks it is.[10]

Price is a concrete, measurable variable for the shopper. In most retail outlets price is fixed—not subject to bargaining. If the shopper were to buy in a store where bargaining over price is the usual practice, he or she would not view price in the role described.

Since price is concrete and measurable, the consumer views it with much confidence. He trusts it more than most cues directly concerned with quality (e.g., quality of technical components and yarn strength). The difficulty in using variables other than price is emphasized by Tibor Scitovsky:

> Today, the consumer is no longer an expert shopper. The rise in the standard of living has greatly expanded the range and variety of consumers' goods and increased the share of complex technical commodities in the consumer's budget. . . . More and more, therefore, the consumer of today has to judge quality by indices of quality. The size of a firm, its age, even its financial success are often regarded as indices of the quality of its produce. . . . Another important index of quality is price.[11]

Willard W. Cochran and Carolyn Shaw Bell concur in their book, *The Economics of Consumption.* They observe that "the constant stream of new and altered goods and services makes the problem of considering available alternatives a continuous occupation."[12] Furthermore, the increasing emphasis on self-service shopping makes it difficult for the customer to obtain product advice from sales personnel.

2. *Effort and satisfaction* In his article, "An Experimental Study of Customer Effort, Expectation, and Satisfaction," Richard N. Cardozo finds that consumer satisfaction with a product depends, at least in part, on the amount of effort which the consumer expends to obtain the product. He states: "The effort invested in shopping may, under specifiable conditions, contribute [positively] to the evaluation of the product."[13] The Cardozo study refers to effort expended by the buyer and to her evaluation of the product. However, it seems reasonable to believe that, in a sense, an expenditure of money may be viewed by the consumer as similar to an expenditure of effort. Some economists, in fact, consider money as stored expended effort. It also seems reasonable to assume that when a consumer is choosing a product, she is likely to predict and consider her feelings after purchase.

   Thus, if expenditure of money is similar to expenditure of effort, and

[10] "The Measurement of Information Value," *Emerging Concepts in Marketing*, Proceedings of the Winter Conference, 1962, edited by William S. Decker (Chicago, American Marketing Association, 1963).

[11] "Some Consequences of the Habit of Judging Quality By Price," *The Review of Economic Studies*, Vol. XII (2), No. 32 (1944–1945), p. 100.

[12] New York, McGraw-Hill Book Company, Inc., 1956.

[13] *Journal of Marketing Research*, August 1965, p. 248.

if, while choosing a product, a consumer considers how she will feel about it after buying it, the Cardozo work helps to explain why a consumer uses price as an indication of quality. The more she spends for a product, the more she has invested in it and the more she probably will like it.

3. *Snob appeal* In 1899 Thorstein Veblen raised the idea of "conspicuous consumption" in his classic, *The Theory of the Leisure Class.*[14] Tibor Scitovsky uses the same general notion to explain the consumer decision process:

> Another basis for price discrimination is the premium some people put on certain goods and services merely for the sake of their expensiveness. A person may know that the more expensive model is no better than the cheaper one and yet prefer it for the mere fact that it is more expensive. He may want his friends and neighbors to know that he can afford spending all that money, or he may feel that his prestige and social position require that he should always buy the most expensive of everything.[15]

To the extent that high price indicates scarcity (as in the case of diamonds and gold), it may convey the impression of individuality. In a society with as high an economic standard of living and as high an emphasis on material wealth as ours, it is likely that scarcity and prestige are factors in many buying decisions.

4. *Perceptions of risk* Another explanation of the price-quality relationship has to do with risk. The prospective buyer balances (a) the dollars-and-cents amount of the extra cost of a higher-priced product against (b) the possibility of losing out because of the assumed lower quality of the lower-priced product. Leavitt states:

> If price sometimes has more than an economic meaning, if it also carries with it some implications about quality or good value or social propriety, then we would expect (1) that the consumer would feel some "conflict" in making a choice and (2) that he would in some cases make the higher-priced choice. The pressures toward the lower price, in other words, deriving from his concern about spending his money, might be balanced, or even overbalanced, by his concern about getting good quality or the "right" product.[16]

To reduce the risk of choosing a product of significantly poorer quality, the consumer chooses the higher-priced brand.

The buying situation itself is a factor. Many consumers, for example, view the purchase of a gift differently from the purchase of an item to be used by themselves. They choose the gift more carefully and spend more to ensure that it will be appropriate and "good." In a sense, this explanation is similar to the prestige concept just discussed; in both

[14] New York, The New American Library, Inc., 1954.
[15] Scitovsky, op. cit., p. 103.
[16] Leavitt, op. cit., p. 207.

cases, the buyer's attitude is influenced by the possibility of public display or exposure.

Because risk is involved in the process, it seems likely that self-confidence, generalized and specific, might also be involved. Donald F. Cox and Raymond A. Bauer have done some significant work in this area.[17] Judging from their findings, women who are self-confident are least likely to feel the need to use price as an indicator of quality.

The concept of apparent justification is related to risk. If a product is priced low, it is common practice for the retailer to give a reason such as an end-of-season closeout, "seconds," and stocktaking. It also seems appropriate for higher-than-normal prices to be accompanied by better packaging, class advertising, and so forth, which reduce the customer's perceived risk by bringing the product image and the price into congruence.

The cost and quality of a component part also have a bearing on the consumer's attitude toward risk. The less important the cost of a component in the finished product, and the more important the quality contribution of the component, the more likely the consumer is to buy a high-priced component to ensure that the finished product will be acceptable.

Finally, pressure to conform is a factor. In a sense, the consumer who purchases a product priced higher than what she would pay normally is reducing risk by conforming. She is accepting the judgment of other people who, she perceives, think that the product is worth a higher price. The pressure to conform is strong, as we all know.

IMPLICATIONS FOR MARKETERS

The concept of price as an indicator of quality must be used very selectively if it is to be effective. It cannot be applied indiscriminately to all, or even most, pricing decisions. It must be applied with finesse and careful thought, and it must be integrated into the company's total approach to its market. Marketers should answer three questions before trying to apply the concept:

1. What types of products are most likely to have positively sloped demand curves (i.e., where demand goes *up* with price increases instead of down, as in the classical model of economists)?
2. What kinds of consumers are most likely to use price as an indicator of quality?
3. What other conditions must or should be present to make the approach successful?

I shall comment on each of these questions, referring again to several useful studies which have been published.

[17] See, for example, "Self-Confidence and Persuasibility in Women," in *Risk Taking and Information Handling in Consumer Behavior*, edited by Donald F. Cox (Boston, Division of Research, Harvard Business School, 1967), p. 394.

Appropriate Products

Judging from the previously mentioned study by Scitovsky, it would appear that products which are difficult to judge on bases other than price would be most likely to have positively sloped demand curves. The difficulty in judging can come either from technical complexity (as in the case of television, tape recorders, and so forth) or from the difficulty of judging future performance by observable aspects of the product (as in the case of carpeting).

Leavitt's work would lead to the conclusion that the product should also have large, perceived quality differences between competing brands even if quality is difficult to measure. Thus, salt or flour, for example, would be poor products for this approach because they are, in general, perceived by consumers as being nondifferentiated commodities.

The product should meet the tests of effort, prestige, and psychic involvement earlier mentioned. And if it is a component or part of a larger effort, it should help the user reduce a risk. For example:

If a consumer is cooking a roast, she is probably aware that both the meat and the spices will affect the quality of the finished product. The price of the meat will be almost the complete price of the finished roast. The quality contribution of the spices may, however, be perceived as much higher than the cost contribution. Thus, by using quality spices, the housewife can decrease her risk of a poor finished product without significantly increasing the cost. The advertising appeal which says, in effect, "Don't risk ruining a good roast with poor spices just to save a few pennies," might be appropriate here.

The same thinking would apply to other products used as ingredients in a finished product, in the household, or in industrial applications. As a case in point, very few chemical plant managers would risk interrupting the production of a multimillion-dollar plant by purchasing anything less then the highest-quality gaskets. The certain savings of less expensive gaskets do not balance the risk.

A number of products possess the characteristics mentioned. One good illustration is scotch whiskey:

Differences in the taste of scotch are not perceived by most people. The price, usually in the $6-$10 range, is large enough to bring the expended effort concept into play. If the consumer expects to serve the scotch to others, risk becomes a factor. Thus, the price of scotch is an effective indicator of quality for many consumers. It is interesting to note that in 1967 the Christmas advertisements for Johnnie Walker Black emphasized that "At $9.40 it's expensive."

Responsive Consumers

Different segments of the population will respond differently to the pricing approach described. For example, Scitovsky states, "Well-to-do people can afford to be more casual and careless in their purchases than the poor."[18] But many people are not in this category. In particular, those who are not capable or confident of their ability to choose a product on its merits will tend toward the use of price. In the camera market, for example, the expert will not need to use price as an index of quality, whereas the novice, without other advice, will tend to use price rather than attempt to understand a morass of technical information. In addition, the prestige-conscious and the risk-averse are likely to use price as an indicator of quality.

Unfortunately, it seems that the poor and the uneducated are highly susceptible to price connotations. They would be the least capable of analyzing most products, and they would be strongly risk-averse.

Other Conditions

Once the price of a product has been established in the consumer's mind, even in the form of a price range, that price will become the "fair" or normal price. If the price is then increased without other perceptible changes, the customer will not receive the price cue as a valid indicator of higher quality. Thus, this pricing approach is most appropriate during the introduction of a product or after a radical (and perceptible) change in the product.

Pricing certainly cannot be separated from the rest of the marketing mix. If the marketer hopes that the consumer will consider his product to be higher quality than his competitor's products because his price is higher, he must make the other perceptible product cues consistent with this image. Advertising, packaging, and other functions must be considered along with pricing.

The general image of the perceived price setter (retailer or manufacturer) becomes important when price is considered as a communication. Raymond A. Bauer, in "A Revised Model for Consumer Source Effect," has advanced some concepts which are useful in this connection.[19] Price will be viewed with confidence only if the source has the correct image.

The nature of the retail outlet might also have an effect. If a product is to be ordered by mail, the price becomes even more important than normally (if the customer has no prior direct experience with the product). The customer cannot examine the product; and thus the measurable price cue is one of the few available solid pieces of information he has.

The pricing approach known as "creaming" a market can be understood in the terms described in this article. If a new product is introduced at a high price, the product may gain an image of quality and prestige. Then the price can be lowered and a broader market tapped. As the price is lowered, many consumers will consider the new price a bargain because it is below the old price, which is perceived as "fair." In addition, the product

[18] Scitovsky, op. cit., p. 103.

[19] Address to the Division of Consumer Psychology, American Psychological Association Annual Meeting, Chicago, Illinois, September 1965.

may retain its image of quality and prestige. In a sense, the high initial price has legitimatized the product.

A fine example of this pricing approach was Du Pont's introduction of Corfam to compete with leather. After introducing it to the high-priced shoe market, the company slowly moved Corfam down into the mass market for shoes. Markdowns illustrate the same principles, and so do price-off deals, such as the soap sold at a permanently reduced price with the "original" price conspicuously marked on the package.

CONCLUSION

The psychological aspects of pricing are important yet neglected. The consumer, in many cases, is knowledgeable about prices and uses them as indicators of product quality. Consumers also respond to some forms of customary pricing.

The concept of price as an indicator of quality can be used in a limited number of situations to attract certain customers to appropriate products. The concept is not a panacea for pricing problems, but, used with finesse, it should lead to higher profitability for perceptive marketers.

QUESTIONS

1. What types of products sold in a department store could have a positively sloped demand curve (where demand increases as prices rise)?
2. What is meant by "psychological pricing"? On what types of products can it be successfully used?
3. In what way does the pricing policy of the retailer affect the manufacturer?

23

Estimating Price Elasticity

Douglas J. Dalrymple

Retail-store managers face several difficult pricing problems. They must develop overall pricing strategies that reflect the strengths and pricing activities of their competitors. In addition, they must consider how the price of an item or group of items affects the demand for other products. Finally, they must understand the consumers' price sensitivity for particular lines of merchandise. The first two of these problems present such serious data

Reprinted from *Journal of Retailing,* Vol. 42, No. 4, Winter 1966–67, pp. 1–4, 64.

collection problems that they are typically handled on an intuitive basis. The problem of estimating price elasticities[1] for lines of merchandise, however, can be resolved by simple statistical procedures and readily available data. This article presents and illustrates a method of estimating these elasticities that should improve retailing pricing methods.

PREVIOUS RESEARCH

The estimation of specific price elasticities usually involves the development of price-demand relationships. One marketing researcher has constructed demand functions for retail grocery services based on prices, trading areas, product lines, and other variables.[2] The price data used by Holdren were based on an index of prices of seventy-four items from each store studied. The relationships derived were store demand functions, and while overall pricing rules could be obtained from this analysis it did not give management a guide to the price elasticity of departments or particular lines of merchandise. Holdren did find considerable variation in pricing within stores and he emphasized the importance of this variation by concluding:

> The existence of imperfectly informed buyers makes it possible for a highly skilled entrepreneur to attain a higher overall gross margin (without adversely affecting volume) than could be attained by a less highly skilled entrepreneur.[3]

This suggests that data on price elasticities for departments and lines of merchandise would be extremely valuable to the individual pricing executive.

MEASURING ELASTICITY WITH CORRELATION COEFFICIENTS

One alternative to the construction of demand functions for stores is to estimate departmental elasticities using simple correlation coefficients.[4] This approach compares the variation observed in prices to the variation observed in sales. The size and the sign of the correlation coefficients obtained from such an analysis provides the retailer with estimates of price elasticities. This method has the advantage that it can utilize readily available data. The data used in this article were monthly operating figures for twenty-one

[1] Price elasticity of demand is defined as: $E = \frac{(\Delta q/q)}{(-\Delta p/p)}$ where q is the quantity taken and p is the price charged and Δq and Δp are small changes in quantity and price. When E is > 1, demand for a product is said to be elastic and sensitive to price changes. When E is < 1, demand is inelastic and insensitive to price changes.

[2] See Robert R. Holdren, *The Structure of a Retail Market and the Market Behavior of Retail Units* (Englewood Cliffs, N.J.: Prentice-Hall, Inc., 1960), Chapter 6.

[3] *Ibid.*, p. 179.

[4] A simple correlation coefficient (r) is a measure of the variation in one variable that is explained by a second variable. The coefficient may range from zero to plus or minus one where a value of one shows a perfect relationship.

departments from a southern California department store organization. Data from twenty-four consecutive months were used to provide a sample of each department's operations. Average monthly markup percentages were correlated with monthly sales for each department. Sales and prices were not correlated directly because reliable price data were not available. Average markup percentages also had the advantage of exhibiting variation over time, and the size of the average markup clearly reflected the pricing policy being followed. Since the elasticity estimates reported in this article were based on variations observed in markup and sales volumes over time, the estimates can be interpreted as averages representing the two-year period. It is quite possible that elasticity itself varied during this period and although it would be desirable to measure this change, it was not possible with the information available.

Average markup percentages were correlated with sales using a standard computer program[5] to give coefficients for each department (Table 1). A review of the data shows wide variation in the coefficients among the twenty-one departments with a range from +.875 to −.694. The high positive correlations suggest that for these departments, months with high

TABLE 1.

Correlation Coefficients Between Initial Markup and Sales, By Departments, 24 Monthly Observations

Department	*Correlation between initial markup and sales r*	*Department*	*Correlation between initial markup and sales r*
Men's Furnishings	.875*	Men's Clothing	.043
Women's Sportswear	.555*	Cosmetics	.014
Moderately Priced Dresses	.467*	Sporting Goods	.011
Gifts	.357	Foundations	−.078
Women's Accessories	.334	Women's Sports Shoes	−.120
College Shop	.266	Infants	−.231
Junior Sportswear	.221	Silver	−.233
Stationery	.109	Housewares	−.310
Hosiery	.096	Women's Shoes	−.435*
Lingerie	.069	Toys	−.694*
Better Dresses	.048		

*Correlation coefficient significantly different from zero ($P < .05$).

Source: Douglas J. Dalrymple, *Merchandising Decision Models for Department Stores* (Lansing, Mich.: Michigan State University, Bureau of Business and Economic Research), forthcoming.

[5] The coefficients were obtained using the Biomedical Computer Program O2D developed by the Health Sciences Computing Facility, University of California, Los Angeles. The coefficients can be obtained using any standard correlation program and a variety of computing facilities.

markups were associated with months with high sales. The negative coefficients suggest that months with high markups were associated with months with low sales. Five of the coefficients were statistically significant, implying that there was a bona fide relationship between sales volume and markup percentages.

The correlation coefficients provide clear indications of the relative price elasticities of the various departments. The high positive correlation between markup and sales for the men's funishings department (+.875) suggests that price elasticity was low and consumers were not concerned with prices. Alternatively, the high negative correlation for the toy department (−.694) indicates that elasticity was high and demand was quite sensitive to price. When the correlation between markup and sales approached zero, as in the case of the men's clothing department, price elasticity appeared to be low. The absence of association between markup and sales for this department suggests that changes in markups did not affect sales, and this finding indicates inelastic demand. This is supported by additional data showing the correlations between markup and department profits (Table 2).

It can be observed that the men's clothing department had a high positive correlation between markup and profits, although the correlation between markup and sales approached zero. This suggests that high markups did not chase customers away and helped produce higher profits for this department.

TABLE 2.

Correlation Coefficients Between Initial Markup and Profits by Departments, 24 Monthly Observations

Department	*Correlation between initial markup and profit r*	*Department*	*Correlation between initial markup and profit r*
Men' Furnishings	.918*	Cosmetics	.173
Men's Clothing	.645*	Women's Shoes	.123
Women's Sport Shoes	.643*	Stationery	.091
Women's Sportswear	.606*	Lingerie	.056
Women's Accessories	.476*	Foundations	.040
Moderately Priced Dresses	.398*	Housewares	.025
College Shop	.349*	Silver	−.016
Gifts	.312	Sporting Goods	−.021
Hosiery	.253	Infants	−.243
Junior Sportswear	.232	Toys	−.371*
Better Dresses	.208		

*Correlation coefficient significantly different from zero ($p < .10$).
Source: Ibid.

A somewhat different situation occurred in the foundation department where there was a small negative correlation between markup and sales (—.078) and a small positive correlation between markup and profits (+.040). This suggests that higher prices reduced sales but that the higher margin achieved on these sales kept profits at about the same level. There would appear to be little to be gained from emphasizing margin in the foundation department, whereas markup was the key to higher profits in the men's clothing department.

It can be observed also that there were two definite groupings of departments with regard to price elasticity as measured by the correlation coefficients. It is significant that six of the departments that had the highest correlations between markup and sales (lowest price elasticity) were clothing departments (Table 1). This may indicate that individual clothing items have few substitutes. While this violates the conventional wisdom that clothing is a shopping good, the frequent use of private labels and the abundance of colors, styles, and sizes probably reduces the amount of shopping consumers are willing, or able, to do. The departments with the strongest negative correlations (highest price elasticity) were departments that sold nationally branded merchandise. This suggests that consumers of these items were acutely aware of prices and were able to substitute alternative sources of supply when prices were not competitive.

SUMMARY

It must be remembered that the estimates of price elasticities reported in this article represent the experience of a single firm located within a particular competitive environment and are not indicative of general conditions in the department store industry. This is particularly important because of the apparent strong consumer franchise held by the firm used in the study. This was shown when in over half of the departments high prices were associated with high sales and profits. This lack of competition cannot be assumed to be typical and other firms should consider the elasticities discussed in this article as untested hypotheses that must be verified before they can be used for pricing.

Although it was instructive to find that price elasticities were generally low, it is more important to realize that relatively simple statistical procedures (correlation) can be combined with readily available merchandising data to obtain valuable estimates for pricing purposes. Further, the necessary calculations can be easily made in most cases through the use of existing programs and excess computer time. Too often retailers have used computers simply to speed up the recording and tabulating of data rather than to analyze relationships among decision variables. It seems clear that the retailers who learn to use computers to assist management in policy decisions will be those who succeed in the future.

QUESTIONS

1. The author notes a high positive correlation between sales and markup in men's furnishings and a high negative correlation in the toy department. Explain.
2. Explain how the findings in the article can help guide management.

24

Turmoil in the Supermarket Industry

Eugene Beem

Denver has been a city of exuberance since the days of Molly Brown; I know most about that exuberance from the history of your retail food industry. Supermarkets came to Denver earlier and in greater numbers than in most other cities. Right now they account for 96 percent of the food business in the greater Denver area compared with a national average of about 70 to 75 percent. My favorite industry, trading stamps, came to Denver early in 1951, and they came here in a *very* big way. By the early 1960s, 90 percent of your grocery business was done by stamp-giving merchants, while only about 47 percent of the nation's retail grocery business offered stamps.

The Denver area price wars have matched price wars anywhere in the country. The housewives' boycott movement started here. It received more publicity and was more effective than in any other place in the country.

Food discounting also began relatively early, and as of now at least 75 percent of all retail grocery business in this area operates on a food discount basis. That compares with a national figure of about 15 to 20 percent of retail food sales.

WHAT IS FOOD DISCOUNTING?

A food discounter is a supermarket operator whose shelf prices for goods of comparable quality average at least 5 percent below what has been traditional for his store's marketing area. Usually, discounting is done without the use of stamps and game promotions, and very often with limited use of price specials. The theme is every day low prices, and there is minimum

Excerpts from talk delivered before American Marketing Association Chapter in Denver, December 1968.

promotion. Even in the area of advertising it is not uncommon for there to be substantially less advertising by the food discounters.

These units may be adjacent to general merchandise discount stores such as your Target and K-Mart discount units, or they may be free standing, as in the case of most of the Kings, Safeways and Del Farms. On a national basis, the best known, most successful food discounters among the chains have been Stop and Shop on the east coast, Lucky Stores on the west coast, and Supermarkets General (in a way, the "Granddaddy of them all") in northern New Jersey.

WHY HAS FOOD DISCOUNTING BEEN GROWING?

There are two important reasons for the trend toward food discounting in recent years. Look at the typical supermarket gross margin trend from 1954 to 1964; in that period there was an increase from roughly 17 to 18 percent of sales to approximately 22 to 23 percent. This increase in store mark-ups was the cumulative result of many factors. One factor has been the remarkable expansion of supermarkets. In the middle 1950s, there was one supermarket around the country for every three or four thousand households; but by the mid 1960s, there was one supermarket for about every 1,700 to 2,000 households. Naturally, the more stores there are, the harder it is for any one store to function at a level of capacity which keeps operating costs per dollar of sales low.

Another important consideration has been the expansion of services during the past decade—such as shopping centers conveniently located in expensive rent areas, boys to carry bags out to the shoppers' cars, increases in store hours, increases in check cashing services, and a remarkable growth in the variety of merchandise offered (stocking a wide variety results in a reduced item-by-item turnover and *increased* labor costs since it costs more to stock partial cases on the shelves than to stock merchandise one case at a time).

Also, until the mid-1960s there were steady increases in many forms of promotion. Take stamps as an example. In 1954, only about 10 percent of all supermarkets gave stamps, but by 1963, about 65 percent of all supermarkets in the country gave stamps. Games also became widespread after the early 1960s, reaching a peak usage by roughly two-thirds of all supermarkets in mid-1966.

Aside from these cost increases for services and promotions, which offered extra shopper benefits, there has been a rising hourly labor cost for supermarkets. Over the past decade, throughout the country, labor costs per hour have approximately doubled.

All of these store factors, no one of which can be isolated, added up to steadily increasing costs of doing business, and consequently margins crept up. One thing we all learned in Economics I is that when a vacuum exists, some operators will, in time, move in and attempt to fill that vacuum. What some of the discounters have done is move into that high gross margin vacuum.

Another very important reason for the exuberant growth of food discounting is the inflationary pressure characteristic of our economy since the middle 1960s. In the retail food area, for example, from 1951 to 1965, prices rose at a rate of less than 1 percent per year. In 1966, there was a jump of about 5 percent in retail food store prices across the country, traceable to a rise in wholesale costs. Although there was little additional increase in 1967, 1968 brough another 4 percent jump in retail food store prices. In an inflationary situation consumers tend to be relatively more sensitive to prices than during a period of price stability. This is particularly true if prices are going up more rapidly than earnings. Factory workers, for example, whose weekly wages after taxes have gone up less than prices since 1965, have been squeezed in the past few years. Research studies clearly document the increasing price sensitivity in Denver. In 1954 (a study done by the University of Denver), price was the most important factor in food stores patronage for about 23 to 24 percent of all the households. In 1961 (a study done by Burgoyne, Inc), the prime importance of price as a factor of patronage had declined to about 12 percent of the Denver area households. By December, 1967 (a study conducted by S&H), price had moved up and become most important for 47 percent of all Denver households.

Of course, there is a bit of a circle here. As food discounting grows, price sensitivity tends to increase. I think, however, that this is a secondary element in the growing price sensitivity as contrasted with the significance of inflation. I can cite one supporting figure. S&H conducted another survey in Denver in June, 1968, after King's Sooper had been out of stamps and into a food discount program for about six weeks. At that time price was the most important patronage factor with about 49 percent of all households. This was only a slight increase over the level of December, 1967. So the explanation for the increase in supermarket food discounting has been both the rise of retail supermarket margins over the decade to the middle 1960s and the inflationary trend of recent years.

THE ART OF FOOD DISCOUNTING

Food discounting is not a simple matter of reducing prices 5 percent across the board on all items, for example. From the research we have done, I feel confident in saying that a straight across-the-board reduction would not have much shopper impact. An art of food discounting has evolved during the past five or six years, and is absolutely critical to the success of the movement. First, let me cite the problem with the effects of a simple 5 percent price cut.

The average customer transaction at a supermarket is about $6. Naturally, it goes to $12 or $14 on the major shopping days, and some may spend

$40 or more; but I am just talking about averages. A 5 percent cut on this $6 average amounts to only thirty cents, not enough to get very many people excited. During an inflationary period it may appear more significant, but it still doesn't seem like very much to most shoppers. Applied to the average item price, 5 percent means one and a half cents saving—again trivial to most shoppers.

To make discounting work well, there must be shoppers who think they are saving not 5 percent, but 18 percent or even 20 percent. How can you do this? The first principle is to concentrate the reduction in the dry groceries area, which accounts for two-thirds of all store items and half of store sales. Most of the dry groceries are exactly the same from market to market, and a lower price will not suggest the possibility of inferior merchandise quality. Also, since these grocery prices tend to be rather stable, compared to meats and produce, common knowledge of the customary price is more widespread. Since the dry grocery department accounts for half of the supermarket volume, you can reduce these prices 10 percent if you reduce only dry grocery prices instead of making a storewide 5 percent cut.

It is quite customary to leave the perishable *margins* alone or to reduce them only slightly. You can do this and still reduce the regular shelf prices of the perishables by backing away from price specials. Specials may have been costing you as much as 5 to 6 percent of perishable sales before the discount program. You put this saving disproportionately into the perishables—bananas, for example—which are most consistent in quality perception from store to store. It costs you nothing to reduce the magnitude of price specials and move to a "low everyday" price policy. You've simply leveled out the purchasing of perishables among shoppers, and eliminated the distortion of purchases created by your specials. You maintain your margins on perishables but get credit for lower prices nevertheless. You've saved your real price cutting ammunition for the dry grocery area, where it will have the heaviest impact.

In dry grocery price cutting, it's important to cut across the board. I would not have thought so, but the "wall-to-wall" policy has been successful enough with Lucky, Stop and Shop, and Supermarkets General that I'm not going to fight it. The "wall-to-wall" tactic prevents the consumer from thinking that you are playing games with her. Consistent across-the-store policy is essential for building confidence. You need to show a saving of at least two pennies per item as compared to conventional competition, hopefully more than two. You can't afford to be just a penny under on very many items, because that doesn't seem like anything to most shoppers. Certainly, to the extent that you can help it, you can't afford to be equal or undersold, unless it's on a competitor's price special.

Private labels play a very important role in food discounting. Lucky and Stop and Shop both expanded their private label programs rapidly when they moved to discounting. Supermarket General probably has the highest percent of sales in private labels of any food chain in the country. King has given a big push to private labels since he adopted discounting. The advantage of such a program is that you can get private labels of reasonable quality that can be priced 15 to 20 percent under manufacturers' brands, and still earn a higher margin than is possible on your discounted groceries. Every sale diverted to a private label from a manufacturer's brand gives you more leverage to cut the manufacturer brand price, or reduce the requirement for sales increases to make discounting profitable. So, private labels can be important in developing a low price image and maintaining that image with the least amount of pain.

Another important principle in the art of food discounting is that, at the outset, prices must be cut by more than 5 percent. The pricing studies we did in Denver suggested that King Sooper's initial cuts were approximately 8 percent. You'd die if you had to remain at that level; there just isn't that much room in conventional grocery margins to survive forever with 8 percent lower prices. But you have to do that at the start to get shock attention—to get people into the store and to sell your new low price image. In this *initial* stage the extra discounting may be through temporary specials or money-back coupons. Of course, also at the start it takes extraordinary advertising—perhaps double the normal newspaper linage for as long as six months. And in-store promotion is critical. If you have been in the King Sooper stores you have seen these little tags that say "other stores charge 29¢, King's discount price 25¢." Some variation of this item tagging is standard; you need to remind the shopper what she used to pay—and perhaps still does elsewhere. Shoppers in the aggregate are highly knowledgeable about comparative prices, but any one shopper can remember only a limited number of *last time* other store prices. No matter what you do, it will be a long battle to convince a majority of the public that your prices really are substantially lower than they used to be. After six weeks' intensive discount promotion, King Sooper had achieved creditably for his claim with only 57 percent of the Denver households who said they had a King Sooper store "easy to get to."

REQUIREMENTS TO MAKE FOOD DISCOUNTING PROFITABLE

I want to turn to the question of how a discounter can make out—offset his average overall reduction of 5 percent or more in prices, and eventually produce increased profits? Of course, discount prices may be partially offset by the elimination of trading stamps. Stamps typically cost 2 percent of sales—perhaps 2.5 percent including bonus stamps. Dropping stamps doesn't give you anything like a 5 percent leverage, but you're on your way. Not all, but most of the people who have gone to discount prices have dropped stamps. You can also pick up a little leverage by cutting back on price specials. I mentioned this earlier in regard to price specials on perishables. Eliminating price specials altogether on dry grocery items is fairly typical—

at least specials that are conducted at a supermarket's cost. You may still run price specials when there is some sort of manufacturer deal to offset the lower price. But you don't sacrifice any margin on these price specials. That gives you a little leverage, in some cases as much as 1 percent, which goes into the 5 percent lower shelf prices.

Some food discounters have cut back on the number of hours they stay open; some have cut back the variety of food assortments, aiming for the point at which almost everything can be stocked a case at a time. This saves labor cost. Some discounters have also cut back on such special services as butcher-cut meat. And then, as I mentioned earlier, some have eventually found it possible to reduce the normal level of their advertising linage. None of these economies provide dramatic saving, and there is a tendency toward maintaining normal services in recent food discounting moves.

When you have done all of these things, there remains, inescapably, the need for substantial extra sales volume. As a rule of thumb, after you have saved in all of the ways I've just suggested, you still need 15 to 20 percent additional sales volume. That compensates for the last 2 percent reduction in your average level of prices.

One other important element for profitable food discounting is having large stores spread out in a community so that trading areas do not bump into each other. I'll explain why in a minute. When Stop and Shop went discount in the east and when Lucky did so in the far west, one of the first things each did was to close up smaller stores. They also closed up some stores that were more or less competitive with one another, preventing this problem of bumping into sister stores as units reached out with low prices to attract more shoppers.

One advantage of the large store is that you can easily accommodate increased customer traffic. Also, you have more nonfood and specialty items which carry margins even at discount prices that are higher than you are used to in the grocery business. So, if discounting draws additional traffic to the store you can offset some of the sacrifice in reduced prices by the higher margin on these specialty and nonfood items.

WHAT IS THE FUTURE FOR FOOD RETAILING?

During your courses in Marketing, some of you were probably exposed to a concept referred to as the "wheel of retailing," developed by Professor Malcolm McNair of the Harvard Business School. According to this concept, margins in retailing tend over time to rise slowly to some intolerable level, at which point they suddenly plunge downward in a discount revolution. The process occurs again and again.

Particularly in food retailing there is evidence of the cycling process. For example, during the World War I era, gross margins were somewhere around the 25 percent level when A&P introduced the economy chain store (1913). These stores were smaller, handled very narrow grocery assortments, and were one-man operations. The store manager, when he went out for lunch, hung a sign on the door that said: "Gone to lunch, back at 1 o'clock." These one-man stores were standardized; they had the same assortments everywhere, I'm told. When the A & P went into economy stores, they dropped trading stamps (which were important at that time too), and they dropped delivery; everything was cash and carry.

As A&P grew, they used their size to develop buying power and scale economies, all of which they poured back into reduced prices. Those early chain economy stores picked up a 10 to 15 percent price advantage against the stores with which they were competitive. They swept the field and turned the plane of competition in food retailing to price, where it remained until roughly the mid-'20s when services and promotion began creeping back into the grocery business. By the early 1930s gross margins were again back to the neighborhood of 25 percent. That marked the arrival of the supermarket revolution.

Whereas the chain stores were very tiny—about the size of a typical college classroom—the supermarkets were large, not unlike the ones we are familiar with now, but spartan in fixtures and decor. There were few, if any, extra services, and the whole appeal was based on price. Since the customer chose her own merchandise and bought more on a typical trip, storing it at home in her refrigerator, the new stores had an important labor saving advantage. These supermarkets achieved a 10 to 15 percent price advantage against the small store competitors, and they forced the plane of competition in food retailing to price for another half generation—really up until the late 1940s or early 1950s.

Once again gross margins have been rising, as I described earlier, and a new food discounting move is spreading quite rapidly across the country. It is appropriate to ask the question—is this another turn of the "wheel"? Is this a revolution, or is it just a merchandising phase? I'm convinced that it is just a merchandising phase.

There are several reasons why food discounting is not going to take over the grocery industry and is not going to stay at the level of importance that is characteristic of this Denver market right now. The first reason for my conclusion is that the record of success in food discounting is quite a mixed one. Many people are in discounting for the reason analogous to the one illustrated by the following story.

I live in Pleasantville, New York, about ten miles from the Yonkers Race Track. When I was there with a friend several months ago, I noticed a priest who was down on the track with the horses. Periodically he would stop in front of a horse, and after several times I noticed that those horses invariably won the next race. Since that looked like a pretty sure formula, I started betting on the horses that the priest had blessed. When the last race approached I took my accumulated winnings and bet them on the horse in front of which the priest had stopped that time. Much to my chagrin that horse, instead of finishing first—finished last. Naturally, when the evening was over, I sought out the priest to find out what had gone wrong. He looked at me in disgust and said, "The trouble with you Protestants is that you don't know the difference between a blessing and the last rites."

As I watch what is happening in food discounting here and elsewhere, it seems that a lot of people are going into it because it's been a blessing for Lucky Stores, Stop and Shop, Supermarkets General or Steele's in Fort Collins. There is *no* magic about food discounting; it's not a panacea for trouble. It's an art which takes outstanding management.

It's not like the supermarket of the early 1930s or the chain economy store of the generation before that. These were radically new forms of retail distribution. They could not be imitated by the competing establishments in existence. Only over time, through the development of new stores or new organizations, could the supermarket or the chain economy store be imitated. This protection against loss of competitive advantage through imitation gave the head start needed to assure business success.

What we have now is a merchandising technique which can be imitated rather quickly, as you have seen in this Denver area and which has, for many operators, produced nothing but trouble.

It is far too early to see what the outcome will be. But at this point Denver may be the only city in the country where every supermarket operator in town is losing money or making less than he was a year ago. Our best estimate, from talking indirectly with a lot of knowledgeable food people in Denver, is that King Sooper has invested (through reduced profits) as much as half a million dollars in establishing its discount program. All this despite considerable sales success. King's sales have gone up—perhaps as much as 20 to 25 percent. Safeway, the largest chain in this market, has sacrificed substantially more in profit than has King—our guess is about $3 or $4 million over an eight-month period; they have met King Sooper prices, but failed to enjoy a significant improvement in sales. This is a great time for the consumer to buy groceries; I advise you to stock up, because the situation can't last.

The first reason, then, why I think food discounting is basically a merchandising phase is because of its uneven success thus far. Secondly, this kind of discounting can be fairly easily imitated or offset. I don't want to overplay that point. One of the operators I would *least* want to compete against in any market area is Lloyd King of King Soopers; he is very capable. As you know, S&H has done business with Lloyd King for years. If anybody can make an idea go, he can. He's good and he may eventually "make it" with a food discount policy. (Whether his half million dollar investment would have been more profitable in a new store or in some other way is another question.) A lot of the other Denver operators will not be successful; maybe *no one* else will. I say food discounting can be more or less easily imitated or offset. Yet there will be room for the exceptional operator who does it much better than anyone else.

Finally, S&H has done enough research on a national basis to be convinced that we know how an operator continuing to use stamps can beat food discounting. The key to beating rather than joining the food discounter is not wholly joyous. There is no substitute for having to meet discount competition part way. I'll give you the strategy as nearly as we've been able to work it out.

Kroger, a chain which uses a stamp other than S&H, appears to have developed this counter strategy quite effectively. When discounting comes into a Kroger trading area, Kroger immediately reduces its prices in line with the food discounters and in general matches their promotional tactics. But Kroger does not cut as many items as the food discounter. Instead, they cut prices enough to prevent the discounter from ever developing a significant price advantage. If, for example, the food discounter goes down by 5 percent, Kroger will go down by two and a half percent and continue offering stamps, justifiably claiming discount prices *plus* stamps. While this policy costs Kroger some profit dollars in the short run, over the long run it pays. Maybe food discounters will make it against someone else, but as a rule they don't make it against Kroger. Kroger has been evolving this strategy for several years, and their profits this year, on the basis of the first nine months, were up about 50 percent, which is virtually as good as anyone else in the food industry.

Now of course, the Kroger strategy has two factors in its favor. One is the value of stamps which cost the store 2 percent of sales, but are worth in retail store merchandise value about two and a half percent of the store patronage. The second element is that Kroger's policies put pressure on the discounter's effort to establish significantly lower prices. If the discounter can't establish his discount price image, he can't generate the 15 or 20 percent extra in sales required to make food discounting profitable.

I can conclude here that the situation in Denver is similar to the cartoon I once saw in the *Saturday Evening Post*. The distinguished board chairman is addressing the other members of his board and he's saying, with a very serious face: "Gentlemen, we've reached the ultimate in cost reduction; we're out of business." A substantial number of Denver's food operators may go out of business in the future. One thing is clear—when 75 percent of your market is operating on a food discount basis, you have an unstable situation.

I am completely confident that the general level of food prices in Denver will rise and that some of these operators who have discontinued stamps and joined the discount parade will return to stamp issuing while continuing to maintain prices low enough to be regarded as competitive. On a national basis discounting will continue to grow, reaching perhaps 20 to 25 percent of supermarket industry sales. But discounting will not dominate the growing industry. It is a merchandising phase, not an industry revolution.

QUESTIONS

1. Why have gross margins increased in the food field in recent years?
2. What must a food store operator do in order to become a successful food discounter?

C. PHYSICAL DISTRIBUTION

Physical distribution in retailing refers to both the physical control of the merchandise in the stores and the decision making involved in choosing the location of the outlets where the merchandise is to be sold.

The first article, by Al Bernstein, demonstrates one of the most widely used techniques of managing and controlling inventories. The next, by Joseph Friedlander, "The 'Maximum' System for Reorder Open-to-Buy," demonstrates the newer techniques, which are presently being computerized.

The article by Donald Thompson, "Subjective Distance," discusses consumer attitudes toward store locations. Barry Berman's "Location Analysis Within Regional Shopping Center" delves into a subject that little has been written about; namely, the strategy of store location within the shopping center.

25

A Control System for Small Items During a Critical Seasonal Operation

Al Bernstein

With the increasing tempo in the development of electronic equipment, Retailing, like all other segments of the business and scientific world, is rapidly being conditioned to the inevitability of its ultimate adoption. At present, everyone in Retailing seems to be consumed with a thirst for statistical information, in the hope that therein lies a panacea for his merchandising difficulties.

Reprinted from *New York Retailer*, April 1962, pp. 14–17.

It goes without saying that the modern aggressive storekeeper must have enough information to conduct his business in the most scientific way possible. But, he must keep in mind at all times the fact that this information can be attained without the installation of expensive equipment.

This is in no way to be construed as opposition to the collection of data by modern electronic methods but—at the present stage—many Retailers find the cost of this equipment prohibitive. In most cases, the information needed can be collected more economically by the people on the job. All that is required is an intelligent appraisal of the data needed, and the planning of a control system that will furnish this information is the most efficient and economical way.

A TOY DEPARTMENT CONTROL

The following is an illustration of a control system that was devised for simplicity and efficiency.

One of the most difficult departments for which a control system can be set up is the toy department—especially during the critical Christmas operation. Bulk items are generally stored in a warehouse and their control is efficient and easy to operate. It is the vast number of small items that do not lend themselves to simple controls.

The toy department is faced with these major difficulties:

1. Over 65 per cent of the toy business is concentrated in approximately thirty business days at the end of the year.
2. Because of this tremendous volume in such a short time, it is extremely difficult to keep the unit control systems operating efficiently. Such operation is of vital importance in so seasonal an operation when the following results must be accomplished:
   a. Sell out as much of the merchandise as possible so as to end with a low physical inventory.
   b. Recognize the best sellers as soon as possible so that their maximum sales may be attained.
   c. Provide an accurate record of the sale of each item so that this information may be used in setting up a buying plan for the following year.

And, above all, to do this with little or no added expense.

The goal, as experienced in a successful toy department, was to develop a system that was inexpensive to set up, inexpensive and easy to operate and one that furnished the buyer with all the information he needed to do a more efficient and productive job.

SOLUTION

The solution that followed was based on a rather novel idea in control. It was based on the fact that we were able to keep only a nominal amount of forward stock in the department. Most of the operation was of the self-service type. The department consisted of an arrangement of booths and counters with the merchandise separated according to classification. The balance was kept in reserve stock rooms situated as closely as possible to the selling department.

The idea, therefore, was to stock the department for the opening day, and then to control the movement of merchandise on the basis of requisitions handed in daily by the stock supervisors.

DUTIES OF SUPERVISORS

Each classification had a floor supervisor whose function it was to check the inventory every day at closing, and to make out a requisition for the goods needed to fill in the floor stocks. The supervisor was furnished with a stock list which indicated every item displayed in his section. This was an exact copy of the buyer's stock control—the only figure left out was the cost of each item. The supervisor, therefore, was fully acquainted with the merchandise for which he was responsible.

The requisitions were handed in daily and the merchandise was brought to the department later that evening or early the next morning—in plenty of time to be put away.

The requisitions were entered into the stock records as they were filled and every few days the balance on hand of every item recorded. Instead of checking off the items as they were sold in units, the control clerk was able to check items off in quantities of 12, 18, 24, the normal amount ordered as a refill.

Please note that every item carried was entered in the control book by classification. This was then arranged by manufacturer, item and price line so that the control book was as easily referred to as a dictionary.

METHOD OF REPLACEMENT

Every time a requisition was filled, the quantity was deducted from the quantity on hand and the new balance indicated. Note, too, that a date was recorded so as to tell at a glance at what rate the goods had sold.

When a markdown was taken, the quantity marked down was recorded as well as the date. If there were unusual circumstances involved, they were indicated also.

One of the most ingenious and surprisingly effective features of control was the check points established. The records for several years past were analyzed and revealed rather accurately on what days of the holiday season the department normally attained 15 percent, 25 percent, 40 percent, 50 percent, 75 percent, 90 percent of the season's business.

These key dates were carefully indicated and used with a great deal of accuracy and success.

ANALYSIS OF OPERATION

Assume that 25 percent of the business was normally in by December fifth. On that date the controls were analyzed to see whether every item was selling at that rate—25 percent of the quantity of every item purchased should have been sold.

If an item was not selling at the proper rate, its display was studied and search made for a reason to explain its slow rate of sale. If no logical reason was found, a markdown would be taken promptly.

Where an item exceeded the pace, its potential was calculated and a reorder was placed, provided quick replenishment was possible. If one-hundred pieces of an item had been stocked and fifty pieces had been sold by the 25 percent check date, it was concluded two-hundred pieces could be sold for the entire season. On that basis, an immediate reorder for one-hundred pieces was placed since there were fifty on hand and fifty pieces actually sold. Reference to the sample control sheet on the next page should make the matter clear.

RESULTS OF ANALYSIS

The most amazing feature of this method was its accuracy—we never found we had ordered out of line. And in most cases, we discovered many strong promotional items whose potentials we had never realized before. We were very rarely left with slow selling goods and our early markdowns were never costly ones. For a department doing over $400,000 in the toy department, we showed such ending inventories as $19,000, $17,000 and $21,000. These were considerably below the national averages.

During the January inventory, we entered our remaining inventory into our stock records so that we now had the following information for each item.

1. Quantity ordered—(initial order and reorders)
2. Quantity left at end of season
3. Quantity sold during season

NEXT YEAR'S PLANS

This information was immediately copied off into the new control book and it served as a complete buying plan for the following year.

As purchases were made, they were entered in the appropriate place in this new buying plan.

This control was effective—it furnished the tools needed to do the best job possible. It was easy to understand, easy to follow and inexpensive to operate. And, it required no expensive electronic equipment.

Classification ‡ Household Toys — *Manufacturers: WM* — *On hand at successive check dates and % of total sales for season anticipated at each date.*

Style	*Item*	*Cost*	*Ret.*	*Initial Purchase*	*11/17 5%*	*11/26 10%*	*12/1 15%*	*12/5 25%*	*12/10 50%*	*12/17 75%*	*12/21 90%*
522	Tea Set	.60	1.00	60	48	36	18	0			
524	Tea Set	1.20	1.98	200	176	150	130	110			
526	Tea Set	2.40	3.98	72	71	69	66	64 (MD)			

Analysis of the three items above

Style 522: All 60 have been sold by 12/5, the date on which 25% of the total potential could be expected. Thus, the potential is 240 and 180 more are needed at once. Also, the item has become a candidate for promotion, if immediate replacement is possible. Normally, a reorder would have been placed before 12/5.

Style 524: Here 90 have been sold at the 25% check point, indicating a potential of 360. Thus, a reorder of 160 pieces is indicated.

Style 526: Only 8 pieces have sold at the 25% point, indicating a potential of 32. Thus, there is an over-stock of 40 pieces, and a prompt markdown is indicated.

QUESTIONS

1. Discuss the weaknesses of the control system described in this article.
2. Are the author's comments on electronic systems still applicable?

26

The "Maximum" System for Reorder Open-to-Buy

Joseph S. Friedlander

The term "Maximum" (M) refers to the maximum requirement, or preparation which must be made *at reordering time*. It is the quantity which will provide for expected sales during:

a. The time which will elapse until the next reorder is placed—called the "reorder period" (RP)
b. Plus the time which will elapse between the placement of that next reorder

Excerpted from *New York Retailer*, June 1962, pp. 8–10.

and arrival of the goods at the selling counter—called the "delivery period" (DP)

c. Plus the reserve (R) necessary to cover normal fluctuation of actual sales *above* the estimated quantity for RP + DP.

$$\text{Thus:} \quad M = RP + DP + R$$

RP + DP is also called *lead time*. It is the period in which fluctuations in sales cannot be compensated for by inventory adjustments. Thus, if sales are 6 a week, reorders are once in 4 weeks and delivery takes 2 weeks, after an order is placed, no further adjustment will take place in the inventory for 6 weeks. (Another order is not to be placed for 4 weeks and it will take 2 more for that to arrive.) During this lead time, sales of 36 are expected, but allowance must be made on a basis of probability for additional sales. This is called the Reserve.

Following is a list of Reserves and Maximums which should protect given estimated average sales so that stocks will prove adequate for about 99 percent of probable demands:[1]

Estimated sales in lead time	*Reserve*	*Maximum*
1	2	3
2	3	5
3	4	7
4	4	8
5	5	10
6	6	12
7	6	13
8	7	15
9	7	16
10	7	17
11	8	19
12	8	20
13	8	21
14	9	23
15	9	24
16	9	25
17	10	27
18	10	28
19	10	29
20	10	30
25	12	37
30	13	43
35	14	49
40	15	55
45	16	61

[1] The reserves are based on the Poisson Distribution where the reserves to provide protection against running out 99 percent of the reorder periods is $2.326\sqrt{\text{lead time sales}}$. This reserve takes care only of chance variation in sales. Delays in delivery are best handled by setting the delivery period somewhat longer than normal expectancy.

Estimated sales in lead time	*Reserve*	*Maximum*
50	17	67
60	18	78
70	19	89
80	21	101
90	22	112
100	23	123
120	26	146
140	28	168
160	30	190
180	31	211
200	33	233

Suppose:

a. Sales are at the rate of 4 a week
b. RP is 6 weeks, which would be 24 sales units
c. DP is 1 week, which would be 4 sales units
d. R is 12 sales units (3 weeks supply)[2]
e. M is RP + DP + R or 40 sales units

The previous table indicates a reserve of 12 units to protect estimated lead time sales of 28 (interpolate-25-30).

Open-to-buy is computed by subtracting the quantity on hand and on order from the above calculated maximum. If, at this reordering point, there were 16 units on hand (OH) and on order (OO), the formula would read:

$$M - OH - 00 = OTB$$

$$40 - 16 - 0 = 24$$

QUESTIONS

1. What is meant by lead time? Why is it important in reordering merchandise?
2. Why is a reserve over and above lead time calculations needed?
3. How does the use of these calculations differ from our previous techniques?

[2] Note that RP + DP = 28 sales units (lead time sales)

27

New Concept: "Subjective Distance" or Store Impressions Affect Estimates of Travel Time

Donald L. Thompson

Models concerned with the distribution of retail trade within any geographic area must include distance in some form as an independent variable. Reilly's law is the best known effort in this direction, although several other simple trading area models are to be found in marketing literature.[1]

Authors who include distance in trading area models do so on the assumption that it is a planning variable of some importance in consumer decision making. Distance, it is assumed, constitutes a "friction" or inertia which tends to keep retail activities localized in any given area. And *actual* distance is assumed to correspond with the consumer's *estimate* of distance, convenience, and travel time.

Since consumers hestitate to undertake the costs and effort of overcoming distance, market researchers conveniently "explain" retail sales volume in terms of local base of demand, or they combine with this an adjustment factor to approximate any "leakage" or "escape" which might take place between communities or clusters of population and establishments. Commonly, distance is used in the formulation of this escape factor, either as a weight to resident population or as an independent variable in a multiple regression.

Our purpose here is to evaluate how much distance really affects consumer decisions on where to shop. If no consistent pattern of consumer "rationality" with respect to distance can be isolated, one can then question the usefulness of this factor as a simple input variable.

THE "EXPERIMENT"

Our research design can best be described as an "experiment"; that is, a conscious attempt was made to control as many outside factors as possible. Four San Francisco Bay area communities were isolated as each having a large, established department store within the immediate vicinity of

Journal of Retailing, Vol. 39, No. 1, Spring 1963, pp. 1–6.

[1] For example, Paul D. Converse, "New Laws of Retail Gravitation," *Journal of Marketing*, 14, No. 3 (October 1949), 379–84; Robert Ferber, "Variations in Retail Sales Between Cities," *Journal of Marketing*, 22, No. 3 (January 1958), 295–303; William J. Reilly, *The Law of Retail Gravitation* (New York: G. P. Putnam's Sons, 1931).

a large-scale discount operation. Investigators then defined survey areas on the basis of the following criteria:

1. The survey areas should be residential in nature, located at points approximately equidistant from the department store and the discount house.
2. The road distances and the driving time from the survey areas to the two types of retail outlets also should be equal. The time standard adopted was the average of five trips by the investigator from the test areas to the destinations, driving at prevailing highway speeds during normal weekday traffic between the hours of 10 a.m. and 4 p.m.
3. A distance of one or two miles and driving time of approximately five minutes were the desired values, although geographic considerations forced some departure from this criterion.
4. There should be only one principal route available for the consumer to travel from his home to each of two types of retail outlets in his immediate vicinity.
5. This route should be sufficiently wide and have adequate access so that travel time would not differ appreciably according to the time of day or the day of the week under consideration.
6. The routes available primarily should be used by shoppers; they should not be major commuter arterials.

LOCALITIES SURVEYED

The following sites were selected as survey areas:

Albany, approximately equidistant from Capwell's Department Store in El Cerrito Plaza and the B.B.B. Discount Department Store in Berkeley.

San Francisco, at a point somewhat closer to the Emporium Department Store in Stonestown Shopping Center than to the G.E.T. Discount House in Lakeshore Plaza.

San Rafael, approximately equidistant from Macy's in downtown San Rafael, and Mac's Discount Department Store.

Walnut Creek, approximately equidistant from Capwell's Department Store in the Broadway Center and the C.B.S. Discount House at Four Corners.

Consumers in test areas were asked whether or not they patronized the retail outlets in question, and if so, to estimate the distance in miles from their residences to the two outlets. They were asked also to estimate the actual driving time spent in travel, not including time used to find a parking place. In San Rafael, consumers were asked, in addition, the distance and travel time via a freeway to a regional shopping center somewhat farther away. In all cases the route was verified, and it was determined that the trip in question was a direct one, with no side journeys involved.

OBJECTIVES

The objectives were:

(1) To probe the extent to which suburban consumers, traveling by private automobile, are capable of evaluating distance and driving time in any consistent fashion

(2) To determine whether or not consumer evaluation of time and distance is affected by the character of the destination

In other words, does the markedly different merchandising character of the department store versus the discount house have any effect on the consumers' evaluation of distance and travel time?

It was not possible to locate a residential area in San Francisco meeting the equidistance criterion. In order to render the San Francisco results comparable with the others, therefore, a series of ratios was computed. The first ratio divides the respondents' averages as to time or distance by the actual measured time or distance. A value of greater-than-one for this ratio indicates an upward bias of consumers in estimating the magnitudes involved. A second ratio was then computed, dividing the above ratio for the discount house by the corresponding ratio for the department store as destination. A value in excess of unity for this ratio indicates that consumers tended to overestimate the distance or driving time to the discount house proportionately more than they did the distance or driving time to the department store.

Obviously, any ratios immediately in the neighborhood of 1.00 enjoy very little statistical significance, although the variance around such central tendency values may be of interest. Ratios near unity, therefore, indicate that consumer differences in estimation are in the aggregate equivalent to a statistical error term, tending to cancel out as the sample becomes large. Models using actual distance and driving time measures would, therefore, under such circumstances, be using an objective independent variable that correctly reflects the subjective evaluation of the consumers whose reactions are effectively captured by means of a mathematical function. This says nothing about the manner in which this variable should be handled in such models, but merely validates the appropriateness of its inclusion.

It is interesting to note from Table 1 that in 13 out of 16 cases the ratios are significantly greater than unity. This shows a general tendency on the part of the sample consumers to overestimate both the driving time and the distance traveled in the satisfaction of their retail needs. Furthermore, when one considers the ratio between the discount house ratio and the department store ratio (with the exception of distance for San Rafael and Walnut Creek), the latter ratios also are significantly greater than unity. One could suggest, therefore, that the sample consumers regarded the discount houses as being farther away from their residences in time and distance than the department store.

Consumers in the San Rafael survey area, as a rule, showed significant upward bias in evaluating the distance to the regional shopping center at Corte Madera, and even greater upward bias in estimating the corresponding time, even though a high percentage of them traded there. Their relative upward bias in estimating the distance to the regional shopping center closely approximated that evidenced in estimating the distance to the

TABLE 1.

Estimated vs. Actual Distances and Driving Times, from Survey Areas to Department Store, Discount House, and Regional Shopping Center (Distance in Miles; Driving Time in Minutes)

	*Albany**	*San Francisco†*	*San Rafael‡*	*Walnut Creek§*
Department Store				
Estimated Distance	1.25	.75	1.65	3.56
Actual Distance	1.50	.75	1.10	3.50
Ratio: Estimated/Actual	.83	1.00‖	1.49	1.02‖
Estimated Driving Time	5.50	3.45	6.07	8.42
Actual Driving Time	5.00	2.50	5.00	7.00
Ratio: Estimated/Actual	1.10	1.38	1.21	1.20
Discount House				
Estimated Distance	1.68	1.46	1.67	3.65
Actual Distance	1.50	1.25	1.10	3.50
Ratio: Estimated/Actual	1.12	1.17	1.52	1.04‖
Estimated Driving Time	6.41	6.77	6.86	9.44
Actual Driving Time	5.00	3.50	5.00	7.00
Ratio: Estimated/Actual	1.28	1.93	1.37	1.35
Regional Shopping Center				
Estimated Distance			5.46	
Actual Distance			3.80	
Ratio: Estimated/Actual			1.44	
Estimated Driving Time			12.71	
Actual Driving Time			6.00	
Ratio: Estimated/Actual			2.12	
Ratio: Discount House Ratio / Department Store Ratio				
Distance	1.35	1.17	1.02‖	1.02‖
Driving Time	1.16	1.40	1.12	1.13
Ratio: Regional Shopping Center Ratio / Department Store Ratio				
Distance			.97‖	
Driving Time			1.75	
Ratio: Regional Shopping Center Ratio / Discount House Ratio				
Distance			.95‖	
Driving Time			1.44	

*Time and distance measured from vicinity of Solano and Carmel Avenues (1950 San Francisco-Oakland Census Trace AC-1) to the B.B.B. discount house and Capwell's Department Store in El Cerrito Plaza.

†Time and distance measured from vicinity of Lagunitas and Beachmont Streets (1950 Census Tract (0—7) to G.E.T. discount house in Lakeshore Plaza and the Emporium Department Store in Stonestown Shopping Center.

‡Time and Distance measured from vicinity of LynCourt and Irving Avenues to MAC's discount house on Highway 101, Macy's in downtown San Rafael, and the J. C. Penney Store at Corte Madera Wye and Highway 101.

§Time and distance measured from vicinity of Eccleston Avenue and Oak Park Boulevard to C.B.S. discount house at Four Corners and Capwell's Department Store in the Broadway Shopping Center.

‖Insignificant at 0.05 level.

department store and the discount house. In their evaluation of driving time, however, they showed a greater tendency to overestimate than they did when the department store or the discount house was the destination (*see* the ratios of 1.75 and 1.44, respectively).

SUBJECTIVE DISTANCE

This investigation poses some interesting questions on trading area analysis of consumer behavior in general. Many authors have pointed out that approximately colocated retail outlets may support trading areas of different size and configuration.[2] This study suggests the further refinement that two retail outlets offering approximately the same merchandise lines—department stores and discount houses—may take on different geographic dimensions in the mind of the consumer. As a rule, the discount houses in the sample generally offered less consumer convenience and fewer services, and usually were more crowded and less desirable places to shop, than were the competing department stores. Apparently the impression made upon the consumer by the fewer conveniences offered in the discount house was further extended by him to influence his evaluation of the physical distance between his own home and the store. This subjective coloring of an objective fact is thus termed, "the concept of subjective distance."

In order to further amplify this concept, detailed information was collected in the San Rafael survey of consumers' estimates of time and distance to retail outlets where they did *not* shop; obviously, the location of these had to be sufficiently familiar to the consumers for an estimate to be made.

Twelve consumers who did not shop at Macy's estimated, on the average, that the store was 2.00 miles and 8.37 minutes driving time distant. The corresponding figures for 87 consumers shopping at Macy's were 1.60 miles and 5.75 minutes, respectively.[3] Fifteen consumers who did not shop at the discount house estimated that it was 1.75 miles away, with an average driving time of 8.03 minutes. On the other hand, 68 consumers shopping at the discount house estimated, on the average, 1.66 miles and 6.60 minutes driving time.

Despite the small samples involved, the results seem to reinforce the ini-

[2] For example: W. A. Bowers and W. L. Mitchell, Jr., *Hardware Distribution in the Gulf Southwest*, United States Department of Commerce, Bureau of Foreign and Domestic Commerce, Domestic Commerce Series No. 52 (Washington: United States Government Printing Office, 1931), p. 116; August Losch, *The Economics of Location* (New Haven: Yale University Press, 1954), pp. 414–20.

[3] One woman regularly *walked* to both outlets in question, and while her results were not included, they seem to indicate the wide range of consumer rationality. Despite the fact that she followed the survey routes, she claimed a 10-minute, 1-mile journey to the department store, and a 30-minute, 3-mile journey to the discount house. Repeated questions as to her route or side trips failed to shake her confidence in the above, highly inaccurate figures.

tial hypothesis—namely, that one's subjective feelings about a retail establishment affect his ability to evaluate its geographic position. In the San Rafael example, consumers stated they did *not* patronize the stores in question; therefore, there must have been some negative factor operating to divert patronage to competitors. A further extension of this negative "image" could have led to the generally higher estimates, or the upwardly biased concepts of distance and driving time could have been part of a larger set of negative factors preventing patronage of the outlets in question.

SUMMARY AND CONCLUSIONS

While the sample in this survey is relatively small in terms of absolute numbers—400 consumers in all—it nevertheless represents a high percentage of persons living in the vicinity of the specific points chosen as approximately equidistant from the two types of retail outlets in question. Further field survey effort is necessary to establish conclusively the relevance of the basic hypotheses suggested by this study.

First, objectively determined distance and driving time measures may not be entirely appropriate inputs for simple models designed to describe or explain geographic patterns of consumer purchasing behavior. Appreciation is necessary of subjective aspects of distance and the varying interpretations of what, from the decision maker's standpoint, may be "givens." Then the idea of "market outreach" or "drawing area" may be restated in more flexible terms than might have been suggested in the past.[4]

Second, the convenience aspects of a retail store can be an important element in fixing its "location" in the minds of consumers. If the discount houses in the survey areas are "farther" away than department stores, other compelling and offsetting factors must be important in attracting consumers to their merchandise offerings.

Third, the general upward bias in estimation of driving time and distance indicates that shopping centers might well publicize these factors more than at present in an effort to broaden their market outreach. By publicizing accessibility of a group of stores, the shopping center might gain further at the expense of smaller, more scattered merchants whose exact location may not be as definitely fixed in the minds of consumers. In short, a "convenient" location from the point of view of the developer is not necessarily as "convenient" to the consumers on whom its profitability ultimately rests. Neat, often circular, market areas drawn on a map, therefore, may be very poor representations of geographic purchasing patterns dependent on the operation of highly variable elements of human behavior.

[4] For example, Reilly's law has been used to determine the breaking point between two retail establishments, substituting their floor space and the distance between them for population and road mileage, respectively. See Richard L. Nelson, *The Selection of Retail Locations* (New York: F. W. Dodge Corporation, 1958), p. 149.

QUESTIONS

1. What does the author mean by "subjective aspects of distance"?
2. How could acceptance of this concept affect decision-making for the management of a shopping center?

28

Location Analysis Within Regional Shopping Centers

Barry Berman

INTRODUCTION

The present large number of shopping centers and their growth, which "... now account for approximately 25 percent of retail volume," calls for a systematic method of examining shopping center locations for their retail trade potential.[1]

This analysis is concerned with studying specific factors which influence the value of locations within regional shopping centers. The empirical data of the study is taken from an analysis of five regional shopping centers in the metropolitan area.

Analysis of retail trade locations is not new. However, existing knowledge cannot be carried over to shopping center studies. By virtue of a different environment, old techniques and concepts such as corner location, traffic counts and trading area analysis need to be reevaluated and revamped.

The importance of location to a retailer cannot be over-estimated. A good location can compensate for certain merchandising deficiencies. A poor location, however, may be such a serious handicap that even the most competent merchandiser could not compensate for it.[2] Indeed, there is no type of economic activity in which the location of establishment is more important than in retailing.[3]

Store location determines the entire marketing strategy of a retailer

New York Retailer, May 1968, pp. 9–23. This article is adapted from Barry Berman's "Analysis of Retail Trade Locations Within Regional Shopping Centers," unpublished, M.B.A. thesis, City College, 1967.

[1] E. B. Weiss, "How Retail Trade Locations Proliferate," *Advertising Age*, (September 23, 1963), Vol. 34, No. 38, p. 102.

[2] William R. Davidson and Paul L. Brown, *Retailing: Principles and Practices* (New York: Ronald Press Company, 1953), p. 11.

[3] *Ibid.*, p. 12.

from product line to pricing and promotion. The entire marketing mix can be interpreted as evolving from a retailer's location. Thus, understanding one's location is a significant merchandising asset.

The need for long-term leases in desirable locations makes the need for proper location analysis quite pronounced. Rental terms have long-term profit implications. Marketers must project into the future when analyzing a given location. This long-term commitment imposes substantial costs for poor locations on the retailer and shopping-center developer, as well as society as a whole.

An unprofitable location has two costs to the retailer: the direct dollar loss, and the opportunity cost (foregone profits from alternative locations and investments). Losses due to poor location can be spread over many units for large chain operations. However, the cost of a poor location to the small businessman is often a financial and consequent personal disaster. Undoubtedly, poor location is an important cause of small business failure, particularly in the retailing field where location assumes so much importance.

Related to poor retailer performance is an unfavorable return to shopping center developers. Shopping center leases generally provide for a percentage of sales to go to the developer as an addition to the fixed minimum rental. Consequently, developers have a definite financial stake in the success of their tenants. Leonard Marx, a developer of shopping centers, claims "that 75 percent of existing centers are financially unsuccessful; they earn less than 5 to 6 percent for their developers."[4] Furthermore, their future prospects may be even dimmer. Competition from roadside discount stores, rehabilitated downtown shopping districts, and from newer centers will cloud future prospects.

Proper layout of stores creating an adequate balance of retailers within a portion of the center, as well as essential traffic, is instrumental to the success of any location. A successful center is properly planned; random choice of a location in a good shopping center does not insure success to the retailer.

Society is probably the most adversely affected by poor location because "it bears part of the extra transportation and delivery costs, plus the loss in time brought about by a poor location."[5] Another significant cost to the consumer is the lack of comparison among competing stores for price, product and service.

Proper location analysis can make an important contribution to retailers, shopping center developers, and the general public. Unlike other methods which increase one of the above's share at the cost of another's, a proper location benefits all simultaneously.

[4] K. Hamill, "Squeeze on Shopping Centers," *Fortune* (September 1963), Vol. 68, No. 3, p. 118.

[5] Eugene J. Kelley, *Shopping Centers: Locating Controlled Regional Centers* (Connecticut: Eno Foundation for Highway Traffic Control, 1956).

Differences Between Shopping District and Shopping Center

Awareness of the differences between the center and the district is essential in appreciating the importance of separate analysis. The greatest difference between the shopping district and the shopping center arises from the newness and the planned concept of the shopping center. The shopping center represents a planned, conscious attempt to create the most conducive shopping environment within the limitations of time, cost and space.

The planned concept of the center is best evidenced in the concept of balanced tenancy. "By this is meant that in a properly planned center, the amount of store facilities in each line of trade is related to the market potential in each line so that no store is subjected to excess competition."[6]

The minimum leases with shopping center developers provide retailers with:

a. The right to control admission of competitive stores beyond a certain size;
b. A restriction on excessive space expansion so that one retailer cannot become too large as compared with the others;
c. A restriction on excessive space devoted to nonfood items by supermarkets; and
d. A right to exclude discount operations.[7]

Parking facilities within the center are planned to be as short a distance from all stores as well as being adequate for maximum crowds. Parking facilities contribute to the value of some corner stores, as they are along the path of shoppers walking to and from their cars.

Retailers' associations are generally much stronger in shopping centers than in central business districts. This advantage stems from aid given by the developer in the form of professional management of promotions, from subsidies, and from the ability to impose involuntary membership on all retailers.

In addition, stores within a center have more freedom in location. In what central business districts could a store choose among several locations? Location has become a variable under the control of the retailer. Furthermore, additional choices are now available insofar as choice of level, number of entrances, etc. Substantial differences exist between the center and district as to shopping habits, means of transportation, and quality of consumer traffic. In fact, the difference is so great that an executive of a national variety store commented, ". . . the formula it uses for new stores in established metropolitan retail districts and also for new units in rural communities does not work so accurately in the case of shopping center stores."[8]

[6] Davidson and Brown, *op. cit.*, p. 58.

[7] Perry Meyers, *The Planning of Branch Stores* (New York: Retail Research Institute, 1960), p. 54.

[8] S. O. Kaylin, "Accelerated Growth Seen for Centers," *Chain Store Age* (May 1958), Vol. 34, p. 16.

Location Considerations in Shopping Centers and Shopping Districts

The greater choice and freedom available to the retailer in the shopping center makes the location problem more complex. Analysis of location within the center must cover the areas analyzed in districts such as: trading areas, affinities, parking facilities, demographic characteristics and traffic counts as well as other considerations unique to the center.

The fault in using the same criteria for both district and center analysis is that some factors are not considered at all and that others are not properly weighted. This paper will concentrate on the additional factors which must be considered, such as location of shopping goods versus convenience goods stores, effect of design of center on location, the relative importance of the corner store in the district, and the effect of non-retail facilities on business.

Location of Shopping Goods Versus Convenience Goods Stores

The main question in this area is whether the department, apparel, and men's wear shops capitalize on the supermarket customer whose shoppers are the steadiest in the center.

The practice is to segregate convenience from shopping goods. This practice is justified by the following phenomena:

1. Most shoppers prefer to buy their food needs close to home. Their inclination is to buy their food needs and go home. The popular use of frozen foods has no doubt influenced their behavior. In addition, the convenience good store has a much smaller trading area. While the regional supermarket may have a trading area of only three miles, the department and apparel stores have a trading area of up to thirty miles.
2. Supermarkets tend to draw their own traffic and are not dependent upon other stores. Nelson notes that supermarkets and other convenience goods stores are generally either slightly compatible or even may have a harmful effect on one another.
3. The parking needs of both type stores are different. Convenience stores have a greater turnover of parking areas. However, their customers will probably walk less to parking areas than customers for shopping goods.

The above factors indicate that convenience goods and shopping goods stores may best be located in different groupings.

Effect of Shopping Center Design on Location

There are three major types of centers: the strip, the mall, and the hub or cluster design.

The strip center is the most popular type deriving its name from its shape which resembles a group of connected stores. Its appearance is similar to a group of buildings in a central business district except that it is set back from the highway to allow for parking, and that it is the result of being planned as a unit.

The limiting factor in the strip type of center is the distance shoppers will travel in shopping. The major advantage in the strip center is the unobstructed path of stores and the visibility of all stores from the highway. Parking is also generally quite convenient in that it is available directly in front of the store.

Modifications of the strip design are common, such as the "L" shaped and "U" shaped center. The present practice is to place high traffic stores on both ends of the center so as to assure maximum traffic.

"The prototype of all centers containing more than 250,000 square feet is the mall center."[9] It consists of two strip centers placed face-to-face with a pedestrian mall. Parking is generally found on all sides. The existence of parking on the extremes of the center allows stores to have two displays: one facing the mall, the other the parking lot. The existence of two entrances can appreciably increase traffic, even though it creates a security problem.

Unlike the other forms of centers, the mall type can be enclosed and made weather-proof. Thus, the stores can be isolated from the outside weather conditions. The problem the mall creates is that a narrow mall creates congestion, while a wide mall may stifle crossings.

The third type of center is the hub or cluster formation, in which the stores are grouped around a center store, usually the department store. The department store is the focal point in the center, all stores are planned around it, all malls lead to the department store.

Often the type of center adopted is based on the amount of land available, zoning considerations, or the desire of several key tenants. Each type of formation has different characteristics with reference to parking facilities, nearness to the department store, nearness to complementary stores, visibility from the road, and existence of outlying shopping areas.

Corner Influence

The value added to a location because of its being at the intersection of two streets is called "corner influence." Corner influence is usually shown in the form of higher rentals, or greater sales value than a standard lot. The advantages present in a corner location include: increased show window display area, greater pedestrian traffic due to converging traffic flows from two streets, and greater ease of traffic flow due to the availability of two entrances.

> Generally, the amount of corner influence is greatest in areas of high land value and decreases as land value decreases. It will also vary with the widths and values of the intersecting streets. Corner influence is greatest in high volume retail areas . . .[10]

[9] Richard L. Nelson, *The Selection of Retail Locations* (New York: F. W. Dodge Corp., 1958), p. 293.

[10] Sanders A. Kahn, Frederick Case and Alfred Schimmel, *Real Estate Appraisal and Investment* (New York: The Ronald Press Company, 1963), p. 287.

The advantages of the corner location are mitigated in the shopping center by the fact that most stores have two entrances. For instance, traffic on the streets perpendicular to the mall is very sparse. Therefore, very little additional traffic passing the store comes from the streets off of the mall. The only traffic on these streets is from those who have parked their cars choosing to walk around several stores, rather than enter the mall through a store. The overwhelming majority of stores within centers go clear through from parking areas to the main mall, thus not making it essential to use corner passageways. In fact, walking through stores is the shortest way to get onto the mall from parking areas.

The advantage of having two entrances to ease the traffic flow is also minimized owing to the fact that most stores have more than one entrance. So do most stores have more than one display window: one facing the mall, the other facing parking areas.

Paying an additional rental for corner locations in shopping centers is questioned by the writer. Traditionally, the corner location in central business districts made much sense. Supplementary empirical evidence will be cited in a later section.

Effect of Non-Retail Facilities on Business

Non-retail establishments include those facilities whose operation evolves upon a service. Included within this framework are medical offices, beauty salons, laundromats, and motion picture theaters.

The effect of non-retail facilities can be measured by the degree of interchange between non-retail facilities and retail facilities. It is generally conceded that there is little interchange of business between most retail and non-retail establishments. Generally, most real estate executives do not object to them as long as they do not interfere with the operation of retail establishments. J. D. O'Connell, director of real estate for Grand Union Company, Paramus, New Jersey states:

> If the facilities are there to accommodate these tenants we do not absolutely prohibit them, but there have to be these facilities for peak periods. It is our experience that people go bowling and to the movies when we have our highest traffic periods. If they are not going to interfere with our business, we do not mind them being here.[11]

A study by S. O. Kaylin has shown that the majority of tenants surveyed like non-retail facilities, if thought was put into the location of the facility in relation to the other tenants and if there is adequate parking.[12] Nelson also notes that non-retail facility users tend to be a large drain on parking as their best hours coincide with the best hours for shopping.[13]

[11] "How Chains Feel About Non-Retail Facilities," *Chain Store Age* (May 1964), 40: 19.
[12] *Ibid.*, p. 18.
[13] Nelson, *op. cit.*, p. 249.

Other Considerations

In locating within a center, stores which may be open on Sunday or in late hours should be located near the front of the center. Shoppers will thus not have to feel uneasy about walking through desolate locations. Secondly, greater visibility is available to allow passers-by to be aware of the store's hours.

Generally, the lower levels of centers are occupied by offices and service establishments. Lack of sufficient window display space, inconvenience of shoppers with small children, etc. are often cited as reasons for the use of these locations for other than retail goods establishments. However, service shops can be in very obscure places and still do quite well.

The question of what portion of a center should be comprised of certain classes of stores received much attention. "Department and apparel stores," in Dr. Hoyt's opinion, "should occupy 70 percent of a regional center."[14] Allied Stores believes that the department store should be approximately one-third of the total size of the center.[15]

The drawing power, not the name of the store, should be the point of orientation. A market-conscious small retailer may often do much better than a big-name chain. Ratios such as those presented above must be used with selectivity and understanding. A real estate executive comments on drawing power:

> The important thing is not the category of the store but the identity of the operation. On the West Coast, one national variety chain (Chain A) has a tremendous reputation as a top-flight merchandiser; a competitor, also a national variety chain (Chain B), has failed to make any impact on the Western market. So if you get Chain A into the center, you can get by with B type supermarket and drug stores—although A type chains for grocery, drug and variety gives you the hottest combination possible.[16]

The point is that at least one of the key stores in the center must be a powerful merchandiser, and that the ideal retail balance must take into account both quantitative and qualitative characteristics.

Summary on Site Location Factors

One cannot be content with merely following other chains into a center. First of all, the choice of center must be made in relation to the store's retailing strategy. Secondly, there is so much disparity among locations within a center that it is quite possible to choose the right center and the wrong location.

[14] Samuel Feinberg, *What Makes Shopping Centers Tick?* (New York: Fairchild Publications, 1960), p. 19.

[15] *Idem.*

[16] "What Combination of Tenants Should a Shopping Center Have?" *Chain Store Age* (March 1960), 36: 37.

Foster E. Sears, manager of site location for J. C. Penney, lists the following factors as site location criteria within a center: store visibility, customer access, proximity to comparison outlets, tenant balance and integration, traffic access, and trading area economic analysis.[17]

EMPIRICAL RESEARCH—ANALYSIS OF REGIONAL SHOPPING CENTERS

Current locational practices of stores within regional shopping centers are examined based on store placement in the following regional shopping centers:

1. Garden State Plaza—Paramus, New Jersey
2. Bergen Mall—Paramus, New Jersey
3. Cross County—Yonkers, New York
4. Roosevelt Field—Nassau County, New York
5. Green Acres—Valley Stream, New York

The above centers have been analyzed according to tenant composition, corner locations, center layout, parking facilities, placement of non-retail facilities, placement of convenience goods in comparison with shopping goods stores, and the number of store entrances.

The writer visited the above shopping centers and listed each store, type of business, number of entrances, number of levels, store affiliation, and whether the store is free-standing, corner or attached. All stores were visited during a thirty-day period. Vacant stores or stores under construction were not included in the tabulation.

At a later date, Standard Industrial Classifications were included so as to make the data more compatible with prior research. Only stores at ground level were tabulated in this survey. Thus, stores on lower promenades or on upper levels were not included in this store census. Store frontage represents the number of front feet facing the mall. If a center contains two stores of the same chain, they were both enumerated separately.

Entrances

Having two entrances gives the store the advantages of a corner store, namely, two display windows, two pedestrian traffic flows, and better traffic flows resulting from two means of egress and ingress. Shopping center developers were quick to recognize the advantages of this; the figures indicate that all the centers surveyed had at least fifty-six per cent of their stores having two or more entrances.

Several interesting observations may be drawn from Table 1. Firstly,

[17] "How Chains Are Stalking Best Locations Within Centers," *Chain Store Age* (May 1964), 40: 40.

TABLE 1.

Number of Stores Having One, Two, Three or More Entrances Within Five Regional Shopping Centers, Individual Centers and Total Classification, in Absolute Amounts and %

Name of Center	*One entrance*	*Two entrances*	*Three or more entrances*	*Total**
Bergen Mall	21 (42%)	25 (50%)	4 (8%)	50 (100%)
Garden State Plaza	30 (43%)	34 (49%)	5 (7%)	69 (100%)
Cross County	18 (31%)	32 (56%)	7 (12%)	57 (100%)
Green Acres	34 (42%)	44 (54%)	3 (4%)	81 (100%)
Roosevelt Field	47 (45%)	40 (54%)	4 (4%)	91 (100%)
Total five centers	150 (43%)	175 (50%)	23 (7%)	348 (100%)

*Totals may not add to 100% due to rounding.

there is no evidence of all centers having the same distribution. For instance, the range in percent among the centers having one and two entrances is 14 percent and 7 percent respectively.

The distribution in no way varies with center size. The range of the size of the centers is large, with Bergen Mall being the smallest with fifty stores, and Roosevelt Field being close to twice the size, having ninety-one stores. (This is an understatement of the size of Roosevelt Field as several vacant stores were not counted.)

Comparing the centers to one another, several interesting observations can be made. Firstly, all variety and department stores surveyed had over two entrances. This is partly due to the fact that most of these stores were "free-standing." In addition, entrances are necessary to ease the traffic flow in these stores. Considering the relatively high traffic volume in these stores, a smooth traffic flow device is essential. Furthermore, several entrances assure traffic being generated from all sides of the store.

The next highest percentage of stores with over one entrance is the shoe store. Seventy-five percent of all the shoe stores had two entrances. Clothing and furnishing stores also contained a large number of entrances.

Retail Balance

Retail balance refers to an optimum grouping of stores within a shopping area. This grouping can be measured by the degree to which pedestrian traffic flows are created within the center, the character of the trading area of the center, and the proportion of the total market which purchases at a particular shopping center. Generally, for a center to be effective it must have a broad span of stores so as to accommodate diverse tastes and needs.

TABLE 2.

Number and % of Stores Within Clothing, Accessory and Shoe Classifications Within Five Shopping Centers, by Individual Center and Total Classifications

Name of Center	*Number %*	*Total Number Stores*
Bergen Mall	22 (44%)	50
Garden State Plaza	30 (43%)	69
Cross County	26 (46%)	57
Green Acres	32 (40%)	81
Roosevelt Field	35 (39%)	91
Total	145 (42%)	348

The largest number of stores within the centers studied is within the shoe store classification. Forty-eight shoe stores were found in the five centers. One hundred forty-five of three hundred forty-eight stores in the centers studied were within the clothing, accessory, and shoe classifications.

The range of the number of stores within this classification varies by center with a low of 39% of the stores within this classification at Roosevelt Field and a high of 46% of the stores within this classification at Cross County.

Interestingly, it appears that there is an inverse correlation between the size of the center and the portion of the stores occupied by clothing accessory and shoe retailers. The larger the center in terms of number of stores, the smaller the portion devoted to wearing apparel.

The second classification in terms of number of stores is the service class. These stores are significant for several reasons. Firstly, a major portion of service purchases are specific intent. Location is not of major importance for these retailers. Secondly, because of their very nature these stores are often occupied and owned by a nonchain retailer. Of the total five centers, only 36 of 348 stores are of the service variety. This figure only includes stores on the main level. Service stores surveyed included: barber and beauty shops, shoe repair and dyers, cleaning and alteration shops, laundry, stock brokers, loan agency, and savings banks.

An important consideration affecting retail balance is the number of chain stores within a center. Even though independent merchants may more effectively gear their operations to the particular market served, center managers are often forced to accept chain stores because of the need for adequate mortgage loans. Thus, lenders through their evaluation principles often have the ultimate say with regard to tenant selection.

Of the 348 stores within the five centers, 205 are occupied by chain tenants. The influence of the chains is greater upon considering the sales of the chain versus the nonchain group. The average store frontage is higher among chain stores, mostly due to the fact that no department stores,

TABLE 3.

Number Chain and Nonchain Stores Within Shopping Centers, Individual and Total Classifications

Name of center	*Chain tenants*	*Nonchain tenants*	*Total tenants*
Bergen Mall	33	17	50
Garden State Plaza	39	30	69
Cross County	37	20	57
Green Acres	47	34	81
Roosevelt Field	49	42	91
Total	205	143	348

variety stores or other users of large frontage were independents. However, among the other types of stores there appears to be no significant difference among store size. Thus, the nature and store type has a greater effect on store size than store affiliation.

Corner Locations

A corner location is defined to be a building of a semi-detached nature. Thus, free-standing locations are omitted from consideration. The purpose of this section is to determine if any type of retail establishment dominates corner locations, and if there is a significant difference among chain and independent retailers in regard to corner occupancy. Thirdly, the effect of a corner location on land use is studied.

Of the 315 stores studied in the above categories, 96 were corner locations (excluding free-standing locations). Particularly high proportions of corner

TABLE 4.

Corner Locations by Standard Industrial Classification Within Five Shopping Centers, Total Five Centers, Absolute Amounts

S.I.C. Classification		*Corner stores*	*Total stores*
52	Paint, Hardware, Wallpaper	1	9
53	Dept. Stores, Variety, Fabric	2	28
54	Grocery, Candy, Dairy	13	29
56	Clothing, Accessories, Shoes	31	145
57	Furniture, Furnishings, Appliances	11	34
58	Restaurants, Eating Places	12	21
59	Drug, Jewelry, Florist, Liquor	11	27
78	Theaters	1	2
	Miscellaneous Services	14	20
		96	315

stores are found in the candy and restaurant fields, among furniture stores, liquor, drug and florists and among services such as banks and stock brokers. Of the 96 corner stores surveyed, 64 were found to be chain stores while 32 were independent operations. This two to one ratio is significantly higher than the 1.4 to 1 ratio of chain stores to independents in the five centers, irrespective of location. (See Table 4.)

Of the 96 corner locations surveyed, less than one-third were of the clothing, furnishing, and shoe type while this type made up 62 percent of the total stores.

Generally, the corner location land use was compatible with the use of the adjacent land. Thus, where sites in the area of the corner location were for distribution of convenience goods, the corner location retailer had a similar function. The advantage received from the fact that the location was a corner one did not give the site a better use.

Shopping Center Layout

Shopping center layout is concerned with the placement of stores to maximize traffic flows throughout the center. The placement of stores is ultimately determined by the size of the center, the amount of land available, and the distance shoppers will walk from one store to another and to parking.

The placement of convenience goods stores is an interesting problem to the developer. Research has shown that few shoppers will buy both shopping and convenience goods on the same trip. In the centers visited, both areas were separated from each other either by distance, or by a highway, as in the case of Bergen Mall. A bridge separated the convenience goods section from the shopping goods section in Bergen Mall. Very sparse traffic was noted during an observation period.

Only in Green Acres was the convenience goods area split into two sections on opposite sides of the center. One area contained a fruit and vegetable stand, a delicatessen, a meat market, a bakery, and a supermarket. The other side of the center also had a convenience section with a meat market, supermarket, laundry, and bakery. The split was probably made to lessen price competition among the stores. However, the cost of this feature is the smaller traffic flows in each section. The areas are far enough away to discourage shoppers from going to both on the same trip.

All of the centers studied are of the modified mall type with the department stores placed on opposite ends to generate traffic. An interesting modification is Roosevelt Field which is designed to appear like a double mall. The advantage of this is that a through store on the central island could appeal to diverse traffic flows. Disadvantages stem from traffic being split into too many directions, and thereby being thin in many areas. Furthermore, parking is now further removed from shoppers who wish to use the central island to shop.

Offices were contained in an underground level in Garden State Plaza and in Roosevelt Field. In Cross County, they were contained in an upper level. The only instance of an office used strictly for record keeping was found in Bergen Mall. In the other centers, less intensive uses of the land were found on the outskirts of the center, or in small malls off the major mall.

Parking Facilities

In all the centers visited, parking facilities were contained around the perimeter of the center. All of the facilities were on ground level, with the exception of Bergen Mall which had some area reserved for parking below ground. Parking areas separate John Wanamaker's from the rest of the center in Cross County. In the centers patterned on a regular mall basis, parking can be found at the rear of every store, a convenience in the rain or when carrying many packages.

SUMMARY

Location analysis in the regional shopping center is more sophisticated than in the shopping district. Not only must the analyst be concerned with complementary stores, trading areas, parking, transportation, and traffic counts, but also, he must be concerned with such areas as effect of design on location, the location of shopping goods versus convenience goods, effect of non-retail facilities, and retail balance. The same rules do not apply to centers and districts as evidenced by the number of entrances minimizing the importance of the corner location in the center.

The analysis of regional shopping centers highlights some of the principles discussed. Some of the findings are:

1. Centers contain a large portion of clothing, accessory and shoe stores;
2. Larger centers appear to offer a greater portion of service facilities;
3. Chain tenants occupy the majority of stores in all the centers studied;
4. Shopping and convenience goods stores were separated in all centers studied; and
5. The added advantage from a corner location does not significantly improve land use.

RECOMMENDATIONS

While much research has been done on the uniqueness of each location and on analyzing locational characteristics, little effort has been made on matching the characteristics of the location with the needs of the retailer. The awareness of the differences in locations within shopping centers provides the necessary prerequisite for the complete study.

One of the voids which is increasingly being filled is the study of consumer shopping behavior. This adds insight to the needs of a particular retailer. Increased emphasis on shopping behavior and on discovering retailer's needs will help solve the problem of finding the ideal location for each retailer in the shopping center.

QUESTIONS

1. What risks and costs are associated with a poor choice of retail location? Do these costs apply equally to both large and small retailers?
2. What factors must a shopping center developer consider in locating a high-fashion specialty dress store within a shopping center?
3. Based on Professor Berman's research, what factors should a prospective tenant look for in choosing a location for a shoe store in a shopping center?

D. COMMUNICATION

Communication refers to the retailer's attempts, through his organization, to communicate with the consumer. It is done through advertising (newspaper, television, radio, direct mail, interior displays, and various forms of promotion) and through personal selling.

Retailers have many choices of ways in which to reach consumers. For the large firms, the overwhelming preference is newspaper advertising. George Fisk, Lawrence Nein, and Stanley J. Shapiro discuss their findings concerning the advertising policies of Philadelphia food chains. The article describes their strategies and offers reasons for the actions of each of the firms studied.

The increasing use of trading stamps and games is examined in the next three articles. In the "Memorandum to the New York City Council" by the Sperry and Hutchinson Company (S & H Green Stamps), the case for using trading stamps is presented succinctly. In the next article, Lord Sainsbury, an opponent of trading stamps in Great Britain, presents his views. The last promotional device that has gained acceptance in the sixties, games, is reviewed in the article from a staff report of the Federal Trade Commission.

The last four readings in this section are concerned with personal selling. In "Retail Reorganization," Wheelock Bingham and David Yunich present the problems faced by the expanding department store in organizing its buying and selling efforts. Alfred Oxenfeldt describes a particular type—the salesman of appliances—and discusses the various types of customers in relation to the function of the salesman. John Wingate describes a different type of selling, that of the auctioneer. In the last article, he demonstrates the use of a statistical technique to help solve a sales hiring problem.

29

Price Rivalry Among Philadelphia Food Chains

George Fisk, Lawrence Nein, Stanley J. Shapiro

Retailers have for some time employed a variety of merchandising techniques that might be considered forms of promotional pricing. Until recently, promotional pricing had not been sufficiently delineated from the more generally accepted constructs of price and nonprice competition. Recently, however, Wroe Alderson (1963) discussed the concept and some of the promotional pricing techniques supermarkets might employ. Among the illustrations provided were the following: advertising a product at its regular price; cutting prices sharply on featured items or moderately "across the board"; cornering supply and offering a desired item at a price that competition cannot match without running out of merchandise; and finally, offering trading stamps or coupons.

Alderson reaffirmed his belief that attempts at enterprise differentiation play an important part in retail competition. Nevertheless, he argues that theories of monopolistic competition and oligopoly both prove inadequate when viewed in light of the competitive behavior of Philadelphia area food chains. Promotional pricing is presented here as an extension of the concept of administered pricing that may prove of real value in studying competitive interaction among retailers.

There is little discussion of promotional pricing, either implicitly or by name, in the literature on retail pricing. The usual practice is to consider every customer appeal other than price as some form of nonprice competition intended to differentiate the product or the enterprise. The concept of promotional pricing, in contrast, implies that the alleged dichotomy between price and nonprice competition has been drawn in an unnecessarily sharp and often confusing manner.

This article reports on research conducted with two objectives in mind—further development of the concept of promotional pricing, and determination of the extent to which Philadelphia food chains use promotional pricing techniques. The following aspects of promotional pricing were examined: (1) the various forms of promotional pricing that could be employed in newspaper advertising; (2) differences in the promotional pricing strategies

Reprinted from *Journal of Advertising Research,* Vol. 4, No. 2, June 1964, pp. 12–20. Advertising Research Foundation.

of competing food chains; (3) the frequency with which prices differed for "comparable" items advertised simultaneously by rivals; (4) competitive reaction to differences in price; and (5) prices charged by four chains for "comparable" items advertised by at least one of them.

The studies also were expected to answer three basic questions concerning the use of promotional pricing by rival food chains:

> What forms of promotional pricing are associated with leader and follower positions in a retail market dominated by a few large supermarket chains?
> What differences exist in the manner in which rival firms use promotional pricing to sell the various classes of grocery products?
> Which major firms usually initiate promotional price challenges, and which limit themselves to responding to such challenges?

FORMS OF PROMOTIONAL PRICING

A more detailed review of the various forms of promotional pricing utilized in newspaper advertising revealed that Alderson's initial list of techniques was illustrative rather than exhaustive. Also, the existence of two equally important dimensions of promotional pricing was recognized: either the amount of money asked for the product, or the amount of product offered for the money could be varied. Appeals involving price cuts, trading stamps, and coupons are obvious instances of promotional pricing, but the concept encompasses much more. It includes deals involving a change in the quantity of the product advertised, or the offering of a second item as an additional purchasing inducement.

Promotional pricing inducements to patronage which stress price may be offered in the store or in advertisements, and may take one (or several) of the following forms:

1. Feature pricing An item is allocated a minimum of four square inches of space in a newspaper advertisement, usually in a prominent position, and offered at an attractive price.
2. A combination recipe or menu ingredient price. The store offers, at a specified price, ingredients for a whole meal or for a particular recipe requiring several items.
3. Price discounts. "Save 8¢," "Regular $9.00, now $4.49."
4. Specials. Neither a price nor quantity discount is offered, but the wording implies a sale below regular shelf price. "Summertime drink sale," "49¢ grocery stockup sale," "butter, egg, milk prices reduced."
5. Offering coupons redeemable for part of the purchase price, or for extra trading stamps. This is a "near money" price reduction.
6. Offering extra stamps with the purchase of an item or a minimum amount of merchandise. This is a second form of "near money" price reduction.

Product or merchandise based promotional pricing inducements include:

1. Quantity discount on multiple purchases of the same item. This is the familiar "toofer" or "six five-cent bars for 25¢."
2. Tie-in discounts. "Half price tickets to Phillies Ball Game with every $5.00 purchase," "One package free when you buy five."
3. Lottery. "Shopper's Sweepstakes—86 valuable prizes. Nothing to buy; just fill in name and address on the entry blank; available from any cashier."
4. Announcement of the availability of a quantity of an item at a shelf price.

The wide variety of ways in which these techniques are combined often makes it difficult to compare the offerings of competing firms. This need not indicate a deliberate attempt to confuse customers, but rather is due to the efforts of competing stores to use all possible appeals in an effort to attract business.

Next, we determined the relative frequency with which various types of promotional pricing were employed by the major rivals—A & P, Acme, Food Fair, Penn Fruit, and Thriftway, a local discount chain. Every item advertised by these five firms in the Wednesday edition of the *Philadelphia Bulletin* was assigned to one of the promotional price or quantity categories. We reviewed 12 issues of the *Bulletin:* those appearing the first week of each month from July 1961 through June 1962. Tables 1 and 2 summarize the results of this examination.

TABLE 1.

Chain Store Advertising in 12 *Bulletin* Issues

	A & P	*Acme*	*Food Fair*	*Penn Fruit*	*Thriftway*
Advertising pages:					
Total	19.9	20.3	15.3	16.8	12.2
Average per issue	1.7	1.7	1.3	1.4	1.0
Item mentions:					
Total	1,646	1,532	1,007	980	619
Average per issue	137	128	84	82	52
Average per page of advertising	83	75	66	58	51

As Table 1 indicates, both A & P and Acme strive to create an image of a large assortment at "low everyday prices." Food Fair, Penn Fruit, and Thriftway avoid this advertising "space race" and mention fewer items per issue. They seek, rather, to use promotional price elements in unique ways to preserve their ability to compete. As Table 2 shows, Food Fair uses lotteries and extra stamps, while Penn Fruit mentions discounts and specials with relatively greater frequency. Thriftway, a would-be shelf and feature price competitor despite its relatively small size, concentrates on features to a greater extent than either Food Fair or Penn Fruit. The relative frequency

TABLE 2.

Promotional Price Appeals Used in *Bulletin* Advertising (12 Issues)

	A & P	*Acme*	*Food Fair*	*Penn Fruit*	*Thriftway*
Total item mentions:	100%	100%	100%	100%	100%
Shelf price	68	69	57	46	54
Features	18	9	11	12	17
Discounts and specials	13	18	25	36	28
Tie-ins	1	1	1	1	1
Extra stamps	—	3	4	5	—
Lotteries	—	—	2	—	—

of mention of discounts bears a rough inverse relation to the market power of the five chains.

Because they advertise more, A & P and Acme mentioned at shelf price nearly twice as many items as any of the other three chains. For the same reason, even though they put less emphasis on discounts and specials, the "tonnage" of A & P and Acme discounts and special appeals exceeds that of Food Fair and Thriftway, and approaches Penn Fruit. Obviously, Food Fair, Penn Fruit, and Thriftway, with fewer item mentions per page of advertising, are allocating more space to certain item mentions than either A & P or Acme. The items given the most space were those featured, discounted, or otherwise incorporated into a special offer.

Features (i.e., mentions covering four square inches or more), as Table 2 indicates, constitute the second most common method in A & P's promotional scheme. A & P advertising, in fact, relies heavily on a relatively large number of bold-print features stating merely the name and price of the item. This approach is used instead of the myriad of special promotional devices, including trading stamps, coupons, and contest promotions, adopted by the other four chains. Such a promotional pattern would seem to be in keeping with the strategy often imputed to A & P—to create a public image of economy and dependable quality without frills.

As Table 3 indicates, A & P avoids both stamps and coupons, while Thriftway avoids stamps. Acme, with one foot in the low-shelf-price camp, is nevertheless a heavy user of both stamps and coupons. Acme's use of every kind of price inducement may have a bearing on its relatively strong consumer patronage in the Philadelphia market area and its indifference to being underpriced in advertising. Food Fair, which is a strong feature price challenger of A & P, uses both stamps and coupons, but offers fewer extra trading stamps than either Acme or Penn Fruit. Tables 2 and 3 thus indicate the existence of wide divergencies in the promotional pricing policies now being pursued.

TABLE 3.

Use of Trading Stamps and Coupons in *Bulletin* Advertising (12 Issues)

	A & P	*Acme*	*Food Fair*	*Penn Fruit*	*Thriftway*
Extra trading stamp values:					
Total	—	2,110	1,720	2,665	—
Average per issue	—	175	145	220	—
Coupons:					
Total	—	49	41	27	14
Average per issue	—	4	3	2	1

PROMOTIONAL VARIATIONS

Variations in promotional pricing by product class was the second topic investigated. How often and in what manner an item is mentioned reflects both the retailer's appraisal of supply-and-demand market factors and of what rivals may do.

An overriding concern with buyers' wishes is indicated by Table 4, which shows that meats were mentioned most by three out of five chains.

TABLE 4.

Ranked Frequency of Item Mention by Product Category in *Bulletin* Advertising (12 Issues)

	A & P	*Acme*	*Food Fair*	*Penn Fruit*	*Thriftway*	*Average Rank*
1. Meat	1	2	2	1	1	1.4
2. Frozen foods	2	3	4	3	3	3.0
3. Canned fruits and vegetables	3	5	3	4	2	3.4
4. Soap products	8	1	1	2	10*	4.4
5. Bakery goods	4	4	8	5	5	5.2
6. Fish	5	7	5	6	7	6.0
7. Dairy products	6	8	6	7	10*	7.4
8. Fresh fruits and vegetables	7	10*	7	10*	4	7.6

*Food classes not within the top eight for a given chain were assigned a rank (weight) of 10.

Interest in the cooperative advertising allowances offered by manufacturers is revealed by the high frequency with which soap products were mentioned by the remaining two chains. Meats, canned fruits and vegetables, frozen foods, fish, and bakery products showed relatively little variation in frequency of mention when compared with soaps and fresh fruits and vegetables.

TABLE 5.

Item Mentions in *Bulletin* Ads by Major Promotion Groups Within Food Classes

	A & P	*Acme*	*Food Fair*	*Penn Fruit*	*Thriftway*
			Meats		
Shelf price	68%	65%	56%	53%	66%
Features	31	17	32	23	32
Discounts and specials*	1	13	9	15	2
Tie-ins	—	—	—	1	—
Extra stamps	—	5	2	8	—
Lotteries	—	—	1	—	—
			Frozen Foods		
Shelf price	82%	73%	79%	62%	73%
Features	9	7	4	4	4
Discounts and specials*	9	17	17	33	21
Tie-ins	—	1	—	—	2
Extra stamps	—	2	—	1	—
Lotteries	—	—	—	—	—
			Canned Fruits and Vegetables		
Shelf price	68%	64%	58%	29%	58%
Features	25	7	2	10	3
Discounts and specials*	7	27	37	59	39
Tie-ins	—	2	—	—	—
Extra stamps	—	—	—	2	—
Lotteries	—	—	3	—	—
			Bakery Products		
Shelf price	50%	68%	28%	30%	38%
Features	7	10	14	6	11
Discounts and specials*	43	20	51	59	49
Tie-ins	—	1	—	1	2
Extra stamps	—	2	4	5	—
Lotteries	—	—	4	—	—
			Fish		
Shelf price	90%	84%	65%	61%	47%
Features	11	8	27	25	33
Discounts and specials*	—	7	3	10	20
Tie-ins	—	—	—	—	—
Extra stamps	—	1	3	4	—
Lotteries	—	—	3	—	—

*Includes all price and quantity discounts and special sales promotional event items.

TABLE 5. (Continued)

	A & P	*Acme*	*Food Fair*	*Penn Fruit*	*Thriftway*
			Dairy Products		
Shelf price	66%	68%	69%	73%	68%
Features	28	16	12	4	14
Discounts and specials*	4	16	7	13	18
Tie-ins	2	—	4	4	—
Extra stamps	—	1	3	6	—
Lotteries	—	—	4	—	—
			Fresh Fruits and Vegetables		
Shelf price	58%	45%	48%	34%	54%
Features	33	50	32	44	46
Discounts and specials*	9	—	10	11	—
Tie-ins	—	—	—	—	—
Extra stamps	—	5	3	11	—
Lotteries	—	—	7	—	—
			Soap Products		
Shelf price	51%	81%	61%	53%	46%
Features	11	—	—	1	8
Discounts and specials*	38	18	35	43	46
Tie-ins	—	1	1	—	—
Extra stamps	—	—	2	3	—
Lotteries	—	—	1	—	—

Of even greater interest is the relationship between the promotional price tactics employed and the market reputation of the firm. Looking at Table 5, we see that Penn Fruit, smallest of the big four, used extra stamps to increase turnover of fresh fruits and vegetables—items on which its original reputation was built. All chains recognized the importance of meats in feature promotions, but Penn Fruit employed discounts and special deals more extensively than its rivals for frozen foods, canned fruits and vegetables, and bakery products. In contrast, Acme, A & P, and Thriftway depended on advertised shelf prices to a greater extent than either Food Fair or Penn Fruit. Thriftway, the smallest chain, does not match A & P or Acme in the amount of shelf price advertising for all categories of merchandise. However, for those items Thriftway features most frequently, it tries to create a discount image by following a promotional pricing strategy similar to that of Acme and A & P.

Differences in the percent of item mentions of the magnitude revealed by Table 5 led us to wonder whether the prices of comparable items varied between chains. To find out, attention had to be paid to store as well as to advertised prices. The remainder of this paper discusses three studies involving, in turn, a comparison of advertised prices, a measure of competitive response to being underpriced in advertising, and a store audit of the shelf prices of competitors.

FEATURE PRICE INTERACTION

Which major firms initiate promotional price challenges and which respond? Because of the difficulties in tracing price changes for thousands of products, the analysis was restricted to featured items. (The analysis also excludes Thriftway, the smallest chain.) Feature pricing interaction was studied by finding features advertised by two or more of the chains in the Wednesday evening *Bulletin*, and then advertised again by one or more of the same chains the next morning in the Thursday *Inquirer*. During each of 12 weeks from Sepetmber 3 to November 29, 1962, prices of all features advertised in common by two or more chains in the Wednesday *Bulletin* were recorded. When the Thursday *Inquirer* contained a reaction to the low bidder, either a price change or a deletion from the advertisement, store audits were conducted.

To be included, an item had to be of feature size (i.e., four square inches

TABLE 6A.

Price Comparison of All Feature Items Advertised in Common by Chains in Same *Bulletin* Issue

	Acme Price Is:			*Food Fair Price Is:*			*Penn Fruit Price Is:*		
	Same	*Higher*	*Lower*	*Same*	*Higher*	*Lower*	*Same*	*Higher*	*Lower*
A & P	27	—	10	16	6	15	21	5	10
Acme	—	—	—	10	7	6	15	5	3
Food Fair	—	—	—	—	—	—	15	4	2

TABLE 6B.

	*Number of Features Advertised in Common**	*Number of Overlaps between Chain and Competitor***	*Price Comparison*		
			Same	*Lower*	*Higher*
A & P	90	110	64	11	35
Acme	62	83	52	22	9
Food Fair	62	81	41	25	15
Penn Fruit	62	80	51	17	12

*Excludes Thriftway, the smallest chain.

**The second column exceeds the first because, for example, when the same item was advertised simultaneously by three chains, three bilateral comparisons of prices could be made.

or more) in the advertising of at least one chain and also appear in the advertising of another. The low bidder, the high bidder, and the total number of common features advertised at the same price or in different units of quantity were recorded. The results of comparing each possible pair of chains to determine the frequency with which they matched and underpriced each other are shown in Table 6A. (In studying Tables 6A and 6B, keep in mind that common features refer to items which may have been featured by only one firm and simply mentioned with the price by competitors.)

Referring to the A & P row in Table 6A, we see that Acme, Food Fair, and Penn Fruit advertised common features with A & P with about equal frequency over the 12 week period. Also, when the data were pooled (Table 6B) so that a major chain could be compared against all three rivals, A & P is revealed as having half again as many features in common with the "other three chains" (90) as did Acme, Food Fair, and Penn Fruit (62 each).

When they matched features with A & P, the other three chains usually had the lower advertised price. In all 10 instances in which it advertised identical units at prices different from A & P, Acme was priced lower. Food Fair underpriced A & P 15 of the 21 times in which there was a price difference, and Penn Fruit was lower than A & P on 10 of 15 occasions. Advertising of the same features among Acme, Food Fair, and Penn Fruit was less frequent and less "one-way" in terms of low and high bidders.

Equally impressive is the relatively high frequency with which each of the chains matched the prices of three main rivals. As Table 6B reveals, all four matched their competitors in more than half of the comparisons made.

COMPETITIVE REACTION TO BEING UNDERPRICED

The relative frequency with which a chain advertised items at prices above, below, or identical with its rivals had now been determined. The next step involved tracing the response of a chain when it found itself priced above a competitor. Philadelphia grocery chains follow up their Wednesday *Bulletin* advertising with advertisements in the Thursday *Inquirer*. This advertising usually contains all those items mentioned in the preceding day's *Bulletin*. The *Inquirer* can make last minute changes if a chain wishes to modify its offering on the basis of competitors' *Bulletin* advertising. Chains which have been underpriced in the Wednesday evening *Bulletin* can thus choose among three courses of action: do nothing—allow prices to stay the same; reduce prices to meet or beat a competitor; drop the items on Thursday.

Table 7 shows the competitive reaction to being underpriced in terms of "reduced" price or "dropped" item from *Inquirer* ad. One could question accepting deletion of an item as proof of a reaction to competition. However, such deletions are highly conspicuous. Invariably the list of *Bulletin* mentions

TABLE 7.

Reaction in Thursday Inquirer Advertising to Common Features Appearing in Wednesday *Bulletin*

	No. of Times "Underpriced"		*Advertised Lower Price in Wednesday* Bulletin:							
			A & P	*Acme*	*Food Fair*	*Penn Fruit*	*FF/ Acme*	*A & P/ Acme*	*PF/ FF*	*Total*
A & P	35	Reduced	—	3	3	—	—	—	1	7
		Dropped	—	3	8	4	4	—	—	19
Acme	9	Reduced	—	—	—	—	—	—	—	—
		Dropped	—	—	1	—	—	—	—	1
Food Fair	15	Reduced	1	1	—	—	—	2	—	4
		Dropped	2	1	—	—	—	1	—	4
Penn Fruit	12	Reduced	—	—	2	—	—	2	—	4
		Dropped	2	1	1	—	—	—	—	4

located above and below the underbid item remain intact in sequence and format on the *Inquirer* page, with only the underbid item deleted entirely or replaced with a different item.

Most prominent in Table 7 is the obvious awareness and concern evinced by A & P at being underpriced. On 26 of the 35 occasions in which A & P was underpriced on common features in the *Bulletin,* a reaction was observed in the *Inquirer* the next day. In most cases (19 out of 26), the item was dropped from the *Inquirer* ad and the price left unchanged in the store.

In contrast to A & P, Acme was relatively unconcerned with being underbid in the *Bulletin* and, though underpriced 9 times, dropped the item from its *Inquirer* advertising only once.

Food Fair was the low price bidder more often than the other chains and elicited a reaction on 15 of the 25 occasions on which it was low bidder.

Most items reduced in the *Inquirer* to meet a lower *Bulletin* bid were priced in the store at the lower *Inquirer* price. However, in at least one observed instance for each of the four chains, an item reduced in price in the *Inquirer* was left in the store at the higher *Bulletin* price.

In only one instance did a chain underbid in the *Bulletin* undercut its rival in the *Inquirer*. When price reductions were made, reactions usually involved just meeting the lowest bidder's price.

Advertised prices of commonly featured items can be extremely misleading as a general index of a chain's price level. In the first place, advertising offers but a limited number of items for comparing prices. Even more important, each chain obviously advertises only those items on which it feels it is being competitive. In order to get at the overall price levels of the chains, a store audit was conducted. Information was gathered on the prices charged by the competing chains for 600 comparable items in twelve classes of food products. (The twelve classes represent over 80 percent of all items mentioned in food chain newspaper advertising.) For an individual item to be audited, it had to appear at least once for any of the four chains in the Wednesday *Bulletin* over the period studied. Private brand merchandise that was not comparable (i.e., in grade) was intentionally excluded from the study.

Stores selected for the audit represent a "chunk sample" chosen on the basis of convenience rather than by a probability mechanism or by expert judgment. The chunk was selected, however, with the intention of providing relatively broad coverage of the Philadelphia market. Auditors checked four stores (one from each chain) in a different sector of the Philadelphia area for each of ten weeks. Thus, a total of forty different Philadelphia area supermarket outlets were visited.

Exact homogeneity of product was a prerequisite for comparison. For example, a five-pound bag of Gold Medal Flour could not be compared to a ten-pound bag by merely doubling the observed shelf price, since greater quantities are generally priced a few cents lower per unit weight than smaller quantities of a given food item. Similarly, three 46-ounce cans of Del Monte Grapefruit Drink could not be compared to four 46-ounce cans of the same item; nor could a pack of eight tomatoes be compared to tomatoes offered by the pound. All items were priced at the lowest offer made in the store. Prices appearing on the container or on the food item itself were the only prices used.

The auditing was conducted in two separate five-week phases, September 17 through November 19, 1962. Each selected item was priced only once during either five-week phase. As shown in Table 8, 295 items were sampled during the first five weeks and 302 during the second five weeks. The intent

TABLE 8.

Items Sampled During Each Five-Week Phase, by Food Class (10-Week Store Audit)

	First Five Weeks	*Second Five Weeks*	*Total*
Meats	65	52	117
Fish	12	18	30
Fresh fruits and vegetables	32	39	71
Canned fruits and vegetables	32	31	63
Frozen foods	26	28	54
Tea and coffee	21	15	36
Toilet articles	20	19	39
Oils and dressings	13	17	30
Canned drinks and juices	9	12	21
Bakery products	20	26	46
Soap products	36	36	72
Dairy products	9	9	18
TOTAL	295	302	597

was to verify the results of the first five weeks against those of the second. Thus, though no item was sampled twice within either five-week period, the items compared during the second period were in large part the same items checked during the first five weeks.

Here are the more noteworthy results of the ten-week store audit, as shown in Table 9A:

1. Food Fair was the only chain where the number of meat items offered at lower prices exceeded the number of meat items offered at prices higher that those of competitors. Of 184 price comparisons in which it differed from competitor's prices on meat, Food Fair's shelf price was lower in 129 cases, or 70 percent of the time, mainly because of its aggressiveness in promoting meat. A & P, Acme, and Penn Fruit, respectively, were *under-priced* in 52 percent, 59 percent, and 64 percent of the instances in which advertised prices were not the same for comparable meat items. Interestingly, meats and toilet articles were the only two out of the twelve

TABLE 9A.

Shelf Prices of Items in 12 Selected Categories (10-Week Store Audit)

		Prices Compared with Other Chains			*Total Price Difference*	
		Same	*Higher*	*Lower*	*Higher*	*Lower*
Meat	A & P	142	79	74	$3.18	$2.16
	Acme	143	95	65	3.77	2.01
	Food Fair	102	55	129	1.71	5.68
	Penn Fruit	141	95	56	3.49	1.80
Fish	A & P	16	14	14	1.19	.49
	Acme	16	4	28	.29	2.10
	Food Fair	19	22	5	1.30	.34
	Penn Fruit	13	13	6	.46	.23
Fresh fruits and vegetables	A & P	37	10	108	.21	3.18
	Acme	64	58	29	1.32	.66
	Food Fair	55	62	27	2.04	.55
	Penn Fruit	60	60	26	1.47	.65
Canned fruits and vegetables	A & P	105	12	27	.25	.68
	Acme	102	11	17	.22	.36
	Food Fair	101	22	15	.53	.30
	Penn Fruit	92	25	11	.60	.26
Frozen foods	A & P	73	14	20	.54	.68
	Acme	75	12	17	.38	.38
	Food Fair	64	20	17	.69	.57
	Penn Fruit	70	20	12	.43	.41
Tea and coffee	A & P	80	7	14	.42	.98
	Acme	75	12	14	.87	.76
	Food Fair	71	24	4	1.66	.49
	Penn Fruit	82	5	16	.25	1.13

TABLE 9A. (Continued)

		Prices Compared with Other Chains			Total Price Difference	
		Same	Higher	Lower	Higher	Lower
Toilet articles	A & P	94	4	2	.18	.02
	Acme	94	7	—	.21	—
	Food Fair	92	2	7	.02	.43
	Penn Fruit	94	2	6	.14	.10
Oils and dressings	A & P	55	11	9	.24	.30
	Acme	54	4	17	.12	.44
	Food Fair	53	11	9	.36	.24
	Penn Fruit	54	13	4	.36	.10
Canned drinks and juices	A & P	32	10	9	.63	.22
	Acme	38	4	11	.12	.41
	Food Fair	36	11	10	.26	.40
	Penn Fruit	38	11	6	.30	.28
Bakery products	A & P	85	8	14	.17	.29
	Acme	70	15	20	.32	.43
	Food Fair	71	20	12	.52	.32
	Penn Fruit	76	14	11	.29	.26
Soap products	A & P	152	4	26	.09	1.18
	Acme	149	19	17	.39	.77
	Food Fair	132	31	11	2.21	.20
	Penn Fruit	155	14	14	.28	.82
Dairy products	A & P	26	6	9	.12	.34
	Acme	21	5	8	.15	.26
	Food Fair	22	6	6	.17	.11
	Penn Fruit	23	11	5	.46	.09

categories in which Food Fair succeeded in underpricing others more often than it was itself underpriced.

2. In fresh fruits and vegetables, A & P was the low bidder to an even greater extent than Food Fair was for meats. Of 118 price comparisons where A & P and a rival had different prices on fresh fruits and vegetables, A & P's shelf price was lower 108 times, or in 91.5 percent of the cases. Thus Acme, Food Fair, and Penn Fruit were each underpriced approximately two-thirds of the time when their fresh fruit and vegetable prices differed from those of a rival.
3. Price levels in the different stores for the meat and produce classes revealed the most extreme variations, while the remaining ten food classes fell more in line with what one would expect from an examination of the cumulative figures in Table 9B. A & P and Acme were priced lower than competitors on the majority of items not having the same price in eight of the twelve classes. Penn Fruit and Food Fair found themselves underpriced more often than not in nine and ten of the twelve classes.

TABLE 9B.

Shelf Prices of Items, Aggregate of 12 Categories (10-Week Audit)

	Prices Compared with All Other Chains			*Total Price Difference*		*Average Price Difference Per Item*	
	Same	*Higher*	*Lower*	*Higher*	*Lower*	*Higher*	*Lower*
A & P	915	179	326	$ 7.22	$11.02	$.0403	$.0335
Acme	901	246	243	8.16	8.66	.0331	.0356
Food Fair	818	286	252	11.47	9.63	.0401	.0382
Penn Fruit	898	283	173	8.53	6.13	.0301	.0354

Table 9B reveals that when prices for all twelve product classes are aggregated:

1. Between 60 and 65 percent of all prices compared were the same for each chain as compared with its competitors.
2. A & P was the only chain which offered more items at lower prices than at prices exceeding those of competitors. That is, Acme, Food Fair, and Penn Fruit were "underpriced" more frequently than they priced below others. When prices were *not* the same on items compared, A & P's shelf prices were lower than its rivals' shelf prices 64.5 percent of the time, Acme's were lower 49.7 percent of the time, Food Fair's 46.8 percent, and Penn Fruit's 37.9 percent.
3. The average price difference for those items on which differences were noted was, for all chains, 3 cents to 4 cents. This was true both for items priced above and for those priced below the offerings of rivals.

CONCLUSIONS

From these studies we can advance certain generalizations concerning the use of promotional pricing by Philadelphia area food chains:

1. The strongest price contender, A & P, emphasizes low shelf prices and breadth of assortment. Seldom the price leader in advertised features, A & P is very quick to match lower prices by its competitors. Its pattern of behavior appears quite logical when considered in the light of past federal anti-trust action against A & P.
2. Acme, the Philadelphia market-share leader, also stresses low shelf prices, but differs markedly from A & P in failing to respond to feature price advertising. Acme emphasizes the added value of the full market basket on which consumers save via trading stamps and coupons. This compensates somewhat for the higher prices charged for certain featured items.

3. Food Fair, the vigorous price leader in meats, is pursuing the same policy A & P used in an earlier stage of its growth to win customers.
4. Penn Fruit, smallest of the four major chains, responds to rivals by promotionally pricing those products for which it initially earned its reputation. Instead of matching its rivals and regularly offering low shelf prices, Penn Fruit seeks to maintain stock turnover on fresh fruits and vegetables by offering extra stamps, coupons, discounts, and specials. The smallest of the chains thus finds promotional pricing a useful strategy in securing a market share. Interestingly, Penn Fruit's heavy emphasis on promotional pricing did not result in its advertised prices for fruits and vegetables being higher than those of Acme or Food Fair.

The empirical findings also have other, and perhaps, more far-reaching implications. First, certain weaknesses in the assumptions underlying conventional economic theory are pointed up. All too often economists and social critics imply or assert that any form of nonprice competition is detrimental to consumer welfare. More specifically, economists generally maintain that the greater the amount of product, enterprise, or service differentiation, the more buyers must pay. This investigation of promotional pricing indicates otherwise. Promotional pricing of the type practiced in Philadelphia offers consumers an opportunity to save on total market-basket costs by dividing their weekly patronage among several stores. On the other hand, promotional pricing offers shoppers who place some value on their own time and effort a wider latitude of choice among variations in price and quantity.

Also significant is the apparent relationship between promotional pricing and market structure. The evidence presented in this report implies that promotional pricing policies are dictated by a store's appraisal of its own strengths and weaknesses. Far from being a tool to assure market domination by one or two price leaders, promotional pricing techniques are used successfully by the weaker as well as the stronger chains. Promotional pricing in general and feature pricing in particular enhance the vitality of supermarket rivalry by encouraging the use of price matching, coupon offers, bonus stamps, deals, discounts, and other hoopla characteristics of that fight for patronage which economists refer to as "competition."

REFERENCE:

Alderson, Wroe. "Administered Prices and Retail Grocery Advertising." *Journal of Advertising Research*, Vol. 3, No. 1, March 1963, pp. 2–6.

QUESTIONS

1. Describe the different strategies of the food chain in reference to the amount of items and space used in each ad. What effect does each strategy have on the firm?
2. What types of pricing techniques are used by the chains in their advertisements?
3. What role do cooperative advertising allowances play in the featuring of product lines in ads?

30

Memorandum in Opposition to New York City Council Bill No. 551 (Intro. No. 473) Introduced September 12, 1967, by Councilman Mario Merola

PROPOSED LAW

This bill would require all retail merchants and business establishments in New York City who use trading stamps to offer their customers either stamps or a 3 percent cash discount in lieu of stamps. Failure to do so would be a crime punishable by a fine of up to $500 or by imprisonment for one year or both. This same bill, introduced in two sessions in the New York State Legislature, has never achieved enough support in the legislature to warrant even a vote.

PRELIMINARY STATEMENT

An understanding of the trading stamp industry and the economics of the market place is most important when considering the merits of the bill. The trading stamp industry has been in existence for almost three quarters of a century. Eight out of every ten families in the United States save trading stamps. Retailers use trading stamps as a promotional device to increase sales volume and to encourage customer loyalty. However, stamps are but one form of promotion used by retailers who also utilize newspaper advertising, special sales, free parking, air-conditioning, baby-sitting service, games and sweepstakes, free coffee, etc. to name but a few.

A trading stamp company and a retailer enter into a contract in which the retailer is licensed to distribute the trading stamps with each purchase made by his customers. The stamp company also provides catalogs and stamp saver books for use in the redemption process. The customer, when he has saved the necessary number of stamps, exchanges them at a stamp company redemption center for the article he desires, such as tables, lamps, bedspreads, clothes hampers, etc. Thousands of different items are available through trading stamp company catalogs.

This memorandum was presented to the New York City Council on April 30, 1969, by Robert V. Dunn, legal counsel for Sperry and Hutchinson Co.

REASONS FOR OPPOSITION

This bill is opposed for the following principal reasons as well as others too numerous to list:

1. There is no reasonable justification for the bill.
2. The proposed legislation is an unwarranted interference with an established and proven business practice.
3. The bill is prohibitive and imposes unduly burdensome requirements upon retailers.
4. Trading stamps should not be prohibited.
5. The bill is discriminatory against the trading stamp industry, the merchants who utilize trading stamps and the consumer who saves them.
6. The bill will adversely affect merchants, stamp companies and the labor market.
7. The bill is unconstitutional.
8. Other inequities dictate against its enactment.

Following is a detailed analysis of each of the principal reasons outlined above:

1. There Is No Reasonable Justification for the Bill

Even if the effect of the bill were not to prohibit trading stamps, there would be no reasonable justification for enacting it. In issuing trading stamps as a promotional device, merchants are attempting not merely to give something of value to the consumer but also—and more importantly—to encourage consumer loyalty. The promotional effect of stamps in retaining customers would be nullified by offering cash.

It has never been suggested that a merchant should offer a cash discount in lieu of any of the scores of other promotions which he uses, some of which have already been enumerated. There is no valid reason why trading stamps should be singled out for such a requirement. During the almost 75 years in which trading stamps have been in existence, it has never been established that the customer would benefit by receiving a cash discount in lieu of stamps. Ironically, trading stamps are the only form of promotion that rewards *every* shopper by furnishing him with additional merchandise worth more than the retailer spent for the cost of the promotion in the first place.

2. The Proposed Bill Is an Unwarranted Interference with an Established and Proven Business Practice

Consumers presently have the privilege of shopping either at stores which give trading stamps or in stores which use some form of promotion other than stamps.

This bill would deprive the consumer of not only the right to receive an extra value by saving stamps but it also deprives the consumer of his right to choose between merchants who give stamps and those who do not. The bill would have the effect of prohibiting the use of stamps by virtue of its price-fixing nature. Under this proposed law, the stamp-giving merchant would be forced to give a 3 percent cash discount on stamps. All other merchants could freely use any other legitimate form of promotion which they might choose and without interference under the law. This type of governmental interference is completely contrary to the principle of the American free enterprise system. Selective legislation such as this does not create sound business practices—it negates them.

3. The Bill Is Prohibitive and Poses Undue Burdensome Requirements Upon Retailers

While the cost of trading stamps to merchants varies, depending upon the kind and number of stamps used, the cost of stamps to a typical large supermarket is equal to about 2 percent of its gross volume. However, this bill would require the merchant to offer an optional cash discount of 3 percent instead of stamps. It is obvious, therefore, that this bill could increase the cost of this one promotion, alone, by *one-third.*

Since trading stamps are issued at a rate of one for each ten cents involved in a purchase, a merchant would be unable to comply with the requirements of the proposed law in any instance in which a sale amounted to less than thirty-four cents. While a three-cent cash discount could be given on each sale amounting to $1.00, no fractional amounts could be given on that part of a purchase which did not involve a thirty-four-cent increment. Inasmuch as criminal penalties are provided for the violation of the ordinance, these technical problems are in fact real, and not academic or theoretical.

Even if it were assumed that these problems could perhaps be overcome, the fact remains that the cash option requirement would, as a practical matter, impose impossible administrative burdens on retail merchants. A busy clerk at a check-out counter could not continually stop to calculate the precise amount of the cash discount to which each customer is entitled in lieu of trading stamps without impairing the efficiency of the supermarket.

Unless trading stamps are given across-the-board to all customers, the owner or manager of a retail establishment would have great difficulty in establishing internal controls to assure that trading stamps are properly accounted for at the check-out counter. A system would have to be devised to keep a separate record of sales in connection with which trading stamps are given, as distinguished from sales in which the cash option is taken.

It is apparent that the actual result of the proposed law would be to discourage any retailer from issuing trading stamps in New York City. Compliance with the cash option requirement would be so burdensome that stamps would no longer be issued.

4. Trading Stamps Should Not Be Prohibited

The direct or indirect prohibition of trading stamps is unjustified. Trading stamps have been used by many different types of merchants in New York City for many years.

There is nothing mysterious about trading stamps. The public knows and understands the basis on which trading stamps are issued. All customers receive trading stamps with all of their purchases on a uniform basis and all stamps are redeemed on a uniform basis. Collectors of trading stamps are easily able to ascertain the value of the stamps through reference to the catalogs of redemption merchandise issued by trading stamp companies.

There is nothing evil about trading stamps. They are not a form of gambling or lottery. They have absolutely no effect on the health, safety or morals of the public. Basically, trading stamps are simply a means of competition used by retailers to attract customers to their stores.

Nonetheless, because stamps are an effective competitive device, certain retail merchants who do not choose to use them seek to deprive their competitors (and the public) of the benefits they derive from their use. Such opponents of trading stamps were effectively answered over sixty years ago in *Ex Parte Drexel*, 147 Cal. 763, 82 Pac. 429 (1905), in an opinion striking down as unconstitutional a similar anti-trading stamp law, wherein the Court said:

> Indeed, an ordinary trading-stamp coupon is in substance a mere form of allowing discounts on cash payments, and its issuance is entirely harmless and within the constitutional right of contract. It may be distasteful to certain competitors in business; but the latter should remember that if a statute suppressing it be upheld then other oppressive statutes might be enacted unlawfully interfering with and hampering business and the right of contract to which these competitors would strenuously but vainly object.

5. The Bill Is Discriminatory Against the Trading Stamp Industry, Merchants Who Utilize Trading Stamps and the Consumer Who Saves Them.

Much of the reasoning underlying this point has been outlined above. However, some serious questions are raised by the singular direction of this proposed law, in that it affects only trading stamp companies and those merchants in New York City who use trading stamps. Some of these questions are: (1) Why should a merchant giving stamps be forced arbitrarily to offer his customers a 3 percent cash discount while his competitor who does not give stamps (and who may or may not use other forms of promotion) is not mentioned in the proposed legislation? (2) Why not require a merchant who *does not* give stamps to offer a 3 percent cash discount in lieu of whatever promotional device he might use that his customers may not want? For instance, free parking, which is another promotional device, is of no use to the customer who has no car. Free delivery service is of no use to the customer who carries his own packages.

Free baby-sitting is of no use to a childless customer. Are not these individuals entitled to a 3 percent cash discount in lieu of these other forms of promotion which they do not need or want?

6. The Bill Will Adversely Affect Merchants, Stamp Companies and the Labor Market

Again, much of the reasoning behind this point has already been outlined and it has been indicated that the immediate effect of this proposed law would be a discontinuance of the use of stamps by merchants unable and unwilling to comply with its onerous requirements.

However, the ultimate result—caused by the wholesale exodus of stamp-giving merchants—would be to wipe out the largest single geographical market available to trading stamp companies in this state or nation. They would be unable to sell the trading stamp service within the boundaries of New York City. Moreover, the eight million citizens of New York would be deprived of their right to obtain additional value for their purchases through saving trading stamps, if they should choose to do so.

Trading stamp companies purchase their redemption merchandise from New York City manufacturers as well as others. The Sperry and Hutchinson Company, alone, buys approximately $15 million worth of merchandise a year from more than ninety-five manufacturers with plants in New York City. It logically follows that the loss of a market such as New York City would definitely result not only in reduced purchases but in a serious reduction in employment by suppliers to the trading stamp industry and, in turn, by the suppliers to those suppliers.

7. The Bill Is Unconstitutional

It is settled law in this state that the trading stamp business may not be prohibited, either directly or indirectly through the imposition of unreasonable burdens. The first case to consider this question was *People v. Gillson*, 109 N.Y. 389. The statute in that case prohibited the giving of a gift, prize, premium, or reward in connection with the sale of articles of food. The Court of Appeals held that there was nothing unlawful about the giving of premiums or similar devices, and that the statute attempting to limit their use served no legitimate purpose which could be invoked under the State's power. In holding the Act unconsitutional, as an illegal deprivation of liberty and property, the Court said at page 399:

> Liberty, in its broad sense, as understood in this Country, means the right not only of freedom from servitude, imprisonment or restraint, but the right of one to use his faculties in all lawful ways, to live and

> work where he will, to earn his livelihood in any lawful calling and to pursue any lawful trade or avocation.
>
> It is quite clear that some or all of these fundamental and valuable rights are invaded, weakened, limited or destroyed by the legislation under consideration. It is evidently of that kind which has been so frequent of late, a kind which is meant to protect some class in the community against the fair, free and full competition of some other class, the members of the former class thinking it impossible to hold their own against such competition, and therefore flying to the legislature to secure some enactment which shall operate favorably to them or unfavorably to their competitors in the commercial, agricultural, manufacturing or producing fields.

The law laid down in the *Gillson* case was followed in *People v. Dycker*, 72 App. Div. 308, 76 N.Y. Supp. 111 where the Court declared unconstitutional an Act which had the effect of prohibiting the issuance of stamps by trading stamp companies.

After the *Dycker* case, the legislature attempted to impose severely burdensome restrictions on trading stamp companies. Again, the Court struck down the statute as unconstitutional in *People v. Zimmerman*, 102 App. Div. 103, 92 N.Y. Supp. 497. Since that time no anti-trading stamp legislation has been enacted in the State of New York.

8. Other Inequities Which Dictate Against Its Enactment

1. The bill restricts itself to the geographical location of the City of New York despite the fact that the nature of the trading stamp industry is state wide, nation wide and, indeed, international in scope. In this respect, it should be noted that the legislature of the State of New York has not passed such a bill nor has any other state, nor the Congress seen fit to do so.
2. Merchants and trading stamp companies operate on a contract basis. This bill calls for an immediate effective date, a most unrealistic approach to a business operation where legal contractual rights and obligations are involved. The imposition of an immediate effective date is even more incomprehensible when one considers that the penal provisions would go into effect overnight, without any opportunity for a change in a business operation.
3. The statute is vague. This is particularly important to consider because of the penal provisions. It is vague as to who would be responsible if there were a failure to give the proper cash discount.

   For example, two trading stamps would be given on a twenty-five-cent sale in a supermarket. If the consumer preferred cash, however, there are no coins minted in the United States of small enough denomination to give her the 3 percent cash discount to which she would be entitled should this bill be enacted. Who would be guilty? Is it the clerk or the gas station attendant who made the sale? Is it the store manager of a busy supermarket who might, at the time of the sale, be required to be in another area of the store? Is it the owner of an establishment who is not even present at the time of the questionable infraction? The question is: *Who would be liable to the imprisonment and/or the fine?*

4. The penal provisions are unduly harsh and call for unwarranted severe punishment for a relatively minor item (assuming the violations were intentional). Such punishment is unrealistic and certainly does not fit the so-called "crime" that this bill would seek to establish.

CONCLUSION

The enactment of this bill is not in the public interest. The consumer will lose, rather than gain. The bill is unreasonable, prohibitive and unconstitutional. It should not be enacted.

QUESTIONS

1. Refute some of the eight arguments presented by the Sperry and Hutchinson Company (S & H Green Stamps).
2. Do you agree or disagree with the memorandum? Discuss.

31

Trading Stamps - An Opposition View

Lord Sainsbury

A fortnight ago an eminent economist wrote an article in these columns entitled "Something for Nothing Makes Bad Economics." Surprisingly, its topic did not involve trading stamps, as I expected. I think, however, that it would be hard to find a more appropriate field with which to illustrate the validity of this statement.

"Something for Nothing" is the slogan which has built a new superstructure on the groundwork of American retailing during the last decade and a similar attempt is being made now in Britain. Stamp companies are trying to impose a permanent levy on retailers in exchange for which they promise increased trade, based on the "Something for Nothing" appeal directed at the consumer.

Reprinted from *The Statist*, Vol. 182, November 29, 1963, pp. 608–609.

Within the space of a short article I am not able to touch upon every aspect of stamp trading. Therefore, I would like to discuss two only, which are at the heart of the matter: the effect of stamp promotions on the cost of distribution and the position of the consumer.

At present, more than a quarter of a million retail stores give stamps in the United States. They buy them from stamp companies, keep them under lock and key, hand them out for each purchase made and account for them like money. They distribute stamp books and catalogues. A large amount of work is involved in all these activities. It is clear that retailing is performing an additional and—in view—unnecessary task; handling millions of paper stickers in addition to money. This inevitably involves more employees and higher retailing costs.

Costs are further boosted by the purchase of stamps which amount to about 2.5 percent of the retailer's turnover. This often quoted 2.5 percent is a misleading figure as it is calculated on the turnover. When considering costs and profitability, the gross margin is a much more relevant figure for the retailer than turnover. The 1957 Census of Distribution found that the average grocer's margin was 15.4 percent in this country (the 1961 figure has not yet been published but undoubtedly will be higher). The gross margin is really the income of the retailer from which he must cover all his expenses. By adopting a 2.5 percent stamp scheme the grocer undertakes an obligation to pay about 16 percent of his gross income *permanently* to a stamp company. A further proportion of gross margin will be absorbed by the additional operational costs.

The enormously high cost of a stamp scheme is demonstrated even better if one compares this 2.5 percent with net profit figures. Speaking of groceries, though no official statistics are available, it is well known in trade circles that very often the total net profit of a multiple retailer is less than 2.5 percent.

Now to cover this extraordinarily high expense, stamp companies suggest that turnover increase will compensate the trader. Figures vary according to the gross margin and the spare capacity of the shop in question and the costs of the stamp scheme itself but, broadly speaking, the required grocery turnover increase should be around one-fifth in order to cover extra costs.

ORIGINAL STATUS QUO RESTORED

To achieve a *permanent* increase of such an order is practically impossible. Rival stores take counter-action and one form of this is the application of other stamp schemes. This process may lead to a situation where the original *status quo* between the shops of a locality is restored. None of them enjoys any advantage over their competitors any more, but they do not drop stamps for fear of upsetting the balance to their disadvantage. The consequence of this situation is clear: prices go up by the cost of the stamps.

Protagonists of stamps, who always consider only the short-term situation, refute this so-called "saturation argument" as a hypothetical and unreal one, which cannot happen in actual life. Yet, it is well known that in the United States there are many localities where the consumers have no choice between stamp and nonstamp stores because every grocer in their neighbourhood gives stamps. The president of the American Safeway Chain, operating 2,063 supermarkets, speaking of stamps some time ago said: "They are a devastating gimmick. They cost Safeway close on $30m. last year. That has to come out in higher prices for food." Stamp trading in the long term inevitably tends to put pressure on prices, and rising prices are bound to have a depressing effect on demand. Rising food prices have a particularly undesirable social effect. Even in our affluent society there are groups of people, like old age pensioners, whose income is wholly spent on the bare necessities of life and they are particularly vulnerable to rising food prices.

As is known, retailing costs in the country, stamp trading apart, are under pressure. The gap between industrial wages and those paid in distribution has been narrowing gradually during recent years and working hours have become shorter. A few days ago, the Union of Distributive Workers submitted a pay claim of an extra £1 a week for the staff of multiple grocers. It is just not possible to satisfy the demand for higher wages and to pay for stamp promotions from the existing grocery margins. In the United States, it is estimated that margins are higher than over here by about 3–4 percent. It would be interesting to investigate to what extent the widespread US stamp promotions are responsible for the difference between British and American grocery margins.

In Britain, shopkeepers are now exposed day by day to the hard-pressure methods of stamp salesmen, and stamp companies loudly advertise their "free gifts" to the consumer. The Distributive Trades Alliance was formed a few weeks ago to counter these activities of the stamp companies and present the true facts of stamps to the consumer.

Opinions have been voiced that there is no need to protect the consumer against the publicity of stamp companies; that he has a mind of his own and is able to make his own choice. But surely the consumer's attitude towards any of his shopping problems is influenced and altered by the publicity which he is subjected to. If this were not the case stamp companies could not advertise and the near £500m. this country spends on commercial advertising would be a completely futile and unreasonable expenditure.

The consumer should be reminded that free gifts are not free because stamp shop prices tend to go up. Similarly, the fallacy of "saving by stamps" should be exposed. It should be pointed out that no saving is included when one gets a discount on higher prices. Furthermore, the catalogues of stamp companies offer only a limited choice of goods and often the brand leaders are not included. In order to put across the facts, the Alliance is about to launch a publicity campaign. The consumer is free to choose between stamps and lower prices, but it is desirable that an informed consumer should make the choice.

Apart from the effect on retailers' costs, perhaps the greatest evils of stamp trading are brought about by:

a. An exaggeration in the customer's mind of the value of the stamps he holds.
b. The measures that are taken by the stamp trading companies to ensure that the customer keeps collecting by making the stamps valueless until a certain number have been saved. Thus to start him collecting all that is needed is to present him with a quantity of stamps that are of no value to him until more are added to them. He is even kept at it by giving him a part-filled book when he collects his gift.
c. The danger that because a newly-established or growing stamp company collects the money from the retailer long before it is to pay it out, the funds might be dissipated before the time comes to pay out.

All these are points that require Government intervention. (a) and (b) could best be dealt with by forcing the stamp companies to redeem stamps for cash in any quantity and to state clearly on them their real value.

The whole matter is one from which the Government cannot remain aloof.

QUESTION

1. Refute the arguments presented by Lord Sainsbury.

32

Games of Chance in Grocery Supermarkets and Their Impact upon Small Business

ORIGIN AND SCOPE OF STUDY

Food retailers employ numerous price and nonprice tactics to maintain and increase store traffic. Since the mid-1950's, trading stamps have been used more extensively than any other form of nonprice competitive device. In 1964–65, however, food retailers began using a variety of so-called "games" or "games of chance" in sales promotion, either as a substitute for or a complement to other kinds of promotional tactics.

From the Appendix to *Economic Report on the Use of Games of Chance in Food and Gasoline Retailing*, Staff Report of the Federal Trade Commission, December 1968, pp. 395, 401–407, 451, 453–54.

Late in October 1966, the Commission adopted a resolution "directing an investigation of sales promotion programs used by food retailers including those involving games of chance." The Commission then issued a press release announcing commencement of the investigation and stating the following objectives:

1. To determine whether these promotional schemes constitute unfair methods of competition or unfair and deceptive practices in violation of the statutes administered by the Commission;
2. To ascertain their economic consequences, including increased costs to food retailers and higher prices to consumers, and their impact on competition in food marketing; and
3. to provide a factual basis upon which the Commission may take such effective corrective action as may be required to enforce the law.

The Commission pointed out that it was "particularly concerned that these promotional schemes, now extensively used by retailers throughout the country, may have increased the cost of food to the housewife and have had the effect of substantially curtailing price competition in food distribution, to the detriment of consumers."

The Commission stated that the first step would be to obtain all the relevant facts through an in-depth investigation, but it also called upon industry members to immediately "discontinue voluntarily any practices that are unfair or deceptive or that unjustifiably add to the American housewife's grocery bill." . . .

BASIC APPEALS AND CHARACTERISTICS OF GAMES

Grocery retailing employs a variety of nonprice promotions to increase store traffic. These include trading stamps, contests, games, sweepstakes, and continuity programs. This report deals with promotional techniques involving "games of chance."[1]

The trade refers to game promotions alternately as "games" and "games of chance." The originators of the various merchandising games have directed their appeals to certain so-called basic instincts of prospective customers. In doing so, they have primarily modeled the games after well-established forms of gambling.

One promoter, Glendinning, states that the games add a "new, exciting element to food shopping." This element appears to be the chance for the consumer to win a prize. The manner in which the chances are made available to consumers is apparently limited only by the ingenuity and imagination of the game promoters. Our survey reveals that when game use in grocery retailing reached its peak in October 1966, some fifty-two different

[1] A Federal Trade Commission staff study dealt with the use of trading stamps by food retailers; see "Organization and Competition in Food Retailing, Technical Study No. 7," National Commission on Food Marketing, June 1966, ch. 21.

TABLE 1.

Types of Games in Use in 55 Major Metropolitan Markets, October 1966

Type of game	*Percent of sales of all stores using games*	*Number of different games used*
Gambling	75	31
Bingo	37	14
Racing	22	7
Card	10	2
Matching	3	4
Punchcard	3	4
Numbers	(*)	
Slot machine	(*)	
Pseudoeducational	16	7
Spelling	13	5
Government-history-geography	3	2
Television	3	3
Pie-in-the-sky	6	11
Total	100	52

*Not used in October 1966 in 55 markets.
Source: Compiled by FTC from Maiers Market Research Co., Weekly Composite Market Survey.

games were being used in the fifty-five major grocery markets (table 1). The diversity of the games is so wide as to make categorization difficult. But broadly speaking, the games may be divided into the following, in terms of their basic appeal: (1) gambling-type games; (2) pseudoeducational-type games; (3) TV parlor-type games; and (4) a residual category which might be called pie-in-the-sky-type games,[2] inasmuch as the one thing they have in common is the offer to consumers of the chance to win large prizes.

Gambling-type games are by far the most important. Of fifty-two games in operation in the fifty-five major grocery markets, thirty-one were of the gambling type. Bingo games numbered fourteen, racing games seven, card games two, matching games four, punchcard games four. Recently a game resembling the "numbers racket" has been adopted.

Games Based on Various Forms of Gambling

More than one-half, thirty-one in number, of the fifty-two games were derivatives of some type of gambling game. These thirty-one games were used by stores accounting for 75 percent of the sales of all game-using stores

[2] For example, a Pennsylvania housewife complained to one grocery chain about its promotions that "dangle diamond necklaces or mink stoles before our eyes . . . [so that] too many people are convinced they are getting something for nothing, that there is indeed pie in the sky" (FTC investigational file).

in the 55 markets in October 1966 (table 1). Five of the seven types of games copied from gambling games were in use at that time. They were:

BINGO-TYPE GAMES. There were 14 bingo-type games in use in the 55 major markets, and the stores using them accounted for 37 percent of the sales in game-using stores.

"Bonus Bingo," owned by Strategic Merchandising Corp., was the most important bingo-type game being used in the fifty-five markets, accounting for more than 60 percent of the sales of stores using such games. A typical "Bonus Bingo" game was "Program No. 83," used by Safeway. Upon the first visit to the store, the customer was given a booklet containing eight bingo cards varying in value from $1,000. Each card contained five rows and five columns, for a total of 25 spaces. All of the cards had a number of "free" spaces, i.e., spaces for which the customer did not have to obtain a number. The number of free spaces per card varied from ten to fourteen. At the initial store visit and at each subsequent visit, the customer was given a slip containing a bingo number and a game value, both covered by a water soluble paint. When sufficient slips were obtained to complete any row, any column, or either of the two five-space diagonals in a specific value game, the customer was a winner and could claim his prize from the store.

RACING-TYPE GAMES. Seven different racing-type games were used in the 55 markets, and stores using them accounted for 22 percent of the sales of all game-using stores in October 1966 (table 1). Of the seven, five were based upon some type of horse race, one upon dog races, and one upon stock-car races.

"Let's Go to the Races," owned by Walter Schwinner, Inc., was the most important racing game in October 1966, accounting for more than 55 percent of the sales of all stores using racing games in the fifty-five markets. Typical of the "Let's Go to the Races" game was the one used by Colonial Stores in Atlanta. In this game, the customer received a card upon each visit to the store. The cards designated a horse by number for each of five races. The value of the winners varied from $10 in the first race to $1,000 in the fifth race. The races were shown on a local TV station and customers had seventy-two hours to claim their winnings if one of their horses won. The winning numbers for each of the five races were also posted in each participating store, and the customer could determine if he was a winner by visiting the store. Winning numbers were not given over the telephone.

CARD-TYPE GAMES. Two different card-type games were used in the 55 markets, and stores using them accounted for 10 percent of the sales of game-using stores. One of the card-type games was based on blackjack and the other on poker.

"3-of-A-Kind," owned by Kayden Industries,[3] was the more important, in terms of use, of the two card-type games. In this game the customer was

[3] Merged with J. & H. International Corp. in January 1967.

given a master card containing winning combinations of cards. For example, in one such game, as used by A & P, the values of the winning combinations were $5, $100, and $1,000. To win a $1,000 prize the customer had to obtain a five of diamonds, a five of spades, and a five of hearts, or a queen of hearts, a queen of spades, and a queen of diamonds, etc. At each store visit the customer was given a punchout containing two cards. These were placed in the appropriate places on the master card and when any designated combination of three cards was completed, the customer could claim his prize.

MATCHING TYPE GAMES. Four matching games were used in the fifty-five markets, and stores using them accounted for 3 percent of the sales of game-using stores in October 1966. The games usually involved both halves of a picture of a piece of money, a trading stamp, or a piece of merchandise. When both halves were obtained, the customer won the amount of money or the number of trading stamps designated.

"Match The Stamp," owned by Spot-O-Gold Corp., is illustrative of the matching games. This particular game is suitable only for supermarkets that dispense trading stamps, but other matching games are available in which the prizes are money. In one "Match The Stamp" program used by National Tea, the size of the prizes varied from 25 to 1,000,000 trading stamps. At each store visit, the customer was given the upper or lower half of a trading stamp picture with a designated number of trading stamps shown on the picture. If a housewife obtained both an upper and a lower half with the same designated number, she could claim her prize.

PUNCH-CARD TYPE GAMES. Four punch-card type games were used in the fifty-five markets in October 1966 and stores using them accounted for 3 percent of the sales of game-using stores. These games all required that either a specified volume of purchases or a specified number of weekly visits be "punched" before the winning amount was discovered.

The winning amount was hidden by a seal. All cards were winners when completed but the amount of the prize could be as little as $1 or as much as $1,000. Thus, the chance element dealt only with the size of the prize.

"Cash-A-Check," owned by Volume, Inc., was the most important punchcard type game in October 1966. When used by firms other than Acme, this game was called "Lucky Check." In this game the customer was given a check-type card which says, "This may be worth $1,000." One such card had a place for punching sixteen weekly visits[4] and $100 in purchases. Each week for sixteen weeks the customer could get the free visit section punched. He could also have the amount of his purchases punched. When either of these was completed, a seal was removed which showed the customer's winnings. The minimum prize was $1. Thus, every customer who completed a card was assured of winning at least $1. The card was not redeemed if the seal showing the winning amount was "tampered with."

[4] The number of weekly visits required varied according to the dictates of the chains using the program.

NUMBERS-TYPE GAMES. One game appears to be a direct derivative of the "numbers game." However, it was not used until 1967. In this game the customer was given cards containing prices for four stocks traded on the New York Stock Exchange. The winners were determined by the actual Friday closing prices of the stocks.

SLOT-MACHINE-TYPE GAMES. Two types of slot-machine-type games were available although not in use in the fifty-five markets in October 1966. In "Dial-A-Winner" an actual machine was used. The customer was given a token which he deposited in a machine and dialed numbers. The machine then whirled and announced whether the individual was a winner or loser. In "3-Way Jackpot" no machine was used. The customer was given a game piece with a picture of a slot machine on the front. Pulling the front tab separated the game piece and showed a picture of a slot machine window. Winners had to collect particular combinations of bells, oranges, cherries, and so forth.

Pseudoeducational Games

Second in importance to gambling games are those of a pseudoeducational character (exhibit B). This kind of game accounted for sixteen percent of the sales of stores using games in 55 metropolitan grocery markets in October 1966 (table 1).

SPELLING-TYPE GAMES. Five spelling-type games were used in the fifty-five markets in October 1966 and stores using them accounted for 13 percent of the sales of game-using stores. The object of these games is to spell some word or phrase. Further, their names are usually suggestive of prizes, for example, "Quik Cash, "Spell Diamond," "Santa Claus," "Love That Money," and "Money Letters."

"Quik Cash," owned by Spot-O-Gold Corp., is typical of the spelling games. In this game the size of the prizes varies from $1 to $1,000. On each store visit the customer receives a card which has from one to three letters concealed by a gold spot. The letters are revealed by erasing the gold spot. If letters or combinations of letters which spell "thousand" are obtained, the customer can claim the $1,000 prize. Other prizes are obtained in a similar manner.

GOVERNMENT-HISTORY-GEOGRAPHY. Two games fit into this group, "Presidents and Prizes" and "Around the World in 80 Ways." In both games, there is a supplemental booklet which gives some facts either about the Presidents or about the countries. Stores using these games accounted for 3 percent of the sales of game-using stores in October 1966. . . .

"Presidents and Prizes," owned by Strategic Merchandising Corp., is typical of the pseudoeducational type games. On the initial store visit the customer receives a booklet with a master game card and a short biographical sketch of every President of the United States. On each store visit the customer also receives a concealed picture of one of the Presidents. Prizes usually vary from $1 to $1,000 and can be claimed if the customer obtains the pictures of the designated Presidents. For example, to win $1 it is only necessary to obtain a picture of George Washington. To win $1,000 it is necessary to obtain the pictures of eight designated Presidents.

Television-Type Games

Three of the games used in the fifty-five markets studied used the names of television shows. They were "The Price Is Right," "Batman Games," and "Tic-Tac-Toe." Stores using these games accounted for 3 percent of the sales of game-using stores in October 1966.

"Pie-in-the-Sky"-Type Games

The remaining eleven games used in the fifty-five markets had little in common beyond the fact that each offered to consumers the opportunity to win a large prize or what we have called the "pie-in-the-sky." Stores using these games accounted for 6 percent of the sales of all game-using stores in October 1966 in the fifty-five markets.

Because these games have little in common other than the lure of a large prize, only two of the ones in use in October 1966 are described below:

"Giant Step" involves a map with numbered steps. On each store visit the customer is given a game piece which tells how many steps to take on the map. Prizes are instantaneous and are whatever is found in the step that the game piece specifies.

"Pic-A-Winner" is a game involving chocolate-coated mints. On each store visit the customer is given a mint. Prizes are awarded to customers who receive mints with colored centers.

Margin Changes in Five Metropolitan Markets

. . . A somewhat better analysis of changes in margins resulting from games may be made on the basis of the experience in the five metropolitan markets proviously discussed. . . .

Referring to the Washington market (chart 1), note that Safeway margins had been running at a lower level in 1966 than in 1965 until the introduction of the "Bonus Bingo" game. At that time Safeway's margins increased. Expressing the gross margin as an index of the 1965–66 average, during the first six months of 1966 Safeway's margin averaged 98.1 percent. In the next four months, while the "Bonus Bingo" game was in full swing, Safeway's margin rose to an average of 101.8. In the final 2 months of the year, the margin dropped to an average of 96.9. It was in these latter two months that the consumer protests were made against high prices and the use of games. These margin changes suggest the following observations. During the first four months of the operation of "Bonus Bingo," the margin increase

CHART 1 Changes in sales per store and gross margins of leading food retailers during use of game promotions

WASHINGTON, D.C., MARKET

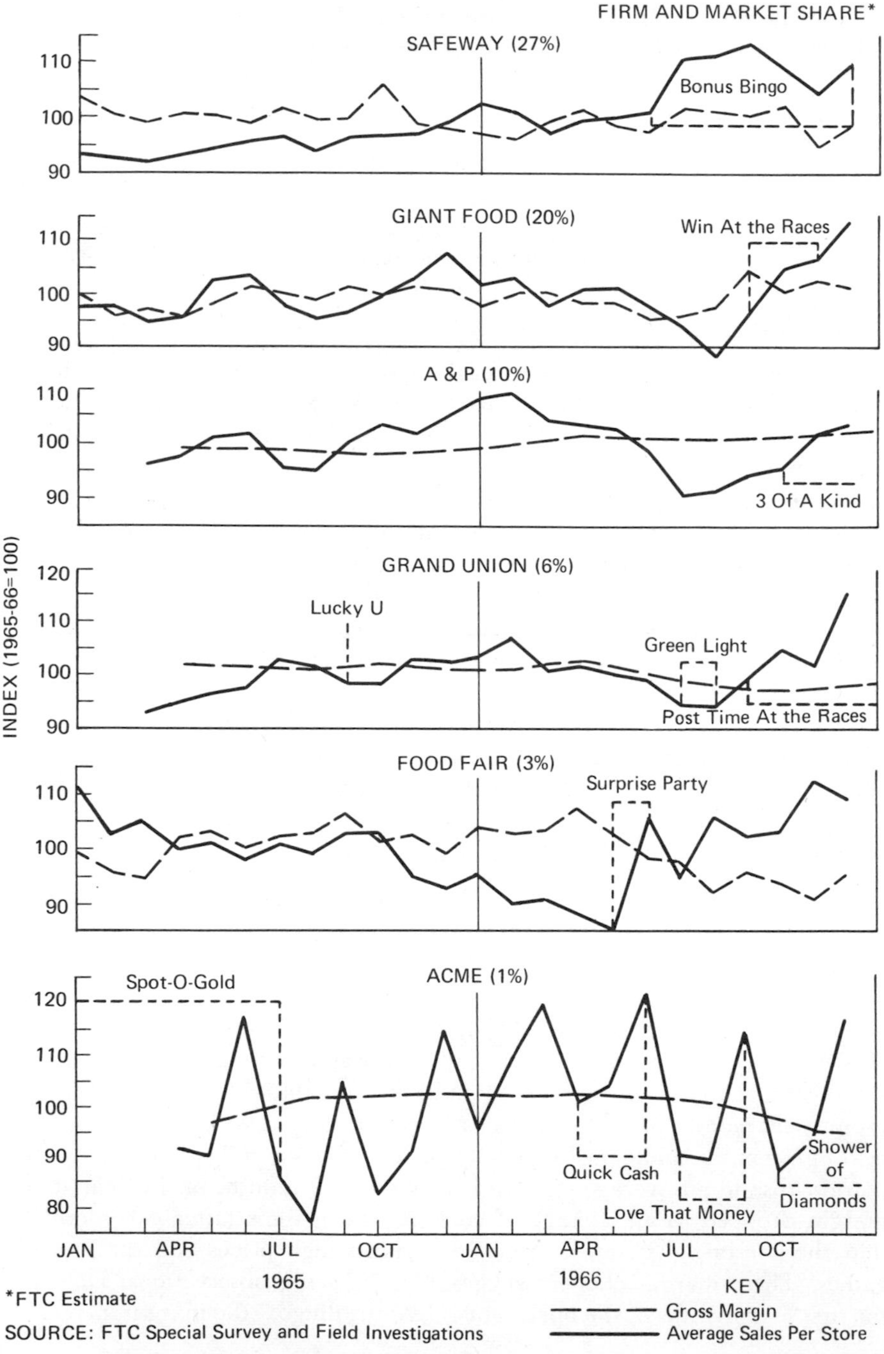

*FTC Estimate

SOURCE: FTC Special Survey and Field Investigations

exceeded the cost of the game. Therefore, it would appear that prices were raised by more than the necessary amount to compensate for the cost of the games.

Giant Food similarly was operating at lower margins in 1966 than in 1965, but raised its margins at the time it introduced the game "Win at the Races," The primary cause of Giant's lower margins prior to the game appears to be the reductions which it made in its gross margin in the three months when Safeway was using "Bonus Bingo" and Giant had no game. After introducing its own game Giant's average gross margin index rose to approximately 103.1 as compared to an average for the preceding eight months of 98.3, and 95.8 for the three months immediately preceding the game.

The data for A & P are less precise, inasmuch as the company only furnished quarterly information on gross margins. The significant observation regarding A & P, as with the others, is that it raised its margin sharply after it introduced a game, "Three of a Kind." In the first full quarter in which the game was in operation, the margin index was raised to 102.9, compared with 100.5 for the full quarter preceding the game.[5]

In short, it appears that in the case of each of the three leading food retailers in the Washington, D.C., market, gross margins, and thus average prices, were raised during the course of game promotions in the latter part of 1966. . . .

QUESTIONS

1. Compare the effectiveness of games versus trading stamps as a promotional tool in the food store.
2. Do games increase food prices in supermarkets?

[5] Interfirm comparisons of gross margins are not reliable because of differences in the degree of vertical integration and thus the allocation of costs as between manufacturing and retailing units within such integrated firms. Nonintegrated firms may show higher margins because all costs are borne at the retail level.

33

Retail Reorganization

Wheelock H. Bingham and David L. Yunich

Major organization changes are not to be undertaken lightly. Changing an executive organization structure inevitably involves the creation of new jobs, new paths of promotion, new executive activities and relationships, the demand for new executive skills—and changing or eliminating those that exist and are familiar. Changes inevitably involve uncertainty for each executive concerned. Instead of remaining in a stable organizational environment, in which he may have found a comfortable niche, he must face a changed environment, in which a new and untried pattern of behavior will be required of him.

In business literature there is a great deal of discussion of organization theory and also, in recent years, much discussion of the human problems of organization; but there are too few case histories revealing how individual companies have perceived their problems of major organizational change, analyzed them, chosen among the alternatives, and put the new organization structure into effect. In this article we undertake to develop such a case history.

Managements often enter on major organization changes to solve the following problems: attaining greater efficiency in operation, accommodating an increased volume of sales, adjusting to changes in products and/or markets, reducing expenses, carrying out the ideas of new top management, and so on. Perhaps less common reasons are the major organizational problems which arise out of sweeping social and economic changes affecting an entire industry, and which therefore confront many companies more or less at the same time. The organizational problem now facing many department stores is of this last type, and the presence of many common elements in the problem as it relates to individual companies is a further reason for believing that a case history may be useful.

BACKGROUND PERSPECTIVE

Perhaps we should first provide some background and perspective on the nature of the organization problem in the typical department store. The

Reprinted from *Harvard Business Review,* Vol. 43, July-August 1965, pp. 129–46.

department store idea appeared around the middle of the nineteenth century, and the stores enjoyed a remarkable popularity during the latter part of that century and the first half of the twentieth. They were the great merchandising innovation of their time. Professor Malcolm P. McNair has said:

> In its rise to prominence, beginning a little less than 100 years ago, the department store displayed the typical innovative pattern: it was the new kind of store, altering distribution channels, selling goods at prices below those of normal competition, arousing the intense hostility of established merchants. No single individual can be said to have invented the department store, but the original John Wanamaker undoubtedly was the greatest protagonist of this innovation in America, and when he bought the old Pennsylvania Railroad freight station in Philadelphia to house his new enterprise he was the unconscious precursor of those hardy individualists who in the early 1930's opened food supermarkets in old carbarns and old garages, and their successors in the next generation who set up soft-goods discount houses in abandoned textile mill buildings in New England.[1]

The department store was a peculiarly urban institution. Its distinguishing feature was the offering of a wide range and variety of merchandise all under one roof, an innovation made possible only by the substantial urban market that had come into existence before it; and as this market grew in size and in income, the department store grew and prospered. Also contributing to its success were the accompaniments of metropolitan growth, such as the vast networks of public transportation facilities, comprising commuting railroads and the rapid transit and bus lines; the soaring volume of newspaper circulation; the rising tide of fashion influence; the enhancement of taste and culture that go with the spread of education; and, up to a point, the increase in automobile use and the development of the highway system.

Organizational Pyramids

Initially, most department stores were founded by merchants with previous experience in retail or wholesale dry goods business or men's wear. As the stores began to grow by adding merchandise classifications, the natural division of labor seems always to have been on the general basis of "Joe, you take the ladies' wear, and I'll keep on with the men's wear." Apparently it never occurred to one partner to say to the other, "You take the selling, and I'll do the buying."

And so, as more lines and categories were added, the method of organization evidently always used was to seek or designate an individual with knowledge of the particular merchandise and its wholesale market. From time to time, also, merchandise groups were brought into stores on a leased-depart-

[1] "Change and Challenge in the Department Store Industry," a speech delivered at a testimonial dinner given in Professor McNair's honor by the National Retail Merchants Association, October 5, 1964, New York City.

ment basis, with the lessee having the ownership of the goods and the full responsibility for both buying and selling. It was as a lessee of the china and glass department that the Straus family first came into the department store established by Rowland H. Macy.

Thus the department store, almost from the beginning, was an assemblage of shops under one roof, with the division of responsibilities running by merchandise departments; and this came to be the all-important merchandising pyramid of the organization. In some respects this departmental arrangement parallels the product manager type of organization found in many multiline manufacturing companies, where responsibility for both producing and marketing a particular product or group of products is placed primarily on a single individual, the group product manager. In this analogy, of course, the buying function in the department store is the equivalent of the producing function in the manufacturing enterprise.

As volume increased and merchandise lines widened, further division of labor appeared within the merchandising pyramid. Instead of reporting directly to the general merchandise manager, the departmental buyer might report to a divisional merchandise manager, or administrator, who might in turn report to a merchandise vice president in charge of a broad commodity grouping, such as soft goods or hard goods.

But what of the other parts of the retailing task—the sales promotion, the store operation, the accounting and record keeping, and the personnel management? In the early days the department buyer might have something to say about these also; for instance, he might write his own advertising copy and do his own hiring and firing. Gradually, however, with specialization and increased division of labor, these other activities were incorporated in other pyramids of the organization, such as sales promotion, store operation and building maintenance, personnel, and accounting and control.

The resulting form of department store organization, as it emerged in the years prior to World War II, was typically represented by four or five functional pyramids: merchandising, sales promotion, store operation, personnel, and control. (Sometimes sales promotion was subordinate, at the upper level, to merchandising; and, more often than not, personnel was subordinate to store operation.) Although merchandising, comprising both buying and selling, was the all-important pyramid, with the other functions constituting sales-supporting activities, the total organization did not have a pure line-and-staff character. There were important line responsibilities in the other pyramids for day-to-day sales-supporting activities. Also, even though salespeople were included in merchandising, a substantial numerical preponderance of the salespeople existed in the other pyramids.

In some of the versions of this functional form of department store organization, especially prior to the 1930s, a system of duplicating supervision was frequently found. Thus floorwalkers, or customer-service supervisors, watched over salespeople to ensure proper service to customers. Floorwalkers reported up through the store-operation pyramid, while salespeople usually discovered that the real boss was the buyer.

In a substantial number of stores this check-and-balance concept led to an organizational setup where salespeople were made at least initially responsible to section managers and floor supervisors who reported to a customer-service manager, who in turn reported to the head of the operations pyramid. The section manager job became a more responsible one, in contrast to the floorwalker job from which it had developed; and section managers began reaching out for more authority over the selling function.

Department Managers

For a few years this section manager development looked like the wave of the future. Then came the impact of a book on department store organization. Paul Mazur, a partner in Lehman Brothers, wrote (with the assistance of Myron Silbert) *Principles of Organization Applied to Modern Retailing.*[2] This book, published in 1927, became a classic. It took a strong position against "checks-and-balances" and urged that a department buyer-manager exercise individual profit responsibility.

The book became a text for the so-called "department manager plan," under which the departement manager-buyer had full control of the selling function and was held responsible for departmental expenses and profits. Salespeople were freed from any line responsibility in the store-operation pyramid, and the former section managers became assistant department managers, responsible for day-to-day operation under the supervision of the manager-buyer.

Ideally, the department manager-buyer was held immediately responsible for the direct expense of the department, including sales force, advertising, traveling, and communication expenditures; and he also was charged, on his departmental operating statement, for many allocated expenses—for such activities as delivery and receiving and marking—for whose efficiency he could not be responsible, but whose volume of work was affected by his decisions.

In the late 1930s, and then particularly in the early postwar years, the department manager plan, in various forms and degrees, swept all before it and became the dominant type of organization for the department store buying and selling functions. But, notwithstanding its practical success in the short run, not all the critics of the department manager plan were convinced. They argued that such an organization was inevitably oriented toward buying rather than selling, that convenience in buying and wholesale-market structure tended to govern the grouping of merchandise in departments, with little consideration given to the combinations of goods that might be most effective in their impact on consumers. Fear was expressed

[2] New York, Harper & Brothers.

that selling leadership would be neglected, that a man who was a highly successful buyer did not often possess the qualities of a good sales manager.

Compared with the product manager type of organization in a large manufacturing business, the weakness of the department manager plan in a department store is that the relatively small scale of operations in a typical department store throws the dual responsibility primarily on a single individual, whereas in the manufacturing situation the typical product division is large enough to enable the product manager to have qualified subordinates for manufacturing and marketing.

In spite of such misgivings, the department manager plan of organization achieved strong dominance by 1950. It afforded simple individual departments; it lent itself to the traditional merchandise-management procedures of customer contact on the selling floor, and "eyeball" and "little black book" control of stocks. All this was congenial to the temperament of a great many buyers and merchandise managers, and it worked reasonably well *so long as the business was all conducted under one roof*. Indeed, if the department store business had remained primarily a single-unit type of enterprise, the organization problem with which this article is concerned probably never would have arisen at all.

Downtown Operations

It may be useful, at this point, to consider why the department store remained so long a predominantly single-unit type of institution, especially in view of the fact that the rate of growth of general-merchandise multiunit enterprises like Sears and J. C. Penney was substantially greater than that of the conventional department store. Part of the answer is that for a long time the general-merchandise chains were not regarded by the department stores as constituting real competiton; but perhaps more significant is the semimonopoly that department stores so long enjoyed in their downtown locations.

In addition, the interdependence of department stores and public transportation systems in the major cities in an earlier period tended to limit the number of good locations, since the pattern of such systems was predominantly radial, and the desirable locations were necessarily close to the hub. Professor McNair has said:

> During the days when the department store was almost by necessity a central downtown type of retail institution, the traditional department stores preempted practically all the feasible locations for that type of business. The number of possible locations for central downtown department stores of large volume was strictly limited. In each large city, up to World War II, and in many smaller cities, the department store districts were sharply and narrowly defined, usually clustering around the hub, or the important interconnecting points of the public transportation system. Repeatedly, location only a few blocks out of

> these magic circles proved disastrous. When, as not infrequently happened, there was a shift in these major department store centers, in response to changing population, residential, and transportation factors, some shrewd merchants among the traditional department stores saw the change coming and moved to anticipate it; the ranks closed quickly, and the stragglers experienced the penalty of their lack of foresight. So long as downtown remained supreme and the customers for the wide range of department store merchandise had no other alternative than to come downtown, the traditional department store was almost invulnerable; sheltered behind its monolithic downtown fortress, with highly limited possible locations, it enjoyed a species of monopoly. Thus was its period of untroubled maturity substantially prolonged.
>
> But when the great social revolution of Suburbia burgeoned in the postwar years, the traditional department store perforce had to sally forth from its protective downtown walls and join the battle in the open plains. With the growth of Suburbia and Exurbia, and the almost universal dependence on the private automobile for personal transportation, the number of potential department store locations multiplied rapidly. The whole terms of the retail contest were changed. Some department store managements intuitively perceived this potential disadvantge and dragged their feet on the establishment of suburban branches; but the social and economic trends of the times were too strong for them.[3]

Suburban Locations

Thus the second phase of urbanization in the United States, the outflow of the higher and middle income groups from the center core areas of cities to suburbia and beyond and the accompanying changes in ways of living and modes of transportation, forced department stores to follow their customers and become multiunit rather than single-unit organizations. At the same time there was a marked development of new competition. The general merchandise chains traded up; the variety chains greatly widened their price lines and offerings; the food chains pushed into nonfood lines; and a formidable new contender—the self-service discount store—appeared on the scene. The department store principle and the multiunit form of organization were being emphasized by almost all important retailers, and all of them were competing for desirable suburban locations.

Thus, even in the years when the department manager plan of organization was achieving its greatest acceptance, the economic and social trends of the period were setting in a direction that threatened ultimately to make this plan unworkable. A department manager might be able to operate effectively by on-the-floor customer contact and eyeball stock control in one unit, or in an organization with up to two or three branches; but when the number of geographically separated units exceeded four or five, the system began to break down. This was the problem we at R. H. Macy and Co. Inc. sought to resolve by a fundamental reorganization.

[3] McNair, op. cit.

BASIC REORGANIZATION

Until shortly after World War II, Macy's consisted of six large, downtown department stores, located in major metropolitan areas throughout the country (one having a small branch). Each of these stores was operated as a separate entity, sharing with other Macy stores only the broad corporate image of large assortments of merchandise oriented principally toward the middle-class buying public. All these downtown stores, except the original Macy store in New York, had been purchased from local merchants as going enterprises with established clienteles.

The Macy management chose to keep the traditional names of three of these stores, designating them for legal and promotional purposes as divisions of Macy's. Thus, in Newark, Atlanta, and Toledo, the local Macy stores were known as Bamberger's, Davison's, and the Lasalle & Koch Company, respectively. On the other hand, management chose to change the names of the remaining two stores, in San Francisco and Kansas City, Missouri, to Macy's.

Strategy Change

Prior to World War II, Macy's management saw its major opportunity for future growth in the purchase of established downtown department stores in the country's major cities and in the establishment of new Macy stores in the developing metropolitan areas, particularly in the West. But the changes in the environment of the department store industry that emerged in the postwar years called into question the adequacy of this strategy for taking full advantage of the new environmental opportunities and for protecting the company against the new threats to the traditional pattern of department store operations. Soon after the war, the Macy management decided that the company would add to its concept of corporate strategy the establishment of operating units in the suburban areas.

Initially, these suburban units were established as branch operations of the main store. More precisely, the suburban units were seen as operating arms, or selling outposts, of the local main store, established simply to extend its reach. These were to differ from the main store only in the range of merchandise offered and, of course, in the size of the merchandise inventories they carried.

This concept, however, was directed only to some of the problems created by changes in the environment—i.e., those having to do with the shift of shopping traffic from the downtown areas to the suburban shopping centers. Many of the problems resulting from the increase in competition from other retail outlets were not solved by this concept of operations. Management soon recognized the limitations of this initial modification of the corporate strategy, and subsequently further modified it to encompass the idea of establishing suburban operating units with enough independence to tailor their merchandising approaches to meet the unique needs of the communities they served.

Macy's opened thirty-nine suburban stores in the period between 1946 and 1964—a large number for a department store corporation to open in 18 years. The earliest of these new stores were added under the branch-store concept. By the mid-1950s, however, we had begun to think of suburban stores as having some independence from the downtown stores, and new stores were added with this latter concept increasingly in mind. During this period no additional downtown stores were added to the company's corporate structure.

Novel Design

Soon after the change in corporate strategy was implemented, resulting in the addition of several suburban stores to the operating pattern of each of the company's existing downtown stores, it was clear that the executive organization structure of the store divisions was ill suited to the new task. The management job of directing, coordinating, and controlling division operations could not be effectively and efficiently performed with the existing structure of executive activities and relationships. A change had to be made.

For many years prior to the change in corporate strategy, the executive organization structure of the Macy divisions was primarily of the "functional" type described earlier in this article. The breakdown of functions was:

> *General management*—responsible for the establishment, within the broad limits set by corporate headquarters, of the total store character, objectives, and major policies.
>
> *Merchandise administration*—responsible for the buying and selling of goods.
>
> *Advertising and promotion*—responsible for assisting merchandise administrators in developing their advertising and promotion programs.
>
> *Personnel*—responsible for administration of personnel policies and practices.
>
> *Operations*—responsible for the conduct of the stores' daily operational activity.
>
> *Control*—responsible for the financial aspects of operations and the preparation of management-and merchandise-control data reports.

Under this long-standing organization structure, the key operating executives of the company were those associated with the merchandise-administration function. This line of executives started at the top with two vice presidents—one for hard goods and one for soft goods. Reporting to each of these vice presidents were five or six merchandise administrators, each of whom supervised ten to twelve buyers, who were essentially department managers. The buyers, with their assistants, were responsible for the purchasing and selling of particular categories of merchandise. Salespeople—who were nominally supervised by store-operations executives but were basically controlled by the buyers—maintained contact with the customers, working with the merchandise as it was bought, priced, displayed, and stocked by the buyers.

All personnel associated with a particular category of merchandise were

EXHIBIT 1. Traditional organization structure of a division

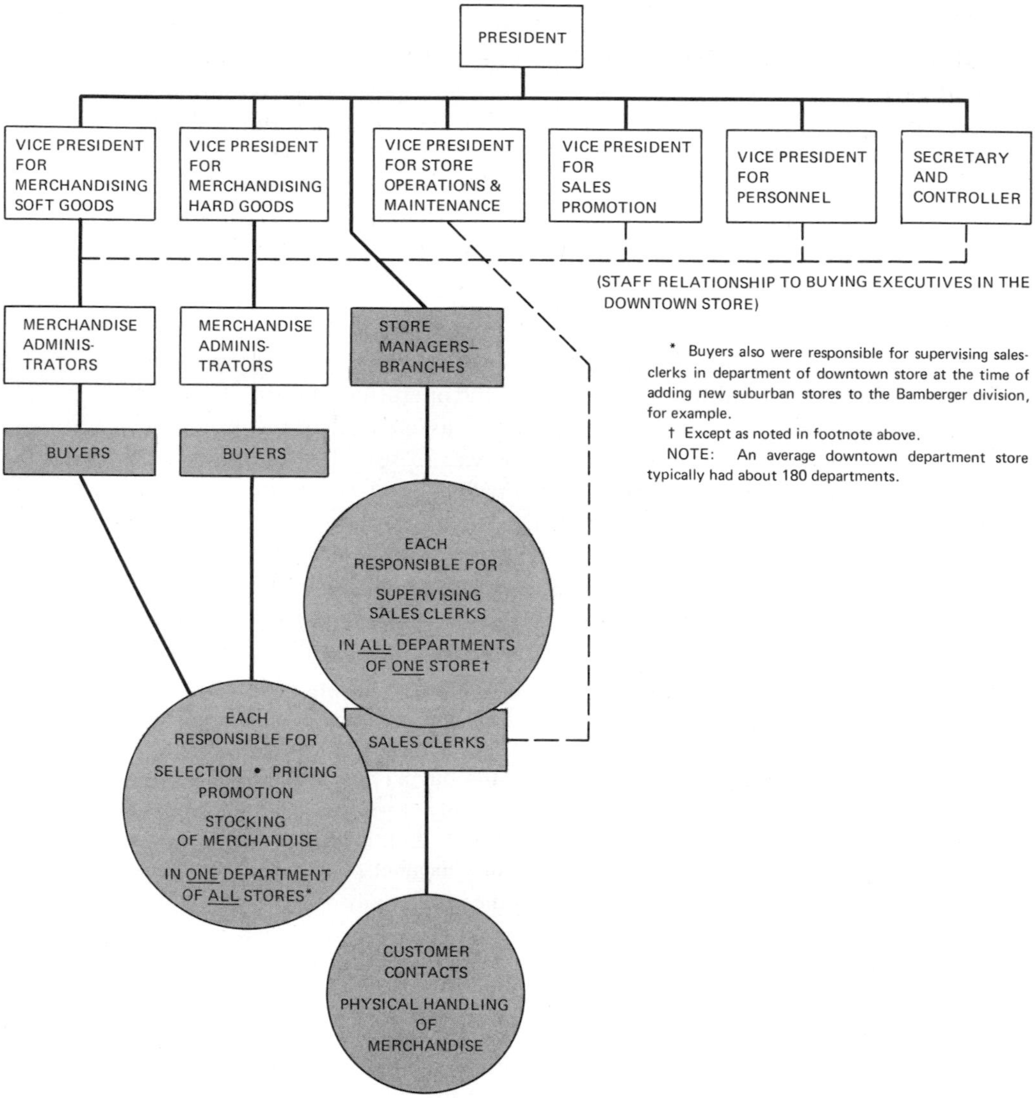

* Buyers also were responsible for supervising salesclerks in department of downtown store at the time of adding new suburban stores to the Bamberger division, for example.

† Except as noted in footnote above.

NOTE: An average downtown department store typically had about 180 departments.

considered part of a department. A chart of the traditional organization structure of one of the Macy divisions is presented in Exhibit 1.

The relationship among the buyers, salespeople, and store-operations personnel had always presented a problem to the Macy executives and to executives of other retail stores similarly organized. On the one hand, the buyers needed complete control over their departments in order to have their total merchandising plans well implemented. On the other hand, they were not able constantly to be on the selling floor to supervise the salespeople, and they were generally too busy with vendor contacts to give adequate attention to the administrative details involved in training, scheduling, discipline, and so on. Thus, as was typical in the industry, the authority relationship between these groups shifted back and forth over time, depending on the speed with which dissatisfaction accumulated with the existing arrangement.

With the addition of suburban stores in each division came a condition of overload on the buyers, because the techniques they had developed to handle the tasks for which they were responsible under the existing structure were inadequate. For instance, by 1954 the Bamberger division had added four outlying stores, and these additions made it virtually impossible for the buyers to keep adequate control over the merchandise stocks and displays in all locations. Also, it was difficult for the buyers to be well enough aware of local buying patterns and competitive situations to tailor their purchases, prices, promotional efforts, and merchandise distribution to the specific needs of each store.

While supervision of the salespeople had been decentralized in the outlying stores, the buyers at this time retained this responsibility in the downtown store. What was a complicated and time-consuming task with one store became an almost impossible task with several stores, especially with the additional responsibility of salesperson supervision in the downtown store. The problems that could be foreseen in following through on corporate strategy by adding even more stores to each division made it clear that the executive organization structure needed to be changed, and changed significantly.

Alternative Concepts

A possible alternative to a basic change in organization structure was to search for ways of extending the capacity of buyers to cope with their enlarged tasks while retaining their traditional functions. The addition of more assistants was a device which came quickly to mind, but this idea was rejected because it would only partly take care of the problem over the long run. If the assistants were located in the suburban stores, they could be of some help in collecting and analyzing pertinent local information for the buyer. But this information would still have to be processed by the buyer before he could make his decisions, and thus his job would be made only slightly more manageable. Furthermore, this approach would involve a substantial increase in executive payroll.

Another alternative was to improve the merchandise-control system of the company, making it possible for the buyer to have timely and usable information on activity at all locations. This alternative was accepted by the company, but not as a complete solution. Soon after Macy's change in corporate stategy, work was begun on the improvement of the merchandise-control system, but the management still was not satisfied that such improvement went far enough. The top executives concluded that a whole new concept of the buyer's role in the organization was required, and they set out to study the problem from this viewpoint.

One of the first ideas considered for making a basic change in the role of the buyers in each store division was the complete decentralization of buying operations. Implementing this concept would involve development of an independent buying organization in each one of the suburban stores as well as in the downtown store. Almost immediately the argument of expense was raised, and also the question of potential losses that might be incurred from inability to buy in division-wide quantities. Other potential inefficiencies of this approach lay in the difficulties it would present in achieving stock transfers between stores when such transfers were justified by variations in the buying patterns facing each store.

SPLIT FUNCTIONS

Management therefore decided that full organizational decentralization of buying and merchandising was not an optimum solution of the problem of excessive work load on the buyer. Some method of organization was required which would combine the advantages of centralized buying with the advantages of greater local responsibility, including responsibility at the downtown store, for the stocking and selling of merchandise. Accordingly, management set about breaking down the functions and responsibilities of buyers, with the objective of seeing which might be delegated to the individual-store personnel without losing the advantages of centralized buying, providing at the same time for the possibility of achieving sharper presentations of merchandise, given the unique demands of the individual communities being served.

The first step taken in this direction was to make a basic separation or split between the buying and the selling functions of the buyers. These functions broke down into specifie tasks as shown in Exhibit 2.

New Structure

Implementing this concept of splitting the buying and the selling functions would involve the creation of a number of new executive positions and the redefinition of existing executive positions both at division headquarters and in the store units as follows:

(1) In each store, as it was brought under the new concept, three selling line levels would be created.

(2) At headquarters, the functions and responsibilities of the senior vice president for stores needed to be broadened to bring about the new emphasis on the selling function in the stores.

EXHIBIT 2

Split between the Buying and Selling Functions of the Buyers

Buying Function	*Selling Function*
1. Prior planning and research to determine what and how much to buy (inventory management). 2. Buying (placing orders and maintaining contacts with vendors). 3. Pricing. 4. Distributing merchandise to the stores. 5. Promoting the merchandise (advertising, flyers).	1. Presenting the merchandise (tags, displays, arrangements, fixtures). 2. Supervising the salespeople and the selling services (deliveries, complaints, adjustments). 3. Maintaining adequate stock on the selling floor. 4. Maintaining customer contacts.

(3) In the larger stores, assistant managers for operations would be created to relieve store managers of some of their traditional duties, in recognition of the need for greater emphasis on selling and customer services.

(4) At headquarters, duties and responsibilities of the divisional senior vice presidents for personnel and labor relations, operations and maintenance control, and sales promotion would be broadened to include service in a staff relationship to the selling lines in all stores, as well as to the buying line in the downtown store.

Under the new concept, buyers were to continue to have their offices in the downtown store building. They were to serve all the stores in the division, including the downtown store. But the downtown store was no longer to be thought of as the "mother hen with her branchstore chickens." Each store was to be regarded as having equal status, and no one store was in any way to have priority over another—for instance, in the allocation of merchandise.

In short, it was to be a true multistore organization. We might remark, parenthetically, that this divorce of buying and selling operations necessitated a high degree of reliance on data-gathering and reporting systems to replace the buyer's previous dependence upon customer contact and personal observation as a means of obtaining vital merchandising information. Without the promise afforded by the rapid technological developments in data-processing systems and their adaptation to retail management needs, the major decision on separation of buying and selling might have entailed significantly greater risk. As previously indicated, management was vigorously pursuing the objective of improved merchandise-control systems.

Exhibit 3 illustrates the divisional organization structure under the new concept.

The new organization structure was tested against the three major requirements set by management. These were:

1. High absorption capacity in the organization for future expansion through the addition of quasi-independent suburban stores.

2. Clear lines of authority and responsibility in the organization, and formal means of coordination between necessarily separate but interrelated functions and duties.
3. Preservation of the advantages of centralized buying with, at the same time, the advantages of decentralized selling.

The design developed by management promised to accomplish these objectives well, and the decision was made to give it a try.

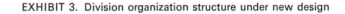

EXHIBIT 3. Division organization structure under new design

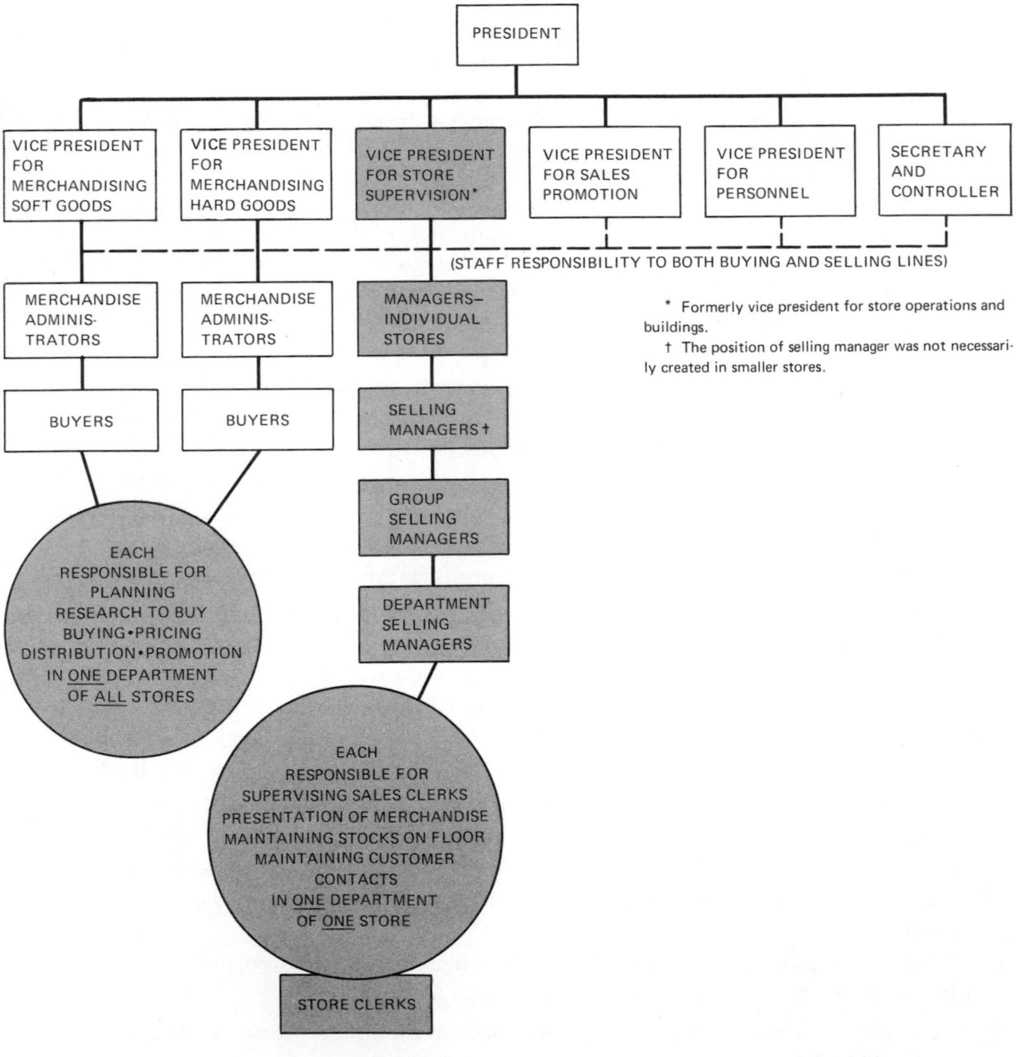

* Formerly vice president for store operations and buildings.

† The position of selling manager was not necessarily created in smaller stores.

PLAN IMPLEMENTATION

The design and the implementation of a new organization structure are closely related processes. While it may be possible to "ivory tower" a new organization structure and then impose it on an existing organization, there is always a strong likelihood that this approach will fail, especially if the executive groups involved stand pat. On the other hand, top management cannot relinquish the job of deciding what the new structure should be to the very people who have the most at stake in maintaining the status quo. Some balance between top management control over the design and executive participation in it must be struck in order for a changeover to be made effectively and efficiently.

Executive Involvement

In general, the Macy management believed that the greater the departure from the existing structure required by new strategy, the less the degree of democracy allowable in the determination process. Also, it believed that if important changes had to be made quickly to meet severe pressures, the participation of the executive groups concerned would have to be minimized, and top management itself would have to take responsibility for essentially imposing the new design on the existing structure.

The situation at Macy's was such that there were no severe time pressures for making needed changes. Operating efficiency in store divisions that had rapidly added outlying stores was being strained, but in most divisions the crisis point had not yet been reached. Nevertheless, the likelihood of further erosion in operating effectiveness and efficiency as more new stores were added in these divisions was great, and management believed that failure to solve the organizational problem in the relatively near future would seriously limit the possibility of further expansion through the addition of new suburban stores. Inability to move aggressively on this strategic front would increase the risk that competitors might snap up choice locations, meaning that Macy's might in a number of instances have to forgo the advantages of getting there first in the new locations.

Consequently, the decision was to choose a path which resulted in putting a high degree of responsibility for the organizational design on top management, though providing for appropriate participation on the part of the rest of the executive group. With this approach, top management believed there would be an important reduction in the length of time necessary to effect the desired organizational change. It also believed that little would have to be sacrificed in the quality of the design itself.

To limit the potential dangers of ivory-towering, however, and also to gain as much support from members of the organization as possible prior to the announcement of a new structure, top management chose to follow a course which emphasized experimental testing of its preliminary formulation of the new design. From these tests, management believed it could obtain useful experience which might, on the one hand, indicate that some revision of the design was necessary, and which, on the other hand, would enable the executive groups to see, to the extent that the experiments proved the validity of the design, that the new ideas were workable.

Experimental Approaches

In addition to limiting executive participation in the formulation of the design, and in addition to employing an experimental approach to test the new design and prove its worth, top management chose to work on the problem initially with a single division—Bamberger's, New Jersey—with a view to taking the process almost all the way to completion before starting on the other divisions. In this way, we believed, we could minimize the total organizational disruption from the changeover, and at the same time add only slightly to the total length of the period required for the changeover. Successful installation of the new structure in one store division would do much to reduce the resistance of executives in the other divisions to the change, and would contribute a body of experience as to the best procedures to follow that would have immediate and direct utility in effecting similar changes in the other divisions.

Within the Bamberger organization, three distinct groups of buying executives could be distinguished with reference to their reaction to the initial design. One group was dead set against any change in a system of organization with which they were very familiar, and which had served the company well in the past. Another group expressed a willingness to look objectively at the result of the experiment with the new design, but could not generate much enthusiasm for the idea of making a change. The third group was quite excited by the prospect of working under the new organizational design, believing it might help solve some of the troublesome problems they had faced for a long time. While precise information on the composition of these groups might have been obtained, the Bamberger management chose to rely on its feel for the situation, believing that the largest group was the one composed of those who were "willing to look."

In order to give the initial experiment the greatest chance of success, a buyer who was one of the executives who were enthusiastic about the preliminary design was chosen as a guinea pig. This buyer was very able, understood the objective of the experiment, and felt privileged to play a significant role in the process of reorganization. Furthermore, he was responsible for a category of merchandise which lent itself well to the new type of organization.

The experiment was four-pronged:

1. Establishment of a revised list of the buyer's duties and responsibilities in accordance with the concept of splitting the buying and selling functions.
2. Elimination of the buyer's responsibility for, and activities associated with, supervision of the selling function in the downtown store.
3. Establishment of a routine of periodic inspection of the selling departments with which the buyer was associated in order to permit him to get a feel for how the merchandise was moving.
4. Establishment of new merchandise-control reports to keep the buyer informed in greater detail about the merchandise being sold in each store, and to provide for comparison of the department in Bamberger's with similar departments in other divisions.

This initial experiment was successful. In each of the Bamberger stores, the experimental department showed significantly better operating results than it had achieved in the past, and it outperformed the corresponding departments in the other divisions by a substantial margin. The buyer who had subjected himself to the experiment became even more vocally enthusiastic about the new organizational design than he had been previously.

Next, another experiment was set up, this time involving several departments, all with high degrees of seasonal and fashion variation in their patterns of sale. Again the experiment demonstrated the viability of the new design.

With this evidence in hand, a number of the Macy top managers were satisfied that the design should be extended throughout the Bamberger division. Before extending the new organizational design to a large number of other departments, however, the question of additional cost had to be met. This question was forcefully raised by some of the remaining doubters in the Macy top management group.

The first experiment had demonstrated the capability of the new structure to handle effectively an increasing number of stores, with little additional personnel required in the buying line. But there was still the question of the cost of additional personnel needed for the selling line—a question sharply focused on the downtown store, which required a whole new set of selling line personnel at the group sales manager level to perform duties formerly handled by buyers.

Initially, it was estimated that in Bamberger's downtown store, for instance, a cost of $400,000 per year for additional personnel would be incurred. While the long-run operating advantages and cost savings of the new structure would in all probability far outweigh this initial additional cost, it was hard for some members of the top management group to face the idea of adding costs when profit margins, normally low in department stores in comparison with many other industries, were continually being threatened by generally rising costs of operation.

To counter this fear, the argument was advanced by the more positive members of the top management group that savings in the total salary bill would result from elimination of the duplicated personnel who had been added fundamentally because of the inefficiencies of the old organization structure. It was impossible, of course, to determine in advance the amount of such savings, but those members of the management group who subscribed to this argument were willing to take their stand on the reasonable faith that savings from this source would be substantial.

This group carried the day, and it was decided that a third experiment, this time including almost half the departments in the store, and thus several of the merchandise administrators who supervised the buyers, would be undertaken. The outcome of this experiment was to be critical in determining the subsequent steps.

The results of this third experiment were even more conclusive than those of the first two. Not only did operating performance improve in the departments, as in the case of the first two experiments, but savings realized in other personnel costs almost immediately offset the expense of adding new selling line executives. At this point, the evidence was sufficient to overcome even the deepest reservations, and the decision was finally made to go the whole distance in installing the new organization structure in the Bamberger division.

Operating Guide

While proving that the general shape of the new structure was fundamentally sound, the experiments did not solve all the problems of operating under it, even for those directly involved in the departments concerned. As in the case of any major reallocation of functions and responsibilities, when executives began to work on a day-to-day basis under the new structure, much confusion was generated about who was to do what, particularly in relation to the downtown store. New people had to be added to the selling lines in all stores, particularly the downtown store; and a number of the store managers, most of whom had grown up under the old structure, were hesitant to move aggressively in staffing their stores appropriately.

In addition, a number of the buyers informally insisted on operating in accordance with the old structure. To these buyers, assumption of sales and stock responsibility by the selling line amounted to usurpation of their prerogatives. Some of them continued to spend a large portion of their time on the selling floor of the downtown store, in spite of the fact that their selling supervision responsibilities had been eliminated, and in spite of the fact that new merchandise-control information had been developed which required that they spend additional time in their offices for study and analysis of reports.

Thus there was enough confusion and pushing-and-pulling between the buying line and selling line to warrant the preparation of a management guide, listing in the greatest possible detail the specific operating duties of each line and of each organizational level within each line. This would also serve to reduce any uncertainty that might still exist as to how strongly top management felt about the need for change in the patterns of executive behavior.

In the preparation of this manual, a concept was developed which helped define more precisely the operating relationships between the buying line and the selling line. This concept separated authority and responsibility into three categories: "line," "primary coordinate," and "secondary coordinate." Line authority was unequivocal and exclusive; coordinate responsibility was, in contrast, shared or divided. Both the buying line and the selling line had coordinate responsibility for some activities, although primary coordinate responsibility belonged in each case to but one of the two lines. The concept of coordinate responsibility was developed in order to give recognition to the fact that the company buying line and the individual-store selling lines were responsible for the same objectives and results, i.e., developing store sales volume at a profit.

The organization manual elaborated the concept of primary and secondary coordinate authority and responsibility as follows:

1. The line with *either* primary *or* secondary coordinate responsibility and authority may *originate* the idea for any action proposed.
2. Any such action may be *authorized only* by the line with *primary* coordinate responsibility and authority, regardless of which line originated the idea.
3. Before such action is taken by the line with *primary* coordinate responsibility and authority, it *must* notify and consult the line with the *secondary* coordinate authority and responsibility. Such notification and consultation is *mandatory*.
4. The goal will at all times be to arrive at *mutual agreement* between the two lines concerning the idea.
5. But, if this is not possible, the line with *primary* coordinate responsibility and authority will take the action, and the *secondary* line may appeal the action to his immediate line supervisor.

The manual listed eighty-four authorities and responsibilities of the buying line and the selling lines, indicating in each case whether the authority was line, primary coordinate, or secondary coordinate. The manual was introduced to the operating executives in the summer of 1960, almost five years after the initial concept of the new organization design had been formulated. The manual and its presentation helped clarify the concept of the new structure, but it still did not solve all the operating problems. Only additional time and experience in operation could be expected to iron them out eventually.

Management Commitment

The initial work on the design of the new organization structure in Bamberger's started in late 1955. It was not until late 1959, however, that the new structure was established in the entire Bamberger division.

Some company executives now believe that this amounted to an excessively long period of time from conception to actual implementation of the plan. According to these executives, top management went further than necessary with the experimentation to prove its point. Others, however, believe that this length of time was necessary to gain within the organization an acceptable level of commitment to the new structure.

The authors personally believe that this period was essential, given the magnitude of the change itself and the need to alter old habit patterns and to achieve at least a minimum degree of executive commitment to the new design.

After complete installation in the Bamberger division, the new structure was introduced to the Macy New York division, in July 1963. Management moved more rapidly with the installation in the New York division than it had in the Bamberger division. The strategy of change was very different, involving a complete formal restructuring all at once. Under this strategy, management anticipated a minimum of confusion and resistance. The new structure was already proven. Division executives knew about it, had confidence in it, were anxious to make the changeover. With no necessity to experiment, needed personnel changes could be made, starting at the top of the division hierarchy, that would ensure continuous reinforcement of the widespread positive feeling toward the new structure. Thus the top management problem in the New York division was one of assisting in organizational adaptation to the new structure, rather than refining the new organization concept and gaining commitment to it.

SUMMARY

Organizational problems in the department store industry have a long history. In the current period the forced evolution of the department store into a multiunit, rather than a single-unit, institution has posed a serious problem for a large number of companies, all within a relatively short time span. How one important firm met this problem has been related in this case history.

When the management of the R. H. Macy & Co., Inc. chose to change its corporate strategy to maximize its opportunities and minimize its risks in the face of the changing economic and social environment, it confronted the task of changing its executive organization structure. The structure which had been well suited to the previous strategy early proved inadequate for the strategy required by the new environment.

In the process of changing from the old to a new structure, the Macy top management faced a series of choices, each at least partly dependent on the choices previously made. The first in this series was a choice between the alternative of making only moderate changes in responsibilities and relationships, in order to cover the weak spots as they appeared, and the alternative of making a bold departure from the existing relationships, with a view to taking care of future as well as current problems.

Since management chose the latter alternative, its next choice concerned the degree of executive participation to be sought in developing the organizational design. And since the decision was to invite participation on a highly selective and limited basis, the next choice involved the method by which the management committee's design would be tested and then established in the organization. The management chose to proceed on a step-by-step basis in installing the new structure and to set up experiments or pilot projects.

It is impossible, of course, to know whether or not a different series of choices would have produced a better organization design, or would have resulted in a speedier and more efficient changeover. We do know, however, that the company was successful in establishing a new organizational structure which by all tests has proved superior to the one that preceded it.

The effectiveness of the series of choices made by the Macy management must have resulted from their appropriateness to the situations faced, plus, as most of the top management group would be quick to add, a little good luck. The authors hope that others may profit in at least some broad way from this account of the Macy experience, even though no two situations are ever the same, and though there is often great danger in attempting to apply in detail what has worked in one company to the situation of another company.

QUESTIONS

1. Has the population movement to the suburbs affected store organization?
2. How did the role of the buyer change in the new organizational structure? What impact could it have on the salespeople?
3. List the arguments a buyer might offer in resisting the new structure.

34

Customer Types and Salesman Tactics in Appliance Selling

Alfred Oxenfeldt

Appliance customer types—each seeking different product features and varied kinds of services—have helped to segment appliance dealers into different types. Any given dealer sells to all customer types, but in very different proportions, for each type finds that certain kinds of stores match his desires best. Retail stores are, increasingly, adapting their operations to cultivate particular types of customers; consequently, retail institutions and methods of operation are changing.

On the firing line with the customer is the retail salesman. He faces the task of diagnosing differences among individual customers and of finding ways of coping with them. In addition, he must also perform other functions for the retail store of a fairly routine administrative character. Increased understanding of customers can be made to produce benefits for the retailer only if he can transmit it to his salesmen. They must implement it in the actual sales situation.

This article is concerned primarily with explaining retailers' perceptions of their customers and the way that their salesmen deal with customers and perform their other duties. It should help to explain some of the ferment that exists today in retailing and might suggest the direction in which retailing institutions are likely to develop in the near future.

This article draws heavily on intensive studies of two suburban (Long Island, New York) markets for television sets. Although these markets are hardly representative, they do include diverse types of retailers. The findings of those studies have been supplemented from other sources.

VARIED CUSTOMER DESIRES

Customers seek different product features and desire dissimilar kinds of service. In the retailing of such things as clothing, drugs, appliances, and hardware, consumers were offered essentially the same blend of service at essentially the same price until relatively recently. The customer who placed overriding emphasis on low price "had no place to go." He would have been willing to forego such niceties as spacious and attractive premises,

Reprinted from *Journal of Retailing,* Vol. 39, No. 4, Winter 1963–64, pp. 9–15, 55–56.

convenient locations, ample parking, numerous and attentive salesmen, and speedy delivery service in order to effect a saving. But no retail institution met his desires.

Other customers place heavy emphasis on pleasant surroundings, attentive and informative salesmen, ironclad guarantees, etc. Clearly, the same kinds of shops do not meet the needs and desires and whims of these dissimilar types of customers. Accordingly, new types of retailers—in particular, the "mass" or "volume" retailer now called the "discount house"—emerged. This type of retailer essentially applies the same principles to the sale of such things as appliances and clothing that had been applied for decades to the sale of food products in supermarkets.

We can hypothesize, then, that the activities of appliance dealers represent adaptations to the nature and behavior of their customers. Similarly, distributors and manufacturers of major appliances pick their marketing strategies, methods of display, hours of operation, salesmen, etc., on the basis of the number, location, and expressed or implied preferences and actions of their customers. To understand, then, why and how appliance dealers and their salesmen do the things they do, one must study the ultimate consumer and determine how the retailer sees him.

Every appliance dealer does business with varied consumers, even though customers of a given type tend to be attracted to a particular kind of retail outlet. At one extreme, there is a substantial and apparently growing class of consumers regarded by retailers and their salesmen as "the enemy." These are aggressive and well-informed but extremely shrewd customers who consider a major purchase a challenge to outsmart the retailer. They place an unreasonably high value on tiny monetary savings because for them it is a matter of pride and principle to make purchases at the lowest possible price. These consumers are found mainly in large cities. They have no store loyalty or personal friendship with a retailer or salesman and buy wherever they can "get the best deal." The notion that the dealer is "entitled" to make a profit is foreign to their thinking; if they were able to buy an appliance below the dealer's actual cost, they would ordinarily boast of it rather than feel compassion for the dealer. Many do not hesitate to invent stories about the low prices they have found in competing stores.

At the opposite extreme are consumers that salesmen call "gentlemen." These customers feel and show genuine concern for the retailer's interests. They would not beat down a price even if they believed that they could. These consumers regard retailers as basically honest and as a general rule trust their advice.

Another important type of consumer, as viewed by appliance dealers and their salesmen, is the "lamb." "Lambs" are very uninformed and unsophisticated buyers; moreover, they are gullible and malleable. Ordinarily they are anxious to own the item for which they are shopping and welcome any advice and sales arguments that facilitate their purchase.

As indicated, every salesman meets all types of customers, though "the enemy" gravitates to the discount houses and appliance chains; he comes out in greatest numbers when those stores are running special promotions. "Gentlemen" and "lambs" are found in all kinds of retail stores. The former tend mainly to patronize local shops and become acquainted, if not friendly, with the retailer and some of his salesmen. "Lambs" are attracted to stores that claim to offer bargains.

Appliance salesmen who have had numerous contacts with "the enemy" tend to become wary. Until they have conducted a reconnaissance to form an estimate of the enemy's intentions and capabilities, they withhold their fire. Once they find an "enemy," most appliance salesmen expect and offer no "quarter." All tactics are considered fair in what they regard as a no-holds-barred struggle—on both sides. Whatever qualms of conscience they might have felt if they used shady tactics with "gentlemen" never arise. They regard their behavior as more than justified—indeed, they consider it necessary for survival—by the nature of the enemy they face.

It is not clear whether all appliance salesmen modify their behavior when they meet, not an "enemy" but a "lamb" or a "gentleman." Doubtless there are substantial differences among salesmen in this regard, with many matching customer consideration if a large financial sacrifice is not involved. On the other hand, some seem to be motivated solely by short-term gain and try to get their customer's name on a contract by any device that might work, regardless of the customer's demeanor.

It is impossible to explain the low ethical standards one finds among metropolitan salesmen of appliances unless one recognizes the aggressiveness and unscrupulousness of many consumers. Consumer avarice certainly reinforces seller deceitfulness.

On the other hand, the aggressiveness and avarice of many consumers can be explained in large measure by the unenviable position they occupy when they come to the marketplace. They confront an enormous variety of similar items among which they must choose. The most important attributes of the product are far too technical for them to appraise. Many of them, moreover, have lost any personal ties with the retailer, for more and more of them buy from department stores or large chains that are impersonal and characterized by rapid turnover of sales personnel.

Moreover, their purchase involves a sizable outlay, so that the penalties of a mistaken choice are substantial. Then, too, every consumer gets to meet the "sharp salesman" who deals loosely with the truth and, finding a trusting consumer, will take outrageous advantage of him. From this strange mixture of dependence, mistrust, insecurity, feelings of inadequacy, and strain because of the large expenditure comes strange and varied consumer behavior. And that is precisely what one finds in the market for major appliances. Consumers vary at least as much as do the stores in which they buy and the salesmen with whom they deal.

THREE CUSTOMER APPROACHES TO PURCHASE SITUATION

Customers have been divided into three broad types on the basis of their approach to the purchase situation and the way they relate to retailers. Within these broad classes of customers are many and very important differences to which skilled retail salesmen are sensitive. Customers differ in income, in education, and in the number and condition of their present television sets. Some are interested in auxiliary equipment (like hi-fi or stereo), some are brand loyal, some are "regular customers," etc. Many salesmen consciously try to identify the types of customers their stores attract and study how best to serve them, as well as other types. No salesman meets only one type. The adaptable salesman is able to serve many classes of customers, even while concentrating his efforts on certain selected types.

CHIEF FUNCTIONS OF APPLIANCE SALESMEN

The appliance salesman performs several distinct functions, often concurrently, that should be distinguished to understand his contribution to the distribution process. First, he communicates product information and frequently demonstrates and displays merchandise in the process. Second, he is a persuader, another form of communication. Third, he participates in record-keeping. Finally, he helps to "manage merchandise," including the floor arrangement of merchandise and some movement from rear spaces to the sales floor; occasionally he also participates in arranging window displays.

Communication of Product Information

Some distribution specialists would describe retail salesmen as purveyors of misinformation rather than as sources of information. This observation partly is a slur on the honesty of the average salesman, who is careless with the truth when he has reason to believe that a fib (whether small, medium, or large, white, grey, or black) would mean the difference between a sale and a lost customer. It attests also to the very limited amount of product information that the average salesman possesses and the dubious sources from which he draws it. Especially retail salesmen who sell a wide variety of technical products of varied brands, all of which change frequently, cannot keep informed about the products they sell even if they have had some technical product training. For the usual kinds of people engaged in retail selling the task is overwhelming. Consequently salesmen of appliances tend to substitute glibness for solid fact. Most of them get by because of the even greater ignorance of the customers and their ability to deceive themselves and most others into believing that they really know what they are talking about.

The retail salesman's communication function has altered greatly in recent years. This change has affected the major appliance salesman almost as much as most others. Although self-service and self-selection date far back to the early Woolworth stores, if not before, arrangements for reducing the participation of the salesman in the purchase transaction have been so extended that they have created a new species of salesman-customer relationship. The salesman's communication function has changed dramatically as customers have been brought in direct contact with merchandise. The merchandise itself, plus point-of-sale printed materials, packages, etc., communicate much of the product information formerly supplied by the salesman.

Other Duties

Television set dealers vary widely in the communication duties they assign to their salesmen. Some relegate their salesmen to the role of the salesman in a food supermarket—to virtual nonexistence. At the opposite extreme, other appliance retailers assign a salesman to accompany each customer while he inspects merchandise. Most retailers fall between these two extremes, displaying their merchandise so that customers can inspect it and narrowing down the range of alternatives without personal assistance. At some point, however, a salesman is summoned or volunteers his services.

Retail salesmen have been criticized harshly by some retailing specialists, such as E. B. Weiss, on the grounds of incompetence, low effort, and limited intelligence. Some salesmen no doubt merit this harsh assessment. On the other hand, most of the major appliance salesmen studied by the author over an extended period deserve the highest praise for skill, effort, and intelligence. The proportions of salesmen who belong in these two opposing classes cannot be assessed reliably on the basis of available information. The author's investigations, which were intensive rather than extensive, suggest that talented appliance salesmen represent a large majority in metropolitan centers and their suburbs, particularly in the appliance chains. The caliber of individual salesmen varies enormously, sometimes within the same store.

The Persuasive Function

The salesman provides information, combined with puffery, allegation, falsehood, implication, and innuendo, mainly in an effort to persuade. He also discusses product attributes when customers ask questions of him. But whatever the proportion, the salesman definitely uses the communication process in order to persuade. He relies almost entirely on words and gestures, combined with occasional demonstration of the product. Consequently, persuasion and communication are inextricably intertwined, even though in intent and effect they are quite different.

Beyond the variety of techniques common to retail salesmen generally, appliance salesmen have some special strategies for their attempts to sell a *particular item.* A favorite is the "bait and switch" stratagem by which the customer is persuaded to buy, not the item advertised, but a more expensive one.

The appliance dealer generally sees his main objective—to make sales at a profit—as having two distinct stages: first, he must lure potential customers into his premises; second, he must induce them to make a purchase. And his assumption is that there is no necessary connection between the item used to lure customers into the store and the item that is ultimately sold. In its extreme form, "bait and switch" involves "loss-leading."

"Switching" should not be confused with the related sales tactic of "trading-up." This tactic is planned by the manufacturer at the time the line of products is designed for the market. Specifically, "stepping up the consumer" consists of leading the customer from the model in the line in which he showed greatest original interest to more costly models by stressing, step by step, the features that may be obtained for "modest" added cost. (These added charges seem even more modest when expressed in terms of payments per month) Each feature added to a television set ordinarily commands a price that is significantly above the added cost of the feature to the retailer (and to the distributor and manufacturer as well). Consequently, the manufacturer, and the various middlemen through whom he sells, has a strong financial inducement to "step up" the customer to more expensive models. And the number and magnitude of the "step-ups" as well as "switches" he engineers is a major measure of a salesman's skill.

These sales tactics can be evaluated from many standpoints. They can be evaluated simply on the basis of effectiveness. On that score they must be rated in the case of television sets very high. Salesmen (with the conscious or unconscious collaboration of consumers) do succeed in "switching" or trading up a very large proportion of their customers. No exact estimate of their number is possible, but the author would venture the guess that at present it exceeds 65 percent of the television sets sold—and it was even higher in years back. (A switch or step-up occurs when the salesman's efforts induce a customer to purchase a set that yields the retailer and/or the salesman a larger margin of profit than the one in which the customer expressed initial interest.)

The social effects of bait-switch selling are not easy to evaluate. Although the salesman's motives are clearly self-interested, some general consumer benefits may still result from the practice. Judged from the standpoint of consumers who seek merchandise at minimum *price* (which may mean high *cost*), the bait-switch stratagem increases the supply of attractive goods available.

In rare cases, a customer literally cannot persuade the retailer to sell him the "lure" merchandise, no matter how strong his determination to do so; such "lure" items usually are called "nailed down models." Likewise, some customers cannot be switched. They know their own minds, are not easily intimidated or persuaded by salesmen, and will not buy an item unless they believe its worth to them exceeds its cost. However, "bait" merchandise often leads other consumers to make an unproductive visit to a store in the expectation of finding offerings that are not available or were misrepresented in the store's advertising. Frequently, the "bait" item is advertised in a manner that conveys a false impression to the customer; it often does so by withholding information from the prospective customer—like the fact that it does not include some essential feature, or that it is a model about to be superseded or even a model from a previous year. Occasionally, the "bait" item is made in a style so unattractive that the consumer would consider his home disfigured by its presence; the large black square box type of table model television set is a relatively familiar example from the recent past.

When some misrepresentation or nondisclosure about the "lures" induces the consumer to make an otherwise unplanned shopping trip, then the bait-switch tactic hurts even the consumer who knows what he wants and will not be diverted. Not only has he made an unnecessary and frustrating shopping trip, but in addition he may be subjected to sales pressure of an unpleasant and embarrassing sort. Or he may make a purchase he will regret—hardly a goodwill builder for the firm! And similar harm to the store image may result if consumers discover that a certain store advertises sets that are "new" in the sense that they have not been used but are not "new models" because they were introduced one or more years earlier.

Record-Keeping and Merchandising Functions

Salesmen are expected to give their employers and their suppliers information as well as to inform their customers about products. Manufacturers, store owners, or managers want information on the following aspects of the market: customer reactions to individual brands and models and specifically to particular product features, such as performance, aesthetic appeal, customers' apparent impressions of the value of the guarantees and service facilities offered by different manufacturers.

Many retailers ask their salesmen to keep a written record of such observations which they collect and analyze and then transmit to their suppliers. The vast majority of retailers do not systematically gather such data, however. They require only that their salesmen do the paper work involved in effecting a sale. Especially when the transaction involves installment credit, this element of salesmen's duties can be burdensome. If the salesmen carry it out inefficiently or ungraciously, it can itself become an important source of lost sales.

SALES MANAGEMENT

In considering the functions performed by retail salesmen of television sets, one must take account of the activities of the store owner or executive of an appliance chain who is responsible for managing the retail sales force. Many retailers do not consider it their responsibility to train salesmen. Apparently they feel that their job has been done when they hire someone who seems to be a good salesman. If they find by examining actual sales records that they were mistaken, they will hire a replacement. What training salesmen get comes primarily from manufacturers' or distributors' representatives and is concerned mainly with product information rather than with sales methods.

There are some exceptions, of course. A few appliance chains describe themselves as "fanatics" on the subject of sales training. Inspection of what they actually do suggests outright neglect far more than fanaticism. The retail salesmen who sell television sets ordinarily constitute a very small group. Perhaps the smallness of their number discourages the owner or store executive from designing and carrying out a program of training. The most common method of preparing a new retail salesman for his assignment is to put him under the wing of a senior salesman for a few days. Just what senior salesmen do at such times is difficult to determine. Although the guidance they give new salesmen can scarcely qualify as rigorous sales training administered by a training specialist, it does familiarize the new salesman with the way that store handles its paper work and with the sales approaches of at least one salesman—who may not be very capable as a salesman, let alone as a teacher. The substantial number of capable people among the ranks of appliance salesmen may be better explained by a selective process—self-selection by individuals who undertake this work and skilled employment practices or quick weeding out of the untalented by owners and managers—than by the conscious development of latent sales talent.

Appliance salesmen must, of course, serve all categories of customers. The best salesmen have always classified customers. Mainly, they divide them by two basic questions: first, "do they have the money to buy?" Second, are they "really interested in buying or just looking"? These days, in addition to such criteria, appliance salesmen divide customers into three personality types: the "enemy," the "gentleman," and "lambs." In turn, customers now perceive a much wider range of retail institutions that they might patronize. They accordingly attempt to match their desires and needs against the offerings of the different types of retail establishment. As customers become more discriminating, retailers will be forced to adapt their operations even further to win the favor of the kinds of customers they seek to cultivate.

In the process, the on-going changes in retailing will culminate in greater segmentation of retail institutions.

QUESTIONS

1. Describe the types of customers as outlined in the article.
2. Describe the function of the appliance salesman.
3. Refute the argument of the store owner who does not believe it is his responsibility to train salesmen, but leaves it to manufacturers, distributors, or simply the salesman's previous employer.

35

Retail Selling at Resort Auctions*

John W. Wingate

There is an intriguing kind of retail selling virtually unknown to many students and store employees. This is the consumer auction conducted at vacation resorts, such as Atlantic City (New Jersey), Ft. Lauderdale (Florida), and Blowing Rock (North Carolina). These are frequented by customers with some mad money to spend and by some who have become auction addicts, attending daily throughout the season.

MERCHANDISE OFFERED

The merchandise offered consists of art objects (such as figurines and paintings), jewelry, silverware, linens, and rugs, along with small specialty items to "warm up" the audience. These specialties are often surplus stocks of articles that almost anyone could use, such as ball-point pens, cologne, novelty opera glasses, and cutlery. Most of the larger items are objects that are not really needed. Nevertheless, many of them are choice pieces that are likely to be treasured and prominently displayed, once purchased. In fact, the auctioneer may say, "If you really need it, buy from your local retailer who is a legitimate merchant. We are different. Buy from us the things you

Reprinted from *New York Retailer*, December 1965, pp. 20–24.

*The auctions discussed in this article are not to be confused with the city auctions of somewhat similar goods that cater to a more sophisticated and knowledgeable clientele. In these, there is much less attempt to talk up the value of the goods and none of the preliminaries discussed below.

don't need and haven't planned to buy but that you can obtain at great savings."

These auctions combine entertainment for the customer along with the opportunity to secure a bargain on a showy article. Many customers on vacation have extra money to spend and enjoy buying unusual items at auction rather than in a regular store.

TIME OF SALE

Typically, two sales are held every day, except Sunday, throughout the season at 10:30 a.m. and 7:30 p.m. The first lasts about three hours and the second about five hours. The season in the northern auctions runs from June to mid-October and the winter season in the southern auctions from mid-November to mid-May. The same auctioneers may sell in both regions, sometimes under the same name and sometimes under different names.

PRELIMINARIES AT THE SALE

At the sale itself, each customer is given free a numbered card with a stub that is deposited in a box for drawings that are conducted throughout the sale. Some customers arrive with free tickets they have picked up in their motels or in local restaurants that may be exchanged for free gifts, maybe a key ring and chain. The sale is preceded and interlarded with drawings for free prizes, such as a serrated-edged carving knife, a ball-point pen or a set of ash trays. Sometimes the proceedings start with a bingo game, with no charge for entry and free prizes for winners.

The auctioneer is a past-master in developing rapport with his audience. He addresses by name those who have attended and bought before. He asks where people are from and exhibits a remarkable knowledge of prominent people in the towns mentioned. He assures his audience that no one is under any obligation to buy and that the successful bidders must be satisfied and will not be forced to take the goods. He also may explain that a purchaser, who later wishes to exchange his purchase for another article on which he is the successful bidder, will be given full credit for the original purchase. One firm has what it calls a "Golden Rule Guarantee" by which it warrants to return the purchase price within thirty days, if the purchaser is not satisfied.

GETTING DOWN TO BUSINESS

After such preliminaries, the auctioneer gets down to business. He usually starts with some small items worth only a dollar or so. There is a good deal of joshing at this point. For example, if no one bids promptly the auctioneer may ask if anyone will take the article for nothing. He actually gives it to the first to respond. Others hold up their hands but are told they are too late.

Often, after the sale of a low-priced article has been completed, the auctioneer will announce that he has a number of identical articles still in stock and offers them to all comers (so long as they last) at the same price. A considerable supply of small but flashy articles is disposed of in this way, virtually all selling for considerably less than $5 each. To show his good faith, the auctioneer sometimes reduces the price on such multiple offerings below the successful bid price. Thus, a carving knife may be bid up to one dollar and the auctioneer may then announce that the purchaser and all others interested may have *two* for one dollar. This usually brings a considerable response.

The first hour of the sale may be devoted to such relatively trivial matters as those mentioned above, and then the auctioneer gets down to serious business. He presents a number of high-priced items, such as a Sheffield silver tea and coffee service, a pair of bisque figurines, an original painting, a set of Sheffield steel carving knives, a banquet cloth and an oriental rug. Each major item is explained in detail—the thickness of the silver in the ornamentation of a tray, the number of pounds of lambs' wool in a rug, the beautifully molded hands on a figurine. If the item is from a fine store that has gone out of business, the original retail price in that store is quoted as its retail value. The alleged value at which the item is insured may also be mentioned. Each item is presented as unusually fine, in "mint" condition, often as a collector's piece.

COMPARATIVE PRICES

The quoted valuations are often three to six times the final selling price. In fact, few articles sell at the auction for more than a third of the price the auctioneer quotes at the start of his presentation. For example, he may start the bidding on a so-called $1000 item by saying he will accept a bid of $500. No one speaks up, so he suggests $400 and $300. Still, there is silence. "Well, what will someone offer. I won't be offended." Someone says $50. The auctioneer treats this as a joke, but nevertheless accepts the bid. Someone raises it to $75 and, with much palaver, further bids are obtained. The price may get up to $200, less than a reasonable price in the auctioneer's estimation. At this point, he may indicate that he has a bid for $225 and bring down his hammer. This price may be a bona fide bid made in advance by a dealer or other customer not present or by a customer present who gives a concealed sign that is hardly observable by others. Such customers have charge accounts and want their identity hidden. In some tricky auction houses, an increased bid may be a phantom one to move an actual bidder to increase his bid. If this attempt fails, the goods will be treated as sold, only to be offered again at a later date. The more reputable concerns insist that they do not stoop to this practice.

STIMULATING BIDDING

When a member of the audience shows interest by bidding but drops out at a price of $200 perhaps when the auctioneer announces a further advance to $225 the auctioneer's assistant may approach the interested customer—and probably his wife—and recommend a higher bid. He may point out that if the customer will bid $250, the auctioneer will immediately stop the bidding, thus assuring purchase at this price. To procure an attractive article at a quarter of its alleged value is more than a good many customers can withstand, especially when assured that they are not expected to have ready cash. Personal checks are freely accepted and deferred payments can be arranged. Also, the goods if bulky or fragile, will be packed and shipped to any address, the buyer paying the express charges, however.

Many items put up for sale are from estates of famous people, estates that are being liquidated, sometimes to establish a tax loss. The glamour of owning something that once belonged to a celebrity adds to the pressure on better heeled members of the audience to bid.

During the sale, an assistant frequently goes through the audience exhibiting fine jewelry: rings, brooches and watches. If anyone wishes one of the items shown it will be put up for auction.

There is usually an intermission or two during a sale. Free cokes and cookies may be served and further drawings held for cheap door prizes. After this, a second auctioneer may take over and sometimes sell a few items for more than $1000 each.

VOLUME MOVED

During a successful sale, a surprising amount of merchandise is sold to people that came in with no particular purchase in mind. In one three hour morning auction observed by the writer, the apparent sales exceeded $10,000. These included two pieces of jewelry, one that sold for $3300 and the other for $2800. At this sale, items with successful bids of less than $100 each brought in $700. Omitting the two pieces of jewelry referred to, eight items selling for more than $100 each brought in over $3000. But another daytime sale observed in another auction room was much less successful bringing in hardly $800. The owner, a man with a poor presence and delivery, took over the selling and a considerable portion of the crowd walked out. Evening auctions are more productive of sales results than day-time auctions.

These auctioneers are among the hardest working of salesmen. They exude enthusiasm and charm; they flatter customers they get to know. One even kisses the ladies who have returned for the season.

FIRST CLASS ENTERTAINMENT

Observation of a number of these auctions leads to the conclusion that they are first class shows, providing a most interesting evening or afternoon for summer or winter visitors. Even if only a few dollars are spent on the low priced gadgets, the customer gets his money's worth, if not entirely in merchandise at least in entertainment. Such participation may be more satisfactory than attendance at a play or sports event. Also, with spare money to spend, the auction route is more fun than buying in a regular store. The auctioneer is an expert in building up the value of the item in the customer's mind to a reasonable market price. He makes the customer who spends $10, $100, or even $1000 feel that he has obtained a bargain. Perhaps he has not, but he has probably paid little or no more than a reasonable market price and probably a lot less than the original price at which the goods may have been offered in a smart specialty shop. The better auctioneers are careful not to "gyp" customers. They wish to develop a following, customers who will visit them in Florida in the winter and in a northern resort in the summer. Their customers must be convinced that they have made good buys and that the particular auction house can be relied upon. As indicated, the house may have a thirty day return policy. One with such a policy reports that its returns are about nil.

CRITICISMS

The chief criticism that may be made of auctions of this type are, first, that their comparative price statements are exaggerated. Second, some of the auctioneers tend to misstate merchandise facts: a cotton and rayon table cloth was called a linen and silk cloth, a ball-point pen of unknown brand a Paper-Mate, a toilet water of an unknown maker Arpege perfume. However, merchandise labels are usually left on the goods and customers can read them when goods are passed around for inspection. The customers seem to take exaggerations good naturedly, probably because the prices they pay are reasonable for the merchandise actually procured. They are given a great show; and, in spite of some questionable selling practices, they generally get reasonably good values.

MARKETING SIGNIFICANCE

From the sellers' point of view, the auction route is an excellent way to dispose of an inventory of objets d'art, perhaps from an exclusive shop that must be liquidated promptly. Also, articles that few customers would buy through normal channels sell this way. For example, large elaborate sets of silver tea sets are a drug on the regular market but will sell at fair prices to auction customers.

There are differences in practice in regard to the title of the goods sold. Some auctioneers own none of the goods and receive commission from the owners of 15 percent to 25 percent on much of the merchandise handled. This is, of course, not profit since income must provide for personnel and overhead expenses. One successful house buys most of its goods outright from estates, importers and manufacturers and must obtain auction prices that will provide an adequate markup overall. But this firm obtains diamonds and other fine jewelry from estates on a commission basis of 3 percent to 4 percent. The high prices at which such merchandise sells makes even such a low commission profitable. It is the auctioneer's interest to get a good, but not exorbitant price. It is his job to convince successful bidders that they have become the proud possessors, for a song, of valuable and choice merchandise —and perhaps they have.

QUESTION

1. Compare the selling techniques of the auctioneer with the selling performance of a door-to-door salesman and an in-store salesman. What similarities exist? In what way are they dissimilar?

36

Formal Decision-Making in the Teaching of Retailing

John W. Wingate

. . . Collegiate schools of business have been saying for some time that the chief function of the business administrator is to make decisions and these schools have been attempting to plan their courses so as to provide students with experience in the decision-making process.

There is no doubt that brilliant merchants of the past, and even of the present, have been intuitive decision-makers, operating or "flying by on the seat of their pants." They seem to have absorbed the pertinent information upon which each decision should be made and have had the drive to make their decisions succeed. But they have apparently not applied an analytical

Reprinted from *New York Retailer*, December 1962, pp. 2–5.

reasoning process to the data. Rather, perhaps through subconscious processes, they have arrived at decisions that have admirably achieved their objectives, but have sometimes been colossal failures.

For the average executive and for the typical executive trainee, not blessed with such intuitive insight, it is dangerous to attempt to emulate the handful of "synthetic" deciders. It is safer to master the formal approach to decisions where the data available, even though generally incomplete, is collected, and weighed, and sometimes probabilities assigned to various outcomes. Thus, each decision becomes a reasoned attempt to maximize something: dollar profit, return on the investment, chance of survival, rate of growth or even customer good will or employee morale.

Perhaps the first major attempt to sharpen the decision-making faculty was the introduction of the case method,[1] by means of which students in college and in executive development seminars faced up to specific situations which called for decisions and attempted to determine a better, if not the best, course of action. While the decision-making process was generally nonmathematical, students did (and do) learn to marshal the various decisions that might be made and to attempt to foresee the probable results of each.

MATHEMATICS IN DECISION-MAKING

More recently, the preoccupation with mathematics and models has led to the attempt to translate real-life situations into mathematical symbols that lend themselves to mathematical solutions. Where many variables are involved, both the statement of the equation and its solution are beyond the ability of most to perform; and experts in programming and computer operation are called in to come up with the answers, or with the changes in the situation that have been caused by the interaction of various decisions made by competitors.

The use of probability ratios is often an important element in the mathematical approach. It may be illustrated by an elementary problem in retail management:

A department manager of a selling department has observed that customers often walk out without buying, apparently because they do not get adequate attention from the existing sales force. Accordingly, he requests the superintendent for one more full-time sales person at a salary of $60 a week. A recent study made in the store reveals that fringe costs to maintain an employee (social security, hospitalization, insurance, etc.) are 15% of the employees' wages, so that the new person would add $69 to direct expense. The department is operating at a 35% gross margin of which about

[1] The Incident Method might also be mentioned. It is a variation of the case method, where students are taught to build up a case calling for solution from an incident that gives a clue to the need for more information to determine whether a problem actually exists.

5% is absorbed by direct handling expenses. Thus, only 30% of the sales is available for salesperson's salaries, overhead expenses and profit.

Past experience with hiring additional help leads the superintendent to the conclusion that sales increases attributable to a larger staff are often not sufficient to cover the additional expenses and thus fail to contribute to overhead and profit. As a tool to arrive at a sound conclusion, he visualizes the various outcomes of hiring another person and sets an estimated probability for each. He might organize his thinking as follows:

Possible Outcomes	*Chance of Occurrence*
1. The new clerk might upset the morale of the department and thus cause a decline in sales of $100 a week.	5%
2. There may be no increase in sales; sales of the new person being offset by less sales of others.	10%
3. An increase in department sales of $100 a week.	15%
4. An increase of $200 a week.	20%
5. An increase of $300 a week.	30%
6. An increase of $400 a week.	10%
7. An increase of over $400 (average $600) a week.	10%
TOTAL	100%

The profit or loss at each outcome may then be calculated. For example, with an increase of sales of $100 a week, the margin available after handling costs is $30. The salary cost is $69, so the loss is $39. The entire table would look as follows:

Outcome No.	*Calculation*	*Profit or Loss*	*Probability*	*Product*
1	− $30 margin −$69	− $99	.05	− 4.95
2	− 69	− 69	.10	− 6.90
3	+ $30 margin − 69	− 39	.15	− 5.85
4	− $60 margin − 69	− 9	.20	− 1.80
5	+ $90 margin − 69	+ 21	.30	+ 6.30
6	+$120 margin − 69	+ 51	.10	+ 5.10
7	+$180 margin − 69	+ 111	.10	+11.10
			TOTALS	−19.50
				+22.50
				+ 3.00

Thus, the chances are that to hire a new salesperson will add only $3 a week to controllable profit, and a positive decision by the superintendent would be the result of the weight he might give to the intangible factor of customer good will.

At this point, the superintendent should consider action that might be taken, should a new person not be employed. It may be possible to increase department sales a few hundred dollars a week with no increase in the force by such devices as the following: simplifying sales check and cash register routine, arranging the stock to make more self-selection possible, retraining the regular force in the techniques of speeding up customer contacts and handling more than one customer at a time.

Such decision-making may be complicated by assuming a highly competitive situation, where a decision made by one competitor is likely to lead to a counter move by another. For example, the hiring of one more clerk might lead a next door competitor to improve his service or cut his prices. If the total market available is regarded as a static one, the chances of the different occurrences may be very different than planned above. The addition of the new clerk might be profitable for a week or so but might prove unprofitable as soon as a competitor revises his tactics.

In all such formal attempts to arrive at an optimum decision, the mathematical results must be checked against the "rule of reason." Since most planners have had much more experience with intuitive thinking, their hunches are often right. If a mathematical solution leads to a contrary result, there should be no immediate decision that the hunch was wrong; rather the elements and weights in the formal decision should be carefully re-examined. Perhaps some possible outcomes were overlooked; the probabilities assigned to the various outcomes may be wide of the mark; and the calculation of the probable outcome in terms of money gain or other advantage may be wrongly calculated. The chief value of the formal analysis is to provide a check on hunches that often leave out many considerations and weigh factors emotionally. The person trained in formal techniques may not use them in very many of his real-world decisions but he will have learned to consider more possible outcomes. . . .

QUESTIONS

1. How are most management decisions made in retailing?
2. What contribution does mathematics make to decision making?
3. Apply your answer to Question 2 to the sales problem presented in this reading.

PART IV

INNOVATION AND CHANGE

A. RETAILING IN THE GHETTO
B. CHANGE IN RETAILING

A. RETAILING IN THE GHETTO

Perhaps no problem is as urgent and perplexing to management as that of retailing in our nation's ghettos. Hardly a day passes that the press or a congressional committee does not present some finding concerning the high prices or lack of competition in the poverty areas of our large cities.

The next three readings address themselves to some of these major issues. The first, by William Cox and Sue Seidman, discusses the present interest in and growth of consumer cooperatives in poverty areas of the United States. The two articles that follow are concerned with the problems of pricing in the ghetto area. The excerpt from the report of the Committee on Government Operations takes up the charge of discrimination in food prices by chain stores in these areas. The article by Donald Dixon and Daniel McLaughlin also presents the results of a study of price discrimination in these areas.

37

Cooperatives in the Ghetto

William E. Cox, Jr. and Sue R. Seidman

Few social and economic institutions have produced the popular interest and the wide differences of personal and business opinion that have been associated with consumer cooperatives. A consumer cooperative is a "marketing organization owned and operated for the mutual benefit of consumer-owners, who have voluntarily

Talk given at a meeting of the American Marketing Association, August 26, 1969, in Cincinnati, Ohio.

associated themselves for the purpose."[1] Consumer cooperatives have been organized to provide insurance, credit, bulk buying, and many other services, but this paper shall be limited to retail store consumer cooperatives, which are stores "owned and managed by a group of ultimate consumers who use the store as a source of supply for merchandise."[2]

Consumer cooperatives are currently enjoying a revival in the black ghettos of the nation's cities. The efficiency of American retailing institutions, particularly the food chains, has provided little opportunity for cooperatives to offer lower costs, better services, or otherwise challenge the profit-oriented retailing institutions. In the depressed neighborhoods of urban areas, however, the relative absence of the most efficient retail institutions, together with the contemporary interest in community participation, has created a new interest in the cooperative as both an economic and a social institution.

The purpose of this paper is to investigate the feasibility of the consumer cooperative as a means to "maximum productivity of the marketing functions as it relates to disadvantaged segments of the population."[3] The research method consisted of extensive reading of secondary source material and numerous interviews with individuals knowledgeable about or active in cooperatives.

The paper briefly reviews the history of the cooperative movement in the United States, and examines two of the most successful cooperatives—Greenbelt, near Washington, and Hyde Park in Chicago. Five currently operating cooperatives in the ghetto are evaluated, based on information gathered in interviews with officials of the cooperatives and from secondary sources:

1. Harlem River Consumers' Cooperative
2. Jet Food Corporation
3. Hunterspoint Neighborhood Co-op
4. Morningside Heights Consumers' Cooperative
5. Hough Family Service Corporation

Successes and failures of these five operating cooperatives are discussed, and the future of cooperatives in the ghettos is assessed.

A BRIEF HISTORY OF THE COOPERATIVE MOVEMENT

The consumer cooperative movement was started in 1844 by twenty-eight poverty-stricken workers in Rochdale, England, in protest against excessive prices and adulteration of goods. They, therefore, decided to pool

[1] T. N. Beckman and W. R. Davidson, *Marketing*, 8th ed. (New York: The Ronald Press Company, 1967), p. 256.

[2] C. F. Phillips and D. J. Duncan, *Marketing, Principles and Methods*, 6th ed. (Homewood, Illinois: Richard D. Irwin, Inc., 1968), p. 286.

[3] Ralph Gillen, "A Challenge for Business: Better Commercial Services for Low-Income Neighborhoods," an unpublished report submitted to the National Marketing Advisory Committee, December 15, 1967, p. 1.

their funds and supply themselves. Since the workers had to earn their living during the day and could not afford to hire labor to manage their business, their store was open for only a few hours weekly and their initial inventory was very limited.[4]

For the operation of their association, the Rochdale workers evolved what have come to be known as the Rochdale Principles and Practices, which are now recognized as "the standards" wherever consumers' cooperatives are formed. The Rochdale Principles are:

1. A consumers' cooperative society shall be democratically controlled.
2. There shall be open membership. No persons shall be denied membership unless it be known that they wish to join for the purpose of doing harm to the organization.
3. Money invested in a cooperative society, if it receive interest, shall receive a fixed percentage which shall not be more than the prevailing current rate.
4. If a cooperative society makes a profit that profit shall be returned to the consumers who patronize the society on the basis of their amount of purchases.

The Rochdale Practices are:

1. A cooperative society shall be composed of members who voluntarily join.
2. Business shall be for cash.
3. Goods and services shall be sold at prevailing prices.
4. A portion of profits shall be used for educational purposes in the field of cooperation.
5. At each inventory, reserves shall be set aside to cover depreciation and unforeseen difficulties arising in the operation of the business.
6. Labor shall be fairly treated.
7. Cooperative societies shall cooperate with one another.[5]

In the United States, the consumers' cooperative movement originated at about the same time as it did in England, when in the early 1840s a buying club of consumers was organized which later expanded into a movement operating 700 stores extending over ten states and into Canada.[6]

Prior to 1900, the cooperative movement in the United States had some brief spurts of success but it is generally conceded that the movement was a failure. Just after the turn of the century, there was a revival of interest in consumers' cooperatives. This period was marked by the formation of many cooperatives among immigrant groups as well as farm and labor organizations. Movement toward nationwide coordination of cooperative activities began with the organization of the Cooperative League of America in 1916.

[4] Florence E. Parker, *The First 125 Years* (Superior, Wis.: Cooperative Publishing Association, 1956), p. xiv.

[5] Ellis Cowling, *A Short Introduction to Consumers Cooperatives* (Chicago, Ill.: The Cooperative League of the United States, 1941), pp. 17–25.

[6] Same reference as footnote 4, pp. 4–5.

Cooperatives started to become popular for the first time in the United States after World War I and the decades of the twenties and the thirties were times of prosperity for the cooperative movement. During World War II, cooperatives continued to grow in importance and apparently reached their peak in the late 1940s and early 1950s, with Census data showing their greatest penetration in 1954.[7] Even then, cooperatives accounted for only 0.2 percent of total retail store sales of consumer goods. Since that time, cooperatives have lost ground and appear to be in about the same relative position in retailing as they were at the close of World War II.

While consumer cooperatives have never been significant factors in American retailing, they are much more important in Western Europe. Carson has estimated that cooperatives handle an average of 6.2 percent of the retail trade in Western Europe, with Switzerland, Sweden, and Great Britain reporting 9.0 percent or more.[8]

Why have cooperatives in Western Europe had greater success than those in the United States? The primary reason appears to be that "under the competitive retail situation in the United States, the cooperative form of retailing cannot offer lower prices to its members."[9] In contrast, the less competitive retail situation in Western Europe has provided a more favorable environment for the establishment and growth of cooperatives. There is some evidence indicating that cooperatives are losing ground in Great Britain and Italy, where there have been significant improvements in retailing efficiency in recent years.[10]

Although the primary economic aim of retail cooperatives is to provide quality merchandise at lower net prices (competitive prices plus a patronage dividend), it is frequently suggested that social and philosophical aims are equally important. Thus a failure to achieve the economic aim might not be disastrous since the cooperative could still provide a basis for community participation in economic affairs, a vehicle for community organization, an attack upon capitalism, and a variety of other aims. Bell, however, sees the consumer cooperative as a "formalized manifestation of an underlying consumer consciousness," and suggests that where cooperatives have succeeded, it is "because of real services rendered, not because of political or philosophical overtones."[11] These questions are further examined in the following review of two successful cooperatives.

[7] U.S. Bureau of the Census, *1963 Census of Business, Retail Trade: Summary Statistics, Vol. 1, Part II, 7A–5* (Washington, D.C.: U.S. Government Printing Office, 1964).

[8] David Carson, "Marketing in Italy Today," *Journal of Marketing*, Vol. 30, No. 1 (January 1966), p. 14.

[9] Same reference as footnote 2, p. 295.

[10] W. G. McClelland, "Some Management Problems Now Facing British Retailers," *Journal of Retailing*, Vol. XLI, No. 1 (Spring, 1965), p. 8. Also see: Giancarlo Ravaggi, "Retailing in a Developing Economy-Italy," *Journal of Retailing*, Vol. 43, No. 1 (Spring 1967), p. 43.

[11] M. L. Bell, "A Revised Concept of the Consumer's Co-operative," *Journal of Marketing*, Vol. 25, No. 3 (January 1961), p. 41.

TWO SUCCESSFUL COOPERATIVES

Two of the most successful retail cooperatives in the United States today are Greenbelt Consumer Services, Inc. of Beltsville, Maryland and The Hyde Park Cooperative Society of Hyde Park, Chicago. The history, membership and financial data, services offered, and the cooperative commitment of the members of these two cooperatives are examined in this section of the paper.

Greenbelt Consumer Services, Inc.

The town of Greenbelt, Maryland, was built during the early 1930s under the auspices of the Government Farm Security Program (1) to give employment to the unemployed who were on relief, (2) to demonstrate the soundness of planning and operating towns in accordance with certain "garden city" principles, and (3) to provide low-rent housing in good physical and social environment for low income families.[12] It was to be built with a large wooded area separating it physically from Washington, D. C., and surrounding suburban areas; hence the name Greenbelt. This physical isolation created the need for a variety of services including a retail grocery market.

The grocery was financed initially by the Consumer Distribution Corporation (CDC), a nonprofit capital fund endowed by Edward A. Filene of Boston. Mr. Filene envisioned CDC as "furnishing top and local management, central purchasing and informational public relations and other services."[13] CDC assumed direct managerial control over the local Greenbelt store for the early years while local responsibility was being developed. Then it was planned that ownership would revert to the members and the store would automatically come under local control.[14]

Initially, the cooperative operated a food store, valet shop, drug store, gasoline filling station, barber shop, and movie theatre, all urgently needed because of the relative isolation of the community and limited transportation. The cooperative was run under CDC management from October 1937 to December 1939. During this period new residents were moving into Greenbelt and the volume of business grew slowly. By the end of 1939, 311 families (slightly over 50 percent of the community) had joined the cooperative and the CDC membership requirements having been met, the association began operating as a true cooperative. At the beginning of 1940, under the name of Greenbelt Consumer Services, the association assumed management of all the businesses.[15]

[12] Same reference as footnote 4, p. 408.

[13] Martin L. Bell, "The Cooperative Department Store: Outgrowth of Filene's Marketing Thought," *Journal of Retailing*, 34, No. 3 (Fall 1958), p. 154.

[14] Same reference as footnote 13, pp. 154–58.

[15] Same reference as footnote 4, p. 141.

The story of the Greenbelt cooperative, now the leading non-farm consumers' cooperative in the United States, is one of continuous growth, expansion, and success. By 1943, Greenbelt's sales passed the million dollar mark and its membership had risen to 1,283. At the end of 1954 the cooperative had over 5,500 members, 75 percent of whom were government employees. Gross volume for the year was over $5,450,000 from which $55,400 was returned on patronage in addition to 5 percent interest on share capital.

Although it operates only in the Washington area, in 1960 Greenbelt opened its tenth shopping center. In 1964 Greenbelt's sales amounted to $22 million and by 1968 they had risen to $40 million.

As of July 1, 1968, Greenbelt Consumer Services had approximately 19,000 member families, each of whom had paid a membership fee of $10.00 per share. Greenbelt now has the greatest appeal for well-educated upper-middle-income people, with 60 to 70 percent of its members employed by the government.

Greenbelt operates a wide variety of stores, including supermarkets; its furniture store, Scan, which is the largest importer of Scandinavian furniture in North America; petroleum service stations, and pharmacies. Other member benefits include life insurance, auto leasing, and insurance; travel programs; and a co-op newsletter, "The Co-op Consumer." In addition, the cooperative employs several fulltime home economists who are available to members for demonstrations or consultations.

As Greenbelt's membership has grown, a single annual membership meeting has become impractical as a method of democratic control. Therefore a "congress" system based on district organization and representative government has been devised and has worked quite well. At present the congress of Greenbelt is made up of 114 delegates elected from the membership. Its primary purpose is to provide a closer link between the members and the board of directors as well as to maintain and promote effective membership control. Another important function of the congress is to provide a training program for future member leadership. The numerous committees of the congress that provide a broad array of services to the Greenbelt membership also provide leadership training.

Hyde Park Cooperative Society, Inc.

The Hyde Park Co-op is in the heart of Chicago's racially mixed south side. Some years ago as the population of Hyde Park began to change and some general deterioration of the neighborhood seemed to be setting in, a general exodus of business establishments began. Instead of moving, the members of the Hyde Park Cooperative Society provided a core of people determined to redevelop Hyde Park instead of abandoning it. Thus around this neighborhood-owned business there began to grow a new community spirit. A redevelopment plan conceived by the University of Chicago and executed by the city of Chicago included a new shopping center to replace several blocks of run-down commercial buildings. The supermarket in that center, the largest in Chicago, was assigned to the Hyde Park Cooperative.[16]

The Hyde Park Co-op was originally organized by a group of families centered around the University of Chicago who needed a convenient place to shop. Today it is owned by some 10,000 member families that have paid $9.00 to join. Its membership is racially integrated as is the community in which it operates. Members are in the upper-middle income brackets and are university-oriented. Mr. Gilbert Spenser, General Manager of the Hyde Park Cooperative Society, estimates that over 60 percent of Hyde Park's members are connected with the University of Chicago in some capacity and over 80 percent are college graduates. The cooperative is the only complete, convenient, and modern supermarket for some five square miles.

Only two commercial operations are directly part of the cooperative: the grocery and the FORM furniture store. The grocery is the largest single supermarket in the Chicago area and not only is it an efficient merchandising business, it also supports many worthwhile community enterprises and welfare agencies on Chicago's south side.[17]

FORM, the cooperative's Scandinavian furniture store, opened in September 1967. It provides quality imported furniture at reasonable prices. The operation was patterned after a similar successful operation run by Greenbelt Co-op which provides Hyde Park with much valuable consulting service. The Co-op has helped its members develop a number of other cooperative activities, though none are directly connected with the society. These services include the Credit Union, Fuel Co-op, Chicago Memorial Association and the Sitters' Swap. Additional membership services of the cooperative are the employment of a fulltime home economist on the staff of the grocery and the twice-monthly publication of the Society's newsletter, *Evergreen*.

Hyde Park's financial operations have been both sound and profitable. In 1963 sales totaled $4,868,591 with dividends on cash stock of 4 percent and patronage refund of 3 percent. By 1966 sales totaled $6,117,449, and dividends and patronage refunds have continued at the same level.

The Greenbelt and Hyde Park cooperatives have a number of factors in common:

1. Emphasize food marketing
2. Relatively little competition from large-scale, efficient retailers
3. Highly educated membership
4. Capable leadership dedicated to cooperative principles
5. Experienced, professional management and
6. Large, modern, fully competitive stores

[16] Elinor Richey, "Splitsville USA," *The Reporter*, Vol. 20, No. 11 (May 23, 1963), pp. 35–38.

[17] Jerry Voorhis, *American Cooperatives* (New York: Harper and Bros., 1961), p. 167.

Members have been drawn primarily from long-term residents of the area, and while incomes were relatively low at the time the cooperatives were formed, members were not at the poverty level or below. Moreover, members for the last twenty years have been at the middle income level. Among the government and university employees that dominate the membership of both cooperatives are many leaders and potential leaders who have been willing to spend considerable amounts of time and energy to insure the success of the cooperatives.

Greenbelt and Hyde Park have survived and prospered as consumer cooperatives primarily because of the special character of the membership of the two associations. Without a sizeable number of members who are deeply involved in the cooperative movement and philosophically committed to cooperative principles, it would be difficult for Greenbelt and Hyde Park to maintain their success over an extended period. These associations have been subsidized by the voluntary contributions of their leadership cores and it is this subsidy that permitted Greenbelt and Hyde Park to remain competitive with the corporate chains, particularly in their early years.

CURRENT MARKETING EXPERIMENTS WITH COOPERATIVE ELEMENTS

Five examples of retail marketing operations that incorporate some cooperative elements and are operating in ghetto areas have been elected for examination. Four of the five: Harlem River Consumers' Cooperative, the Hunterspoint Neighborhood Co-op, the Jet Food Corporation, and the Hough Family Service Cooperative have been established in the last four years. The fifth example, about which very little has been written, The Morningside Heights Consumers' Cooperative, has been operating successfully for well over a decade.

The Harlem River Consumers' Cooperative, Inc.

Many residents of black ghettos believe that their retail stores are poorly stocked and charge exorbitant prices; the Harlem River Consumer Cooperative was organized to help change this situation. Several business firms aided the Harlem co-op in opening its doors in June 1968 by advancing funds to buy refrigeration equipment and improve store facilities, helping the co-op to hire and train employees, and serving as consultants.

The cooperative is located on the ground floor of the Esplanade Garden Apartments and serves as the principal market for the residents of the 1,870 apartments, as well as the surrounding neighborhood. Although the store is relatively small (10,000 square feet), its bright interior and range of nationally branded merchandise compares favorably with any suburban market.[18] Most of the cooperative's merchandise is purchased through Mid-Eastern, Inc., a regional wholesale agency that serves some thirty-five local coopera-

[18] "Enterprise: Helping Themselves," *Time* (June 7, 1968), p. 88.

tive associations. About 60 percent of the volume is in national brands; the remainder is sold under the Co-op label.

The community itself has provided most of the sixteen members of the Board of Directors and the 4,300 members, who have purchased $264,000 in shares at $5.00 each.

After reaching an annual volume level of $2 million in early 1969, the Harlem Cooperative began to encounter a series of problems. A new board of directors was elected in February 1969 to replace the ousted board that had attempted to remove Miss Cora Walker, the director.[19] Twenty-two of the market's twenty-seven employees have been on strike since April and the other five employees refuse to cross the picket line. Two managers and several volunteers now run the store. As a result, revenue has dropped to an estimated $4,000 per week. In addition, a court ruling is expected on the legality of the present board of directors, based on a suit filed by a group of members. It appears that Miss Walker will lose her position regardless of the outcome of the strike and the court ruling.[20]

The Jet Food Corporation

The Jet Food Corporation was organized in October 1966 as a franchise program to develop modern supermarkets in the inner city. The cooperative element of the program is that stock is sold to residents of the areas where stores are constructed.[21] In November 1967, the Jet Food Corporation opened the first Super Jet Store in Baltimore as a prototype unit. Stock subscriptions at $5.00 per share were sold to area residents and $180,000 of the store's $500,000 initial costs were raised in this manner. Jet Food plans to expand their operations into ten other cities and opened their first supermarket in Cleveland in June 1969.[22]

Jet Food emphasizes the need to adapt the product assortment of its stores to the buying habits of ghetto residents. Thus national brands, rather than a co-op brand, are featured and little prepackaging is used. Forty percent of the Baltimore store's volume is in meats, compared to the 25 percent national average for all supermarket chains. Two additional examples of the recognition of low income buying habits are the absence of large size packages and containers and little use of multiple pricing techniques.[23]

Hunterspoint Neighborhood Co-op

Since its opening in 1965, the Hunterspoint Neighborhood Co-op has been in trouble. Among the reasons cited for the difficulties of this San

[19] C. Gerald Fraser, "A Strike Plagues Co-op in Harlem," *New York Times*, May 25, 1969, p. 80.

[20] Same reference as footnote 19.

[21] "Ownership Brings Dignity," Information Pamphlet of the Jet Food Corporation (Baltimore, Md.: The Jet Food Corporation, 1968).

[22] "New Chain for Ghetto Shoppers," *Chainstore Age* (March 1968), Vol. 44, No. 3, p. 80.

[23] Same reference as footnote 22, p. 82.

Francisco ghetto cooperative are: (1) poor location with insufficient parking facilities, (2) lack of consumer interest, (3) inexperienced management, and (4) an insufficient and inappropriate inventory high in gourmet items (such as imported wines) and low in national brands.[24] In 1965, the Co-op was robbed of $12,000, and with only $2,000 insurance, suffered a severe financial setback.

Safeway Stores learned of the Co-op's problems and for the past year has been providing management consulting services for $1.00. Safeway personnel have supervised interior and exterior alterations to the Co-op store, restocking the shelves with a more appropriate inventory, and moving in new equipment. Many other supermarket chains are watching the Hunterspoint-Safeway venture with interest, for this form of cooperation may be a necessary feature of successful cooperatives in the ghetto.

Morningside Heights Consumers' Co-op

Many cooperatives both within and outside low income areas fail from an inability to compete successfully, but New York's Morningside Heights Consumers' Co-op, not far from Harlem, has been a going concern for nearly a decade. Last year it returned a 4.8 percent cash rebate to members and twelve per cent dividend on their $25.00 a share stock.[25]

The Morningside Heights membership is racially mixed, as is its neighborhood. Approximately 50 percent are Negroes and Puerto Ricans, the other half are whites. Though the members are predominantly low income, many of the Co-op's white members with upper-middle incomes are connected with nearby Columbia University and are deeply committed to the principles of cooperation and to the Co-op itself.

Morningside Heights furnishes an excellent example of effective cooperative action in a predominantly low income area. Over a decade ago, the Morningside Heights area had a substantially unfulfilled need for more efficient grocery services. This need was recognized by both the low income families in the area and some members of the university, also living in the area, who were willing to furnish a leadership core. This leadership core carefully studied and analysed the lack of adequate marketing services and decided that a pooling of resources of interested individuals in the area would provide the most effective method for meeting their marketing needs.[26] Today the Co-op has been so uniquely successful that four of its board members, three of them nonwhite, have been asked and agreed to serve on the Board of Harlem River Consumers' Cooperative. These four hope to be successful in communicating not only their commitment to cooperation but also their know-how in competing effectively.[27]

[24] "Safeway Credited with Management Aid to Struggling Co-op," *Grocer's Beacon* (July 12, 1968), p. 3.

[25] Same reference as footnote 18, p. 90.

[26] Philip J. Dodge, "People Help Themselves Through Cooperatives," Public Affairs Pamphlet No. 358 (New York: Public Affairs Committee, Inc., April 1954), pp. 8–9.

[27] "Harlem is Proud of Its Co-op," *Business Week* (June 1, 1968), p. 90.

Hough Family Service Cooperative, Inc. (HFSC)

HFSC was started in April of 1968 in Cleveland, Ohio, by Mr. William Stewart, project director of the Urban Demonstration Program of the Cooperative League of the United States. It is funded jointly by the Office of Economic Opportunity and the Cooperative League of the United States. Since 1968 it has enrolled 473 members at a $5.00 per share membership fee and a $2.00 non-refundable joining fee. Any member obtains full membership rights with the purchase of his first share. Among these rights are: using any services of the Co-op, voting in all elections, and helping to make policy decisions. Among the services HFSC plans to offer are:

1. Discounts on food purchased in bulk (primary current service)
2. Discounts on appliances
3. Tires and batteries
4. Home maintenance and appliance repair service and
5. Consumer education and information to help members get better values for their money.

HFSC eventually hopes to pool the purchasing power of thousands of members to allow purchases of a variety of goods and services at close to or below wholesale cost while retaining all of the services normally available to consumers. At present HFSC has one small store that depends heavily on outside funding for its continued existence.

Among the five cooperatives in ghetto areas reviewed in the preceding section, the oldest and most successful (Morningside Heights Consumers' Co-op) is very similar to the Greenbelt and Hyde Park cooperatives. The only significant difference is that a higher percentage of Morningside's membership is nonwhite. Morningside Heights has the same advantages of having many members affiliated with a university and is therefore able to draw leadership resources from an educated membership with a strong commitment to cooperative principles. In each of the other four cooperatives in ghetto areas, there is no sizeable group of members with a high educational level, government or university affiliation, and a strong dedication to cooperative principles. Although these organizations appear to meet some criteria as cooperatives, the absence of the traditional membership base that has been associated with successful cooperatives raises serious questions about the ability of cooperatives to succeed in the ghetto.

If the ghettos of America were as well served by corporate chains as the suburbs, it is unlikely that there would be any significant interest in consumer cooperatives in the ghetto. The relative absence of the chains, especially supermarket chain stores, has meant that the ghettos and their residents have not benefited from the dynamic, competitive retailing system that has historically limited the appeal of consumer cooperatives in the United States. Rather than relying on cooperatives to fight the ghetto's lack of competitive marketing services, emphasis might be better placed in finding ways to bring the large-scale, efficient corporate chain stores into the ghetto on a basis that is profitable and satisfying for all concerned.

QUESTIONS

1. Discuss some of the reasons for the successes and failures of a cooperative retail firm.
2. How importantare the social and philosophical attitudes of the participants?
3. Are the Rochdale Principles still applicable to today's cooperative movement?

38

Raising Prices of Selected Food Items on Dates Welfare Checks and Food Stamps Are Received

ALLEGATION

The charge that certain food chains' outlets in low-income areas raise prices on selected food items on days welfare checks and food stamps are received by the poor formed the basis of the hearings in Washington, D.C. The charge was also raised at the New York City hearing. Before detailing the specific charges, certain pertinent factors should be noted:

First, smaller individual sales transactions, the lower profit margin on food items customarily purchased by the poor, and limited sales of high-margin gourmet items tend to restrict the profit of food chain outlets in low-income areas.

Second, food sales experience an upsurge at supermarkets located in low-income areas on and around the dates welfare checks and food stamps are received.

Third, managers of stores are under pressure to operate at optimum profit, either out of a desire to earn a bonus or out of a fear of being glossed over for promotion.

Fourth, store officials and supervisory personnel may lack the interest to oversee official policies of price and quality uniformity because their focus is primarily on optimizing the profits of outlets within their districts.

Additional factors frequently mentioned by those alleging discriminatory

Reprinted from *Consumer Problems of the Poor: Supermarket Operations in Low-Income Areas and the Federal Response*, 38th Report by the Committee on Government Operations, August 7, 1968, pp. 16–27. Footnotes deleted.

practices are the small numbers of chainstore outlets in low-income areas and a general absence of effective competition for the food dollar there. This subject receives separate treatment later in the report.

During the three days of hearings in Washington, D.C., New York, and St. Louis, the subcommittee heard testimony from five witnesses, including three Federal officials, on the practice of increasing food prices on the day welfare checks are issued.

a. The ad hoc committee for equal pricing testified at the Washington hearings on the results of a price survey involving nine Safeway stores in poor and affluent neighborhoods on August 15, September 1, and September 15, 1967. Welfare checks are received on September 1, in Washington, D.C.

It reported that twenty food items popular in low-income areas were selected for the survey and priced in three low-income and six affluent area stores. Eight of the original items were not available in all stores on each of the three shopping days, and were, therefore, discarded from the survey. Of the twelve food items still under survey, only two were priced the same at all stores on all dates.

The ad hoc committee found that on September 1, the average cost of the remaining ten items was 9.1 percent higher in the three stores serving large numbers of welfare recipients than in the six serving middle-to-upper income families. This disparity they characterized as a "tax on poverty."

A summary of the findings of the ad hoc committee is contained in the following three tables:

TABLE 1.

Increase in Prices in Safeway Stores Serving Welfare Clients, Aug. 15 to Sept. 1

(Note: Welfare checks are distributed on Sept. 1)

	Average Price on Aug. 15 (cents)	*Average Price on Sept. 1 (cents)*	*Percent Increase in Price to Families on Welfare*
1. Bananas (2 lbs.)	29.0	34.0	17
2. Town House peas (1 lb.)	21.3	25.3	19
3. Del Monte peach halves (2 large cans)	63.0	67.0	6
4. Crisco (3 lbs.)	80.0	89.0	11
5. Cheerios (7 oz.)	26.0	30.0	15
6. Eggs (1 doz. grade A medium)	39.0	49.0	26
7. Domino sugar (5 lbs.)	61.0	65.0	7
8. Lettuce	35.7	35.7	—
9. Washington flour (5 lbs.)	64.0	66.3	4
10. Gerbers strained bananas (6 jars)	65.0	69.0	6

TABLE 2.

Comparative Prices at Safeway Stores on Sept. 1, 1967
[Note: Welfare checks were distributed on Sept. 1]

Item	*Average Price in 3 Stores Serving large Numbers of Families on Welfare (cents)*	*Average Price in Six Other Stores (cents)*	*Higher Price Percent Paid by Families on Welfare*
1. Bananas (2 lbs.)	34.0	29.8	14
2. Town House peas (1 lb.)	25.3	19.5	30
3. Del Monte peach halves (2 large cans)	67.0	63.0	6
4. Crisco (3 lbs.)	89.0	82.0	8
5. Cheerios (7 oz.)	30.0	25.0	20
6. Eggs (1 doz. grade A medium)	49.0	37.0	32
7. Domino sugar (5 lbs.)	65.0	62.3	4
8. Lettuce	35.7	22.8	57
9. Washington flour (5 lbs.)	66.3	64.4	3
10. Gerbers strained bananas (6 jars)	69.0	64.7	7

TABLE 3.

Safeway Prices on Sept. 1, Chevy Chase Store Compared with 6th and H ST. NE.

[Note: Welfare checks were distributed on Sept. 1]

	Chevy Chase Price (cents)	*6th and H St. NE. Price (cents)*	*Percent Higher in Store Serving Welfare clients*
1. Bananas (2 lbs.)	29	34	17
2. Town House peas (1 lb.)	19½	24½	26
3. Del Monte peach halves (2 large cans)	63	69	10
4. Crisco (3 lbs.)	82	89	8
5. Cheerios (7 oz.)	25	28	12
6. Eggs (1 doz. grade A medium)	37	49	32
7. Domino sugar (5 lbs.)	63	65	3
8. Lettuce	29	29	—
9. Washington flour (5 lbs.)	63	65	3
10. Gerbers strained bananas (6 jars)	65	69	6

Further analysis of the ad hoc committee data shows that while the average market-basket price (ten items) in the three low-income stores rose $9\frac{1}{2}$ percent between August 15 and September 1, the average market-basket price (same ten items) in the six middle-upper income area stores also rose—but only $2\frac{1}{2}$ percent. On September 1, this identical market-basket cost the average low-income shopper 18 percent more than the average middle- or upper-income shopper buying in their respective neighborhoods.

A spokesman for the ad hoc committee summarized their findings, as follows:

> Mrs. SCHLOSSBERG. The charts and graphs that we have prepared from our research speak for themselves. They point up without question the unfair pricing practices which exist. They show the prices on a given item on a given day are not consistent throughout the city. And further, they are consistently higher in certain areas serving large numbers of welfare and low-income families. The most shocking and outrageous of our findings is the fact that the prices of items we used in our survey increased by from 3 to 57 percent in some lower income area stores on the first of the month, at which time welfare checks are issued and the largest numbers of food stamps are spent.
>
> It is just this kind of practice that causes great discontent and bitterness in the slum areas of our major cities and is a primary factor in making situations ripe for violence, riots, and bloodshed (hearings, p. 7).

b. In New York City, the Consumer Action Program of Bedford-Stuyvesant, Inc., charged that five supermarket chains or affiliated stores raised prices on the dates that welfare checks are distributed in outlets in low-income Bedford-Stuyvesant (Brooklyn, N.Y.). With one minor exception, prices in outlets in middle-income Flatbush (Brooklyn, N.Y.) either remained steady or decreased.

The executive director of the consumer action program testified that their study was made in response to numerous complaints by residents of the area that food costs rise on the 1st and 16th of the month, the dates when welfare checks are distributed. Residents were asked to submit a shopping list of the "items, amounts, brands, and chainstores where they regularly buy. Tabulation and analysis of the submitted lists was made: the outcome being a resident's typical shopping list of twenty items and five major chainstores. Plans were made to conduct a survey on the five different chainstores on November 14 and November 16 . . . . The five major chainstores were surveyed on the same dates in Flatbush, a middle-class-income area. The actual purchase of the items took place on November 14 in five major chainstores in Bedford-Stuyvesant and the same twenty items were purchased on the same day in the same major chainstores in the Flatbush community. On November 16, the same five residents purchased the same twenty items in the same Bedford-Stuyvesant major chainstores as well as in the corresponding major chainstores in Flatbush."

The results of the CAP survey are tabulated in Table 4.

c. The Commissioner of Labor Statistics, Department of Labor, testified as to the results of a small Bureau of Labor Statistics study made in Watts, Los Angeles County, during the first week of March and directed to the

TABLE 4.

Comparison of Price Increases in Retail Store Outlets in Bedford-Stuyvesant and Flatbush Between Nov. 14 and Nov. 16, 1967

Location and Store	*Nov. 14, 1967*	*Nov, 16. 1967*	*Increase*	
			Price	*Percent*
BEDFORD-STUYVESANT				
A. & P.	$10.29	$10.41	$0.12	1.2
Key Food Stores	12.60	12.78	.18	1.4
Waldbaum's	8.41	8.70	.29	3.4
FLATBUSH				
A. & P.	10.08	10.08	—	—
Key Food Stores	11.82	11.78	−.04	—
Waldbaum's	8.33	8.21	−.12	—

question of whether prices are raised on the first of the month to coincide with the receipt of welfare dollars:

> Mr. Ross. We came back into a few stores and checked on . . . eighteen items only in the area of Watts in the first week of March, which was after the welfare checks were disseminated in Watts. We did find that among the items where the prices were changed there had been more price increases in the Watts area than there had been in the higher income areas of Los Angeles. We found also that the price increases were more frequent for the items that were the volume sellers in the low-income area than they were for the items that were the volume sellers in the high-income area, where there was a difference. . . .

d. The deputy-mayor of the city of New York and the chairman of the New York City Council on Consumer Affairs testified on this subject both as to chain and nonchain foodstores as follows:

> Mr. Reid. Have you seen instances . . . of price variations on welfare check days. . . ?
>
> Dr. Costello. Yes. Our surveys have evidence, provide evidence. . . . We did a survey of food prices across some twenty-five stores in the ghetto area on June 26, which would be several days before welfare checks were distributed and established what we call our price for the food basket. We went back on July 1 and July 3, and found that there was an increase in the average cost of about 15 percent.
>
> This kind of survey has got to be continued, has got to be done over neighborhoods, has got to be done over a course of time, but the one test of this that we did, we did find there was a differentiation in cost between June 26 and July 1 and July 3. In between those two events, of course, welfare checks had been distributed in neighborhoods.
>
> Mr. Reid. So that you have found at least in one instance correlation between an increase and the dates when welfare checks or factory pay checks might have been available?
>
> Dr. Costello. Right.

e. In testimony before the subcommittee on two separate occasions, officials of the Office of Economic Opportunity referred to the problems of price hiking on "mother's day," the date welfare checks are distributed:

> Mr. ROSENTHAL. Have you had any complaints made to any of your consumer groups or community-action groups that prices in supermarkets were raised on "mother's day?"
>
> Mr. BOZMAN. We have heard some indication about prices going up on the days that checks are known to be in the poor community.
>
> Mr. ROSENTHAL. Where have you heard this from? How about your colleague from California?
>
> Mr. TAYLOR. We have this documented in California. We did a survey immediately after the riots . . . and when this Safeway thing came up, I was particularly interested, because they were our number one offenders in California.

During a hearing held one year earlier on the subject of price hiking in low-income area stores of all kinds, Mr. Theodore Berry, then Director of Community Action, OEO, testified:

> Mr. BERRY. Dr. Caplovitz referred to the youth-in-action survey in the Bedford-Stuyvesant section of Brooklyn, which is the survey that was founded by our office, for the conduct of an in-depth inquiry into the problems of the poor consumer in that community.
>
> This survey found that some merchants raised prices on the first and sixteenth of the month, the days that the welfare checks arrived . . . (hearings, p. 329).

DENIAL

The food chains involved denied unequivocally the specific charges of price hiking on welfare-check day and any general suggestion of discriminatory practices in low-income area outlets.

Before detailing these denials, it is important to note the means by which chainstore food prices are established and implemented. As a general rule, prices are set by merchandizing managers at a central or home office and set forth in price books furnished each outlet of the chain. All outlets in any given pricing area, such as Safeway's Washington, D.C., metropolitan area or A. & P.'s New York metropolitan area, are furnished the identical price book on the same day containing the prices for all items carried in the store. These books are supplemented, updated, or replaced from time to time, reflecting special sales or price changes up and down.

In response to the charges brought by the ad hoc committee for equal pricing Safeway Stores testified that: "There is no truth to the accusation that Safeway charges higher prices or that Safeway raises prices in its poverty stores at the time welfare checks are issued. . . . All Safeway supermarkets in the entire Washington, D.C., metropolitan area are included in the same Safeway pricing area. We do not distinguish between poverty neighborhood and other stores within the pricing area."

Safeway further testified that one of its outlets, identified as being in a middle-income area, was actually located in a poverty area.

Similarly, officials of the Great Atlantic & Pacific Tea Co. testified at the New York hearings that it was A. & P.'s policy and practice to have "completely uniform prices in all . . . stores in . . . metropolitan New York area. These prices are the same in the approximately 450 A. & P. stores in that area, regardless of whether the store is located in the high-, low-, or middle-income neighborhood."

All store officials testifying stated that store managers have no authority at any time to charge a price higher than the book price.

Store managers are authorized to deviate from the book price by marking lower than book but only when it is necessary to move overstocks of perishable merchandise or to meet local competition.

Policies of Uniformity

At the very heart of the denials of price hiking on welfare check and food stamp days lies a policy of absolute price and quality uniformity throughout any one pricing area of the chain, backed up by a system of audits and inspections. Safeway's division manager for the District of Columbia stated that "Safeway's general philosophy and policies as to retail pricing in our stores reflect a total commitment to fairness and equity in the prices of products offered. . . . Any other policy would be sheer folly. . . . This means that it is Safeway's policy, implemented in practice through careful procedures and controls, that a given item bears the same price on the same date in each and every Safeway supermarket in the District of Columbia that handles the item and that even the occasional human error is caught and corrected promptly."

Oversight and Enforcement of Price and Quality Uniformity

In rebutting charges of price hiking on welfare check day (and other forms of discrimination alleged such as day-to-day higher prices and inferior quality in low-income area outlets of a chain), all of the major supermarkets testifying placed great emphasis and reliance on the comprehensiveness and sophistication of their audits and inspections. Safeway officials testified, for example, that "any store manager attempting to sell 'over book' would be detected in short order, and subjected to severe discipline, including termination." Safeway's District of Columbia division manager testified that district managers, each with approximately fourteen outlets under his jurisdiction, are primarily responsible for insuring the accuracy of prices.

> Mr. Winstead. The district managers are totally responsible for the management and the operation of the stores in their particular district, and price checks are a part of both their responsibility and duty. And they are completely responsible to see that proper prices are charged in those stores under their supervision at their level (hearings, p. 93).

The manager of one of Safeway's poverty-area stores involved in the ad hoc committee's survey testified:

> Mr. ROSENTHAL. Now, your district managers or supervisors, do you ever see them checking prices in your store?
>
> Mr. MILEY. Yes, sir. Yes, sir.
>
> Mr. ROSENTHAL. They walk around and look at the cans?
>
> Mr. MILEY. He doesn't walk around. He takes me with him.
>
> Mr. ROSENTHAL. And looks—how often does he do that?
>
> Mr. MILEY. I would say once, perhaps every week, sometimes I do not see him for two weeks.
>
> Mr. ROSENTHAL. Why do they do that?
>
> Mr. MILEY. Because they want to see if we are in line and following our rules and regulations, which is fair practices (hearings, p. 73).

A. & P. officials testified similarly that price integrity is maintained in large part by periodic reminders to store personnel and by store supervisors who spot-check prices:

> Mr. VITULLI. Store personnel are periodically reminded, by bulletins to the store managers, of the necessity of strictly adhering to the company's policies on accurate pricing. I have samples of such bulletins here with me today. These bulletins are followed up by our store supervisors, who generally are responsible for a group of about fifteen stores and who periodically spot-check prices to be sure they are correct.
>
> Mr. REID. How often is periodically?
>
> Mr. VITULLI. Approximately once or twice a week (hearings, p. 155).

Further price accuracy, according to A. & P. store officials, is maintained by a system of periodic audits:

> Mr. VITULLI. Making sure that each of these thousands of items is properly marked with the appropriate retail price in each of the thousands of A. & P. stores is a monumental task. We recognize that 100 percent accuracy is not possible because of human error, but I am happy to say that we have approximately $99\frac{8}{10}$ percent accuracy. You may wonder how I am able to make such a statement with such confidence. The answer is that A. & P. has for decades followed a very exacting and expensive but worthwhile procedure of having audits taken of the prices in its stores. This is done not only for purposes of inventory (which was taken about three times a year in each of our stores in this area) but also by way of unannounced or surprise price audits at least twice a year. These audits are not taken by the store personnel themselves, but by a staff of field auditors who report to our unit office managers. The store managers have absolutely no jurisdiction over these auditors (hearings, p. 156).

In specific rebuttal to the charges brought by the Bedford-Stuyvesant consumer group, A. & P. cited the results of regular and surprise audits taken in A. & P. stores in the Bedford-Stuyvesant area as compared with the Flatbush-Bayridge area in Brooklyn sometime prior to the November 14 and 16 surveys:

> Mr. Vitulli: This survey shows that the average number of items found erroneously priced on each audit was only about 10 items out of more than 5,000 items which were subject to these price checks, so that our percentage of error is less than one-fifth of 1 percent, and those errors included underpricing items as well as overpricing them (hearings, p. 156).

Kroger Co. store officials testified at the St. Louis hearings that they "have developed, and forcefully administer, a system of controls intended to eliminate as many errors as it is humanly possible to eliminate":

> Mr. White. A wall-to-wall check of all prices in each store is made regularly in connection with store audits. Additionally, an independent, professional shopping service is constantly checking prices in our stores, along with other aspects of store operations. We also employ a man experienced in price checking to inspect our competitor stores, and he keeps tabs on our prices too. Furthermore, store personnel are expected to frequently and regularly check prices in their store. Store managers and department heads, especially, are actively engaged in these frequent checks. In addition, more than two dozen experienced management people spend much, if not most, of their time in our stores, and price checking is something all of them always do.

Further testimony on the subject of store audits as a guarantee of price uniformity was provided by the St. Louis division manager of Kroger in a colloquy with Chairman Rosenthal.

> Mr. Rosenthal. Somewhere in the statement you indicated that you do make checks on prices and I know that all of your colleagues in the industry do that. How often does someone under your jurisdiction or your command make a check on prices in any of these stores?
>
> Mr. White. Well I am what we call manager of operations for the St. Louis stores division, as I stated. My responsibility is the operation of the stores within the division. I have supervisors who report to me who by themselves supervise a certain number of stores. On their regular visits to these stores, as I indicated with other management people visiting the stores also, they make arrangements for price checks as a regular part of their work.
>
> Mr. Rosenthal. How often?
>
> Mr. White. They visit stores every week.
>
> Mr. Rosenthal. Are the supervisors or someone in their ranks directed by you to examine prices once a week?
>
> Mr. White. That's correct. They are directed to examine prices as a regular part of their duties when they visit stores; yes, sir (hearings, pp. 258–259).

National Food Stores audit procedures closely parallel those of the other large chains:

> Mr. O'Neal. Some of you may not realize it, but price marking for supermarkets, speaking as a former store manager, is a tremendous, difficult and tedious job. It requires the constant attention of district managers, field specialists, auditors, and we have, unknown to our store employees

> and managers, shoppers who visit our stores, check prices, not only do they check prices, they check quality, service, friendliness, cleanliness, many other items. We have regular auditing crews that check prices unknown, unannounced price checks. In a highly competitive business like ours, the correct price on the merchandise is an absolute must (hearings, p. 278).

Goodwill and Repeat Business

The third line of reasoning profferred by all the food chains in response to the allegation of welfare-day price hiking, relates to the need for maintaining customer satisfaction and goodwill. Typical was the statement of the St. Louis division manager of Kroger:

> Our business is based on repeated patronage. Unless we continue to satisfy our customers, no matter who they are and no matter where they live, they can quickly take their business elsewhere (hearings, p. 256).

Absence of Bonus System in A. & P. Operation

Finally, A. & P. witnesses stated that a possible factor given as motivating price hiking on welfare check day—the store manager's desire for earning a bonus—was absent in the case of A. & P.'s operation:

> Not only does A. & P. insist on strict accuracy of retail prices, but there is no reason for the store manager or anyone else to increase the prices at A. & P. stores. There is no compensation or bonuses which might possibly reward any such misconduct at A. & P. stores.

COMMITTEE COMMENT

In the case of charges of price hiking on welfare check and food stamp days, a brief factual summary of the most cogent points on both sides, should suffice:

At the Washington, D.C., hearings Safeway officials brought in store managers to deny the charges, pointed out that none of the items involved in the allegedly incriminating survey were purchased, criticized the fact that food prices surveyed in poverty-area stores were observed and recorded by only one shopper without independent verification, cited their official policies of uniformity, presented the results of an October 2, 1967, surprise audit of the three poverty-area stores showing fidelity to book prices, and argued the complexities of food price comparisons to the uninitiated shopper.

Representatives of the Ad Hoc Committee on Equal Pricing, while they lacked financial resources to purchase all of the grocery items on the survey list, asserted the integrity of their shoppers and the reliability and objectivity of their survey techniques.

The Bedford-Stuyvesant consumer action shoppers purchased their groceries and retained their cash register tapes. The tapes, now in the committee's files, support substantially the shoppers' findings and conclusions. The A. & P. officials, in pointing out the possibility of human error on both sides, noted that their stores have never carried one-quart jars of Tropicana orange juice as reported in the Bedford-Stuyvesant A. & P. survey.

There is considerable evidence to support the case of those who charged such price hiking. Other factors, not dealt with in this part, may also contribute to price differences.

1. Data published by various agencies of the U.S. Government as well as testimony of witnesses show that food chain outlets located in poverty areas generally have smaller "per customer" transactions and that the low-income consumer spends less for food and purchases fewer high markup items than the affluent shopper in middle-and upper-income neighborhoods—all of which reduce profit.
2. Information available to the committee does indicate that there is an upsurge in the expenditure of welfare dollars and food stamp redemptions within 2 or 3 days after issuance; and that an outlet's profit picture could be most favorably affected at this time.
3. The bonus system, under which almost all nationwide retail food chains operate, provides an incentive for store managers to maximize store profits particularly in those instances where competition is absent. Certainly, however, the mere existence of a bonus-incentive system does not automatically bring abuse, anymore than its absence precludes abuse.
4. Also of considerable importance is an apparent inability by top management properly to oversee policies of price uniformity. Since, as Congressman Reuss observed during the Washington hearings:

   > If a large national chain were in the business of systematically discriminating against low-income people . . . you would not expect them to memorialize it . . . in their books and records (hearings, p. 61).

   the chains' denials would seem to stand or fall primarily on the effectiveness of their audits and inspections designed to insure compliance with policies of uniformity and equality. Let us examine, then, the efficacy of these audits and inspections.

It should be noted, preliminarily, that there is no testimony or other evidence to suggest that stores located in low-income areas receive more frequent or more comprehensively conducted audits or inspections than stores located in affluent neighborhoods; or indeed that top management was, in any general way, sensitive to pricing problems in low-income area stores.

Testimony from poverty area Safeway managers in Washington, D.C., indicates that on the average, supervisory personnel visit stores from once a week to once every three weeks and that one of their responsibilities during these visits is to check prices. Although no information was offered or received as to the extensiveness or thoroughness of these price checks, the District of Columbia division manager's inability to furnish even a rough estimate of the time spent by district managers in checking prices would seem to be relevant:

> Mr. GUDE. Would there be any rough estimate that could be made of what percentage of their time is to be spent checking food prices, or is it lumped in with the many other duties on visiting the stores?
>
> Mr. WINSTEAD. We have not made a complete time study on this particular facet of our business. We do not have that information (hearings, p. 93).

While the failure of Safeway's top local management to possess this knowledge does not necessarily imply the ineffectiveness of these inspections as a tool for maintaining price uniformity, it does suggest that price verification has never been of extraordinary importance to management.

A. & P. oversees price accuracy in its stores through a system of spot checks, "once to twice a week" by supervisors who are generally responsible for fifteen stores; and by a team of auditors who visit stores, sometimes unannounced, twice a year. A. & P. claims for itself 99.8 percent accuracy in price marking as an average for all of its stores. Against this claim of near-perfection, it is necessary to contrast not only the results of the Bedford-Stuyvesant survey but the results of the onsite inspection of an A. & P. store in mid-Harlem by members of the subcommitte, showing innumerable instances of multiple price markings on items.

Also an article from Modern Grocer magazine of August 18, 1967, circulated by top management to A. & P. store managers, stated that "many local chains still fail to price mark all items. Clerks are still careless and managers are failing to follow through when clerks are ordered to price mark."

As indicated earlier, Kroger administers a comparable system of controls intended to eliminate pricing errors, including checks by store personnel and supervisory personnel and a 13-week "wall-to-wall check of all prices in each store" by auditors.

It should be noted, however, that Kroger store managers are advised several days in advance of these "wall-to-wall" audits:

> Mr. WHITE. Well, we have our stores audited by an audit team, as I indicated, wall-to-wall price checks, approximately every thirteen weeks during the year. Now, at this time they checked the prices, both over and below what they should be, whether they be advertised or at book retail.
>
> Mr. ROSENTHAL. Do the managers know when your audit check is coming?
>
> Mr. WHITE. They may know two days in advance.
>
> Mr. ROSENTHAL. You've got to get your money back the same way we have to get our money back on the Bureau of Labor Statistics study. You can't check something and let somebody know you are coming (hearings, p. 264).

QUESTIONS

1. Criticize the surveys presented indicating a rise in food prices in ghetto areas when welfare checks are issued.
2. Assuming that some of the studies are accurate and do reflect a difference in prices at the time welfare checks are issued, what could account for this differential in the chain food stores?
3. Testimony indicated that all food chains regularly check on the shelf prices of their stores. Why does so much effort go into this practice?

39

Do the Inner City Poor Pay More for Food?

Donald F. Dixon and Daniel J. McLaughlin, Jr.

HYPOTHESES

The recent riots in major cities have been viewed as an attempt to call the attention of the white community to problems faced by Inner City residents. The President's Commission on Law Enforcement and the Administration of Justice found that these riots were specifically directed against those who represented the principal forms of oppression, including white merchants, especially those who charged high prices or sold inferior goods.[1]

This paper compares the prices charged by stores located in the North Philadelphia Inner City with prices charged in higher income areas throughout the city. An effort was made to obtain prices of the same products in neighborhood stores and supermarkets.

THE SPECIFIC HYPOTHESES TESTED ARE:

1. Prices rise when welfare checks are distributed.
2. Prices in supermarkets are higher in low income areas than in higher income areas.
3. Prices in small neighborhood stores are higher in low income areas than in higher income areas.

Reprinted from *Economic and Business Bulletin*, Temple University, School of Business Administration, Spring 1968, pp. 6–12. Some footnotes deleted.

[1] *The Challenge of Crime in a Free Society*, a Report by the President's Commission on Law Enforcement and Administration of Justice. Washington, D.C.: U. S. Government Printing Office, 1967, pp. 37 and 38.

These hypotheses are established to test the proposition that "The Poor Pay More," which has been advanced in hearings before the House Government Operations Subcommittee. News reports have mentioned information such as that presented by three Washington, D.C. housewives who priced ten food items in nine stores,[2] six New York City housewives who priced twenty items in ten stores,[3] and a St. Louis consumer group which studied two stores.[4] Such reports apparently have been accepted by the Committee as supporting the thesis of economic discrimination by food stores in low income areas.

Small sample studies reported in the public press have serious limitations. Prices in a single chain may differ from store to store because of pricing errors, oversights, or competitive conditions. Thus, it is necessary to choose a sample large enough so that price variations between low and higher income areas may be compared with price variations normally found within an area.

A second difficulty in comparing chain store prices in different income areas is that residents of low income areas often do not have the same opportunities to shop in chain supermarkets as do residents of higher income areas. Hence, price comparisons must take into account the type of store in which purchases are made, rather than proceeding on the assumption that only chain store prices are relevant to the inquiry.

Third, Inner City residents seldom buy the same market baskets as families elsewhere. There is little reason to assume that Negro, Puerto Rican, and white families in low income areas have identical purchasing patterns, or that these families purchase the same items as do families in higher income areas. If the same commodities are priced in low and high income areas, there is an implicit assumption that these items are consumed in relatively equal amounts in each area.

Several studies, each of which avoids one or another of these difficulties, have been published. A summer-long study of food prices in New York City produced no evidence that chain stores charged higher prices in poor areas. However, "There are fewer large stores in the poor areas and prices tend to be lower in large stores".[5] Similarly, in a study conducted for the National Commission on Food Marketing, the Bureau of Labor Statistics reports:[6]

> no significant differences in prices charged by food stores located in low income areas vs. those charged by stores in higher income areas, when the same types of stores . . . the same qualities of foods, and the same sizes of packages are compared. Prices are usually higher, however, in the small independent stores which are most common in low income neighborhoods, than in large independents and chain stores which predominate in the higher income areas.

[2] *New York Times*, October 13, 1967.
[3] *Ibid.*, November 25, 1967.
[4] *Wall Street Journal*, January 4, 1968.
[5] Same reference as footnote 3.
[6] *Special Studies in Food Marketing*, Technical Study No. 10, National Commission on Food Marketing, Washington, D.C.: U. S. Government Printing Office, 1966, p. 122.

Although the B.L.S. study explicitly considered different types of stores, the results may be questioned because of the use of a weighting system which assumed that the distribution of stores in low income areas is the same as that in high income areas. This means that the distribution of the sample could not be interpreted as representative of the distribution of full line stores in each area. Another problem with the B.L.S. study is that products of the same qualities were not always priced in the low and high income areas.

A study by Alexis and Simon, conducted in Monroe County (Rochester), New York, overcomes the problems of store distribution by sampling stores identified by a previous study of shopping behavior.[7] Low income shoppers patronizing chain stores did not pay more than higher income shoppers, if the least expensive among the available items were purchased; but low income shoppers patronizing independent stores did pay higher prices than those patronizing chain stores.

The procedures followed in the studies differ markedly. The Alexis-Simon study centered the definition of low income on the shopper, whereas the B.L.S. study designated the store as low or higher income according to the median income of the census tract in which it was located. Furthermore, although there was considerable overlap among items, the market basket differed in the two studies. The B.L.S. attempted to identify items relevant to the budgets of low income families; the Alexis-Simon market basket was chosen to "obtain a representative group of commodities purchased across income classes and to include food items with positive, zero, and negative income elasticities".[8] The qualities may also have differed, for the only control was the price of the items.

Goodman[9] conducted a study analogous to that of Alexis and Simon in a small area of West Philadelphia. Consumer interviews identified the stores most often patronized, and prices in these stores were compared. Market basket composites, based upon Pennsylvania Department of Welfare criteria, indicate that the prices charged by the small stores in the low income area are higher than prices charged by the supermarkets in an immediately adjacent area. However, it concluded that because most residents go outside the immediate area to shop, they do not pay more than residents of the higher income area.

FINDINGS

The data do not support the hypothesis that prices are raised at the end of the week, or after the distribution of welfare checks. Some products in the

[7] Marcus Alexis and Leonard S. Simon, "The Food Marketing Commission and Food Prices by Income Groups," *Journal of Farm Economics*, May 1967, pp. 436–446.

[8] *Ibid.*, p. 439. "To be included . . . an item had only to show noticeable use across all income classes," p. 441.

[9] Charles S. Goodman, "Do the Poor Pay More?," *Journal of Marketing*, January 1968, pp. 18–24.

market basket were slightly higher in price at the end of the week, but an equal number were lower, so that over-all there was no appreciable change. The average price of the market basket in the small stores, in both low and higher income areas, was two tenths of one percent lower in the latter part of the week, after welfare checks had been distributed. Although the supermarket chains offered end-of-week specials on one or another of the products which were sampled, these lower prices were not sufficient to affect the market basket price.

The results also show that, on the average, the market basket cost in the three Inner City supermarkets is not higher than in the sample of higher income supermarkets. Similarly, the market basket cost for the small Inner City stores is not higher than that for the small stores in the higher income area. (See Table 1.)

TABLE 1.

Market Basket Cost, by Type of Store, and Income of Area, in Dollars

Area	*Type of Store*	
	Supermarket	*Small Store*
Higher Income	8.63	9.38
Inner City	8.54	9.01

But it is apparent that low income families shop in a different type of store than do families who live in higher income areas. The sales of the three Inner City supermarkets represent only 8 or 9 percent of the area's estimated total food sales. Furthermore, the limited mobility of the residents suggests that a small number of purchases are made in supermarkets located in higher income areas. Hence, it may be assumed that the largest part of the food purchases in the Inner City are made in the small stores.

Those who patronize the small stores in the low income area pay an average of $0.38 or 4.4 percent more for the market basket than do those who patronize supermarkets in the higher income area, when comparable brands and package sizes are purchased. This result does not imply economic discrimination against the poor; such a hypothesis can be tested only by examining prices in comparable stores which are in low and higher income areas.

The small stores in the low and higher income areas were roughly comparable. The median selling area of the small stores in the low income area was 570 sq. ft., as compared to 750 sq. ft. for these stores in the higher income area. The majority of the stores in both samples were counter-service—only 27 percent of the low income area stores and 32 percent of the higher income ones were self-service. Furthermore, wholesale prices for a large number of the commodities sold in the small stores were the same, for most of the small stores are members of a retailer-owned cooperative group.

The study shows that those who shop in small stores in the low income area pay less than those who shop in small stores in the higher income area. The difference is $0.37 or 4.3 percent. The data also suggest a tendency for the market basket price in the small stores to rise as income rises. When the small stores are grouped according to the income level of the census tract in which they were located, there was little difference in market basket price between the lowest and second quartiles, but a pronounced increase in the upper quartiles, when the same brands and sizes were compared. (See Table 2.)

TABLE 2.

Small Store Prices, by Income Area, Lowest Cost Market

Basket = 100.0

Income of Area	*Price*
Lowest Quartile	100.0
Second Quartile	101.3
Third Quartile	103.8
Highest Quartile	103.5

These results fail to support the hypothesis of price discrimination against low income families. On the contrary, it appears that if costs in the small Inner City stores are comparable to the costs of stores located in the higher income area, then profits earned by the Inner City stores may be less than average. This inference is reinforced by the often repeated argument that costs are especially high in low income areas where merchants suffer heavily from thefts and property damage. More complete knowledge of store costs is needed if the issue of discrimination is to be determined accurately.

Although the total market basket costs do not suggest discrimination, it is possible that prices for some products are higher in the low income area, so that discrimination occurs within the market basket. However, the results of the study indicate that the pricing pattern is consistent over the entire market basket. The supermarket prices are lowest for all but two products, and for these the prices of the Inner City small stores are the lowest. Furthermore, the prices of the Inner City small stores are less than the prices of the small stores in the higher income areas for fifteen of the twenty products in the market basket. (See Table 3.) In the case of many products, the differences are small, relative to the price ranges reported. In other instances, the number of observations in one or more store groups is small. Thus it is the consistency with which the lower prices are found, first in the supermarkets, and second, in the small stores in the low income area, which is most significant.

The results of the study are unchanged when items other than those specified are introduced. Substitutes for thirteen branded products were priced where the specified brands were not available in the store. Substitution did not occur often in the supermarkets, but was significant in the small stores. In the small stores located in the low income area, 42 percent of the prices reported were for specified items; among the small stores in the higher income area, the comparable figure was 43 percent.

TABLE 3.

Product Prices, by Store Type, in Cents

	Supermarkets (Higher Income Area)	*Small Stores (Inner City)*	*Small Stores (Higher Income Area)*
Pork	114.7	95.8	112.1
Chicken	40.5	41.0	44.4
Canned Fish	33.5	39.4	38.9
Milk	30.8	32.4	33.3
Cheese	40.6	42.6	43.4
Flour	56.5	65.8	64.1
Cereal	30.1	33.5	31.3
Bread	27.5	27.6	28.2
Bananas	13.4	16.8	17.1
Potatoes	44.9	38.3	44.8
Coffee	76.7	86.6	84.7
Canned Fruit	30.5	31.8	32.1
Canned Vegetables	25.4	27.4	27.6
Eggs	49.8	58.7	60.0
Butter	85.3	87.7	94.3
Margarine	31.7	33.4	38.2
Sugar	63.4	66.7	67.8
Candy	5.0	6.1	6.2
Peanut Butter	41.9	46.7	45.7
Frozen Fruit Juice	20.9	23.0	24.1
TOTAL	862.8	901.2	938.1

An examination of the seven items which accounted for most of the substitutions indicates that, on the average, the substitute items were lower in price than the specified items. The market basket price for these seven items in the small Inner City stores was 6 cents lower when the substitute items were included; it was 9 cents less in the higher income area stores. In many instances the lower priced product was a private brand, supplied by the cooperative with which most of the small stores are affiliated. The availability of a private brand, at a lower pricc, is an important element in maintaining lower prices in the small stores. Furthermore, the fact that small stores offer lower priced items instead of the higher priced branded products, does not appear to offer support to the discrimination hypothesis.

DO THE POOR PAY MORE?

The results of this study indicate that price differences for comparable products are explained by the type of store rather than by store location. We can answer the question "Do the poor pay more?" only if several assumptions concerning purchasing behavior are correct. It is known what prices are charged, but what prices do low income families pay? To answer this, it is necessary to know where low income families make their purchases, and what they purchase.

It has been assumed that most higher income families shop in supermarkets, while most of the low income families shop in small stores. The associated assumption is that small stores in higher income areas largely serve the function of fill-in stores, but the extent of this is not known. The associated assumption regarding the Inner City supermarkets is less obvious. Do residents of the immediate area surrounding these supermarkets compose the majority of the customers, or do customers come from greater distances? There is a great need for further work regarding shopping behavior among low income families.

The study also has been concerned with the prices in the core of a large, low income area. It is assumed that most purchases in this area are confined to the small neighborhood stores because supermarkets are geographically remote. There are, however, "poverty pockets" in higher income areas of the city in which residents have a greater opportunity to shop at supermarkets selling both to low and higher income customers. It is important to discover the pattern of prices in such situations as these. There is a need for further research into these areas, along the lines of the Goodman pilot study.[10] In our study prices were obtained for specified sizes of packages, generally those employed in determining the Consumer Price Index. However, it is known that low income shoppers often purchase food items in smaller size packages. Prices actually paid will differ from the prices reported in this study if smaller packages are actually purchased.

The extent to which quality differences affect pricing must also be examined. No effort to determine quality was made in this study, although there

[10] *Ibid.*

was room for variation in the meat and produce items. The prices of pork and potatoes were found to be lower in the small Inner City stores, and chicken was sold at essentially the same price as in supermarkets. This implies that a quality difference may exist, but that it seems to be associated with the small stores, regardless of their location. The important point, relative to the discrimination hypothesis, is that the prices for these items are not higher in the low income area. Yet pork and chicken supposedly comprise a larger proportion of the Negro market basket and hence would most likely be subject to discriminatory pricing.

Furthermore, if a quality difference exists, how is it to be related to a price difference? The sale of lower quality products is not evidence of discrimination if lower prices are charged. In fact, if lower quality is unrelated to nutrition, such a pricing practice would seem to be socially beneficial. Such problems as these do not lend themselves to self-evident answers, especially when U.S.D.A. grades are not directly related to consumer preferences.

There may be difficulty with the market basket employed. Although care was taken to devise a reasonable list of items to be priced, it is possible that another list would lead to different conclusions. Yet, because the results reported here are compatible with those of previously reported studies, it is unlikely that such differences would be significant.

A more important problem is that utilizing a market basket which consists of food items alone is misleading, because products other than food are obtained from the small neighborhood stores, and services such as delivery, credit, check cashing, and other conveniences are also offered. Thus prices charged by the small Inner City stores cannot be compared directly to those charged by supermarkets, which do not offer such services.

The conclusion drawn from the study—that the poor who shop in small neighborhood stores do pay more for food items than higher income families who shop in supermarkets—is not surprising. However, it is clear that the reasons why the poor pay more are too complex to be determined by a study of prices charged by food stores. It is possible that there are forms of discrimination practiced, which have not been determined in this study.

Discrimination can be but a part of the entire system of marketing in the Inner City. Very little is known about marketing in low income areas, and there is a clear and immediate need for work to determine the shopping behavior of Inner City residents, the pattern of expenditures by low income families, and the services provided by small Inner City stores, together with the associated costs of operation. Our results suggest the possibility that the small Inner City store represents a form of marketing which is surprisingly efficient, in the light of the task which is accomplished and the constraints under which such stores are operated. . . .

QUESTIONS

1. Does this article strictly support the view that "the poor pay more"?
2. Does this study support the view that there is economic discrimination against the poor?

B. CHANGE IN RETAILING

Businessmen are constantly under pressure if only because the environment in which they operate is always undergoing change. The environment may change in many ways. For instance, the composition of the population in the trading area may alter, or competitors may increase or may change their tactics.

The two articles in this final section discuss some aspects of change that retailers are presently facing. In the first article, "The Supermarket Challenged," Fred Allvine describes the problems of the changing competition and how they will affect this outlet, which dates back to 1916.

The second article, by Louis Bernstein, describes the more recent development of the franchise outlet and presents the challenging idea that franchising has served as a boon to the small retailer by offering him "promising opportunities."

40

The Supermarket Challenged! New Competitive Strategies Needed

Fred C. Allvine

The one-time revolutionary concept of the supermarket is under severe competitive attack. The challenges to its dominant position are coming from several innovative types of retailers using a variety of approaches that make it difficult for the supermarkets to effectively adjust their operations to the competitive threats. The profit margins of supermarket chains are at a fifteen-year low, and the situation is likely to grow worse before it becomes better. To effectively maneuver a supermarket chain through difficult times, the executives of these companies will have to analyze what is happening to their business and why. Once this has been accomplished, a strategy—based on defensive skills—to minimize the competitive vulnerability of a chain can be devised. This article, designed to help the troubled administrator, covers the following questions: Why are supermarkets experiencing severe competitive pressures? What are the forms that the stores of the future are taking? What can supermarket chains do to reduce their competitive vulnerability?

PROBLEMS OF SUPERMARKETS

The history of the supermarket dates back to around 1916 when Clarence Saunders opened one of the first self-service stores in Memphis. Later attempts were made to establish large self-service, cash-and-carry grocery stores in southern California and other parts of the country. When the first store in the King Kullen chain was opened in 1930, the principles of the supermarket business tended to become established—low prices, combinations of product lines, mass merchandising, and cash-and-carry.[1] However, the growth of the supermarket was slight from 1930–45 because of the depression and World War II. Supermarkets grew very rapidly from 1945–60 (see Figure 1). The dearth of financial investment from 1930–45 created a pent-up demand for this new self-service store, and the migration of the population

Reprinted from *Business Horizons*, Indiana University, Graduate School of Business, Vol. 11, No. 5, October 1968, pp. 61–72.

[1] William Applebaum and David Carson, "Supermarkets Face the Future," *Harvard Business Review*, XXXV (March-April, 1957), pp. 123–24.

to the suburbs gave it impetus. In response, vast sums of capital flowed into the construction of supermarkets; financial returns were initially outstanding (see Table 1, page 384.).

As the construction of supermarkets continued at near-record levels into the later 1950s, the nature of competition changed. Early in the postwar period, well-located new supermarkets offering lower prices, better assortment, and newer facilities became almost immediately profitable by attracting shoppers from the smaller service-type stores. However, in the early 1950s, the demand then existing for large supermarkets was coming closer to being met. Newly opened supermarkets were attracting an increasing share of their business from existing supermarkets. As one executive told me, "The industry changed; instead of looking for relatively untapped areas, supermarkets began identifying high-volume competitors' stores to locate near in order to divide the business."

FIGURE 1. Share of grocery store sales by size of store

	Supermarkets	*Superettes*	*Small Stores*
1952	39%	22%	39%
1954	46	20	34
1956	52	19	29
1958	58	17	25
1960	65	15	20
1962	68	14	18
1964	70	13	17
1966	71	13	16
1967	72	13	15

Source: "Grocery Business Annual Report" in *Progressive Grocer* (April, 1966 and 1967). In 1967 a supermarket was defined as a store doing $500,000 worth of business a year or more (previously $375,000 or more); a superette as a store doing from $150,000 to $500,000 (previously $75,000 to $375,000); and a small store as doing less than $150,000 (previously less than $75,000).

The initial pressing demand resulted in growth too rapid for the long-run good of the emerging industry. Management's attention was focused on crucial financial and physical distribution problems instead of on improved merchandising techniques and distinctive approaches. As a result, competitors' operations were quite similar in size, choice of location, product assortment, and price. As long as demand for the new large self-service type of store was relatively unsaturated, this was no problem. However, as was inevitable, the day came in most markets when demand was close to being satisfied, and the early oversight became a major problem.

The changing nature of the consumer market contributed to the difficulty. The pedestrian shopper is limited to one or two nearby stores; in contrast, the shopper with a car has a number of alternatives to select from, and is inclined to split his patronage among several stores and to be fickle in the sense of changing the mix of stores he patronizes.[2]

The near-saturation of demand for supermarkets, the sameness of competitors' operations, and the mobility of shoppers contributed to market instability—the industry's reference to that vacillating share of the market that is "up for grabs" every week. Estimates given to me by chain store executives of the size of this unstable group of shoppers ranged from a third to a half of the market. During the early 1950s, supermarket chains found that they were being forced to bid for their share of this vacillating segment with more specials in their weekly ads. This was one of the reasons for depressed industry profits from 1951–55 (Table 1).

TABLE 1.

Net Profit After Taxes as a Percent of Net Worth

1946	18.6%	1957	15.8
1947	17.6	1958	15.2
1948	16.5	1959	13.9
1949	17.8	1960	13.0
1950	17.9	1961	12.2
1951	11.7	1962	11.5
1952	10.7	1963	11.5
1953	12.7	1964	12.5
1954	13.9	1965	12.5
1955	13.4	1966	12.3
1956	15.5%	1967	11.0

Source: Economics Department, First National City Bank of New York, New York City.

The severity of price competition and depressed profits during the first half of the 1950s caused supermarket chains to turn to a variety of forms of nonprice promotion. This new approach included offering more services, operating longer hours, doing more extensive advertising, distributing trading stamps and game cards, and the like. One of the most important types of nonprice promotion was stamps, which were adopted by major supermarket chains starting in 1954.[3] Trading stamps were important in the short-run because they helped the chains to differentiate among themselves. To the extent that a chain differentiated itself in the minds of shoppers the problems of split-patronage purchasing and the fickle shopper were reduced.

[2] Ross M. Cunningham, "Customer Loyalty to Store and Brand," *Harvard Business Review*, XXXIX (November-December, 1961), pp. 130–31; *1967 Study of Supermarket Shoppers* (Cincinnati, Ohio: Burgoyne Index, Inc., 1967), pp. 10–11.

[3] Harvey L. Vredenburg, "From First Stamp to Major Industry," in Albert Haring and Wallace Yoder, eds., *Trading Stamp Practice and Pricing Policy* (Bloomington, Ind.: Bureau of Business Research, Indiana University, 1958), pp. 4–9.

In contrast, the use of price as the primary competitive tool pulled that vacillating segment of the market back and forth between chains, which had a depressing effect on profits.

The weakness in many types of nonprice promotion is that almost every chain is capable of imitating the various elements of this strategy (longer hours, extended advertising, trading stamps, and so on). For example, over a period of nine years (1954–62) practically all major chains in most markets adopted trading stamps, so that the definition of a conventional supermarket became a "stamp-giving store." The early givers profited most from trading stamps (see Table 2), while the late-comers essentially neutralized their effectiveness (note in Table 1 the improvement in profitability through 1958 and the decline from 1959 to 1962).[4] By 1962, when practically all competitors had stamps, chains were once again bidding for customers with both stamp giveaways and special prices. The giveaways included bonus stamps associated with the amount of purchase (usually equivalent to double stamps), extra product stamps, double-stamp days and weeks, some triple-stamp periods, and stamp jubilees involving thousands of extra stamps.

TABLE 2.

Effect of Trading Stamps on Supermarket Sales

Years Compared	*Average Sales Gains With Stamps*	*Average Sales Gains Without Stamps*
1953–54	18%	12%
1954–55	25	12
1955–56	13	14
1956–57	14	14
1957–58	10	12
1958–59	9	10
1959–60	8	10

Source: The National Commission on Food Marketing, *Organization and Competition in Food Retailing* (Technical Study No. 7; Washington: U.S. Govt. Printing Office, June, 1966), p. 455.

In this process of "competitive innovation" followed by "competitive neutralization" elements of nonprice promotion become necessary for doing business. As this happens with hours of operation, advertising, trading stamps, customer games, and so on, institutionalized costs mount, driving upward the cost of doing business. This phenomenon contributed heavily to the spiralling gross margins of large-scale supermarket chains. From 1951 through 1963, the period during which nonprice promotion grew to a peak, the

[4] This competitive process is described by Wroe Alderson in *Dynamic Marketing Behavior* (Homewood, Ill.: Richard D. Irwin, Inc., 1965), pp. 184–210.

gross margin of three of the five largest chains increased by 40 percent to 20.6 percent, and for a larger cross-section of chains it increased by 31 percent to 22.8 percent.[5]

Some supermarket shoppers approved of the expanded and costly services, but a large and growing segment became disenchanted. Public pressure on government to investigate why food costs were rising resulted in the rather unfavorable report of the National Commission on Food Marketing. Public displeasure broke into the open in the fall and winter of 1966; shoppers, boycotting in more than a hundred cities, held placards pleading for lower prices and the elimination of stamps and games.[6] Similar sentiments were found in the annual Burgoyne survey of shoppers' attitudes. For example, four out of five shoppers interviewed during 1967 said they preferred a store offering prices 2 percent lower to one giving stamps.[7]

INNOVATIVE COMPETITION

The homogeneous nature of supermarkets made them vulnerable to innovators who would shape their offer for those shoppers preferring different combinations of costly services. This price dimension is illustrated in Figure 2 as a continuum running from high price at one extreme to low price at the other. The retailer selects his price strategy through the combination of services offered to shoppers. The greater the number of services, the higher the price; conversely, the fewer the services, the lower the price.

The other basic dimension that innovators are using to attract particular segments of shoppers is product assortment and an associated number of

FIGURE 2. Price dimension of a retail strategy

High Price	*Medium Price*	*Low Price*
	Customer Services	
	Location convenience	
	Hours of operation	
	Trading stamps and games	
More	Store decor and upkeep	Less
	Cleanliness of store	
	Employee courtesy	
	Quick checkout	

[5] National Commission on Food Marketing, *Organization and Competition in Food Retailing* (Technical Study No. 7; Washington: U.S. Govt. Printing Office, June 1966), p. 223.

[6] "Behind the Boycotts: Why Prices are Higher," *Time* (Nov. 4, 1966), p. 89; "Trading Stamp Tumult," *Sales Management* (Dec. 1, 1966), pp. 31–34.

[7] *1967 Study of Supermarket Shoppers* (Cincinnati, Ohio: Burgoyne Index, Inc., 1967), p. 33.

FIGURE 3. Product assortment dimension of a retail strategy

Narrow Assortment	*Medium Assortment*	*Broad Assortment*
2,000 Products		*20,000 Products*
	Product Line	
	Dry groceries	
	Fresh meats	
	Produce	
	Dairy	
	Frozen foods	
	Health & beauty aids	
	Fancy bakery	
	Delicatessen	
	Housewares	
Less	Lunch counter	More
	Pharmacy	
	Cosmetics	
	Camera & film	
	Magazines	

product lines. The product assortment dimension is shown in Figure 3 as a continuum. A narrow product assortment might be as few as 2,000 items from three basic product lines, as contrasted with a broad assortment of 20,000 items from fifteen product lines.

FIGURE 4. Matrix of basic strategies for segmenting grocery business

Product Assortment \ Price	High	Medium	Low
Narrow	Convenience store Superette		
Large		SUPER MARKET	Discount Store
Broad		Combination Store	Food Emporium

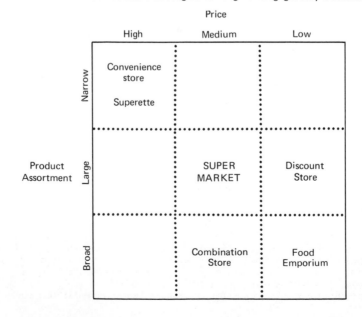

When the price and product assortment dimensions are joined in a matrix, the basic strategies that innovators are following can be more clearly seen (see Figure 4). In the center is the supermarket, the dominant grocery institution. Surrounding it are the four primary challengers who are attacking with distinctively different approaches to satisfy shoppers' demands. These challengers are the discount store, the combination store, the food emporium, and convenience stores and superettes.

The Discount Store

The increasing cost of services offered by supermarket chains and the growing segment of the market preferring lower costs to services caused the chains to become vulnerable to innovative retailers with lower costs. The "discount food stores in discount centers" and the "free-standing" discount stores (f.s. discount stores) moved in to fill this void. In both cases, the formula has been similar. First, discounters pared the excessive costs that supermarkets had acquired over a decade of vying with one another. These included savings from eliminating stamps and games, operating shorter hours, reducing nonessential services, and having "everyday low prices" that do not require remarking hundreds of prices every week. In addition, discounters are generally larger, more readily accessible to large numbers of shoppers, and often more serviceable than the typical supermarket. This combination of lower costs and greater efficiency permits discounters to offer prices approximately 4 percent less than the traditional supermarket.[8]

The development of discount stores in discount centers is a byproduct of the discount revolution in general merchandising. Grocery operations were often excluded from the early discount centers. However, as the discount center concept matured, the synergistic effect of combining general merchandise and food was recognized; in 1966, 1,465 discount food operations (primarily leased) were located in 3,503 discount centers. Grocery sales in these stores amounted to $3.8 billion for 5.5 percent of the industry's sales. The growth of discount food stores and their penetration into the food business is tied to the growth of discount centers. As the discount industry has matured, the annual rate of growth of new centers has decreased from 30–50 percent to around 8 percent at the present.[9] Therefore, it is likely that food stores in discount centers will slowly increase their penetration from the current 6 percent level to 7.5–8 percent within five years, and will conceivably reach a plateau of around 10 percent in ten years.

The second type of discount store invading the traditional supermarket business, the f.s. discount store, is more difficult to define because the

[8] A comprehensive study by the government found that the gross margin of conventional supermarkets was 19.4–20.1 percent in comparison to 15.8 percent for discounters. See U.S. Department of Agriculture, *Food Retailing for Discount Houses* (Washington: U.S. Govt. Printing Office, February, 1967), p. 5.

[9] Figures on discount food operations from *Discount Merchandiser* (Aug. 21, 1967), p. 32-TL and p. 8–TL.

concept came into wide use only during the last three years and is still evolving. My definition of this store is a highly accessible supermarket, larger than average size, that does not give stamps or use games; that has "everyday low prices" in the grocery department (approximately 50 percent of sales) that are 5 to 7 percent less than in the traditional supermarket; that has trimmed its services to the basic ones; and that probably operates shorter hours and has a wider variety of merchandise.

The original f.s. discount store can be traced back to 1956 when trading stamps were invading New Jersey. Most food chains seemed to be resigned to the inevitability of stamps and rapidly adopted them, but there was one major exception—Shop Rite. This organization decided not to join the trend to stamps, but to follow instead a dramatically different approach of across-the-board lower prices in the grocery department (approximately 50 percent of sales) and stress the advertising theme of "Why Pay More." Since 1956 Shop Rite has followed this strategy, better serving a segment of the market in a meaningfully different way. This has included, in addition to lower prices, the development of bigger stores, centrally located in larger trade areas and with a wider assortment of products. By following this creative approach, Shop Rite members have achieved record inventory turnover, sales per square foot, and return on investment.[10]

Another source of f.s. discount store development was the experience of some chains with leasing "discount food stores in discount centers"; lessons were learned that could be applied to their own supermarkets. The discount centers required that the chain with the food concession maintain competitively lower prices consistent with the parent's discount policy. This essentially entailed a reduction of gross margins in grocery departments (50 percent of sales) to a maximum of 17 percent from 21–22 percent of the typical supermarket operation. Here, as in Shop Rite's case, some supermarket chains learned the new mathematics of food retailing—in some situations lower prices will be more than offset by increased sales.[11]

The f.s. food discount stores grew rapidly in the middle 1960s and are still growing at the expense of the traditional supermarket chains. On both coasts, several powerful regional chains have adopted this price-oriented strategy with considerable success. There are now more than a thousand f.s. discount operations, and the number will increase as price pressures mount in the Midwest and South. Some of the more important f.s. discounters include the 165-store Shop Rite chain in New Jersey; 160-store Stop & Shop chain in New England; 290-store Lucky chain primarily on the West Coast; the 90-store Borman chain in Detroit; and 162 of Food Fair's 565 stores. F.s. food discounters commonly command 20–30 percent of the busi-

[10] The success of the Shop Rite approach is indicated by the amazing growth of the organization from sales of around $100 million in 1956 to near a billion dollars by 1968. See "Changing the Rules," *Forbes* (June 15, 1967), p. 54.

[11] "Behind the New Wave Discount Super Revolution," *Chain Store Age* (November, 1967), p. 88.

ness in markets where they are operating, and within five years the national share of market held by these stores could be near 25 percent as market segments are more uniquely recognized.

Combination Store

While discounters rely heavily on price to undermine the position of the conventional supermarket, the "combination store," with its greatly enlarged assortment of products and low prices, poses a serious threat of a different nature (see Figure 4). This merchandising strategy brings together the product offerings of both the supermarket and the super-drugstore, and saves shoppers the indirect transaction costs of time and energy. The developers of this more complicated store concept are benefiting in two important ways. First, the combination store is a means of diversifying into the growing drug and prescription field. Second, synergism was found to exist when a supermarket and super-drugstore were combined. This was nicely expressed by one of the leaders in the field who said that, based upon his company's experience with the combination store, "2 plus 2 equals 5."[12]

Several questions concerning the combination store need to be resolved. One of these is the best method for joining the grocery and drugstore operations. The three basic types of arrangements that I have studied are side-by-side separate operations; drugstore integrated to one side; and drugstore integrated center. The most common and the oldest approach is the side-by-side operation with different entrances or a common vestibule. The Kroger Company seems committed to the side-by-side arrangement and, where able to, locates a SupeRx drugstore adjacent to a Kroger food store. The strength of this approach lies in the fact that the drugstore and supermarket are run as distinct operations, each with its own image, requiring little departure from past management practices. The major shortcoming is that customer shopping convenience is not maximized, thereby reducing the opportunity for cross-over shopping. Furthermore, construction, operating, and inventory costs are somewhat higher.

The most common integrated design for the combination store places the drugstore to one side. The Jewel Company prefers this design. This plan gives shoppers easy access to both departments. The other integrated plan—the drugstore centrally located and food on both sides—is now being tested by Borman's in Detroit. The purpose of this design is to force more cross-shopping and to give greater emphasis to the drugstore phase of the operation.

In addition to choosing the scheme for combining two operations, management must also decide the relative amount of floor space to give to the drugstore section (generally ranging from a sixth to a third); the width and depth

[12] George Clements, "The Philosophy and Arithmetic of Growth Through Diversification," speech before the Western Association of Food Chains, March 29, 1966.

of product lines in the drugstore section; and the number of manned departments (pharmacy, cosmetics, film and cameras, tobacco and candies, and liquor).

Operating methods for the combination store are still being developed, and some chains have already had bad experiences with this new concept. However, the number of combination stores rose to over 400 at the end of 1967 from very few in 1963.[13] Early market evidence and discussions with supermarket executives lead this writer to believe that the integrated combination store could command 25 percent of the food business within ten years.

The Food Emporium

Another store innovation brings together the low price of the discounter with the broader assortment of the combination store. The name "food emporium" seems to best describe what this store is really like. It is a gigantic food-combination store that covers from 40,000 to more than 100,000 square feet ($3\frac{1}{2}$ to 8 times larger than the average supermarket) and that does from $7–14 million of business annually (5 to 10 times the business of the average supermarket).

These huge stores are generally located on major highways; 90 percent of their trade area may extend outward five miles with some regular customers travelling more than fifty. To draw customers from such a large trade area, the food emporiums offer the following advantages: prices 5 to 6 percent lower than in conventional supermarkets; greater variety; larger number of product lines; wider aisles; bargain lunch counters; twenty-four hour service; and a carnival-like atmosphere.

The size and business volume of these stores give them certain economic advantages over the supermarkets. The relative construction cost and physical operating costs are less because of scale economies. In addition, the in-store cost of merchandise is less because the emporium purchases more of its products direct from manufacturers. Finally, labor costs are lower; these warehouse-type stores can utilize mechanized handling and processing of merchandise.

The food emporiums are to be found in only a half-dozen markets, but there are signs that the concept is spreading. The share of market they can command is illustrated by the 17–25 percent of grocery sales that the food emporiums control in Norfolk, Memphis, and New Orleans. In cities where protracted trade areas are possible and the grocery business is dominated by moderate-sized supermarkets (12,000–15,000 square feet), the food emporiums are a "natural." Their development, however, is held back because a single store requires a large investment. However, because of its many

[13] "In-Store-Free-Standing Drug Units 'Multiply'," *Supermarket News* (Feb. 5, 1968), p. 44.

marketing advantages, it is conceivable that the food emporium could capture between 5 and 10 percent of the grocery business over the next ten years.

Convenience Stores and Superettes

The innovative stores discussed so far have offered shoppers lower prices, greater product assortment, or both. The convenience stores and superettes have used a quite different approach in their bid for a share of the supermarket's business. They cater to shoppers who wish to make quick "fill-in" purchases at conveniently located stores with a relatively limited assortment of products that sell for relatively high prices and that are generally open sixteen hours a day. The analytical distinction between the convenience store and superette is one of size and product assortment. The superette is the larger of the two and has a wider variety of products including fresh meat and produce. Of these small stores a larger portion of the new ones are superettes that are competing more directly with supermarkets.

The growth of the convenience stores and superettes has been spectacular —from only 500 in 1957 to 8,000 by 1967. Currently, these stores account for approximately 2 percent of the retail grocery business, and some members of the industry believe that the share could climb to as much as 8–10 percent.[14]

COMPETITIVE SUGGESTIONS

Executives of conventional supermarket chains are responsible for deciding over the long-run how best to remold and develop their future store operating concept to meet the assault of innovators who have segmented the market by appealing to shoppers preferring lower prices, greater assortment, or more convenience. This task is essentially one of deciding in what box or boxes of the decision-making matrix (see Figure 4) the firm wishes to be in order to more closely satisfy the needs of certain groups of shoppers.

Management has a more urgent shortrun problem, however, in deciding what should be done now and over the next few years to reduce the vulnerability of supermarket chains. Of the four types of stores discussed, the discounters pose the most serious immediate threat. The movement is spreading, and supermarket chains need to assess their own position and decide whether they wish to join the discounting movement or to adopt a strategy aimed at reducing the impact of the discounters.

The primary attraction of the discounter is lower price. The greater the difference in prices between the discounters and conventional stores, the easier for the discounter to establish a price image and make large competitive inroads. Therefore, it is imperative that supermarket chains carefully analyze their operating costs and determine which ones are not essential to meaningful differentiation from the discounters. These nonessential costs

[14] *Progressive Grocer* (April, 1968), p. 87.

should be pared from the operation so that prices can be reduced and the competitive threat lessened.

An analysis of the difference in operating costs of supermarkets and discounters reveals one area that usually accounts for most of the difference—the cost of trading stamps and games. This is a point that stamp companies tend to automatically dispute, and they cite a number of so-called authoritative studies as evidence in their favor. However, most of these studies have followed the "market-basket approach," which compares the prices of a relatively small number of products. This approach is far too simple. When one compares the *gross margin* of supermarkets giving stamps with the gross margin of discounters, a truer picture is revealed.

In two separate studies of the difference in operating costs of conventional supermarkets and discounters, the cost of stamps and games accounted for from 60 to 88 percent of the difference. The gross operating costs of a traditional supermarket and a discount store were compared for three chains. The *total* gross operating cost for the three supermarkets was 44.2 percent and for the three discount stores 35.0 percent. Of the difference, 88 percent (8.1 percent divided by 9.2 percent) represented the cost of the stamps and promotions.[15]

The question is now whether stamps and games are important to supermarkets for useful differentiation from discounters. Two hypotheses can be directed at this question: the "equilibrium hypothesis" that supports the continued use of stamps and games and the "total immersion hypothesis" that predicts a bleak future for these tools. Based upon my discussion with several chain store executives, the equilibrium hypothesis is as follows: the primary reason why stamps have lost much of their effectiveness is that there are too many chains giving them; this will be remedied when a few competitors drop stamps so that the segment of the market wanting stamps is balanced with the number of chains offering them.

In contrast, the total immersion hypothesis suggests that practically all supermarket chains will eventually find it necessary to discontinue trading stamps; the time and rate will depend upon local conditions. The catalyst that starts the process is a discount grocery chain that is aggressive and expanding in the market. Within a few years catalysts can be expected in all markets.

The test of the marketplace tends to refute the equilibrium hypothesis. In a small but growing number of large markets, the chains giving stamps have dropped to one or none. For example, in Boston all six of the principal supermarket chains—A & P, First National, Stop & Shop, Star (Jewel), Elm Farm, and Supreme—at one time were distributing stamps. Then, one at a time, the chains with the exception of First National dropped them.

[15] See Robert J. Minichiello, "The Real Challenge of the Food Discounters," *Journal of Marketing*, XXXI (April, 1967), p. 40. If the difference in the gross margins is near 4 percentage points (see footnote 8) and the cost of stamps is 2.5 percent of sales as Minichiello found, then the cost of stamps drops to 60 percent of the difference.

In Omaha, all the chains ultimately gave up stamps, finding that they were not effective in the face of lower prices. In Detroit and northern New Jersey, where discounting is widespread, only a limited number of chains are holding on. One in a large eastern market watched all but one competitor drop stamps, but the effectiveness of its stamp did not improve. Instead, this chain found that it was standing out increasingly in shoppers' minds as that "high-price chain" its competitors were indirectly referring to in their ads. This chain also dropped stamps finally, wishing that the decision had been made sooner.

The facts, as I interpret them, indicate that trading stamps will not help supermarkets to meaningfully differentiate themselves from discounters. Instead, those chains holding on to stamps when facing a severe discounting situation are going to be hurt. Therefore, either in anticipation of discounters, or following their penetration, supermarket chains are going to have to drop stamps and strengthen their price images. The pricing strategy to adopt when dropping stamps is of major importance. A few chains have found that the programs substituted for stamps have not worked, and as a result they humbly had to return stamps to the stores that dropped them. There are essentially two bipolar strategies that chains can pursue: they can simply become stampless supermarkets reducing prices by about the cost of stamps (approximately 2 percent), or they can become one of the f.s. discount food stores, where prices are reduced about 4 percent.

The decision as to which basic pricing strategy to follow requires a careful analysis of several factors. This study of many competitive situations resulted in the following set of questions.

Are your store locations more accessible to larger numbers of shoppers than those of your principal competitors? Some chains have chosen to locate away from major intersections and off major arteries, preferring rather exclusive locations where they have a semimonopoly. Chains with a relatively large number of such locations are poorly suited to switch to discounting; under these circumstances, it is difficult to extend trade areas enough to draw the volume required.

Can your stores efficiently handle increased volume of from 20–100 percent so that the average cost of doing business will appreciably decrease? If stores are generally operating at near-capacity levels so that increased volume cannot be handled more efficiently, discounting is ill-advised.

Can your stores handle increased volume of from 20–100 percent without excessive customer inconvenience?

Are your stores larger than those of your principal competitors so that you can have additional long-margin departments? Over the long run, chains that are going to make a discount program work will be these that have larger stores, more departments, and greater assortment. The additional departments of larger stores are the longer-margin departments that help make up for the lower prices on basic grocery products.

Is your management truly aggressive and prepared emotionally for the possibility of conflict with competitors?

Is your organization financially capable of withstanding a prolonged price war? Experience has shown that it will take six to eighteen months to establish a discount program before profits will return to a normal level. Unless a company is financially prepared to make such a capital investment in its future, a discounting program is ill-advised. I have talked with chains that were forced to give up their discounting programs after a few months because they were unable to see the program through financially to the time when profits could be expected to return to normal and keep growing.

Will your chain's actions be more or less ignored because its share of the market is relatively small? When a chain's market share is relatively small, larger competitors are inclined to ignore what is sometimes called "maverick behavior." The reason for this comparative safety is that the decisions of the smallish competitors are of little over-all importance to the larger organization. Furthermore, competitors are often afraid that the consequences of meeting such behavior, because of the unsettling impact it could have on the larger market, would be greater than giving up a small share of the market.

Do your principal competitors have middle-sized stores that are rather run down and poorly merchandised?

Are your primary competitors unlikely to take harsh retaliatory measures to counter a strategic move on your part?

If the answers to all of these questions are a qualified yes, then a chain should seize the opportunity to establish a discounting program. Similarly, if the majority of answers are generally in the affirmative and the negative answers do not seem to be over-riding, then discounting may still be a preferred strategy. However, should the answers to these questions be generally negative, then a defensive strategy is called for. Stampless chains should of course strive to develop that combination of costly services that will help them better serve the segment of the market they are trying to attract.

After many years of homogeneous growth, the supermarket industry has become sluggish, and its preeminent position is being eroded by stores better designed to serve the heterogeneous demands of the market. Innovative retailers have attacked the three precepts of supermarketing: price, merchandise assortment, and convenience. The discount food stores, either in discount centers or free-standing, are using lower prices to undermine the position of the supermarket. The combination store has greatly enlarged upon the merchandise assortment of the supermarket, and the food emporium combines both lower prices and a wider merchandise assortment. Finally, convenience stores are better satisfying the demand of shoppers for quick shopping.

Supermarket chains must try to adapt to these competitive threats in order to minimize their consequences. In part, chains can meet the price challenge by discontinuing stamps, games, and gimmicks, and lowering prices. However, before doing this, a chain must carefully study its competitive environment and decide what price strategy it should follow. Supermarket chains will not be able to adapt in the short-run to the larger product assortment of the combination store and food emporium. Rather, in the long-run, they may well find themselves emulating these stores.

QUESTIONS

1. What has caused the crisis in supermarket profits?
2. What types of firms are challenging the supermarket?
   What techniques do they use to challenge the supermarket?
3. What are the problems faced by a supermarket that decides to engage in price competition?

41

Does Franchising Create a Secure Outlet for the Small Aspiring Entrepreneur?

Louis M. Bernstein

The demise of small enterprises has been predicted for centuries, most notably by Karl Marx in the nineteenth century and by defenders of small enterprises since the great depression. Whether or not the announcement of their death is premature, small businesses in many fields find it increasingly difficult to survive the impact of intensified competition from large firms added to the ever-present small businessman's difficulties of insufficient capital and inadequate management skill. Of late, many friends of small business have been greatly encouraged by the tremendous growth of franchising systems.[1] They see these as creating many promising opportunities for small-scale enterprises.[2]

Reprinted from *Journal of Retailing*, Vol. 44, No. 4, Winter 1968–69, pp. 21–38.

[1] In number of franchise systems, number of franchisees and number of persons employed by them, the expansion in the past twenty years has been exceedingly large and rapid. While not all systems have been equally successful, it seems clear, for the reasons that are developed here, although documentation by hard data is not possible, that the failure rate among franchisees has been, and probably will remain, below the usual experience for small business.

[2] The publication by the Business and Defense Services Administration of the United States Department of Commerce of *Franchise Company Data for Equal Opportunity in Business*, February 1968, though no endorsement or recommendation of any plans listed, is part of a "special effort to inform minority groups of the opportunities in franchising. . . ."

The purpose of this article is to assess the effect of franchising systems on the present status and future role of small firms in the economy. Specifically, it discusses the kinds of franchise systems that are now offered and are likely to be offered in the future, explores the motives and resources of would-be enterprisers and evaluates the probabilities of their finding franchise opportunities. Thereafter, it will examine the types of assistance that franchising systems provide for their members. Finally, it will evaluate the price franchisees pay for the results obtained and comment on some of the implications of those results.

Stated most simply, a franchise combines know-how supplied by the franchisor with capital and willingness to work hard supplied by the franchisee into a business system that is intended to produce good results for both. Obviously all know-how is not assignable to the franchisor, nor is capital or effort forthcoming solely from franchisees, but the previous statement is, in general, broadly representative of franchising systems. And it should be noted that the very phrase, "franchise system," implies that it is built on a pattern or formula for the conduct of the particular kind of business, not just a sales agreement.

FRANCHISE OPPORTUNITIES

Franchises are being offered in ever-widening fields and in ever-increasing numbers. In 1964, the Department of Commerce found franchising firms in ninety-eight SICs, the largest proportion in retail and service fields. Since that analysis, hundreds of additional plans have been presented to prospects, many of these plans being in fields not previously cultivated by franchisors.[3]

Franchise opportunities are available today in the well-publicized categories of take-out foods, fast food and specialty eating places, of which there are well over 100 different systems; they are also available in motels, car rentals, laundry and dry cleaning stores, auto service and auto supply stores, all of which are widely recognized as franchise fields. Franchises are being offered also in business aids, travel agencies, art galleries, entertainment, nursing homes, beauty salons, pet shops, duplicating services, sales training, computer programming, shoplifting controls, diet programs, social introductions, to name a few of the newer types.

As new developments take place in the business world, we can expect corresponding new franchise opportunities to arise. Newly developed machines for duplicating print, etc. have led to franchised copy centers. The surge in Americans traveling stimulated franchising of travel agencies.

[3] There is no single complete list of franchises. The 1964 data was reported by the Task Force for Equal Opportunity in Business, printed in *Hearings* on Sen. Res. 40, 89th Cong., Part 1, *Franchising Agreements*. It was based on 556 firms listed in *Franchise Annual* 1964. In 1968, *Franchise Annual* listed 780 firms, and this did not include several dozen firms listed by the Department of Commerce in its *Franchise Company Data*, February 1968.

The success of "go-go" fashion stores has led to franchising new types of specialty retail stores. The computer revolution has resulted in franchised programming schools and franchised service bureaus. A few years ago there were no such franchise systems.

If a successful business can be developed that specializes in performing a service, or in purveying a particular product or group of products in an individual way, then the system by which it is done—the know-how—can, in all probability, be packaged and form the basis of a franchise system.

GOALS WITHIN FRANCHISING

People often ask, "Does this growth of franchising bode well for the aspirations of would-be small business enterprisers?" Such a question cannot be answered in the abstract. The chance for future success depends in substantial degree on who the small businessmen are, what they want and what they have to offer.

Men want their own businesses for a variety of reasons, undoubtedly interrelated and complicated. Stated very broadly, they strike out on their own for one or more of the following reasons:

- To do better economically than by working for someone else or to hire themselves when no one else will
- To prove themselves, to prove that they can accomplish something on their own
- To do things jointly with family members
- To get away from supervision, control, the structure of large business or government
- To be free and independent

They can seek to achieve these goals today by:

- Starting a business from scratch
- Buying an existing business
- Acquiring a franchise

Would-be entrepreneurs differ in the level of skill and experience they can bring to the business, in the uniqueness of their ideas, in the effort they are prepared to expend, part time, full time or in unlimited time and energy. They differ also in the capital available to them—hundreds, thousands, tens of thousands of dollars—and in the expectation of returns from the enterprises. For most of them, the results that they attain obviously will bear considerable relationship to what they bring into the enterprise.

What are the probabilities for them under franchising? Their chances of success, again, can be indicated only quite broadly. It must be recognized that, with the vast variety of franchise plans and the flexibility within many of them, only the most general statements will be substantially correct and that there will still be many exceptions even to these. In a very general way, however, Table I suggests the different kinds of franchises that men with varied background and resources might seek.

By-and-large, would-be enterprisers can expect to succeed in most franchise systems only by hard work and fulltime effort. Plans based on part-time work do exist, but the franchisees can, at best, expect only modest results. The exception is the investor who intends to devote only some of his attention to a franchise, planning to rely on hired full-time management. Some systems will consider such candidates.

The returns, the income that franchisees might obtain in the different types of franchise, range so widely as to defy classification. Obviously one which is based on the franchisee performing simple services will probably yield a limited return; $10,000–12,000 might be a good result. And yet a

TABLE 1

Relationship of Prospective Enterprises to Types of Available Franchises

Prospective Enterprisers	*Resources*	*Kinds of Franchise*
Men with limited background and experience	Minimum (under $5,000)	Those involving personal services, *i.e.*, On-location cleaning of carpets Mobile distributorships Routes and vending machines, rack jobbing
	Modest ($10,000) area	Convenience food outlets Small take-out food operations Equipment rentals
Men with background and some business experience	Modest	Credit and collection services Security systems Hearing aids
	Moderate ($25,000–50,000)	Many fast food operations Auto service operations Retail store systems Travel agencies Art galleries
Men having broad business experience with responsibility	Modest	Business consulting services
	Moderate	Employment agencies Temporary help agencies Computer schools
	Substantial ($100,000 area)	Regional franchises Motels Large food operations Entertainment Major car rentals Nursing homes

franchisee involved in distributing business systems might well, if he is an aggressive, effective salesman, earn several times that amount.

Those franchises involving larger operations and greater capital investment can likewise show wide disparity in results. The fast food and specialty food operations have reported average volumes of $200,000 and $300,000 or above, and pretax profits ranging from 10 to 15 percent of gross.[4] Similar wide ranges in results have been reported in other systems. But the general tendency would still hold that income will vary with size of capital investment and amount of franchisee's application.

Those who enter franchise programs in the earlier stages of an idea's development and before imitators are on the scene, may well expect to invest less to join and to obtain greater results than later participants who pay increased fees, get perhaps less choice areas and meet increased competition in the market. On the other hand, those established systems, by having built the brand name, offer presold customers for newly opened outlets, especially so in areas previously developed, whereas with new franchise programs this is a goal, not yet a reality.

Within the broad spectrum of franchising, there are plans in which almost every variation of the economic goals of would-be small business enterprisers can be met. This does not mean, however, that all who seek the franchise channel to get into business for themselves can do so, nor does it mean that anybody can readily get into the business of his choice. The task of an individual seeking a franchise is only slightly alleviated by the published lists and guides. He needs to do a lot of research to find out enough about the various plans to select the one that appears to meet his requirements. Then, in turn, he has to be acceptable to the franchisor.

FRANCHISORS' SELECTION

While would-be entrepreneurs are anxious to find suitable franchises, there is comparable pressure on franchisors to sign up prospects. As might be expected, the position in the life-cycle of the franchise program affects the franchisor's attitude.

A franchisor with a well-established record and substantial geographical coverage may pick and choose. McDonald's, for example, has applicants waiting for nearly a year for franchises. They don't have to seek out franchisees. On the other hand, many other established systems must constantly search for candidates to support their expansion programs. And those with new concepts, as distinguished from duplications of existing successes, can well have considerable difficulty in finding suitable applicants.

Regardless of how they obtain candidates, those businessmen running

[4] See, for example, *Business Week*, June 15, 1968, on *McDonald's* and *Kentucky Fried Chicken* before New York Society of Security Analysts, May 31, 1968.

established, on-going franchise systems take great pains to pick people who seem to fit in with their kind of business and program. The demands in personality, interest, aptitude and ability differ markedly among the several franchise fields. The franchisor seeks to avoid the costs, damage to his reputation and the difficulties in the administration of the system which the wrong operator can cause.[5]

Franchisors use a variety of tools to screen out improbable candidates. The questionnaire on background, business and personal history is a basic instrument used almost universally. Personal interviews and an applicant's visit to existing operations are regularly included. Some of the franchisors, e.g. Manpower and Automation Institute, insist that the candidate visit the parent company headquarters. Psychological testing has been used by at least a few concerns, among them International House of Pancakes, 7–11 Stores and Mister Donut.

The basic financial requirements established for those who seek a franchise also serve a screening function. Presumably they are designed to keep out applicants with insufficient capital for the undertaking. Of course, franchisors who find it difficult to attract franchisees may deliberately state the requirements lower than they should be, or compromise properly-set requirements when they are under pressure. To the extent that initial financial requirements do screen out individuals with insufficient capital, a major source of failure for many independent businesses is avoided.

Those franchisors whose profit comes primarily from the sale of franchises, or from the sale or lease of equipment to the franchisee, can be expected to put major emphasis on getting franchisees signed up. Where sales of product to franchisee or monthly fee based on his sales or profits are the major contributors to the franchisor's profit, his interest will be focused on the best prospects for successful operators.

There are undoubtedly more people thinking about businesses of their own than there are franchise openings. Some will exclude themselves from the market. The man with the true innovative skill, with the ability to start a business *de novo*, will go on his own. He may well become the franchisor of the future. These ambitious men with business experience, with management capacity and capital are most likely to find the kinds of opportunities they desire. Franchisors are eager to find them. Typically these men can, and do, wait to get what they want. On the other hand, those with limited experience and little capital cannot have access to many plans. There are usually many more of these people than there are franchise openings that they can get. Too frequently it is this type of person who is exploited by the fringe operators in the franchise business.

Those running the continuing, expanding franchise systems may be expected to continue to be highly selective. They will demand applicants

[5] Charles L. Vaughn in a talk before Seminar of the American Management Association: "Effective Marketing Through Franchises," April 26, 1967.

with energy and strong motivation, and preferably with adequate capital to push their operations ahead. Many would-be entrepreneurs will be excluded. But those who *are* accepted can anticipate substantial aid in many places. How franchisors help is our next concern.

FRANCHISOR ASSISTANCE

While the financial requirements of the parent company will screen out many applicants for various franchises, the numerous financial aids they offer franchisees provide many small businessmen with financial help that would be inaccessible to them if they were completely on their own. As the Task Force for Equal Opportunity in Business reported, ". . . the well-qualified applicant may often find that the franchising company is willing to go further in assisting him than one might believe on the basis of its bare statement."[6]

In short, the prospect is the determining factor. The franchisor in a good position can afford to and will extend assistance—lower cash requirements—to get the "right man." The franchisor may also provide or arrange for additional financing in order to get people with the most potential.

A most important kind of financial help is provided in some franchise programs where the physical premises are crucial for the operation. Some parent concerns contract for the construction of the facilities and then lease them to the franchisees. This arrangement enables the franchisee to get into business with much less capital than would otherwise be required. This method typically relieves him also of liability for the property if he gives up the franchise. While the franchisor's motivation for such an arrangement may well be to maintain control of his distribution, such concerns are making available substantial capital for the franchisee's use on a rental basis. The franchisee could not obtain such assistance as an unaffiliated independent. What small businessman on his own can expect to get an investor to build and lease him a special-purpose, distinctively designed building?

Among the firms that have leased premises to franchisees are *McDonald's*, *Denney's Restaurants*, *Chips*, *Mister Donut*, *Burger Chef*, *Rayco*. (We should note that many service stations are owned by the oil companies and leased to dealers, even though many do not consider them part of a franchise system.)

The lease arrangement may require the franchisee to forego certain privileges. Anyone doing business in rented premises can have his enterprise upset or ended when he cannot renew his lease. Where lease and franchise are interrelated, the franchisee will not be able to continue in business at the same location if he gives up the franchise. If he controls the location, he can. Thus, while he gains in the use of capital invested, his vulnerability is

[6] Hearings Before the Subcommittee on Anti-Trust and Monopoly, 89th Congress on Sen. Res. 40, part 1, *Franchising Agreements*, p. 480.

increased greatly when he leases his facilities. This restriction has been a subject of concern and complaints to government authority.[7]

Companies that don't themselves secure locations and lease them to franchisees frequently provide help in the location and development of the place of business. The need for the franchisor's approval of a location is a limit on the entrepreneur's freedom of choice; it can, however, provide a solid base for a successful operation. Well-operated franchise systems will issue a franchise only for a location or area where the applicant has good prospects for success.

Depending on the nature of the program, franchisors may provide assistance in real estate negotiations, building or alteration plans, equipment and layout specifications and even construction supervision. The intent is to help the franchisee start out with a business location and facilities suited to the particular needs of the business. Where a distinctive building is a basic part of the brand promotion, the company makes certain that all locations support that effort.

The franchisee is thus not as free as he would be if entirely on his own. On the other hand, the restraints involved provide another kind of freedom: freedom from the mistakes of improperly located or badly designed facilities and hence attendant limitations on his business.

TRAINING

All franchisors purport to train their franchisees. Training may consist of only one day's indoctrination. It may also mean attendance for an extended period at a "college" run by the franchisor; while attending such a "college," the franchisee is usually paid a nominal salary.

Since it is true that most franchisees are without specific experience in the businesses they enter, good training greatly increases their chances of success. But it also has another important aspect. Without the franchise system type of training and management support, the man seeking to operate his own business tends to be limited to fields in which he has already accumulated some experience and know-how. Franchising widens his horizon, giving him a much more extended choice of fields. A franchisor's training program can readily encourage applicants to enter a field they would not otherwise consider, and to do so with good chances of success. The backgrounds of many franchisees bear no relation whatever to the businesses they join.[8]

Initial training at the franchisor's central location is an integral part of many programs, the duration varying. *Duraclean*, *United Rentals*, *Ziebert*

[7] Hearings Before the Subcommittee on Anti-Trust and Monopoly, 89th Congress, on Sen. Res. 191, Part 2, *Distribution Problems Affecting Small Business.*

[8] In *Advertising Age*, April 22, 1968, *Dunkin' Donuts* quoted the success of a former account executive at a major agency—currently a franchisee—as an inducement to secure applications from others in the advertising field.

provide for a week in the central "school." Some of the food service operations call for extended periods in "school" and training operations; five to ten weeks for concerns like *Dunkin' Donuts* and *International House of Pancakes.*

On-the-job training with an established dealer may supplement the school or it may be the basic tool. In many systems, training continues when the franchisee begins his operation. The franchisor assigns a company field supervisor or store coordinator to work with the franchisee and his staff at this time. Implicit in the management assistance discussed below is the opportunity for subsequent training.

When the franchisor provides good training opportunities—and there is no question that many do—the franchisee enjoys brighter prospects for survival and prosperity than if he were on his own. Such training usually enables him to cope with the specific tasks he must perform in the particular business he has chosen. He could, of course, find some sort of training on the outside, but hardly as direct and pointed as that which an established franchisor can provide by drawing on his and existing operators' experiences.

CONTINUING MANAGEMENT ASSISTANCE

We have been examining franchisors' help in getting the franchisee into business. The continuing relationship between franchisee and franchisor is reflected in the various kinds of assistance provided after the business has been established. Some of them are specified in the franchise agreement, but more often than not only a broad and general commitment is included. It is through such assistance that the franchisor's knowledge and experience are made available to the franchisees; this is "one of the best justifications for the whole franchise system."[9]

The quotations below illustrate types of aid extended by franchisors:

> *International House of Pancakes* "using information obtained from each restaurant . . . prepares a detailed weekly operating statement on a central computer. This statement enables the company to compare a restaurant's current operating results with the unit's past performance, as well as with the performance of other units in the chain. (*The New York Times*, August 4, 1968.)
>
> *Schraffts* (motels) will make recommendations to the owner and cause its "supervisory personnel to check by conferring with the owner . . . and employees and checking furniture and furnishings, equipment, supplies, operating methods, accounts and other details in accord with high standards. . . ." and though not in operation control, Schraffts "shall nevertheless control the nature and quality of service available to the public. . . ." (Excerpted from its contract.)
>
> *Lum's* "provides central purchasing and commissary arrangements, recordkeeping, audits, cost controls, employee training programs, and

[9] *Facts About Franchising* (New York: National Better Business Bureau, 1965).

periodic inspections by independent shopping services for quality and service." (As reported in a Prospectus dated December 6, 1967.)

Lindsay in its contract calls for a variety of assistance including "furnishing a business analysis service on request and general financial and management advice and assistance." However, the commitment to furnish "services and assistance to the dealer during the term of the agreement (is) subject to such modification as Lindsay in its sole discretion may deem necessary or desirable." (Excerpted from its contract.)

Advertising assistance is explicitly provided for in many contracts, with the plans almost as varied as the businesses themselves. National advertising, cooperative local advertising, mat services and circulars are some of the items covered in the agreements. Dealer contribution to the national advertising is part of some agreements, as are provisions for accounting to them on how their money is spent.

Regular visits of the franchisor's representatives, which are a part of most plans, can serve the double purpose of checking on the operator's performance as well as helping him to improve the results he obtains. Some plans call for specific payment for assistance. Thus *Kentucky Fried Chicken* charges licensees for on-the-job training after his opening at the rate of $50 per day and expenses.

One area of assistance that franchisors can and do provide is research and development, which can enable the franchisee to adjust better to changing market conditions than he could on his own. Many well-run franchise systems offer help in perfecting labor-saving machinery to cope with help turnover and rising wage rates. They may also do market testing of new lines in company-operated units, offering these lines to franchisees only when perfected.

The franchisor's objective in providing help to his franchisees is to ensure *his* success by contributing to theirs. The more his existing franchisees prosper, the more he profits and the more prospects will want to join his system. At the same time, the consumer acceptance of his products, the value of his brand name and trademarks will be enhanced by the good performance of his franchisees or adversely affected by their failure to meet customer expectations. Assistance can also serve to limit and audit franchisee performance. Thus Lewis and Hancock concluded:

> the line between management aid furnished by the franchisor and franchisor controls is frequently a very thin one. . . . Many of the control devices . . . have a double-barreled purpose: (1) they give the desired degree of standardization throughout the system and thus make it possible to develop customer goodwill on a broad geographical base, (2) they serve as operating guides to the individual franchisee and enable him to benefit from the expericence of both the franchisor and other franchisees.[10]

[10] E. H. Lewis and R. S. Hancock, *The Franchise System of Distribution* (Minneapolis, Minn.: University of Minnesota, 1963), pp. 46, 47.

WHAT FRANCHISEES CAN ANTICIPATE

We have seen that many would-be enterprisers' economic goals can be met within franchise systems, and we have looked at ways in which franchisors help them achieve those goals. Although few franchisees can attain the fantastic profits sometimes promised in franchise promotions, as well as in some human interest stories about franchising, many of them do quite well financially.

Earnings commensurate with the size of the business were evident in the relatively low level of franchisee dissatisfaction with profit that Lewis and Hancock reported in their study.[11] Actual operating statements of present franchisees are used by franchisors in presentations to applicants. Discounting their selectivity, they still give evidence of substantially successful operations. Also, as a further indication of success, franchisees in many systems want to—and are encouraged to—own and operate additional outlets.

Risk of failure, the concern of most independents, is clearly reduced by their participation in a well-run franchise system in which they get the kinds of support described here. Granted that they have been the beneficiaries of our extended period of prosperity, existing franchisees' recommendations lead many to seek similar opportunities. Although hard data are not available, an observer like Eugene P. Foley has been led to conclude that "it seems a safe assumption that the casualty among franchisees is lower, far lower, than that among other small businesses."[12]

WHAT PRICE IN FREEDOM DOES THE FRANCHISEE PAY?

Every fully developed franchise plan calls for commitments by the franchisee. In effect, he thereby gives up some of his independence by agreeing to the extent specified to conform to a certain course of action. But does he yield significantly, and does he gain sufficiently by so doing?

A commitment by the franchisee to spend a specified percent of his gross sales in local advertising may be clearly in the interest of his success, but it is also a restraint. A provision in the agreement specifying hours of operation may be designed to ensure availability of product or service to customer and help build the business, but this too certainly constitutes a restraint on the franchisee. Provision for prior review by the parent company of a franchisee's local advertising may be designed to help him to maintain the brand image

[11] *Ibid.*, p. 81.

[12] Hearings, *op. cit.*, *Franchising Agreements*, p. 8. Some franchisors claim failure rates under 1 percent; some observers believe a rate of 8 to 10 percent would be more factual. Franchisee turnover, stimulated in many cases by the franchisor to eliminate "unsatisfactory operators," undoubtedly keeps down actual failures.

or both, but this is surely a limit on his action. The commitment by a franchisee to purchase supplies or products from the franchisor may have quality control justification, but it is a limitation on him, almost certainly designed to provide franchisor income. The agreement may give a franchisee exclusive rights to a territory in order to protect him, and restricting a franchisee to his defined territory is justified as a necessary part of this arrangement. Nevertheless, it is also a restraint, and the validity of some of these restraints under existing laws has been questioned.

But despite these restraints and limitations, the franchisee still runs his own business; his operation of it will, in final analysis, determine its success or failure. That is why the SBA concluded that a franchisee could qualify for a Small Business Loan: that he "only must show that he has the right to the profits of his operation and accepts the risk of loss."

Depending on the nature of the business and his skill, those profits can be large and the growth of his realizable equity in the business substantial. Obviously, to many men this is more important than maintaining completely their theoretical independence.[13]

EXTERNAL CONFIRMATION OF FRANCHISING

Some of America's major firms have added their confirmation of the value of the franchisor's know-how in their willingness to take on franchises to obtain trademarks, know-how, etc. Standard Oil of Ohio, for example, will operate restaurants as a franchisee of *Dutch Pantry*.[14] American Broadcasting Company and Great Lakes Carbon Corporation both have *Holiday Inn* franchises.[15]

The moves by major firms to acquire franchisor companies is clear-cut confirmation of their belief that franchising works and that those systems will continue to be successful. They must be so for the franchisee if the franchisor is to remain profitable.

The list following, by no means complete, shows major concerns that control a franchise activity and the franchise involved. Some recent acquisitions are listed first.

The financial community clearly envisages franchising as a growth industry, as evidenced by the way stocks of franchise companies have been sought in the past three years. *McDonald's Corporation* and *Kentucky Fried Chicken Corporation* with 1,000 and 1,600 outlets respectively in May 1968, mostly franchised, are outstanding examples, but stocks of other smaller operations like *Dunkin' Donut* and *Lum's* have been snapped up also.

[13] In a recent survey, the franchisees in the A & W Root Beer System, rather than having "a strong preference for steering their own destiny," as had been believed, "showed, however, a great receptivity to direction and guidance from the parent company." *Fast Food* (New York, June 1968), p. 83.

[14] *National Petroleum News* (New York, October 1967), p. 117.

[15] *The New York Times*, March 5, 1967.

Major Company	*Franchise System Controlled*
General Foods	Burger Chef
Pillsbury	Burger King
Ralston Purina	Jack-in-the-Box
United Fruit	A & W Root Beer
United Fruit	Baskin-Robbins Ice Cream
City Investing	Franchises International
Control Data	Automation Institute
Great Western United	Shakey's Pizza Parlor
Pet, Inc.	Stuckey's
Household Finance	Ben Franklin
Household Finance	White Stores
Union Tank Car	Lindsay
B. F. Goodrich	Rayco
Consolidated Foods	Chicken Delight

SOME PROBLEMS OF SUCCESS

When applicants seek a franchise, many quite readily accept the limitations of the system. As noted above, the price appears small for the pospects the franchise offers. But as the business matures and initial goals are met, the problem of "rising expectations" can become quite serious. The franchisee's sights on profits or the number of units he wants to operate can be increased.

A franchisee, who when new might have followed readily the guidance provided, can upon becoming successful feel the urge to try his own ways of doing things. Thus franchisees who, as potential dealers, accepted restraints (as the Supreme Court recently noted) "because their acquiescence was necessary to obtain an otherwise attractive business opportunity"[16] later sued the franchisor for triple damages under the antitrust statutes.

The very success of some franchising systems holds potential for trouble. When franchisees become aware of the earnings of some of their parent companies and the values put on those companies in acquisition, they can well have reason to believe that they have been paying too high a price. They may conclude that their agreements have given the franchisor too big a share of the results of their joint efforts.

The differences between car factories and their franchised dealers have been regularly brought to government attention, as have complaints from service station groups. Other franchise systems have not had that degree of attention, nor have the franchisees sought the aid of government to redress unequal economic power of franchisor and franchisee. It is, however, con-

[16] Perma Life Mufflers *et al. v.* International Parts Corporation *et al.* #733, decided June 10, 1968. The Court remanded the case for trial, holding that plaintiffs were not barred from suing by having "allegedly agreed to do business on anticompetitive terms."

ceivable that one of the byproducts of franchisor acquisition by major companies may be an acceleration of some such effort to protect the franchisees from the control of "big business."

SUMMATION

Despite the limitations on entry into the franchise arrangement and on the operations of small businessmen within the systems, the growth of these systems has made for actual enlargement of opportunities for many small businessmen. Specifically, the entrepreneur's economic security is increased by the contributions made by the franchise programs to his ability to operate profitably and to reduce his risk of loss.

The very fact that franchising represents a method of combining the know-how of the franchisors with the energy and capital of the franchisees suggests that opportunities will increase rather than decrease. There is every reason to believe that know-how in fields that have not yet been exploited will be packaged profitably under franchise programs. And there will be many people seeking their own businesses; people ready, able and willing to participate.

Of course, there are problems in the franchise field—in programs and operations—and of course abuses are not absent from this area any more than from other areas of American business. The fact remains, however, that many would-be entrepreneurs are annually choosing the franchise route to get into business for themselves.

These would-be entrepreneurs are doing so because they have concluded—rightly so, for most of them—that their economic opportunities and security will be greater under a franchise system than in remaining employed or in striking out completely on their own. At least, under the franchise system, they retain the essence of what they consider to be independence.

QUESTIONS

1. Why has franchising appealed to so many individuals?
2. Discuss the differences between the franchisor and the national chain.
3. Discuss, from the point of view of retail strategy, the operation of a franchise firm in your city.